Nuclear India in the Twenty-First Century

Nuclear India in
the Twenty-First Century

Edited by

D. R. SarDesai

and

Raju G. C. Thomas

palgrave

NUCLEAR INDIA IN THE TWENTY-FIRST CENTURY
Copyright © D. R. SarDesai and Raju G. C. Thomas, 2002.

First published 2002 by **PALGRAVE-MACMILLAN™**, 175 Fifth Avenue, New York, N.Y. 10010 and Houndmills, Basingstoke, Hampshire, England RG21 6XS.Companies and representatives throughout the world.

PALGRAVE-MACMILLAN is the new global publishing imprint of St. Martin's Press LLC Scholarly and Reference Division and Palgrave-Macmillan Publishers Ltd. (formerly Macmillan Press Ltd.).

ISBN 0-312-29459-X

Library of Congress Cataloging-in-Publication Data

Nuclear India in the twenty-first century / edited by Damodar R. SarDesai and Raju G. C. Thomas.
    p. cm.
    Includes bibliographical references and index.
    ISBN 0-312-29459-X
    1. Nuclear weapons—India. 2. India—Military policy. 3. World politics—21st century.
    I. SarDesai, D. R. II. Thomas, Raju G. C.

    UA840 .N827 2001
    355.02'17'09540905—dc21

                                     200153134

A catalogue record for this book is available from the British Library.

Composition by autobookcomp

First edition: May, 2002
10 9 8 7 6 5 4 3 2 1

Printed in the United States of America.

CONTENTS

PREFACE

In October 1998, a symposium was held at the University of California at Los Angeles (UCLA), a few months after the Indian and Pakistani nuclear tests were conducted in May 1998. The symposium was organized and sponsored by Professor Damodar SarDesai under his Navin and Pratima Doshi Chair in Indian History at UCLA. The conference was then appropriately called "India and the Nuclear Question." India's security directions at the time remained ambiguous and there were serious questions about the Indian nuclear decision and the possibility that India may revert back to a nonnuclear status as it did in 1974 under pressure from the West.

Apart from some of the contributing authors in this book, the participants at the conference included the nuclear weapons specialists and notable scientists, Chancellor Albert Carnesale and Vice Chancellor Kumar Patel of UCLA, and the strategic nuclear analyst and Director of the Burkle Center for International Relations, Professor Michael Intriligator of UCLA. Other participants included Indian security specialists Ashley Tellis of the RAND corporation (now special advisor to the U.S. ambassador in New Delhi); Neil Joeck of Lawrence Livermore National Laboratory (now on the Policy Planning Staff of the U.S. State Department); K. Subrahmanyam, former Defense Production Secretary and Chairman of the National Security Advisory Board in India; and P. R. Chari , Director of the Institute for Peace and Conflict Studies in New Delhi. Presentations were also made by Ambassador T. P. Sreenivsan, Deputy Chief of Mission at the Indian Embassy in Washington (now India's ambassador to Austria and the International Atomic Energy Agency in Vienna); the noted Indian historian, Professor Stanley Wolpert of

UCLA; and Gary Larsen, Executive Director of the Asia Society California Center. They provided a variety of assessments, some supporting the Indian nuclear decision, and others opposing it.

A year later, Professor Raju Thomas, the Allis Chalmers Professor of International Affairs at Marquette University, in cooperation with Professor SarDesai of UCLA, decided to put together a volume based on the UCLA conference. The participants at the 1998 UCLA conference, together with other experts, were invited to submit chapters for a volume based on the theme of the conference. At the turn of the century, based on some feedback from the potential contributors, the editors felt that as long as India showed no signs of doing what it did in 1974, that is, reverting back to a nonnuclear position, it would be best to recognize what India is today while allowing for the same assessments for or against India as a nuclear weapons state. Thus the emphasis shifted from whether India should have gone nuclear, to an assessment of the strategic, political, technological, economic, and military dimensions of a nuclear India.

The contributors represent a mix of pro-bomb and anti-bomb observers of varying degrees. Raju Thomas explores the various strategic motivations and domestic compulsions underlying India's nuclear policy over the last 4 decades. These include changing perceptions of regional and global nuclear threats, pressures arising from inter-party politics and coalition governments within India, and the search for great power status. In the aftermath of the terrorist attack on the United States on September 11, 2001, he raises the question whether India's nuclear capability is relevant when faced with transnational terrorism by nonstate actors. George Perkovich traces the origins of the Indian momentum towards a nuclear weapons capability, examining especially the domestic politics, strategic thought, and technological factors surrounding India's nuclear decisions. T. V. Paul adopts a more theoretical-strategic analytical scheme in explaining the Indian decision. He examines the relationship between great powers and rising powers determined to challenge the prevailing world order.

Foremost among those supporting a major nuclear program by India are K. Subrahmanyam and Bharat Karnad, two members of India's National Security Advisory Board (NSAB) who drew up India's draft nuclear doctrine in 1999. In many ways, they provide justifications for their advisory decisions on the NSAB. While Subrahmanyam takes a minimalist approach to deterrence, Karnad takes a maximalist approach. Subrahmanyam criticizes the world order of nuclear apartheid especially in the post-Cold War era of Western dominance and an unrivaled NATO alliance willing to use force to resolve the internal affairs of sovereign states. Karnad argues that India's nuclear policy should be based on national interests and not be subject to Western pressures. Taking such an approach will compel the West to treat India on par with China as a great power.

On the other hand, the main opponent of India's nuclear decision in 1998 in this volume is the Indian-American scientist, Rajendran Raja, who considers India's actions as incongruent with Mahatma Gandhi's philosophy, and a demonstration of irresponsibility by the Indian scientific community which he believes should be using its talents to reduce economic poverty and social ills. He suggests that in the context of the infinite universe of billions of galaxies, the acquisition of nuclear weapons that may destroy the tiny third planet from the sun in this solar system constitute the height of irresponsibility by world leaders who have now been joined by India and Pakistan. Siddharth Varadarajan takes a more middle ground between hawks and doves among the contributing Indian and Indian-American analysts. He argues that going nuclear has not advanced India's security. All that India has done is emulate blindly the folly of the formal nuclear powers merely to show that this can be done. Nobody appears to be more secure.

Jacques Hymans compares the political motivations in France and India in their decisions to go nuclear, much of which he argues revolved around both strategic considerations and prestige factors. Benjamin Sheppard focuses on the missile programs in and around the subcontinent, and Rajesh Kadian explores the role (or non-role) of the Indian armed services in the Indian nuclear decision. Chapters by Deepak Lal, Devesh Kapur, and Peter Lavoy examine the economic aspects of the decision, with Lal focusing on the economics of nuclear weapons, and Kapur and Lavoy on the impact of international sanctions on the Indian economy. Kapur claims little or bearable economic impact, while Lavoy claims substantial adverse impact. Raju Thomas explores the links between India's nuclear energy program and its nuclear weapons capabilities. He argues that the U.S. nonproliferation policy that imposed economic and technological sanctions on India after its 1974 atomic test did not stem the advances in India's nuclear weapons capabilities but instead stymied its nuclear energy program and overall energy goals with adverse opportunity costs on its economic growth. In the final section, George Quester draws on the lessons for the region and the world from the failure to stem the proliferation tide in South Asia.

The editors would like to thank Anthony Wahl, Roee Raz, Donna Cherry, Sara Safransky, and Aimee Hartmann (editors, copy, and production editors at Palgrave) for their cooperation and assistance in bringing this book project to fruition. Lisa Rivero in Milwaukee complied the index. Buddhika Jayamaha, a graduate Research Assistant at Marquette University, helped in finalizing the manuscripts for the publisher.

D. R. SarDesai
Navin and Pratima Doshi Professor of Indian History, UCLA
Los Angeles, California

Raju G. C. Thomas
Allis Chalmers Professor of International Affairs, Marquette University
Milwaukee, Wisconsin

CONTRIBUTORS

Jacques E. C. Hymans is a postdoctoral fellow at the Olin Institute for Strategic Studies, Harvard University, 2001–2002. Earlier, he was a predoctoral fellow at the Center for International Security and Cooperation, Stanford University. In September 2001, he defended his doctoral dissertation in the Department of Government at Harvard University. In his doctoral dissertation, "Pride, Prejudice, and Plutonium: Explaining Decisions to Acquire Nuclear Weapons," Jacques Hymans develops a theory of national identity and emotional decision-making in order to explain global patterns of nuclear proliferation and non-proliferation. His analysis focuses on the nuclear weapons decisions of India, France, Argentina, and Australia, countries in which he conducted extensive field research. He has published articles on nuclear issues in the *Non-proliferation Review*, the *Journal of East Asian Studies*, and the *Cahiers du Centre d'Etudes d'Histoire de la Defense*, as well as in the *Hindustan Times* and the *Telegraph* (India). Hymans' article on Argentine nuclear history, entitled "Of Gauchos and Gringos: Why Argentina Never Wanted the Bomb, and Why America Thought it Did," is forthcoming in *Security Studies*. He has given numerous conference papers at the American Political Science Association, the International Political Science Association, and other professional meetings, and he also has given lectures on nuclear weapons at the French Ecole Militaire, the Pugwash Association, and the University of London. Hymans' bachelor's, master's and doctoral degrees are all from Harvard University.

Rajesh Kadian is a physician, author, and consulting editor. Between 1978 and 1990, he was a practicing gastroenterologist in Kansas City, and the assistant clinical professor of Medicine at the University of Missouri at Kansas City. He has been an adjunct associate professor for the School of Medicine at Annandale Campus in Fairfax, Virginia. He is the author of *India And Its Army* (Vision Books, 1990); *India's Sri Lanka Fiasco: Peacekeepers At War* (New Delhi: Vision, 1990); *The Kashmir Tangle: Issues and Options* (Westview Press, 1993); and *Tibet, India & China: Critical Choices, Uncertain Future* (Vision Books, 1999). He contributed four entries on the Indian military to *Reader's Guide to Military History* (Fitzroy Dearborn, 2001), and has published in newspapers such as the *Washington Post* and the *Wall Street Journal*. He is the recipient of a U.S. Institute of Peace grant to undertake research on the Tibetan question. He has lectured widely on geostrategic issues at numerous forums including those held at the American University, the College of William and Mary, Georgetown University, the Henry L. Stimson Center, the University of California, Los Angeles, and the University of Wisconsin, Madison. Kadian has testified on Kashmir before the Human Rights Caucus of US House of Representatives; and has appeared on National Public Radio, The News Hour, and numerous Indian-American TV and radio programs. He has published numerous articles in medical journals in the field of gastroenterology, received the Vita and Clarence Goppert Award for Outstanding Work in Gastroenterology in 1975, and was elected a Fellow of the American College of Gastroenterology. Kadian received his M.D. from the Armed Forces Medical College in Poona, India in 1971, and his American Board of Internal Medicine Certification in 1976.

Devesh Kapur is Associate Professor in the Department of Government at Harvard University, Director of Graduate Student Affairs and a faculty associate at the Weatherhead Center for International Affairs, and a faculty associate at the Center for International Development at the JFK School of Government at Harvard University. Earlier, he was a program associate at the Brookings Institution in Washington, D.C. His research examines local-global linkages in political and economic change in developing countries, particularly India, focusing especially on the role of international institutions and diasporas. He is the coauthor of *The World Bank: Its First Half Century* (Brookings, YEAR/) and the author of *The Reverse Midas Touch? The Indian State and Economic Development: Lessons from the Indian Petrochemical Industry* (Oxford University Press, forthcoming). He has been a consultant for the G-24 and the UNDP. He received a B.Tech. in chemical engineering from the Institute of Technology, Banaras, India; an M.S. in chemical engineering from the University of Minnesota; and a Ph.D. from the Woodrow Wilson School at Princeton University.

Bharat Karnad is a Senior Fellow in National Security Studies, Center for Policy Research, New Delhi (since 1996). He was a member of the first National Security Advisory Board (specifically a member of its Nuclear Doctrine Drafting Group, and of the Strategic Defense Review of the External

Security and Technology Security Groups), and of the National Security Council, Government of India (1998–1999). He was Adviser on Defense Expenditure to the Tenth Finance Commission, Government of India. He also has been consultant on foreign/military affairs and a speechwriter (1990–97) for Jaswant Singh who presently holds the portfolios of both Minister for Defense and External Affairs, and to K. C. Pant, currently Deputy Chairman, Planning Commission. Karnad was the editor of *India Week,* occasional op/ed page columnist for *The Asian Wall Street Journal,* Hong Kong (1988–1991), Washington correspondent of *The Hindustan Times,* New Delhi (1984–1987); assistant editor and roving foreign/war correspondent of *The Hindustan Times* (1980–1983); and special correspondent in South and Southwest Asia for the *Field/World News Service/The Chicago Sun-Times,* and *The Atlanta Constitution* (1979–1983). He has been a visiting fellow, Henry L. Stimson Center in Washington, D.C., and a Ford Senior visiting Scholar in the Arms Control, Disarmament and International Security Program, University of Illinois, Urbana-Champaign (1995). His publications include *Nuclear Weapons and Indian Security* (Macmillan, forthcoming); editor and contributor of *Future Imperilled: India's Security in the 1990s and Beyond* (Viking, 1994); chapters in several books; and numerous articles in professional/academic journals. He received his B.A. from the University of California, Santa Barbara, and his M.A. in Political Science from the University of California, Los Angeles.

Deepak Lal is the James S. Coleman Professor of Development Studies at UCLA. From 1984-1993, he was a professor of political economics at the University of London, where he became an emeritus. Professor Lal is the author of several books, including *Wells and Welfare* (Organization for Economic Cooperation and Development, 1972), *Methods of Project Analysis* (Johns Hopkins University Press, 1973), *Appraising Foreign Investment in Developing Countries* (Heinemann, 1975), *Men or Machines* (International Labor Organization, 1978), *Prices for Planning* (Heinemann, 1980), *The Poverty of Development Economics* (Harvard University Press, 1983, MIT Press, 2nd edition, 2001), *Labor and Poverty in Kenya* (Oxford University Press, 1986), *The Hindu Equilibrium* (Oxford University Press, 1988), *Public Policy and Economic Development* (Oxford University Press, 1990), *Development Economics* (Elgar, 1992), *The Repressed* Economy (Elgar, 1993), *The Political Economy of Poverty, Equity and Growth* (Oxford University Press, 1996), and *Unintended Consequences* (MIT Press, 1998). He was educated at Stephen's College in Delhi and Oxford University.

Peter R. Lavoy is Assistant Professor of National Security Affairs, Associate Chair for Research, and Director of the newly formed Center for the Study of Asymmetric Conflict at the Naval Postgraduate School. He has published numerous articles and book chapters on weapons proliferation and on South Asian security issues. He coedited, with Scott Sagan and James Wirtz, *Planning the Unthinkable: How New Powers Will Use Nuclear, Biological and Chemical*

Weapons (Cornell University Press, 2000). His next book is *Learning to Live with the Bomb: India and Nuclear Weapons, 1947–2000* (forthcoming). During 1998–2000, Lavoy served in the U.S. Office of the Assistant Secretary of Defense for Strategy and Threat Reduction, most recently acting as Principal Director for Requirements, Plans and Counterproliferation Policy. From June 1998 to June 2000, Lavoy served as Director for Counterproliferation Policy in the Office of the Secretary of Defense, a position he occupied as an International Affairs Fellow of the Council on Foreign Relations. At the Pentagon, Lavoy oversaw a staff that was responsible for developing policies to improve U.S. military capabilities to successfully deter, combat, and defend against the use of nuclear, biological, and chemical (NBC) weapons and missiles, and to help allies and coalition partners to prepare their armed forces and populations to counter NBC threats. Lavoy received a Ph.D. in Political Science from the University of California, Berkeley and a B.A. in Government from Oberlin College. He has held research positions at the Center for Security and Technology Studies at Lawrence Livermore National Laboratory and at the Center for International Security and Cooperation at Stanford University.

T. V. Paul is Professor of Political Science at McGill University, Montreal, Canada and Director of the University of Montreal-McGill Research Program in International Security (REGIS). From 1997 to 1998, he was a visiting scholar at Harvard University's Center for International Affairs (CFIA) and the Olin Institute for Strategic Studies. He served as the assistant editor of *Canadian Journal of Political Science* from 1995 to 1999. Paul is the author of the books: *The World Power and India: Challenge and Integration in the Major Power System* (with Baldev Raj Nayar, Cambridge University Press, forthcoming); *Power versus Prudence: Why Nations Forgo Nuclear Weapons* (McGill-Queens University Press, 2000); *Asymmetric Conflicts: War Initiation by Weaker Powers* (Cambridge University Press, 1994); and coeditor and contributor to the volumes: *International Order and the Future of World Politics* (with John A. Hall, Cambridge University Press, 2000); *The Absolute Weapon Revisited: Nuclear Arms and the Emerging International Order* (with Richard Harknett and James Wirtz (University of Michigan Press, 2000); and *The Nation-State in Question* (with G. John Ikenberry and John A. Hall, forthcoming). He is currently working on the book projects: *The World Order and India: Challenge and Integration in the Major Power System* (with Baldev Raj Nayar), and *Transitions without War.* He received his B.A. from Kerala University, his M.Phil. from Jawaharlal Nehru University in India, and his M.A. and Ph.D. in Political Science from the University of California, Los Angeles.

George Perkovich is a Senior Associate at the Carnegie Endowment for International Peace and a consultant to the Nuclear Threat Initiative. From 1990 to 2001, he directed the Secure World Program of the W. Alton Jones Foundation. He is the author of *India's Nuclear Bomb* (University of California Press), which received the Herbert Feis Award from the American Historical

Association, for outstanding work by an independent scholar, and the A. K. Coomaraswamy Prize from the Association for Asian Studies, for the outstanding book on South Asia. Perkovich's writing also has appeared in *Foreign Affairs, Foreign Policy,* the *Atlantic Monthly, World Policy Journal, The Bulletin of Atomic Scientists,* the *New York Times,* the *Washington Post,* the *Los Angeles Times,* and other publications. He has served on various advisory panels and tasks forces related to South Asian security issues, including the 1997 Council on Foreign Relations Task Force that published "A New U.S. Policy Toward India and Pakistan." Perkovich received his Ph.D. in Foreign Affairs from the University of Virginia in 1997, his M.A. in Soviet Studies from Harvard University in 1986, and his B.A. in Politics from the University of California at Santa Cruz in 1980.

George H. Quester is Professor of Government and Politics at the University of Maryland, where he teaches courses on International Relations, United States Foreign Policy, and International Military Security. He has taught previously at Harvard and Cornell Universities, at UCLA, and in the Department of Military Strategy at the National War College. From 1991 to 1993, he served as the Olin Visiting Professor at the United States Naval Academy. Quester is the author of nine books and numerous articles on international security issues, and on broader questions of international relations, including *The Politics of Nuclear Proliferation* (Johns Hopkins University Press, YEAR) and *Nuclear Monopoly* (Transaction Books, YEAR), and he is a member of the International Institute for Strategic Studies and the Council on Foreign Relations.

Rajendran Raja was educated at Cambridge University, England where he was successively elected Exhibitioner and Senior Scholar and awarded a Prize Fellowship of the college in 1973. In 1969, he was elected President of the Cambridge University India Society and organized the Gandhi Centenary Debate in Cambridge that year. He got his Ph.D in particle physics from Cambridge University's Cavendish Laboratory in 1975, during which time, he shared an office with Professor Otto Frisch, the father of atomic fission. Partly as a result of a suggestion by Frisch, he sought work at Fermi National Accelerator Laboratory (Fermilab), where he is currently Senior Scientist. Since 1985, he has played a major role in the D-Zero experiment at Fermilab, which resulted in the discovery of the top quark in 1995. He is currently heavily involved in the Neutrino Factory/Muon Collider collaboration which attempts to invent a new form of particle accelerator using Muons, a heavy version of electrons, to study neutrino oscillations. He is the author of over 200 articles in leading physics journals and has edited several conference proceedings.

Damodar R. Sardesai is the Navin and Pratima Doshi Professor of Indian History at the University of California at Los Angeles (UCLA). He has been on the faculty of UCLA since 1966. He was the Department of History's Vice-Chair and Chair and has also served as Director of the University of

California's Education Abroad Program in New Delhi. He was invited to be the visiting Chairman of the Department of History of the University of Bombay from 1971 to 1973, to reorganize the university's History Department. The recipient of many academic awards, SarDesai was elected President of the prestigious (formerly Royal) Asiatic Society of Bombay (1989–99), and Fellow of the Royal Historical Society, Great Britain in 1979. SarDesai has authored and edited a dozen books on history and international studies. These include: *Indian Foreign Policy in Cambodia, Laos and Vietnam, 1947–1964* (University of California Press, 1968); *British Trade and Expansion in Southeast Asia, 1870–1914* (South Asia Books, 1977); *Southeast Asia, Past and Present*, Fourth Edition (Westview Press, 1997); *Vietnam, Trials and Tribulations of a Nation* (Promilla, 1989); and *Vietnam, Past and Present*, Third Edition, (Westview Press, 1998). He was educated at Bombay University and UCLA. from where he received his Ph.D. in History.

Ben Sheppard is Defense Analyst at Jane's Information Group and a regular contributor for various *Jane s* publications, writing on ballistic missile proliferation. Publications Sheppard has written for include *Jane s Defence Weekly, Jane s Intelligence Review, The Bulletin on Arms Control*, and *The War Studies Journal*. In addition Sheppard contributed a chapter on missile proliferation in India and Pakistan to *India's Nuclear Security*, and authored and coedited a *Jane's Special Report* titled "Ballistic Missile Proliferation: Identifying the Real Threats". Sheppard also organizes the annual *Jane's Missile Proliferation* conference. He received his M.Sc.Econ. in Strategic Studies at the University of Wales, Aberystwyth in 1996, after concluding a B.Sc.Econ (Honours) in International Politics at the same institution. During this time he spent a year as an exchange student at the University of Illinois, Urbana-Champaign. He is working currently on his Ph.D. thesis at Kings College, University of London, dealing with ballistic missile proliferation.

K. Subrahmanyam joined the Indian Administrative Service in 1951. He served as the Home Secretary for Tamil Nadu from 1975 to 1976. From 1968 to 1975 and from 1980 to 1987, he served as the Director for the Institute for Defense Studies & Analysis, New Delhi. Mr. Subrahmanyam was also a Rockefeller Fellow at the London School of Economics, a past Visiting Professor and Nehru Fellow at St. John's College, Cambridge University. He has published over a dozen books, including *India and the Nuclear Challenge, Nuclear Proliferation and International Security, and Indian Security Perspectives*. He is now the Consulting Editor (Foreign Affairs) for the *Times of India* and the *Economic Times*.

Raju G. C. Thomas is the Allis Chalmers Professor of International Affairs at Marquette University in Milwaukee, Wisconsin. He was a Visiting Fellow at Harvard University (1980–1981 and 1988–1989), UCLA (1982–1983), the Massachusetts Institute of Technology (1988–1989), the International Institute for Strategic Studies in London (1991–1992), and the University of Wisconsin-Madison (1994). Between 1992 and 1997, he was the Co-director of the University of Wisconsin at Milwaukee and Marquette University's Joint Center for International Studies. Thomas' dozen books and edited/coedited books include *The Defence of India: A Budgetary Perspective* (Macmillan-India, 1978); *Indian Security Policy* (Princeton University Press, 1986); *South Asian Security in the 1990s* (IISS-London/Brasseys, 1993); *Democracy Security and Development in India* (St. Martin's Press/Macmillan, 1996); *The Great Power Triangle and Asian Security* (Lexington Books, 1982); *Energy and Security in the Industrializing World* (University Press of Kentucky, 1990); *Perspectives on Kashmir* (Westview Press, 1992); *The South Slav Conflict: Religion, Nationalism and War* (Garland Publishing, 1996); *The Nuclear Non-Proliferation Regime* (Macmillan & St. Martin's Press, 1998); and *India's Nuclear Security* (Lynne Rienner/Sage, 2000). Between 1997 and 2001, he wrote most of the sections on India for Jane's Sentinel/Jane's Information of Great Britain. Thomas has published over 35 book chapters and 30 articles in academic journals. He has delivered numerous overseas lectures in India, Pakistan, Sri Lanka, Britain, Canada, Australia, Japan, Malaysia, Singapore, South Korea, Sweden, France, and Germany. Between 1965 and 1969, he worked for British multinational corporations in India. Thomas was educated in economics at Bombay University and the London School of Economics, in international relations at the University of Southern California, and in political science at UCLA from where he obtained his Ph.D.

Siddharth Varadarajan is a senior editor and Deputy Chief of the National Bureau of *The Times of India*. He has been one of the main foreign correspondents for the *Times of India* having reported extensively from the war zones in Iraq, the former Yugoslavia (the only Indian journalist to report out of Belgrade as NATO bombs fell in 1999), and from Afghanistan during the civil war there. He has covered Pakistan and Bangladesh frequently on special reporting assignments. Apart from writing regularly on international affairs and Indian politics, he is the author of a major study on the Indian media and communalism, published as "The Ink Link Media, Communalism and the Evasion of Politics," in K. N. Pannikar, *The Concerned Indian's Guide to Communalism* (Viking, 1999). He is currently writing a book on Indian foreign policy. He studied at the London School of Economics and Columbia University, and taught at New York University before returning to India in 1995.

Part I

General Dimensions

CHAPTER ONE

Whither Nuclear India?

Raju G. C. Thomas

Summary

The logic of India's nuclear weapons policy has fluctuated over the last 4 decades. India's present nuclear weapons posture must be viewed in the context of broader regional, global and domestic political compulsions, and from the standpoint of India's long-term and cumulative historical experience. India's nuclear threat perceptions were first focused on China during the second half of the 1960s following the Chinese atomic test in 1964. India's main attention then shifted to Pakistan's pursuit of nuclear weapons over the next three decades. At the end of the twentieth century, India perceived nuclear weapons as a deterrent against an unrivaled U. S.-led NATO alliance that appeared willing to intervene in the internal affairs of sovereign states on humanitarian grounds.

One domestic hypothesis is that inter-party politics, nationalism, and self-images as a rising power propelled India's decisions to join the ranks of nuclear weapons states. If India could not compete for international recognition as a major economic power such as Japan, perhaps the clout of nuclear weapons would provide that recognition. After all, nuclear China in the 1960s was recognized as a major world player before its rise as a global economic giant in the 1990s. A second domestic hypothesis is that India's economic and technological growth that made nuclear weapons and missile delivery systems possible, also made them strategically desirable, thereby provoking Pakistan to respond in kind, so justifying the initial Indian decision to go nuclear

In the aftermath of the terrorist attack on the United States on September 11, 2001, India (along with Russia and China) joined the U. S.-led global campaign against transnational terrorism. Traditional perceptions of nuclear threats from the nuclear great powers dissipated suddenly. However, whether a nuclear-armed India can deter cross-border terrorism, especially nuclear terrorism, by radical and irresponsible nonstate actors, is questioned. Perhaps India's nuclear policy has not adjusted to the realities of the new world. Whatever the new substance and direction of India's nuclear policy at the beginning of the twenty-first century, U. S. nonproliferation policy in South Asia has failed with potential ramifications for the nonproliferation regime elsewhere in the world.

South Asia: The Most Dangerous Place on Earth?

In the years following the series of nuclear tests conducted by India and Pakistan in May 1998, U. S. officials and the American media have called South Asia the most dangerous place on earth. A *New York Times* editorial, "Danger Within Pakistan," stated that "the world cannot afford to allow the region's two nuclear-armed nations to increase their tensions."[1] This view of impending nuclear war on the subcontinent unless something was done by the United Sates was voiced notably by President Clinton prior to his visit to South Asia in March 2000. Likewise, Deputy Secretary of State, Richard Armitage, told reporters on October 11, 2001 that Kashmir "is the most dangerous place in the world," and that "the main purpose of [Secretary of State] Powell's trip would be to ensure that tensions between the two countries do not escalate."[2] Indeed, during the American bombing of Afghanistan to root out Osama Bin Laden and his Al Qaeda terrorist base, tensions escalated over Kashmir between these two newly-armed nuclear weapon states. India pointed out that radical Islamic groups, including some supported by Al Qaeda, were conducting terrorism in Indian Kashmir from across the Pakistani border. Pakistan claimed that this was a freedom struggle and accused India of state terrorism in Kashmir. The Indo-Pakistani rhetoric escalated as international attention focused on Afghanistan, Pakistan, and India.

Premonitions of an impending Indo-Pakistani nuclear war in the midst of the 2001Afghanistan crisis appear somewhat overblown although precautionary measures to avoid such an eventuality are necessary. There is no reason to believe that Indian and Pakistani leaders are less rational and responsible with their nuclear weapons than American, Russian and Chinese leaders. Some danger may lie on the Pakistani side where radical Islamic extremists, especially those who sympathize with Al Qaeda in the military establishment, could gain control of the nuclear weapons and delivery systems. Besides several Pakistani leaders have threatened the use of nuclear weapons if India were to launch a conventional attack on Pakistan.

The periodic warnings by the West that India and Pakistan are on the brink of nuclear war may compound the dangers of nuclear war and become a self-fulfilling prophecy. While the Indian government and its supporters disagree with such dire predictions, Pakistan and its allied Kashmiri separatists support this thesis of imminent nuclear war. Raising the specter of nuclear war by Kashmiri separatists is intended to bring about U. S. intervention while the world's attention remains focused on South Asia. Pakistan claimed that it was not enough for the US to wage war against the Taliban and Al Qaeda in Afghanistan. If Southern Asia is to be stabilized, then Kashmir too must be settled. General Musharraf of Pakistan considered this one payoff for his country's cooperation with the United States in its war against Al Qaeda and the Taliban in Afghanistan. Stemming the hemorrhage in Indo-Pakistani relations and the slide towards a nuclear war constituted a concurrent challenge for the United States as it pursued its war objectives in Afghanistan and the elimination of terrorist networks everywhere. Meanwhile, there continues to be no basis for a settlement on Kashmir. Pakistan will not give up its goal to make Indian-held Kashmir part of Pakistan. India insists on the territorial status quo in Kashmir.

Threats to the territorial integrity of India are compounded also by domestic inter-religious and linguistic conflict, violent secessionist insurgencies and weak and unstable coalition governments. Can a nuclear-armed India ward off domestic insurgency, terrorism and potential state disintegration? As discussed later, India's atomic test in 1974 and nuclear tests in 1998 were intended, at least in part, to distract the domestic audience from political and economic problems at home. In both instances, the tests generated national unity and solidarity. However, testing more nuclear weapons is unlikely to produce the same unifying and stabilizing effect in the future. All the nuclear weapons accumulated by the erstwhile Soviet Union did not prevent its collapse. Likewise, can the deployment of nuclear weapons by India deter cross-border and transnational terrorism conducted by nonstate actors? Effective nuclear deterrence may apply only to another state. Nuclear weapons cannot deter transnational terrorists. And if such weapons were to fall into their hands, nuclear deterrence will fail. Irresponsible or irrational nonstate actors carry greater credibility in the threatened use of nuclear weapons.

Graham Allison has pointed out that attempts to steal nuclear weapons or weapons-usable material have been a recurring fact, especially in Russia and some of the former Soviet republics.[3] Acquiring some "40 pounds of highly enriched uranium, or less than half that weight in plutonium, it could, with materials otherwise available off the shelf, produce a nuclear device in less than a year." Allison concluded that "terrorists would not find it difficult to sneak such a nuclear device into the United States. The nuclear material required is actually smaller than a football. Even a fully assembled device, such as a suitcase nuclear weapon, could be shipped in a container, in the hull of a ship or in a trunk carried by an aircraft." A private Pakistani group that may have sought to develop such nuclear bombs for Al Qaeda operations worldwide (against India as well as Al Qaeda's other enemies), is the Ummah Tameer-e-Nau (UTN). Founded by a nuclear scientist, the UTN claimed to be a relief organization helping deprived civilians in Afghanistan. UTN was put on Washington's list of suspect terrorist groups.[4] Nuclear weapons in the hands of the more extreme Kashmiri separatist groups may compel India to capitulate in future confrontations over Kashmir. This has complicated India's ability to maintain its territorial integrity and political unity at the beginning of the new century. Against such threat conditions, the Indian deployment of nuclear weapons may be an exercise in strategic futility.

The Antecedents of a Nuclear Weapons State

In May 1974, when India tested its first atomic device, thus exercising its nuclear weapons option, the international outcry caused the Indira Gandhi Congress government to pull back immediately to a nonnuclear status. The Indian atomic test of 1974 was described at the time as a Peaceful Nuclear Explosion (PNE), permissible under Article 5 of the 1970 Nuclear Nonproliferation Treaty (NPT). In retrospect, there was nothing peaceful about that single explosion, as admitted in 1998 by the BJP government. Reasons for the 1974 test may be found in the strategic circumstances of the prolonged East Pakistani civil war of 1971 when India's ability to intervene in the conflict was deterred by the new thaw between the long standing antagonists, the United States and China, both also allies of Pakistan, and both nuclear weapons states. China already had threatened India that it would support Pakistan if India were to intervene in its civil war.

In order to thwart such a possible move, India's military intervention in East Pakistan and its war with Pakistan in December 1971 was preceded by the signing of the Indo-Soviet Treaty of Peace and Friendship in August 1971. The treaty included security clauses calling for military consultation and cooperation if either country was attacked. From the Indian standpoint, the treaty was intended to reduce the risks of either American or Chinese military intervention in a South Asian war. Nevertheless, during the Indo-Pakistani war, China issued an ultimatum demanding India dismantle certain military installations on the Chinese side of the border across the northeast frontier of India, and the United States sent its nuclear powered carrier, the *USS Enterprise,* into the Bay of Bengal in a show of gunboat diplomacy against India. Given this experience, India began to consider seriously the need for an independent nuclear deterrent where it would not have to rely on the Soviet Union under similar circumstances. The 1974 atomic test may be seen as a delayed response to the events of 1971.

However, the immediate decision by Indira Gandhi's Congress party government to go nuclear in May 1974 had much to do with distracting the public's attention from India's domestic political and economic problems. Indira Gandhi's popularity at the height of the Bangladesh war of independence had declined. A major nationwide railway strike paralyzed the country.

Opposition parties demanded Indira Gandhi's resignation for having violated election laws during her reelection campaign in 1970. These conditions eventually led to the declaration of a national emergency and the suspension of fundamental rights in 1975. Yet, for more than three decades after the 1971 Indo-Pakistani war, the *USS Enterprise* episode is still mentioned in Indian strategic circles as one good reason for acquiring or maintaining an Indian nuclear deterrent.

As in 1974, reasons for the BJP-led government decision in 1998 to conduct the nuclear tests stemmed from both an assessment of long-term Indian security concerns and immediate domestic political pressures. The BJP, and its predecessor, the Jan Sangh, had always declared that should it ever constitute the ruling government of India, it would immediately transform India into a nuclear weapons power. Such Jan Sangh declarations were made after China conducted its first atomic test in October 1964, two years after Chinese forces had crushed the Indian Army along the Himalayan frontiers in the Sino-Indian war of 1962. While the BJP's January-February 1998 election platform had declared that it would consider going nuclear if it won the national election that Spring, it may have been motivated subsequently by its inability to win a majority of the parliamentary seats and its need to consolidate the disparate coalition that it had put together.

The coalition consisted of a motley group of parties, including the All-India Annudurai Dravida Munnetra Kazhagaham (AIA-DMK) of Tamil Nadu led by Jayalalitha Jayaram. Amidst demands by smaller members of the coalition government for ministerial posts and favors, especially those by the AIA-DMK, the nuclear tests of May 1998 may have been a method of consolidating the coalition government by inducing feelings of pride and patriotism. The tests produced widespread support throughout India, including praise from the opposition Congress party led by Sonia Gandhi. Indeed, the earlier Congress government of Prime Minister Narasimha Rao was on the brink of conducting nuclear tests in 1995. However, the United States discovered the plan before the tests were conducted and compelled India to step back from the brink under the threat of dire economic consequences.

After the euphoria, more cautious and rational calculations began to be made about India as a nuclear weapons state. Was this to be a permanent state until the five nuclear "haves," who were also the permanent members of the Security Council, agreed to comprehensive nuclear disarmament as required by Article 5 of the NPT? Thereafter, a new debate arose. Should India sign the Comprehensive Test Ban Treaty (CTBT) and the proposed Fissile Materials Cut-Off Treaty (FMCT) while refusing to sign the NPT? Should adherence to these pacts be conditional on India being accepted as a formal member of the nuclear weapons club, and even as one of the permanent members of the UN Security Council?

The CTBT was completed and opened for signature in 1996. During its deliberations in the Disarmament Commission at Geneva, India was one of the strongest opponents of the treaty. Ironically, India had always supported such a treaty in the 1950s and 1960s as a first step towards comprehensive nuclear disarmament. But by the time the treaty was finalized in 1996, there were fears in India that the five nuclear "haves" having already conducted sufficient tests, would be able to continue with simulated tests under laboratory conditions. The gulf between "haves" and "have-nots" would be widened under the CTBT. India now wanted a Comprehensive Nuclear Disarmament Treaty (CNDT) and not just a CTBT. Meanwhile, the proposed draft of the FMCT was still pending.

Western economic sanctions against India after May 1998 only increased the Indian resolve to ride them out without yielding to pressures to renounce its nuclear ambitions. And indeed, unlike Pakistan which was brought to the brink of economic collapse by the sanctions and had to be bailed out by Washington, India survived the economic blows. India's economic growth rate was only marginally affected from about 6 to 7 percent of the GNP between 1994 and 1998, down to 5to 6 percent in 1998-99. It was back to 6.5 percent at the end of 1999 with expectations of higher growth rates in the future, although these expectations were not fulfilled as the world economy began to decline in 2001. While economic sanctions, especially the cutoff of loans and grants from the World Bank, the IMF, and the Export-Import Bank, had deleterious effects on the development and growth of India's infrastructure, the pro-bomb lobby believed that such sanctions would not last long as the West got accustomed to an economically prosperous India providing markets and investments opportunities. Subsequently, America's need for coalition partners during its war in Afghanistan, led to the lifting of all economic sanctions against both India and Pakistan. India's gamble to exercise its nuclear-weapons option had paid off.

Some three years after the 1998 tests, nuclear nationalism subsided in India. As the leading member of the ruling coalition government that included parties that professed socialism and regional linguistic nationalism and parochialism, the BJP had to tone down its Hindu nationalist fervor. And as its Hindu nationalist ideology began to drift towards the need to maintain the secular nature of the Indian state as enunciated and professed by the earlier Congress Party, the public declarations by the BJP for a major nuclear weapons program also mellowed. A greater willingness to sign the Comprehensive Test Ban Treaty emerged compared to the strong resistance that prevailed among its party members towards the treaty in the mid 1990s. However, calls continue for expanding India's nuclear capabilities among the more conservative Hindu nationalist organizations, such as the Rashtriya Swayamsevak Sangh (RSS) and the Vishwa Hindu Parishad (VHP), and among India's strategic hawks in the security policy-making community. Although the official government rhetoric became more muted, there appeared to be no parallel change in the pace and development of India's nuclear and missile programs.

NATO and India's Nuclear Weapons Rationale

Meanwhile, support for the continuation of India as a nuclear weapons state received a boost following NATO's assault on Yugoslavia in 1999. The global security climate in a Western dominant world was perceived to have dramatically changed following the 50th anniversary celebrations of NATO in Washington in April 1999. NATO's formal expansion to include three more European states, and the lofty rhetoric of new nuclear doctrines and humanitarian interventions in the internal affairs of other states, were viewed with concern as having relevance for Indian security.

The permanent representative of India to the UN Security Council stated on March 24, 1999: "The attacks now taking place on Yugoslavia have not been authorized by the [Security] Council, acting under Chapter VII, and are therefore completely illegal ... What NATO has tried to do is to intimidate a government through the threat of attack, and now through direct and unprovoked aggression, to accept foreign military forces on its territory ... There are several traditional descriptions for this kind of coercion; peacekeeping is not one of them."[5] Defense Minister George Fernandes stated in December 1999: "Like the majority of the Indian people, I saw the aggression against Yugoslavia as the greatest injustice of the 20th century, the defeat of international law, a manifestation of UN impotence, and a violation of all human and moral norms."[6] The Indian defense minister continued that India was against a "unipolar world" and "favored a world without a world policemen, and in which the UN would act in accordance with its charter." Foreign policy analyst T. V. Rajeshwar stated that "the war unleashed by the North Atlantic Treaty Organization (NATO) on the sovereign nation of Serbia on March 24 was a clear case of aggression."[7] Former Foreign Secretary of India A. P. Venkateswaran wrote: "The aerial attacks launched by NATO against Yugoslavia once again establishes the truth of the axiom, 'Power tends to corrupt, and absolute power tends to corrupt absolutely.' There is no legal sanction whatsoever for this unilateral action by NATO carried out at the behest of the US, following the failure of the talks on Kosovo. ... "[8]

Regarding how far NATO's future military operations could extend in the future, Siddharth Varadarajan (a contributor to this volume) pointed out that NATO's new "Strategic Concept" included an expanded definition of what constitutes a threat to the security of the "Euro-Atlantic area." The term North Atlantic no longer refers to a specific geographical region. "Like Vamana, the diminutive avatar of Vishnu, the 'NA' in NATO has an immense capacity to expand across the three worlds."[9] According to Varadarajan, one factor triggering NATO's right to intervene is weapons of mass destruction. This is found in the NATO summit's "Defense Capabilities Initiative" operations outside alliance territory. "Obviously, we are talking about operations that are pretty far afield. In line with this, the proliferation of nuclear, biological and chemical weapons and their means of delivery is identified as a threat to NATO."

Amidst a series of official and nonofficial Indian condemnations of NATO's use of force in violation of the UN Charter, several Indian analysts declared that India's decision to go nuclear a year earlier was justified. Former Foreign Secretary of India, Mukchund Dubey, referred to the "NATO Juggernaut" and condemned its unmitigated act of aggression against Serbia. He declared that NATO's actions had justified India's decision to acquire a strong nuclear deterrent to avoid Western nuclear monopoly and Western pressures during times of crisis that affect the Indian national interest.[10] K. Subrahmanyam (a contributor to this volume) pointed out that the three strongest critics of NATO's military actions, Russia, China and India, were all nuclear weapons states.[11] Other analysts argued in 1999 that India should consider seriously Russia's proposal for a strategic partnership among Russia, China and India.[12] Thus, NATO's military actions in 1999 provided India with a post hoc rationalization for the nuclear weapons tests it had conducted a year earlier.

The absence of a system of countervailing conventional military power in the post Cold War era and the ability of the United States to undertake military operations without opposition or resistance by other major powers, generated some ominous assessments in India and China. Reflecting the widespread strategic sentiment in India at the time regarding the new unipolar security environment, a 1999 *Times of India* editorial noted the dangerous new American-dominant world, the American development of new missile defense systems, the legitimization of wars of intervention abroad on self-determined moral grounds, and the ability to fight wars without casualties to American forces because of its new high-tech weapon systems.

> "In these circumstances two major trends are likely to emerge. Independent powers like Russia and China are bound to develop their own military capabilities to deter U. S. dominance to the extent possible and to defend their own national interests and sovereignty. In this, the nuclear weapons and long range missiles are bound to play a crucial role. Secondly, the deep resentment against U. S. hegemonism is bound to unleash various terrorist activities by nonstate actors against U. S. interests and personnel in various parts of the world. India has to take note of these developments and formulate its own national security strategy to safeguard its strategic autonomy. That calls for the country to accelerate its acquisition of a credible minimum deterrent, [and a] programme of ballistic and cruise missiles."[13]

The prospect of U. S. military intervention against Russia, China and India over Chechyna, Tibet or Kashmir for alleged human rights violations in these provinces is remote. All three are large and heavily armed states with nuclear weapons capabilities. Whether there was a direct link or not, less than two months after NATO's assault ended on June 8 1999, India issued a highly generalized and globalized nuclear doctrine. The doctrine was not directed specifically at either China or Pakistan, its two traditional adversaries, but merely laid down the reasons for acquiring an independent nuclear deterrent and the conditions under which they would be deployed. The doctrine called for a credible and survivable nuclear deterrent, with appropriate command and control facilities, and conditions that would ensure the security and safety of the weapons. It declared a no-first-use policy, indicating that nuclear weapons would be held only for retaliatory purposes to deter an attack, or would be used if such deterrence were to fail. It stated that India's nuclear weapons would never be used to threaten nonnuclear-weapons states who were not aligned with existing nuclear-weapons states. The issuance of the nuclear doctrine, albeit merely a "draft," indicated that there would be no reversal in India's pursuit of a nuclear weapons capability until the nuclear "haves" were willing to give up theirs as well.

Are then India's nuclear weapons and missile capabilities intended to serve as a regional deterrent against Pakistan and China, or as a global deterrent against the other major nuclear-weapons states, especially the United States and Britain? Facing no military restraint from Russia and China and little risk of death and destruction to themselves, the United States and Britain have opted for military ultimatums designed to be rejected, and for quick military solutions as in the cases of Iraq, Yugoslavia and Afghanistan.

The growth of India's missile capabilities may provide some clues regarding the intent and direction of India's nuclear deterrent posture. The May 1998 Indian nuclear tests were followed in April 1999 with the successful testing of the *Agni-2* missile with a range of 2000 kilometers. The *Agni* series of missile development and tests have continued into the new century. The *Agni* missile range constitutes a retaliatory strike deterrent capability that could reach much of the Middle East, Central Asia, China and Southeast Asia. In May 1999, the Indian government sanctioned a major missile development program including the proposed deployment of the ICBM, *Surya*. Initially, *Surya* will have a range of 5000 kilometers with no payload, and 2000 kilometers when carrying a nuclear warhead. The range of the *Surya* ballistic missile may rise from 5,000 km to 12,000 km, giving India an inter-continental ballistic missile capability that could reach the United States, Britain and France.

The development of the geosynchronous and polar satellite launch vehicles (GSLV and PSLV) in India's space program also contributes to India's ICBM technology and capability. According to Ben Sheppard (a contributor to this volume), the GSLV and the PSLV, when given a ballistic missile trajectory, could serve as ICBMs that could strike targets at a distances of 12,000 km and 14,000 km.[14] India successfully launched the GSLV in April 2001 and a PSLV in October of the same year. Meanwhile, India's Defense Research and Development Organization is developing two missiles to be equipped on its proposed nuclear-powered submarines, the *Danush* and the *Sagarika*. The first would be a short-range Submarine Launched Ballistic Missile (SLBM), and the second a Submarine Launched Cruise Missile (SLCM). Both have been stalled for the time being by technological difficulties. These ballistic missile and space rocket programs suggest the intention to create a global nuclear deterrent that goes beyond India's regional nuclear rivals, China and Pakistan, to the other major nuclear powers.

The Afghanistan Crisis and
South Asian Nuclear Security

Political and strategic conditions changed in the aftermath of the terrorist attack on the United States on September 11. The United States and India—and indeed much of the rest of the world including Russia and China—found common cause in the war against terrorism. India was among the first countries to rush to the American side to offer military bases and logistical support to fight the Al Qaeda organization in Afghanistan, having also been the subject of Al Qaeda's terrorist operations in Kashmir. The United States, however, sought such facilities in Pakistan instead which is adjacent to Afghanistan while attempting to soothe India's fears of a return to the old Pakistani-American military alliance of the Cold War. The American policy has been to encourage rapprochement between India and Pakistan over Kashmir in order to facilitate its larger campaign against transnational terrorism.

After the September 11 terrorist attack on the United States, the Russia-China-India quasi-alliance momentum had stalled, if not halted. During the visit of President George W. Bush to Shanghai in October 2001, President Jiang Zemin of China declared his support to the United States in its war against terrorism. And during the visit of the Indian prime minister to Moscow in November 2001, President Vladimir Putin of Russia and Prime Minister Atal Vajpayee of India proclaimed a common cause against transnational Islamic terrorism in Chechnya and Kashmir, as well as a common cause with the United States in combating global terrorism.[15] Russia now seeks to become a partner, or even a member, of NATO, perhaps expanding the organization into a Russia-North Atlantic Council.[16] All states have jumped on the American anti-terrorism bandwagon with various degrees of conviction and support. The dreaded unipolar world was getting more unipolar under U. S. control and domination.

The lingering remnants of East-West confrontational politics declined further when Presidents Bush and Putin agreed on November 13 to reduce their nuclear warheads on strategic delivery systems to between 1,700 and 2,200 over the next ten years.[17] This agreement overrides the START-II agreement which required both the United States and Russia to reduce their strategic nuclear warheads to 3,500 by 2003. Therefore, progress is being made by the two major nuclear weapons powers towards comprehensive nuclear disarmament as required by Article 6 of the Nuclear Nonproliferation Treaty (NPT). India's attempt to achieve global nuclear deterrence with its projected long-range missile program would appear less justifiable amidst the new nuclear arms reductions agreed to by the United States and Russia, and its common global cause with the United States against world-wide networks of terrorism.

It would seem unlikely that Article 6 of the NPT will be fulfilled in the near future. Comprehensive nuclear disarmament by the five formal nuclear weapons states may encourage "rogue states" to acquire nuclear weapons as the possession of a handful would make them major military powers instantly. Moreover, the earlier Indian *post hoc* rationalizations for nuclear weapons based on NATO's assault on Serbia over its Albanian Muslim majority province of Kosovo would not become entirely redundant. The absence of countervailing conventional military power against the United States has enabled it to conduct bombing campaigns against other states without much fear of casualties to American forces. Under such conditions, quick military solutions are likely to be preferred over other more prolonged peaceful policy alternatives. Washington wants other states to trust its noble intentions, but the record of U. S. military interventions in Vietnam, Iraq, Panama, Afghanistan and other places, would give rise to doubts.

As Indian analysts pointed out in 1999, weaker states may perceive the deployment of nuclear weapons as a means of deterring such Western military interventions, notwithstanding the new wave of global unity and amity among states to combat global terrorism. Realists and balance of power theorists would argue that, lacking a system of global countervailing conventional power, nuclear deterrence would remain a more acceptable long-term strategy (assuming that the strategy of terrorism is not a viable option for states) against the threat of Western military interventions, no matter how remote this prospect may seem at present. Conditions in Chechnya, Kashmir, and Xinjiang, provinces seeking to secede by violent means, are not fundamentally different from that which were found in Kosovo. They are all Muslim majority provinces of a larger sovereign state seeking independence through violent means. Only the degree of state violence invoked to defeat the violent separatist movements have varied. What makes Western military intervention unthinkable in these cases is that Russia, India and China are major states with large military establishments and nuclear weapons capabilities.

Two Nuclear War Scenarios

Whether a nuclearized South Asia is the "most dangerous place on earth" remains to be considered. Two Western-conceived scenarios of nuclear war came into prominence during the crisis in Afghanistan: (1) escalation from insurgency and cross-border terrorism to conventional war and to catastrophic nuclear war; (2) fissile materials falling into the "wrong hands" who are able to make nuclear weapons and willing to use them.

The Escalation Scenario
Under the first scenario, Indian frustration with fighting an indefinite war against insurgents and terrorists operating from Pakistan and Afghanistan, may tempt New Delhi to escalate the situation by conducting a conventional war

against Pakistan to destroy the bases of the *mujahideen* across the border. There have been some discussions in India of the legality and viability of "hot pursuit" of the insurgents and terrorists into Pakistan. Following the terrorist attack on India's parliament in New Delhi in mid-December 2000 by the *Lashkar-e-Tayeba,* calls intensified among Indian politicians and the attentive public to attack the terrorist sanctuaries in Pakistan.[18]

If the United States could use massive conventional force to eliminate terrorist bases in faraway Afghanistan from whence terrorist operations were planned and conducted in the United States, then why cannot India launch attacks on terrorist bases in Pakistan and further afield across the Hindu Kush? Western fears of an impending Indo-Pakistani war escalating to nuclear war rose dramatically in mid-December.

India's acquisition of nuclear weapons has not alleviated its difficulties in dealing with insurgency and cross-border terrorism in Kashmir. Nuclear weapons did not prevent a limited conventional border war in Kashmir, as illustrated in the Indo-Pakistani war along the ceasefire line in the Kargil sector in mid 1999. India has no relative advantage in fighting a conventional war that is confined to Kashmir. In the 1999 Kargil war, Indian forces suffered immense losses before it eventually pushed back Pakistani forces that had seized the sector within the Indian line of control. However, because of the threat of Pakistani nuclear retaliation, India could not consider an all-out conventional war in 1999 that would have compelled Pakistan to defend the entire country against India's superior conventional forces. Thus, when Pakistan attempted to seize Kashmir by force in 1965 and 1971, India escalated the war across the international frontiers sending its forces towards the major Pakistani cities of Lahore and Karachi. That strategy lessened the military pressure on India in Kashmir as Pakistani forces had to be diverted south to defend its Punjab and Sindh provinces. The situation is different in the new South Asian nuclear context. Pakistan's possession of nuclear weapons now deters the Indian initiation of a full-scale conventional war for fear that Pakistan may retaliate with nuclear weapons leading to an all-out catastrophic Indo-Pakistani nuclear war.

However, there are several factors that mitigate such an outcome. The decision-makers in India and Pakistan have generally remained quite rational and responsible during crises. Past Indo-Pakistani wars have been essentially "gentlemanly" wars. Cities and other civilian targets were never attacked; prisoners-of-war were treated humanely and returned after the cessation of hostilities. Nuclear responsibility between the two sides was demonstrated also in a formal treaty signed by India and Pakistan in 1988 not to attack each other's nuclear energy installations in case of war. Second, the geographical proximity of the two countries and the inter-related nature of societies on either side may in themselves constitute a deterrent. An attack by India on Pakistan may cause radioactive fallout in India, and vice versa. Even if Pakistan were to attack distant targets in India with intermediate-range ballistic missiles, it will inflict death and destruction on millions of Indian Muslims for whose protection Pakistan was created in 1947.

Moreover, the relationship between Indians and Pakistanis are not quite the same as Israelis and Arabs who come from different ethnic and cultural backgrounds and do not share a common centuries-old historical experience. There is still an overarching unity to the subcontinent based on common history, language, cuisine, music and culture. Indians and Pakistanis know and understand each other well. In an interview with the *Washington Post*, Prime Minister Atal Bihari Vajpayee was asked what role India would like to see the United States play in settling the Kashmir dispute between India and Pakistan. He replied that "there can be no place whatsoever for any third party involvement, in any aspect of our bilateral relations. When two people can speak the same language, why should either side suddenly seek an interpreter?"[19] Note that Musharraf's family is originally from Delhi, and his wife's from Lucknow, the seats of Muslim culture in the subcontinent. During the 1965 Indo-Pakistani war, some family members of then Indian president, Zakir Hussain, lived in Pakistan. I recall while living in Bombay in September 1965, there were discussions as to whether Pakistan would bomb Bombay. The popular local assessment was that Pakistan would not do so because Pakistani Foreign Minister Zulfikar Ali Bhutto's mother lived in Bombay—whether or not this local belief was factual, or whether Pakistan had the military range to conduct such an attack at the time. Thus, the Indo-Pakistani relationship may be viewed, in one sense, as merely a family quarrel where nuclear weapons may be brandished but never used.

Third, the possibility of deterrence failure between India and Pakistan because of inadequate command, control, communications and intelligence systems, may be resolved by providing both sides with the appropriate technologies to avoid nuclear wars through miscommunications or accidents. Fourth, covert nuclear weapon capabilities in India and Pakistan since the late 1980s, have prevented major conventional wars from taking place for fear of escalation to nuclear war. No major wars have occurred between India and Pakistan since 1971, except the localized Kargil border conflict in 1999 across the ceasefire line in Kashmir.

The "Loose Nukes" Scenario

A second Western-mooted scenario of a prospective nuclear war on the subcontinent revolves around the speculation of "loose nukes" in Pakistan with radical Islamicists gaining control of them. This danger may be more serious. A coup against the Pakistani military dictator, General Pervez Musharraf, may result in such a situation. Under these conditions, Pakistani threats to use nuclear weapons against India would be no bluff if India fails to comply with Islamabad's demands on Kashmir. In turn, India would feel compelled to preempt a Pakistani nuclear attack, or retaliate after the attack has taken place.

This remains the U. S. nightmare. Two weeks after the September 11 terrorist attacks on the United States, there were fears in the Bush administration that a war in Afghanistan and instability in Pakistan may result in the loss of control of Pakistan's nuclear arsenal which holds about 30 to 50 nuclear weapons.[20] According to David Albright of the Institute of Science and International Security in Washington D. C.: "If domestic instability leads to the downfall of the current Pakistani government, nuclear weapons and the means to make them could fall into the hands of a government hostile to the United States and its allies."[21] According to Pervez Hoodbhoy, a Pakistani nuclear scientist teaching at Qaid-e-Azam University in Islamabad, "Nukes everywhere are susceptible to hijacking. There are special dangers here."[22]

Such fears were aggravated in October when it was learnt that two retired Pakistani nuclear scientists, Sultan Bashiruddin Mahmood and Abdul Jajid, ran a relief organization for three years in Afghanistan, although both denied providing Al Qaeda or the Taliban nuclear blueprints and materials. Mahmood was the former chief designer and director of the country's Khoshab Atomic Reactor. Abdul Jajid, worked in Pakistan's Atomic Energy Commission. However, Pakistani President Pervez Musharraf assured U. S. officials that he had ordered an emergency redeployment of the country's nuclear arsenal to at least six secret new locations and had reorganized military oversight of the nuclear forces in the weeks since Pakistan joined the U. S. campaign against terrorism.[23]

Rising Indo-Pakistani tensions over Kashmir and the prospect of a nuclear war may be fueled by such fears. However, it is not coincidental that South Asia appears to be "the most dangerous place on earth" only when the United States and its media pay attention to the region and say it is so. The more extreme groups among the Islamic militants such as the Lashkar-e-Toyeba, the Harkat-ul-Mujahideen and the Jaish-e-Mohammed may become encouraged to escalate the war of insurgency and terrorism in Indian Kashmir in order to invite U. S. intervention. Although these groups have been declared terrorist organizations by the United States since September 11, they could re-surface under other names, or newer like-minded organizations could rise.

Pakistan and the Kashmiri militants hope that the internationalization of the Kashmir issue may then lead to a Western enforced settlement that would lead to the separation of the Kashmir Valley from India and its eventual annexation to Pakistan, not unlike the de facto severance of Kosovo from Yugoslavia following NATO's military intervention and the likelihood of that province's eventual attachment to Albania. On the other hand, nuclear tensions may ease if South Asia was subjected to a policy of benign neglect by the United States and especially its media. Without Western attention and the prospect of military or diplomatic intervention—as in the case of Kosovo and East Timor prior to their detachment from Yugoslavia and Indonesia—the continuation of the insurgency and terrorism in Kashmir by Islamic militants may appear futile against the sustained and prolonged resolve of Indian forces to thwart Pakistan's war by proxy against India.

Technological Capacity and the Status Question

Nuclear compulsions arising from domestic politics and the need for deterrence against regional and global nuclear threats appear to be declining. And

India's possession of nuclear weapons will not deter acts of terrorism, even nuclear terrorism, by nonstate actors. Then does a nuclear India at the beginning of the twenty-first century make any sense? One possible root cause of the problem may be that the development of nuclear weapons and missiles in India is made possible from the growth of technology in the nuclear energy and space programs. The Indian educational system continues to churn out an abundance of scientists and engineers capable of developing bombs and rockets who need to be employed and cannot all be absorbed by the civilian sector. Otherwise, they would be lost to the West, or remain within India as an unemployed or underemployed, disgruntled, and underprivileged class of workers. Nuclear and missile technological capabilities in India have no doubt generated perceptions of external threat conditions that required an Indian nuclear deterrent.

Itty Abraham argued that that the evolution of India's nuclear capabilities arose from an unusual mix of autonomous scientific growth within a highly protected domestic strategic enclave that was not subject to public political scrutiny.[24] Various scientific personalities and egos ran India's atomic establishment, especially those of Homi Bhabha and Raja Ramana, the "grandfather" and "father" of the Indian atomic bomb. The idiosyncrasies and inconsistent beliefs on the role and nature of nuclear weapons of Prime Minister Jawaharlal Nehru and his successors contributed to the sense of infallibility among the scientists and engineers working within this protected strategic nuclear and missile enclave.

In India, there are differences in the expectations, criteria and strategy of acquiring technological self-sufficiency in sophisticated conventional weapons through indigenous sources on the one hand, and that of nuclear weapons and missiles on the other. Unlike conventional capabilities, the technological sophistication of nuclear weapons and perhaps even missiles developed in India need not match the quality of those found in the US, Britain or France. The minimum expected requirement at present of nuclear weapons and missiles is that the bomb must detonate and the missile must land in the approximate target area. That would constitute minimum deterrence.

Technological comparisons with the capabilities of existing nuclear weapons states, including China, are not considered important although this attitude may change if India decides to embark on an overt nuclear arms buildup to rival that of the medium nuclear powers. However, the designated range, payload, accuracy and other operational requirements of missiles must be reasonably assured. In the case of short-range tactical missiles to be used by the Army on the battlefield, Indian military expectations of comparative technological quality are that such missiles must match those available to India's adversaries, not unlike that of other major conventional weapons. Medium and intermediate range missiles intended for strategic deterrence need to fulfill less stringent requirements of sophistication and accuracy since they serve a somewhat more flexible and ambiguous purpose. Ultimately, missiles developed and produced in India need only demonstrate its own pre-defined and projected range, payload and accuracy and not necessarily the missile capabilities possessed by China, Pakistan or other countries.

The indigenous development of nuclear weapons and missiles in India carries another major advantage over the similar development of other major conventional weapons. There is a parallel "peaceful" civilian program being undertaken by the Departments of Atomic Energy and Space that more directly contributes to India's nuclear weapons and missile capabilities. Indeed, despite all the technical setbacks, cost overruns and prolonged delays in India's nuclear energy programs and schedules, nuclear reactors and reprocessing facilities have provided India with the crucial plutonium for the development of atomic and thermonuclear bombs. Similarly, the civilian space program shares with the military missile program common needs such as cryogenic booster engines, special aluminum alloys, launch motors, gyroscopes, liquid and solid propellants, stabilizers and guidance systems. No doubt, civilian technological development in the areas of aeronautics, shipbuilding, automotive, and electronics also carry benefits for the defense sector, but they do not tend to be as comparable in the technical standards required or technologically compatibility as in the case of nuclear energy and space programs. The spin-offs and spin-ons between civilian and military endeavors in nuclear and space technologies have been much more direct and beneficial.

Jacques Hymans (a contributor to this volume) points out that, as in the case of France, the need for international status, in addition to the need for nuclear deterrence for security reasons, were inextricably intertwined in India's decision to go nuclear. With respect to India's civilian nuclear program, Itty Abraham too notes the similarity in the Indian case compared to that of France. "With nations turning so often to the past to authenticate themselves, incorporating the hyper-modernity of this technology into existing national discourse was often a complex feat of rhetorical shifts . . . The contrasts of modernity and tradition, however defined, find frequent mention in France, for example, where reference would be made to nuclear reactors in terms of past technological marvels like the Eiffel Tower, the Arc de Triomphe and even the Cathedral of Notre Dame . . . One can easily see in both a similar aesthetic of triumphant rationalism in which atomic energy was the proof of the relative superiority of their own ideology."[25] Abraham continued that like France, Nehru, in particular, linked Indian history and culture with the concepts of science and nation, "where modern science is appropriated to authenticate the Indian nation," and conversely "where science makes the Indian nation modern. . . . "[26] The result was an unusual mix in the Indian rhetoric that combined Sanskritic Vedic verse and the need for nuclear energy power and weapons. George Perkovich (a contributor to this volume) points out that even first prime minister Jawaharlal Nehru, for all his "idealistic, anti-nuclear leanings . . . recognized that India could gain international power, standing, and a measure of security if it acquired a nuclear weapon capability. Thus Nehru hedged many of his anti-bomb statements with qualifications that India could develop nuclear weapon capability and might choose to do so some day."[27]

India has complained repeatedly that it does not get enough respect compared especially with China. Until the mid 1980s, before China forged ahead with sustained economic growth rates of between 8 to 12 percent of its GNP, the per capita incomes of India and China were between $300–400. The population sizes of the two countries also put them in the same bracket. But India pursued economic development and population control through the democratic process compared to the authoritarian measures and totalitarian conditions found in China. Instead, the West, and particularly the United States, equated India with Pakistan, a country once one-fifth the size of India before the separation of Bangladesh in 1971, and now only one-eighth the size of India. A nuclear India was expected to resolve this discrepancy. But it failed when Pakistan matched India in the tests of bombs and missiles. Arguing against India signing the CTBT under American pressure, Bharat Karnad (a contributor to this volume) declared: "Nothing is better appreciated and better guaranteed to create respect—the vital aim always missing in Indian foreign and military policies— in the world than a country that stands up for itself and its national interests whatever anybody else may think or do. China is respected and allowed every consideration. India is badgered and asked to behave because Washington is convinced that the threat of punitive actions is enough to turn Indian resolve to jelly. Or, it is tempted by offers of freer access to high technology or whatever else New Delhi puts a policy premium on, because it is believed that India (and Indians) can be bought off or won over with blandishments. That is the principal difference in the American treatment of China and India."[28]

The search for international status, recognition and respect, and especially the frustration arising from such denial to India by the international community as compared to China, extends to other areas. With reference to Indian female contestants winning international beauty pageants such as Miss World and Miss Universe (India swept both in 1996 and 2000, and one of them twice in other years in the 1990s), the noted Indian novelist, Shobe De observed: "For so long we've considered ourselves to be losers and second-raters, we crave success at anything at all in the international arena."[29] Vir Sanghvi, the editor of *The Hindustan Times,* declared that "Indians especially longed for recognition from the West, anything showing that they are major players in the world, whether with nuclear weapons, a seat on the United Nations Security Council, Western book prizes, movie deals with Hollywood or top jobs with multinational corporations. There is a sense that we can be a contender. At least we certainly want to be."[30]

Did U. S. Nonproliferation Policy Make Any Difference?

It would be a truism to say that U. S. nonproliferation policy failed to stop the nuclear tide in South Asia. In the midst of the U. S. military campaign against the Al Qaeda terrorist network and the radical Islamic regime of the Taliban in Afghanistan, India, and especially Pakistan, were rewarded for their support of the United States with the lifting of almost all sanctions that had been imposed in 1998 following their series of nuclear tests. The decisions to "proliferate" appear to have paid off. Will others, especially Iran and Israel, follow India and Pakistan since there may be no penalties for proliferation?

However, it was not as though the United States did not try.[31] Nuclear nonproliferation was not a priority during the Nixon administration or earlier administrations which were more concerned about anti-communist "containment" policies, the Vietnam War, and domestic political scandals. It was only after President Carter took office in January 1977—almost three years after the Indian atomic test of May 1974—that U. S. policy took on a degree of earnestness. President Carter threatened the economic sanctions stick on both India and Pakistan. Subsequently, President Reagan used the economic and military aid carrot on Pakistan. Neither approaches worked. Just before and during the Carter administration, a series of internal legislation was passed to contain proliferation tendencies in South Asia. In 1976 and 1977 the Symington and Glenn Amendments were passed to the U. S. Foreign Assistance Act which prohibited American economic and military aid to countries attempting to acquire reprocessing and enrichment capabilities for weapons purposes. Both Amendments then were essentially directed at Pakistan.[32]

In 1978, Congress passed the Nuclear Nonproliferation Act (NNPA) that called on the U. S. government to withhold cooperation on peaceful nuclear programs with countries that would not allow the IAEA inspection of its nuclear facilities. This Act was expected to be enforced retroactively, the target clearly being the 30-year Indo-American agreement of 1963 that had assured the supply of enriched uranium to the two General Electric light water nuclear power reactors set up at Tarapur near Bombay. In accordance with the NNPA, the supply of enriched uranium to the Tarapur power plants was withheld by the Carter administration. In doing this, India claimed that the United States had violated an international agreement. The United States claimed violation of the peaceful nuclear uses clause because American heavy water was allegedly used in the Canadian-supplied *Cirus* research reactor from where India had obtained the plutonium for the 1974 atomic test. Subsequently, to circumvent the NNPA and Congressional pressures, and to fulfill the contractual obligations arising from the 1963 agreement, the Carter administration allowed India to obtain the enriched uranium from France, and later Germany. As discussed in my chapter later in this volume on India's nuclear energy and weapons programs, the U. S. nonproliferation policy essentially retarded the pace and quality of India's nuclear energy program without affecting its ability to divert to a weapons capability.

The Reagan administration took a laissez-faire approach to the proliferation issue in order to maintain Pakistani cooperation and goodwill in the U. S. policy of assisting the Afghan *mujahideen* in its war against Soviet occupation forces in Afghanistan. The reward for such Pakistani cooperation was large-scale economic and military aid to Pakistan, the third largest U. S. aid to any country after Israel and Egypt, and a U. S. policy of minimizing the seriousness of Pakistan's clandestine nuclear weapons program. The Reagan policy succeeded enormously on the Afghan front, but contributed heavily to the shambles that is now found in the nonproliferation regime in South Asia. Whereas India had ended its efforts to acquire nuclear weapons after its 1974 test of an atomic device, Pakistan had accelerated its own nuclear weapons program leading to an Indo-Pakistani posture of mutual nuclear brinkmanship and eventually to the tests and countertests of 1998.

However, there was an effort on the part of the Senate to link American economic and military aid to Pakistan to combat the Soviet occupation of Afghanistan, with U. S. nonproliferation policy in the region. The passage of the Pressler Amendment in the Senate in 1984 required the U. S. administration to certify every year that Pakistan was not attempting to acquire a nuclear weapons capability. The Pressler Amendment was Pakistan-specific and did not apply to India. But India had already been denied a variety of economic and technological assistance following the 1974 atomic test. Thus, if U. S. intelligence were to indicate that Pakistan was pursuing such a capability, then the U. S. government would be compelled by law to cut off all economic and military aid. During the Reagan administration from 1981 to 1988, Pakistan had acquired the materials and technology to put together uranium-enriched bombs. As long as the Soviets occupied Afghanistan, the need to stop Pakistan's search for weapons was not an American priority.

By 1991, based on clear evidence, the Bush administration declared that it could no longer certify that Pakistan was complying with its nonproliferation requirements and the terms of the Pressler Amendment. Economic and military aid was cut off to Pakistan, including the transfer of some 40 F-16 fighters that Pakistan had already paid for. But these actions were too little and too late. Following Pakistani president Pervez Musharaff's support for the American military campaign in Afghanistan in Fall 2001, economic sanctions were lifted against Pakistan, its debts were rescheduled or written off, and $1.3 billion in economic aid was offered immediately. The F-16 fighters are likely to be delivered now. Economic and military sanctions to enforce the U. S. nonproliferation policy against Pakistan was sidelined again amidst the new U. S.-led campaign against terrorism.

Whither Nuclear India?

Domestic compulsions based on India's nuclear technological capabilities and the desire for great power status are insufficient explanations for India's decision to maintain its nuclear weapons capability. Despite newer trends in global economic interdependence, and terrorist threats stemming from nonstate actors against which nuclear weapons appear ineffective, India's older regional and global security concerns have not become entirely irrelevant. The use of force remains an instrument of foreign policy of the great powers as demonstrated in Iraq, Yugoslavia and Afghanistan. Indeed, the willingness of the United States and Britain to use overwhelming conventional military force against weak states inflicting enormous death and destruction has increased both in intensity and frequency since the end of the Cold War, especially when wars may be conducted without casualties to themselves. And while the nuclear weapons capabilities of the United States and Russia are being reduced, the expansion of NATO and the buildup of technologically advanced conventional weapons by the United States continue unabated.

Therefore, India's nuclear policy must be viewed in the longer and broader context of its varied and cumulative security experience since its independence in 1947. It remains, as the American phrase goes, a "work in progress." No doubt, there will be further shifts in India's nuclear policy in the decades ahead as security conditions go through anticipated marginal shifts or unexpected major convulsions. For the time being, however, India is likely to remain a nuclear-weapons power until the other nuclear-weapons states agree to comprehensive nuclear disarmament, a somewhat remote possibility at the beginning of the twenty-first century.

Notes

1. *New York Times*, January 26, 2000.
2. See "Kashmir Most Dangerous Place: US," *Times of India*, October 12, 200. External Affairs and Defense Minister, Jaswant Singh, stated: "I disagree with the assessment. We have disagreed with earlier also to this type of thesis being put up by the West. Rather than Kashmir, it was Afghanistan which is a flashpoint." See "India Rejects US Assessment of Kashmir as 'Most Dangerous,'" *Hindustan Times*, October 12, 2001.
3. Graham Allison, "Why We Must Act As If He Has The Bomb," *Washington Post*, November 17, 2001.
4. John F. Burns, "Uneasy Ally in Terror War Suddenly Feels More U. S. Pressure," *New York Times,* December 21, 2001.
5. Quoted by A. P. Venkateswaran in: "The Arrogance of Power," *Hindustan Times*, April 1, 1999.
6. "Indian Minister Praises Yugoslav Resistance to NATO," *Agence-France Presse*, Friday, December 31, 1999.
7. T. V. Rajeswar, "A Warning to All," *Hindustan Times*, May 1, 1999.
8. Foreign Secretary of India, A. P. Venkateswaran, "The Arrogance of Power," *Hindustan Times*, April 1, 1999.
9. Siddharth Varadarajan, "Ruses for War: NATO's New Strategic Concept," *Times of India*, May 10, 1999.
10. Mukchund Dubey, "The NATO Juggernaut: The Logic of an Indian Defence Deterrent," *Times of India*, April 8, 1999. See also A. P. Venkataswaran, "The

Arrogance of Power," *Hindustan Times*, April 1, 1999; Siddharth Varadarajan, "NATO on a Dangerous and Illegal Course," *Times of India*, March 29, 1999; C. Raja Mohan, "Kosovo: The Liberals War," *Hindu*, April 6, 1999; and Lt. General Satish Nambiar, "NATO Celebrates Its Fiftieth Anniversary by Destroying Yugoslavia," *Mediterranean Quarterly*, vol. 10, no. 3, Summer 1999, pp. 15-24.

11. See K. Subrahmanyam, "Clear and Present Danger: US Path to Unipolar Hegemony," *Times of India*, May 3, 1999.

12. Endorsing the prospect of a Moscow-Beijing-New Delhi trilateral security relationship, an editorial in the *Hindustan Times*, May 31, 1999, noted that "NATO's ruthless action in Yugoslavia may bring India and Russia (and possibly China) even closer together as they realize the danger of a world with only one superpower."

13. See *Times of India* editorial, "Securing Our Future," April 3, 1999.

14. See chapter in this volume by Ben Sheppard entitled, "Ballistic Missiles: Complicating the Nuclear Quagmire."

15. Shekhar Gupta, "Putin-PM Declaration Today to Reflect Common Enemy (terrorism) and Common Ally (U. S.)," *Indian Express*, November 6, 2001.

16. See "NATO Proposes Closer Security Link with Russia," *New York Times*, November 22, 2001.

17. See Karen Deign and Dana Milbank, "Bush, Putin Agree to Slash Nuclear Arms," *Washington Post*, November 13, 2001; Peter Baker, "A Familiar Bush Strategy on Disarmament," *Washington Post*, November 13, 2001; "Look Deep Into Putin's Eyes and Seal the Deal," *The Los Angeles Times*, November 14, 2001; Michael Gordon, "U. S. Arsenal: Treaties vs. Non-Treaties," *New York Times*, November 14, 2001.

18. *India Network News Digest,* December 18, 2001, Volume 13, Issue 20; and *Hindustan Times,* December 19, 2001.

19. *Washington Post*, November 9, 2001.

20. See Steven Munson, "U. S. Nightmare: Broken Arrow From Pak N-Arsenal," *Indian Express*, November 6, 2001. This article was reproduced in this Indian newspaper from *The Los Angeles Times*. See also David Willman and Alan C. Miller, "Nuclear Threat is Real: The Former Soviet Stockpile is Seen as a Likely Source of Weaponry for Terrorists," *The Los Angeles Times*, November 11, 2001.

21. Cited in Steven Munson, "U. S. Nightmare: Broken Arrow From Pak N-Arsenal," *Indian Express*, November 6, 2001.

22. See Molly Moore and Kamran Khan, "Pakistan Moves Nuclear Weapons," *Washington Post*, November 10, 2001.

23. *Washington Post*, November 10, 2001.

24. See Itty Abraham, *The Making of the Indian Atomic Bomb: Science, Secrecy and the Postcolonial State*, London: Zed Books, 1998.

25. Abraham, pp. 9-10.

26. Abraham, p. 28.

27. See George Perkovich's chapter in this volume.

28. Bharat Karnad, "Policy on CTBT," *Hindustan Times*, November 4, 1999. Karnad 's observation may also be found in his chapter in this book.

29. Barry Bearak, "India, Beauty Superpower, Is Becoming Jaded," *New York Times*, December 13, 2000.

30. From Barry Bearak, "India, Beauty Superpower, Is Becoming Jaded," *New York Times*, December 13, 2000.

31. For a useful and comprehensive study of U. S. actions, see Henry D. Sokolski: *Best of Intentions: America's Campaign Against Strategic Weapons Proliferations*, Westport, Conn.: Preager Publishers, 2001.

32. A detailed description and evaluation of U. S. nonproliferation policy in India and Pakistan may be found in Leonard Spector, *The Undeclared Bomb*, pp. 80-148.

CHAPTER TWO

What Makes The Indian Bomb Tick?

George Perkovich

Summary

This chapter summarizes the history of India's nuclear-weapons development program and the central factors that shaped it. The history is divided into four somewhat distinct phases, with the third culminating in the nuclear tests of May 1998. The chapter then chronicles unusually dramatic events of the fourth phase, beginning in 1999—the Lahore summit; the Kargil War; the draft nuclear doctrine. The chapter suggests that these events indicated some of the difficulties India would have adjusting to the benefits and liabilities of overtly possessing nuclear weapons. The chapter concludes by noting that after a fifty-year epoch, in which India took a singular approach to nuclear weapons, Indian strategists and officials are now on a slippery slope toward convergence with the dominant, realpolitik conception and management of nuclear weapons, which India always had derided as irrational, immoral, and excessively dangerous.

Introduction

What are the major factors that have shaped the evolution of India's nuclear capabilities and policies, including the 1998 nuclear weapon tests? What do developments since the Indian and Pakistani tests say about the future of nuclear security in South Asia?

The conventional Western explanation is, in the words of Bradley Thayer, that the "central cause of Indian nuclear proliferation is a realist one, it was to match the capabilities of China."[1] As the U. S. Defense Department put it, "The bitter rivalry between India and Pakistan remains the impetus behind the proliferation of NBC [nuclear, biological, and chemical] weapons and missiles in the region."[2]

This essay will argue that domestic factors have been at least as important as external security considerations in determining India's nuclear policies. China doubtless has affected Indian interests in acquiring nuclear weapons capability, but the concern has been more about keeping up with China's status as an emerging great political-economic power than with countering a particular military security threat. Moreover, India's quest for nuclear weapon capabilities began before a Chinese threat emerged and was driven not by the military or national security experts, but rather by a charismatic nuclear physicist, Homi Bhabha, who wanted to establish himself and his nation at the apogee of modern scientific-technical achievement. From Bhabha onward, India's ambitious, persuasive, and prestigious nuclear scientists have pushed nuclear capabilities forward with little studied reference to the security situation. The nation's moral norms and post-colonial identity also have affected nuclear policymaking much more extensively than military-security models would hold. Peculiar institutional processes of nuclear policymaking, too, have been enormously important, reflecting domestic imperatives. These and other domestic factors tell us as much about the evolution of India's nuclear capability than does the external security environment.

India's nuclear history to date can be divided into three phases.[3] The first phase began with the formation of the Atomic Energy Commission in 1948 and ended with the conduct of India's first nuclear explosion, in 1974. During this period, the Indian nuclear establishment gradually acquired the materials, know-how, and technology required to detonate nuclear explosives. The second phase ran from 1975 to 1995 and was marked by singular self-restraint in not conducting further nuclear tests and deploying a nuclear arsenal. The transition to the third phase began in 1995 and led to the 1998 nuclear tests that seemed to put India on a course to weaponizing and deploying a nuclear arsenal. Several important events occurred in 1999 to suggest that the trajectory of Indian nuclear policy remained uncertain.

Phase One: 1947–1974

With Jawaharlal Nehru's backing, the physicist Homi Bhabha launched India's nuclear program even before independence.[4] No overt plans existed for building nuclear weapons in this early period, and, indeed, Nehru decried nuclear weapons in all of his pronouncements on the subject. Nehru sought to position India as a moral exemplar, a state that could lead the transformation of the international system away from over-militarized power politics and toward a more equitable global order. He and other Indians also saw nuclear weapons in the context of the colonial narrative wherein it was no accident that nuclear weapons had been used by a white-led nation against an Asian people. However, notwithstanding his idealistic, antinuclear leanings, the worldly Nehru also recognized that India could gain international power, standing and a measure of security if it acquired nuclear weapon capability. Thus, Nehru hedged many of his antibomb statements with qualifications that India could develop nuclear weapon capability and might choose to do so someday.[5]

Homi Bhabha, who remains the dominant historical figure of India's nuclear program, sought to create a world-class nuclear complex. Joining the nuclear euphoria of the early 1950s, Bhabha asserted that nuclear power would fuel a tremendous rise in India's economic development and would speed the country toward the upper echelon of modern industrial states. While almost all of his efforts in the 1950s were dedicated to building a multifaceted civilian nuclear complex, Bhabha (and his successors) did intend to develop dual-use nuclear capabilities. They drew adeptly on international assistance to do it. While playing a major role in 1956 international negotiations on nuclear non-proliferation safeguards, Bhabha outlined how a state could create a parallel nuclear weapon program drawing on "know-how obtained" from safeguarded International Atomic Energy Agency (IAEA) programs.[6] Rather than urge measures to reduce the prospect of such parallel programming, Bhabha tried successfully to weaken the grip of prospective IAEA safeguards. With weakened safeguard provisions accepted, Bhabha in 1958 ordered the construction of a plutonium reprocessing plant that could extract weapons-grade plutonium from spent fuel. The plant was based on American blueprints and was engineered by an American contractor. It began trial runs in 1964, decades before any commercial use of plutonium existed. Bhabha's plans to acquire this key requisite for nuclear weapons emerged prior to threats from China or other sources and, indeed, without reference to such threats.

Bhabha's and Nehru's early interest in acquiring the technical option to build nuclear weapons stemmed more from a desire to manifest Indian prowess, modernity, and sovereignty than from a sense of military threat. Several times in the late 1950s and early 1960s the two men made vague and seemingly reluctant references to India's capacity to build nuclear weapons.[7] Nehru said in 1958: "We have the technical know-how for manufacturing the atom bomb. We can do it in three or four years if we divert sufficient resources in that direction. But we have given the world an assurance that we shall never do so." Nehru's statement revealed the advantages he believed India could accrue from its unique, ambiguous approach to nuclear weapons. By claiming the technical capacity to build the bomb, India (and its scientists) would win international prestige on scientific-technical-military grounds, while the resistance to the temptation actually to build nuclear weapons would earn moral prestige. In 1958, and indeed even the early 1960s, India did not have the bomb know-how Nehru claimed. Had such boasts of nuclear weapon capability been technically valid, they could have conveyed a deterrent message against a potential adversary. As it was, India would not have the material, equipment, and designs necessary for detonating a nuclear weapon in anything like three or four years from 1958. But Bhabha and the nuclear establishment operated under such autonomy and secrecy that there was practically no one outside this establishment who could question its claims about current capabilities and future achievements.

If in the 1950s Bhabha and Nehru welcomed the dual-use, military-civilian potential of the nuclear program they were building, the interest in potential military applications grew from 1962 through 1964. After the 1962 war with China, Indian leaders recognized the need to pay much greater attention to national defense. They dramatically increased defense spending.[8] In December 1962, the Jana Sangh party called for building nuclear weapons, the first political stirrings against Nehru's apparent peaceful-uses-only policy.[9] Yet, few if any changes were made within the nuclear establishment to reflect a new course. This owed much to the fact that the plutonium production reactor and reprocessing facility required for building nuclear weapons were already being constructed.

It was China's initial nuclear blast, on October 16, 1964, that ignited the first major debate over India's nuclear policy. The somewhat surprising delay in openly addressing the nation's national security requirements stemmed from the dominant role that Nehru had played in international affairs. Nehru's death in May 1964 therefore opened the door for rethinking India's positions, and the Chinese test pushed politicians and pundits through it. Throughout October and November, parliamentarians staked out competing positions, ranging from Prime Minister Shastri and Krishna Menon's stalwart opposition to building nuclear weapons, to the Swatantra Party's preference for alliance with the West, to the Jana Sangh's advocacy of a bomb-building program. Bhabha, as before, played a central role in the debate. Advocates of nuclear weapons cited his misleading October 18 radio broadcast as "proof" that India could build a nuclear arsenal cheaply, while critics urged that Bhabha had been misleading and was improperly trying to affect policy decisions.[10]

The most instructive debate occurred in Parliament on November 23 and 24, 1964. Pro-bomb speakers argued in a realist vein that China would now grow into "a giant," and that India would "remain a dwarf" if it did not build nuclear weapons.[11] Others argued that China did not develop nuclear weapons to threaten India, but rather to deal with Russia and the United States. These arguments were countered with charges of pro-Chinese or pro-American bias. Still other commentators argued that China did not pose as much a military threat to India as a political-psychological one. As the journalist Inder Malhotra put it, China would gain global support at India's expense by giving "the colored peoples in the world a sense of pride that one of them has been able to break what has hitherto been a monopoly of the white nations."[12]

Opponents of a bomb-building program argued that the cost would undermine India's economic development that had to be a greater priority. This in turn could sabotage India's democracy. As one parliamentarian, M. R. Masani noted, "the brutal, heartless dictatorship" in China could "get away with" a crash nuclear weapon program, "but can any democratic government, whatever the party, hope to survive in a democracy if it asks the people to do without food and clothing so that the wretched bomb may be made?"[13] Critics also argued that nuclear weapons did not provide readily usable military power, as France was finding in Vietnam, and Great Britain had found in Suez. Prime Minister Shastri closed the two-day debate by saying that moral imperatives and economic costs should keep India from departing from its position of abjuring nuclear weapons.

However, Shastri was a new and beleaguered prime minister whose position within his own Congress party already was eroding due to domestic problems. He clearly felt political pressure to take a more robust nuclear policy line, especially since the Congress party's foreign policy acumen was already doubted in the aftermath of the 1962 defeat at the hands of China. Thus, Shastri closed by saying that the no-bomb policy could be subject to change. In the ensuing days he found himself under growing pressure to make a change. The hardline Jana Sangh and a left-wing grouping of Socialist parties demanded that India build bombs. In doing this they cited Homi Bhabha's low cost estimates and apparent advocacy of building explosives. Thus, on November 27, in yet another Lok Sabha debate, Shastri announced a barely noticed but major shift in nuclear policy.[14] He declared that the Atomic Energy Commission would pursue development of *peaceful* nuclear explosives for purposes such as tunneling through mountains.

Shastri's shift owed much to Homi Bhabha. The prime minister talked with Bhabha twice on the day of his announcement, and then invoked Bhabha's name in explaining why peaceful nuclear explosives should be pursued. Indeed, the best explanation for the shift was domestic: Shastri's leadership position within the Congress party was in jeopardy, largely due to internal economic problems, and his colleagues, generally citing Bhabha, wanted a more robust nuclear policy to demonstrate the party's leadership capacity. Unless and until Shastri could align his nuclear policy with Bhabha's apparent preference, Shastri would be attacked. Once Bhabha was satisfied, there was little basis for others to criticize Shastri. And so the prime minister and the scientist hit on a compromise that actually was optimal from Bhabha's point of view. Little technical difference existed between a peaceful explosive and a bomb, but declaring the interest in the former would not jeopardize the international nuclear assistance India needed. Pursuing a bomb would undermine the overall nuclear program. Moreover, a peaceful nuclear explosive effort could be reconciled with India's normative rejection of nuclear weapons, in which Shastri personally believed, and on which some of India's world prestige depended.

Thus, the 1964 decision to proceed toward a peaceful nuclear explosive capability was clearly precipitated by the need to respond to China's acquisition of nuclear weapons, but was a much more complicated move than a security-first explanation would convey. Indian decision-makers were conflicted over whether and why to build explosives. Even those who advocated nuclear weapons did not offer any detailed military-security strategy to buttress their advocacy, beyond the rather vague feeling that India and China were competitors for major power rank in Asia, and China now was getting ahead. Remarkably, the Indian military were largely excluded from the debate and the policymaking process. This left the field to politicians and Bhabha, with pundits making arguments from outside. The policy that emerged also reflected the influence of morality and economics: India stood for the moral improvement of the international system and Shastri shared the moral aversion to nuclear weapons enunciated by Gandhi and, with ambiguity, Nehru. To preserve India's moral standing, any work on nuclear explosives had to be seen as peaceful.

Shastri's endorsement of a peaceful nuclear explosive project did not turn out to signal a major change in the nuclear program's course. In 1965, Bhabha and his colleagues privately confronted the fact that they were not close to being able to build a nuclear explosive, notwithstanding years of claims to the contrary. As detailed in George Perkovich's *India's Nuclear Bomb*, Bhabha then quietly pursued American technical assistance, which was not forthcoming.[15] Meanwhile, Shastri elliptically sought international security guarantees to protect India in the event of nuclear threats from China. The Indian military rehabilitated its reputation in 1965 by defeating Pakistan in war, but Indian elites were alarmed by an ultimatum China had given (and then ignored) to India to withdraw construction works from Tibet. The victorious war had the paradoxical effect of re-igniting the bomb debate in India. Yet, unbeknownst to many of the debaters, Atomic Energy Commission (AEC) scientists already had begun nuclear explosive design calculations.

The surprise death of Homi Bhabha in an airplane crash in January 1966 led to personnel changes that slowed the nuclear explosive work. The task of choosing a successor to Bhabha fell to Indira Gandhi who had been named prime minister upon Shastri's sudden death from a heart attack, also in January 1966. Mrs. Gandhi selected Vikram Sarabhai who proved once again that individuals matter in nuclear policymaking. For Sarabhai, more than Bhabha, had a moral objection to nuclear weapons and did not share Bhabha's enthusiasm for grandiose (and self-aggrandizing) projects that did not further India's development needs. Early in his tenure he ordered scientists such as Raja Ramanna to stop working on explosive designs.[16] Sarabhai's order reflected his moral commitment, temperament, and assessment that India's well being depended more on economic development than on nuclear explosives. As before, national security experts and the military were not consulted.

By 1966, international negotiations on a prospective nuclear nonproliferation treaty were in full swing, with India playing a major role. Among other things, India demanded that a fair treaty must obligate existing nuclear-weapons states to freeze and then eliminate their nuclear arsenals, and must provide security guarantees to states that do not acquire nuclear weapons. While professing its own abjuration of nuclear weapons, India refused to surrender the right to develop and detonate peaceful nuclear explosives as long as the recognized nuclear-weapons states retained the right to conduct nuclear detonations. India's position on the treaty reflected the now traditional duality of its nuclear policy: It took strong moral positions against nuclear weapons and against discrimination by "haves" against "have-nots," and it also reserved the right to acquire nuclear explosive capabilities as long as any other states enjoyed such rights. At the core of India's position was a demand for equity and a perception that the emerging nonproliferation regime amounted to "nuclear apartheid."[17] This racially laden perception of the problem informed Indian debates and policies for decades to come.

At the end of 1967 it appeared unlikely that the United States and the USSR would agree to the kind of nonproliferation treaty India sought. In April 1968 Prime Minister Gandhi explained to the Lok Sabha that India would vote against the treaty but at the same time, in her view, India would find no security benefit in acquiring nuclear weapons. Indeed she said that pursuing nuclear weapons would weaken the country by diverting its resources from more productive uses, something that only India's enemies would welcome.[18]

It has been argued that India's prime motivation in rejecting the treaty was to keep open its bomb-building option, but this neglects the depth of Indira Gandhi's ambivalence, the doggedness of Morarji Desai and other leaders' moral opposition to nuclear weapons, and the lack of support for anything resembling an ambitious nuclear-weapons-building program. The general public outside of New Delhi knew almost nothing about these matters, meaning that the subject was an elite affair. With the military excluded from decision-making, the matter fell to a small circle of central government officials and scientists. There was near consensus against accepting the inequities of the Nuclear Non-proliferation Treaty (NPT), while there was no consensus on building bombs. For their part, the scientists did not seek or want a major military nuclear program. They wanted to design prototype nuclear explosives to show their countrymen and the world that India could accomplish world-class technological feats. At the same time, they wanted to keep the military out of the nuclear policymaking councils.

Thus, behind the scenes, and without prime ministerial authorization, the physics director of the Bhabha Atomic Research Center (BARC), Raja Ramanna secretly instructed the physicist Rajagopala Chidambaram to calculate the equation of state for plutonium, a calculation needed for the design of nuclear weapons. This was a major challenge that Chidambaram and a few colleagues eagerly pursued over ensuing months. Other scientists and engineers within the AEC and the Defense Research and Development Organization (DRDO) also quietly began to prepare the scientific and engineering ground for building a nuclear explosive. At some point Sarabhai realized what his subordinates were doing, and although he had not authorized them, he did not now try to stop them. Sarabhai and the then-director of BARC, Homi Sethna, deeply disliked one another, and it was Sethna and Raja Ramanna who determined to push ahead on explosives. None of these nuclear establishment leaders had any background or expertise in international security affairs or foreign relations, nor did they consult with people who did. They wanted to build nuclear explosives in large part to demonstrate to themselves, their country-men, and the world that they could do it, and to provide the strength and power generally associated with nuclear weapons.

India's Nuclear Bomb reveals a number of scientific and technological hur-dles that still had to be overcome by the nuclear establishment. For brevity's sake it can be said that by the time of Sarabhai's fatal heart attack in December 1971, much of the job had been completed. (However, one absolutely vital component—the neutron initiator—was not completed until 1974, belying many claims that India could have built a bomb much earlier.) What remained to be obtained was the prime minister's authorization to build and detonate a nuclear device.

By fall of 1971 Indira Gandhi had made statements revealing that momen-tum was building for a peaceful nuclear explosion. U. S. government officials were concerned enough to urge Canadian Prime Minister Pierre Trudeau to write to Indira Gandhi and declare that use of Canadian inputs to develop a peaceful nuclear explosive would seriously threaten Canadian-Indian nuclear cooperation.[19]

In December 1971, war intervened. A violent internal crisis in East Pakistan dragged Pakistan and India into a direct military confrontation that ended in India's victory and the transformation of East Pakistan into the independent country of Bangladesh. Although the war was first and foremost an Indo-Pak affair, it was seen, especially by Washington, against the background of the newly formed triangular balance of power relationship among the United States, China and the Soviet Union. Henry Kissinger had in July 1971 made his breakthrough visit to China, with Pakistani assistance. Less than a month later, India and the Soviet Union signed a Treaty of Peace, Friendship and Co-operations (that had been negotiated earlier).

Given the drama of the war and its background, it is reasonable to search for its bearing on India's subsequent nuclear policies. Sumit Ganguly aptly notes that "India emerged" from the war "as the preeminent power on the subcontinent."[20] Moreover, Ganguly adds, the Friendship Treaty with Moscow "greatly assuaged India's fears about military pressure on its borders from a recalcitrant and nuclear-armed China." This analysis undermines his and other writers' conclusions that "security concerns" were what "pushed the country further down the nuclear path" toward the Pokhran test. In the post-war period, India's military security situation did not require nuclear but-tressing. A closer look at the decision to conduct India's first peaceful nuclear explosive in 1974 shows that issues of scientific ambition and momentum, interpersonal relations, and an intuitive desire to demonstrate India's prowess and greatness were more important than any grand national security strategy.

Chronicling the rationale and sequence of decisions that led to the 1974 peaceful nuclear explosion remains difficult. Very few people were involved and, according to participants, they did not make notes of their discussions. The key decision-maker, Indira Gandhi, never unburdened herself of her thought processes on the matter. We can say that in September 1972, Indira Gandhi authorized the chairman of the Atomic Energy Commission, Homi Sethna, to build a nuclear explosive device, with the assumption that it would then be detonated in a "peaceful" experiment. It took the small team of AEC and DRDO scientists and engineers another year and a half to ready the device, in part because of difficulties making the neutron initiator that is vital to spawning the efficient chain reaction of a nuclear explosive. In January and February 1973 the key decision makers, Prime Minister Gandhi, AEC Chairman Homi Sethna, the director of the key nuclear laboratory Raja Ramanna, and two close personal advisors to the prime minister, met to discuss the pending decision with Gandhi. Ramanna, who enjoyed an unusually close relationship of mutual respect with Mrs. Gandhi, was the chief advocate of detonating the device. The two political advisors, P. N. Haksar and P. N. Dhar, opposed the move, arguing that it would raise the likelihood of militarization, and divert India from its economic priorities, and cause international political trouble. It is vital to note that no military representatives were involved in the decision-making process, and none of the participants had expertise in military-strategic affairs. According to Ramanna, Prime Minister Gandhi did not ask questions during the deliberations or otherwise reveal her thinking. She listened and then said simply to Ramanna, "Let's have it."

The PNE generated temporary euphoria and lasting celebration of the scientists. The nuclear establishment soon announced that the explosive yield was about 12 kilotons, or the same as the U. S. weapon dropped on Hiroshima. This claim has been maintained ever since. However, reliable sources within the Indian nuclear establishment have acknowledged privately that the yield was "much lower."[21] The lower-than-claimed yield had several lasting implications. It reaffirmed a pattern of excessive projections and claims by the nuclear and defense science establishments in a system where no independent body of scientists existed to evaluate such claims on behalf of the public interest. The nuclear (and DRDO) establishment has used its aura of prowess to win widespread public adulation, bureaucratic autonomy, funding, and political influence—gains that would have been undermined had the proficiency of the tested device been proved unimpressive. Similarly, if doubts about the performance of nuclear explosives grew, the military, which could someday have to rely on these weapons in life-or-death conflicts, could press for a greater voice in nuclear policymaking and a possible checking role on the scientists. Knowing this, the nuclear establishment was motivated to win permission for other tests to allay any doubts. When these tests were finally approved in 1998, the questionable yield of the 1974 explosive came back into play: The top scientists in 1998 based their declarations of those tests' explosive yields on calculations that took the 1974 yield as the benchmark. In doing this they insisted falsely that the 1974 yield was 13 kilotons. This raised anew all of the problems mentioned here.

In the years following the test, Indira Gandhi did not offer any detailed explanation of her decision. She told the American writer Rodney Jones in an interview, "The PNE [Peaceful Nuclear Explosion] was simply done when we were ready. We did it to show ourselves that we could do it. . . . We did it when the scientists were ready."[22] The strategic nature of the decision was acknowledged (and lamented) by many Indian commentators in subsequent decades. The scientists complained that they were not allowed to conduct follow on tests, which they had assumed would be the natural progression. The military bemoaned that it had been left out of the loop before the test and not brought in afterwards, despite the fact that the test would likely affect Pakistan's and China's military strategies against India. Professional diplomats regretted that the scientists had mistakenly convinced Prime Minister Gandhi that the international repercussions of the test would be minor, failing to anticipate the international sanctions that arose against India's nuclear program.

Thus, after the Pokhran test India found itself with the demonstrable capacity to build nuclear explosives, but with no policy actually to go ahead and do so. The government maintained the traditional commitment only to use atomic energy for peaceful purposes and declared it would not make nuclear weapons. This position reflected the Gandhian self-image of India as well as the press of competing economic and political priorities. Indira Gandhi and others hoped that self-restraint would bring international respect for the nation's moral singularity. Other states that detonated nuclear devices went on to build horrible arsenals of war; India showed it could do the same, but chose virtuously to abstain. The explosive technology demonstrated that India was among the world's leading technological powers and could become a major military power if it chose to.

India's nuclear decision-making remained in the grip of the prime minister, a handful of close political advisors, and the leaders of the nuclear establishment. Now, as before, the scientists wished to move forward and design more sophisticated, deliverable nuclear explosives, but they were stymied by a reluctant prime minister. While the scientists conceivably could have built a potent bureaucratic-political alliance with the military to favor a more robust policy, they chose not to. The nuclear establishment leaders did not want to let other actors into their bailiwick. The scientists—mostly Brahmins—had been granted great autonomy, resources, and freedom from oversight, and they did not want to open themselves to questioning and pressures from military officials who the scientists felt probably would not understand the issues involved. In this, the scientists were joined by successive prime ministers who also wanted to keep the military at arms distance from decision-making and who also worried that militarization of the nuclear program could drive up costs enormously.

Phase Two, 1975–1995

The categories of personality, morality, institutional structure, and political economy that so strongly affected the journey from 1947 to the first Pokhran test in 1974 remained important in the following years, too. Remarkably, and contrary to most expectations, India did not conduct follow on tests for the next 24 years. If external security considerations had determined Mrs. Gandhi's decision to test in 1974, then this variable could not explain the subsequent restraint, unless the one test so fundamentally improved the security situation as to obviate the need for further tests and robust weaponization. There is no reason to believe that this "peaceful" nuclear explosion was so decisive in security terms. Indeed, realists like Henry Kissinger, strategists like K. Subrahmanyam, and scientists like those at the helm of the Indian AEC all assumed that India would *and should* proceed steadfastly toward developing a nuclear arsenal. It is well then to try to explain why India instead adopted a policy of self-restraint.

The first major "event" in the post–1974 phase of India's nuclear history was the state of emergency declared by Indira Gandhi in June 1975. This reflected a degree of domestic turmoil that made the popular euphoria following Pokhran an ironic and distant memory. Mrs. Gandhi and the polity at large simply had more important things to worry about than nuclear policy. The prime minister displayed little interest in the issue.

The state of emergency ended in 1977 and Morarji Desai was elected prime minister. Desai evinced a strong moral aversion to nuclear weapons and a mistrust of the leadership of the Indian nuclear establishment. In his first press conference, on March 24, 1977, he told a West German interviewer, "I will give it to you in writing that we will not manufacture nuclear weapons. Even if the whole world arms itself with the bombs we will not do so."[23] Desai frequently criticized the decision to conduct the 1974 nuclear explosion.

Desai was a quirky man, and his moral position was unusually rigid, but he nonetheless represented a durable and important strand of Indian thinking about nuclear weapons. His thorough opposition to nuclear weapons was matched with an insistence that India would not sign the NPT because the treaty was inequitable. Both positions reflected India's moral self-image, a desire to express and demonstrate internationally India's moral superiority to the Cold War powers. This position could then earn international respect and prestige for the nation that lacked the economic and military strength to win international due. Leaders of the pro-bomb Jana Sangh, including then Foreign Minister Atal Bihari Vajpayee, went along with this nuclear policy despite the fact that Pakistan was gearing up construction of the Kahuta uranium enrichment plant.

Indira Gandhi returned to power in 1980, following the collapse of Desai's fragmented government. She immediately repudiated Desai's pledge not to conduct further nuclear explosive tests and criticized him for not heeding the interests and advice of the nuclear establishment.[24] However, she did not say that she would actually reverse Desai's policy and order nuclear tests.

External security considerations could have warranted a more robust line: The Soviet Union was now deep into its war in Afghanistan; Pakistan's nuclear-weapons program was advancing steadily; the United States was providing enormous levels of military aid to Pakistan; China was deepening its ties to Pakistan, in part to counter the Soviet advance into Southwest Asia. Still, much of the attention Indian leaders gave to nuclear policy at this time centered on negotiating with Washington an escape from the congressionally mandated cut off of nuclear fuel for the Tarapur reactors. These negotiations succeeded in late 1982.

Shortly thereafter, the leaders of the Atomic Energy Commission and the Defense Research and Development Organization pressed Prime Minister Gandhi to authorize another nuclear test (or tests). The process for considering this request was more developed than the one leading to the 1974 test, with Defense Minister R. Venkataraman playing an important role. However, once again, the scientists and the top politicians excluded the military from deliberations on nuclear policy. Eight years after Pokhran, Indira Gandhi once again acceded to the recommendation of the top scientists and authorized a test. However, within 24 hours she changed her mind and canceled the authorization. Thereafter, according to one of the scientists involved, she "refused to entertain a meeting with us on that subject."[25] Whatever arguments security and military analysts made about the growing external challenges to India, the prime minister remained unswayed. She felt personally uncomfortable with the idea of India's building nuclear weapons, did not see what real gains would accrue from it, and preferred to concentrate on matters closer to home.

Throughout the mid-1980s, under both Indira Gandhi and her successor son Rajiv, Indian leaders recognized that Pakistan's nuclear-weapons capability steadily advanced. China faded to the background of India's security concerns. Top Indian officials, including now military officers, considered three alternatives for dealing with the looming Pakistani threat: Destroy Pakistan's nuclear infrastructure with a pre-emptive air attack; increase India's own nuclear strength; and third, use diplomacy to stabilize relations with Pakistan and improve ties with the United States. The first alternative was considered seriously several times but ultimately rejected as unduly provocative and counterproductive. Indira and Rajiv Gandhi did pursue the second course—increasing India's nuclear strength—but did so ambivalently. They approved no nuclear tests and generally resisted the advice of hawkish strategists and military officers who pushed for a weapon-building program. However, in 1983 Indira Gandhi did approve an ambitious program to develop, test, and produce ballistic missiles. This program would be the basis of a future nuclear arsenal if India so chose. In 1985, India opened its second plutonium production reactor, Dhruva, 12 years after construction on it began. The modest and generally self-restrained approach to nuclear weapon development in the mid-1980s coincided with diplomatic efforts to warm relations with the United States. India hoped that the United States would help constrain Pakistan's nuclear program and open the gates to high technology cooperation with Indian industry, particularly in the defense and computer sectors.

Strong cases could be made for the wisdom of Indian policy in the mid-1980s, but from a security-first, realist perspective, India's response to the growing Pakistani nuclear threat was remarkably self-restrained. One reason for this restraint was Rajiv Gandhi's general aversion to nuclear weapons and preference for nuclear disarmament. The ascendancy of Mikhail Gorbachev in the Soviet Union, just months into Rajiv's tenure, raised the prospect of dramatic progress in global nuclear disarmament, and Rajiv genuinely sought to augment this. This was somehow fitting: Gorbachev said that his desire to pursue peace (and hence nuclear disarmament) stemmed in part from his attendance at a 1955 speech in Moscow by Rajiv's grandfather, Jawaharlal Nehru, who, according to Gorbachev, "linked the question of peace to the preservation and progress of all human civilization."[26] Rajiv also got along poorly with the chairman of the Atomic Energy Commission, Raja Ramanna, and felt that the nuclear establishment had failed miserably to live up to its promises to fuel India's economic development with abundant and cheap electricity. This dissatisfaction inclined the prime minister against satisfying the wishes of the nuclear establishment as his mother had. And indeed, the nuclear establishment suffered many ills at this time. Among them were a series of failures in the heavy water production program that led to a shortage of heavy water to moderate power reactors.[27]

India's restraint also owed to a desire not to disrupt high technology cooperation with the United States. Rajiv Gandhi and his top science advisor, DRDO head V. S. Arunachalam thought that India's ultimate development and strength depended more on enhancing technological expertise and resources across the board, with American help, than in focusing on nuclear weapons. Here they differed with others such as AEC Chairman Ramanna who preferred the more traditional, post-colonial insistence on being self-reliant in policy, if not in fact. In 1986, when the American researcher Gary Milhollin published a report that India had bought and clandestinely received heavy water from China, Ramanna reacted in a way that revealed the recurrent and vitally important issue of racist colonialism in India's perceptions of the nuclear arena. "We are all used to white people having a low opinion of us and I can see how jealous some of them become when we achieve total independence in our nuclear requirements," the AEC chairman said.[28]

By the end of 1987 and the aftermath of the Brasstacks military crisis between India and Pakistan, Pakistan had all the necessary components to assemble a nuclear weapon. In this, Pakistan benefited enormously from Chinese assistance in supplying weapon designs, components, and technology for fissile material production. Indian scientists at this time, drawn from the Atomic Energy Commission and the Defense Research and Development Organization, were working on designs and components for lighter and smaller nuclear weapons and were designing more sophisticated boosted-fission weapons. Characteristically, the Indian effort was driven and directed by the scientists, while the Pakistani program was controlled by the military. Pakistani teams, led by the Atomic Energy Commission (belying the engineer A. Q. Khan's self-aggrandizing propaganda that he was "father" of the Pakistani bomb), concentrated on producing deliverable nuclear weapons based on a simple, robust design, while the Indian scientists pursued sophistication over weapon utility. The net effect was that Pakistan began to outpace India in the militarization of nuclear capacity, while Indian scientists outdid their Pakistani counterparts in the elegance and technical ambition of their prototype designs. All of these developments, of course, occurred under cover of secrecy. This greatly complicated the capacity of Indian and Pakistani officials to know how they stacked up against each other. This ambiguity arguably allowed the maximum deterrent effect at the lowest financial cost.

Had the Indian military been given a voice or roll in nuclear policymaking, the professional predilection for worst-case assessments probably would have spurred Indian leaders to authorize a more robust weapon development effort. As it was, however, the military was still excluded from significant influence. Nuclear policy remained in the hands of the prime minister who was in turn influenced by a small circle of advisors, most prominent among them DRDO head Arunachalam, who himself took council from strategists such as K. Subrahmanyam and Arun Singh. Rajiv assented to the scientists' desire to intensify preparations of militarily deliverable nuclear bombs in 1988, though weapons were not made operational at this point and little effort was made to provide the kind of exercising that Air Force leaders felt necessary to have a serious nuclear capability.[29] Rajiv and the scientists had no desire to emulate Western and Soviet deterrence doctrines and practices which seemed to them unrealistic, excessively sanguine about the utility of nuclear weapons, immoral, and unaffordable. Instead of a hyperactive quest for escalation dominance and nuclear war-winning capabilities, Rajiv and his advisors believed that sufficient deterrence was achieved if an adversary contemplating a first strike on India could not be certain that he would *not* receive retaliatory nuclear devastation. Given India's vastness and the opportunity to disperse nuclear assets widely enough that an adversary, especially Pakistan, could not figure on destroying all of them, this sort of deterrence did not require deploying an active nuclear arsenal. And if deterrence obtained without active deployment, India's actual nuclear capabilities could be left ambiguous. This ambiguity in turn allowed a more minimalist array of capabilities to be produced. An adversary could not know how much of what nuclear weaponry India had. Given the stakes, an opponent could not afford to underestimate and therefore would likely be deterred from strategic aggression.

Nevertheless, India's and Pakistan's new and ambiguous nuclear weapon capabilities did not prevent the two states from falling into another political-military crisis in spring 1990 over Kashmir. The new Indian prime minister, V. P. Singh, recognized that he needed to assess what sort of threat Pakistan posed. To do this he gathered top scientists and government advisors, but did not invite military officers to attend. Only later did he consult the Air Force Chief of Staff in a one-on-one conversation, to the exclusion of other service chiefs and any systematic analysis of military factors.[30] This series of conversations concentrated on assessing Pakistan's likely nuclear doctrine and how India should respond under various conflict scenarios. When the 1990 crisis later peaked, in April and May, U. S. intelligence detected Pakistani preparations to assemble at least one nuclear weapon. President George Bush dispatched a team to Pakistan and India to urge calm. The visiting Americans found Indian leaders seemingly unaware that Pakistan was mobilizing to bring a nuclear weapon into the equation, for diplomatic leverage if not military use. The Indians correctly saw the crisis as a political one emanating from unfortunate developments in Kashmir and did not think war, especially nuclear war, was likely. Because neither India nor Pakistan actually sought war, it should not be said that nuclear weapons deterred war in this crisis. However, once the crisis ended, the Indian prime minister, at the urging of DRDO head V. S. Arunachalam, did constitute a secret committee to think through how India should plan to maintain governmental authority and manage nuclear responses in the event of a nuclear attack on New Delhi.[31]

Before the committee could complete its task, political tumult once again derailed nuclear policymaking, as V. P. Singh's government collapsed in November 1990 and was replaced by a short-lived government headed by Chandra Shekhar. Eventually, in May 1991, the Congress party's Narasimha Rao emerged from national elections as prime minister and took the reins of nuclear policy for what would turn out to be five years. Rao demonstrated again that the personality and outlook of prime ministers play major roles in shaping India's nuclear policy. His tenure also showed the economic considerations in a democratic polity can challenge the valuation that the rich nuclear-weapons states and their theorists have put on nuclear weapons.

Officials who worked closely with Prime Minister Rao recalled that he had moral and practical reservations about nuclear deterrence and did not see nuclear weapons as particularly useful for India.[32] While leaders of the DRDO and AEC continued to work on designs for sophisticated nuclear weapons and continued to test nuclear capable Prithvi and Agni ballistic missiles, Rao did not authorize a concerted nuclear weapon production program. India's nuclear capability remained modest, covert, and therefore ambiguous, while its nuclear policy remained ambivalent. This was the case, notwithstanding increasingly detailed revelations of Chinese technical assistance to Pakistan's nuclear and missile programs.

The Rao government believed that economic development and integration into the global economy were more important than nuclear weaponry in strengthening India. "If we cannot make our economic sinews strong," Rao said India would have no "political clout no one is going to take it seriously."[33] Here he articulated a view that could also be traced back to Nehru, Shastri, Desai, and other Indian leaders, a view that academics, nuclear strategists, and policymakers in rich Western countries tended to overlook thanks to their over-valuation of nuclear weapons.

Recognizing that the United States was emerging as the sole global super-power, and that Indian interests required closer ties with America, the Indian government in the early 1990s showed increasing interest in American-initiated proposals to constrain nuclear weapon development. The United States and

Russia by now had imposed moratoria on nuclear-weapons tests and sought progress in international negotiations on a test ban. Washington, Moscow, Paris, and London also proposed negotiations to end production of fissile-materials for explosive purposes. In December 1993 India cosponsored a UN General Assembly resolution calling for a treaty to ban unsafeguarded fissile material production, adding support of this potential constraint to the traditional Indian call for a test ban.

However, Rao's tentative interest in constraining India's nuclear option generated a concerted backlash from the nuclear and defense science establishments, the BJP, and the small but vocal circle of strategic analysts. These actors found much to react to in the spring of 1994 when the Clinton administration launched a diplomatic campaign to induce Pakistan to safeguard its fissile material production facilities in return for release of 28 F-16 aircraft that Pakistan had paid for but never received, due to Pressler Amendment sanctions. The administration's initiative contained other elements, including a regional ban on ballistic missile deployments, but the incentives for Pakistan were not matched in detail or magnitude by incentives for India to stop its production of fissile materials for explosives. Moreover, the domestic and external complexities of persuading the U. S. Congress and the governments and citizenry of India and Pakistan to fall into alignment around this initiative were simply overwhelming.[34] Revealingly, the prospect of such a bargain prompted AEC Chairman Chidambaram to make himself available for press interviews wherein he clearly denounced the U. S. proposals.[35] DRDO head Abdul Kalam also mobilized to invoke the issue of racism and colonialism in denouncing Washington's nonproliferation policy. Reminding an interviewer that India had entered "the rarefied strata of strategic missile competence" despite outside pressures, he said that denigration of India's technical achievements "is deliberately communicated because of racial prejudice where one group of people believes only they can do it."[36]

While the United States was preaching arms control to resistant South Asian officials, and Kalam was trying to invigorate support for the lagging missile program, DRDO teams joined with a handful of designated Air Force officers to conduct the first realistic test drop of a nuclear weapon from a Mirage 2000 aircraft. The event occurred near Basalore in May 1994, according to Raj Chengappa. A nuclear weapon, minus the fissile core, was affixed to the aircraft and released, falling a prescribed distance until triggering sensors released safety locks and detonated the high explosives package that compressed the dummy "nuclear" core in a simulation of an actual nuclear-weapons detonation.[37] After years of "relying" on a rudimentary capacity to deliver a retaliatory nuclear blow *in extremis,* India finally possessed what the Air Force could accept as an operational deterrent.

The U. S. nonproliferation initiative quickly died with the world and the Indian public none the wiser about the quiet advancement of India's deterrent. American officials shifted their attention to winning indefinite extension of the Nuclear Non-Proliferation Treaty, which was due to be decided upon in an

April-May 1995 conference of states parties to the treaty. As a nonparty to the treaty, India would not participate in the conference. But Indian diplomats and strategic pundits sought to rally nonaligned countries and others around the world to use the negotiations to press the five recognized nuclear-weapons states to commit themselves to concrete steps toward nuclear disarmament. In this they were joined by many nongovernmental activists within and outside of the nuclear-weapons states. To the dismay of many, the five nuclear powers rebuffed these pressures and generated a consensus by the 179 parties to extend the treaty indefinitely without further binding commitments to undertake disarmament. The only "concessions" extracted were contained in a parallel, non-binding statement of "Principles and Objectives for Nuclear Non-Proliferation and Disarmament." This included pledges to complete a comprehensive test ban treaty "no later than 1996," and to reach early conclusion on a ban against fissile-material production for explosive purposes.

This result left India more isolated than ever. One option now would have been to adapt to the mainstream and forego further nuclear-weapons development and possible testing. The option that India took instead was defiance. Indian commentators blasted the NPT extension as an eternal legitimation of "nuclear apartheid." India's anti-colonial identity then required deepened resistance to the nonproliferation regime. At the same time, the fact that the United States, China, Russia and the other nuclear-weapons states had managed to overwhelm any resistance suggested that they would also be able to push through a test-ban treaty soon. This meant that if India's strategic security interests, and/or the interests and desires of its nuclear scientists, required testing of nuclear weapons, India would have to move quickly or face enormous external pressure. More broadly, India's hawkish strategic community felt that the nation's moralistic approach to international nuclear politics had been repudiated decisively and that the only way to command international respect was to adopt the rhetoric, logic, and policies of realpolitik as defined and spoken by the West and China.

Thus, the second phase of India's nuclear history—a period of remarkable self-restraint and quiet scientific-technical advance—ended ironically with the indefinite extension of the NPT. Morality, individual personalities, institutional circumstances (the exclusion of the military), and economic priorities had combined to keep Indian leaders from conducting nuclear weapon tests and developing operational nuclear doctrines. Indian leaders knew that Pakistan had steadily acquired nuclear weapon and ballistic missile technologies, and that China had assisted decisively in this acquisition, even as Beijing also worked with New Delhi to improve bilateral ties. Where Western theorists and policymakers operating in the realist paradigm would have moved to deploy a nuclear arsenal long ago in these circumstances, India's leaders tried to hold out. But in the process, these leaders had less and less to show for their restraint, and a political opposition with a competing vision of India's interest, destiny, and the international community gained ascendancy. China's rising rank as an emerging global power heightened the sense that India must act more decisively to manifest the economic, military and political strength necessary to stand proudly on the global stage.

Phase Three: 1995–1998

The NPT extension and apparent momentum toward completing negotiations of a comprehensive test ban treaty suggested that outside pressures might limit India's nuclear options. At the same time, internal politics, particularly the growing power of the pro-bomb BJP, pushed India towards a more robust nuclear policy. Both trends augmented the influence of India's nuclear and defense science establishments. The fear that arms control might ensnare the nuclear program drove strategic analysts publicly to amplify the nuclear establishment's private advocacy of nuclear testing. Military officers more decorously intimated that if India were to need nuclear weapons, then such weapons needed to be tested.

Given these trends, it was not surprising that Narasimha Rao in the late summer of 1995 relented partially to the scientists' requests to conduct nuclear tests. Rao's Congress party had suffered ominous defeats in state elections in December 1994 and March 1995, and the BJP's political might was growing. The BJP sought to raise the electoral salience of security policy by exclaiming that it would end the days of Congress party pusillanimity and exercise the nuclear option. As the national elections loomed, Rao sometime in late summer endorsed the nuclear establishment's request to prepare for nuclear tests. The scientists told the prime minister that tests were needed to perfect and demonstrate India's technological capacity, and to prove the effectiveness of India's deterrent. They also stated that explosive tests were needed to recruit and retain talented scientists and engineers in the nuclear and defense programs. Without dramatic, full-scale tests, morale would fall and the aging scientific cohort that had prepared the first explosive in 1974 would not find suitable younger replacements.[38] Just as American presidents and the U. S. Senate in 1999 found such arguments persuasive in rejecting the CTBT, Rao, too, found it hard to rebuff the nuclear laboratories' pleas.

However, Rao had not yet decided actually to authorize a test(s) and, moreover, he did not have a nuclear strategy in mind to rationalize a test. He felt that the U. S. position on nonproliferation was so hypocritical as to be immoral, but this did not lead him to embrace Indian reliance on nuclear weapons either.[39] According to a knowledgeable former official in New Delhi, the prime minister "did not have a nuclear deterrence strategy. He didn't think about when it will be used, against whom, or these questions of doctrine. He didn't think these things were useable, and he was not planning to use them, so why spend a lot of time thinking about such things?"[40]

Before Rao reached a final decision, the *New York Times* revealed that U. S. spy satellites had detected test preparations.[41] The Clinton administration already had mobilized quietly to dissuade the prime minister from testing; now that the matter burst into public, a raucous debate erupted in India. As in the 1960s, two main narratives emerged in the debate. One centered on whether India needed to or should conduct nuclear tests. The other, which was more energetic, focused on the imperative to resist colonial pressures *not* to test. Rao was prepared to defy U. S. demands but decided that a nuclear test was not in India's interest, primarily because he concluded that the economy was not yet strong enough to withstand the inflationary effects of international sanctions. He concluded that inflation was more important to the national interest and in electoral politics, than was nuclear weapon testing.[42] The CTBT negotiations offered a forum for putting a sharp edge on this seemingly soft position: India would put off a decision to test, but would make severe demands for nuclear disarmament a condition for signing the CTBT. If those demands were not met, India would retain the right to test and blame the nuclear-weapons states for leaving it with no choice.

As national elections neared in the spring of 1996, foreign policy and national security issues did not receive serious attention and debate, despite the December imbroglio. The BJP made enough gains in the elections to cobble together a large coalition government.

During and immediately after the election, BJP spokesmen had made confusing and contradictory statements on whether or not a BJP government would conduct nuclear tests. In hindsight the confusion stemmed in part from the fact that only a handful of party leaders knew what it would do. Clearly the BJP did advocate a major break from India's traditional normative position against nuclear weapons. Where Nehru and his successors hoped and claimed that India could achieve global recognition and power by helping transform the international system through moral leadership, the BJP argued that India would receive its due only when it displayed a more robust and militarily stout sense of national purpose. Becoming a nuclear-weapons power was the way to demonstrate the resolve, purposefulness, strength, and defiance necessary to be taken seriously by the leaders of the new world order. More specifically, if India's main rival for global power status was China, then India should act more like China. As the strategist Raja Mohan put it, "Why cannot we be like the Chinese" and display the "combination of defiance and dealmaking" that get taken seriously by the United States and others?[43]

Almost immediately after being sworn in, Prime Minister Vajpayee authorized Rajagopala Chidambaram and Abdul Kalam to proceed to prepare for nuclear tests. Unknown to all but a handful of actors, at least one nuclear device was emplaced in a shaft at the Pokhran test grounds where it stayed at least into the summer of 1996.[44] However, Vajpayee then brought the preparations to a halt when he reflected on the fact that he had not yet received the Lok Sabha's vote of confidence. In case his government was not affirmed, he did not want to saddle a successor with the major consequences of nuclear tests. To the scientists expressed dismay, Vajpayee asked them to pause. Vajpayee's democratic caution proved well founded when his government failed to receive the required support in the Lok Sabha and fell, less than two weeks after its formation.

Vajpayee's successors, Deve Gowda and Inder K. Gujral, were each asked to authorize nuclear tests but demurred, believing that India had greater economic, political, and diplomatic priorities. However, development and testing of ballistic missiles continued. The short-range Prithvi was prepared for induction into Army units, and in 1997 a group of these missiles was dispatched to an operational base in Jalandhar, near the border with Pakistan. The longer-range Agni missile had not been flight tested since 1994 and had never reached half of its advertised range of 2,500 kilometers. The Agni program's problems were largely technological, but Abdul Kalam and his supporters sought to blame weak-kneed politicians for caving into U. S. pressure. Kalam had by now become adept at this sort of media-political campaign to press governments toward bolder strategic policies.[45]

By the summer of 1996, negotiations in Geneva on the Comprehensive Test Ban Treaty assumed a major role in the Indian nuclear narrative. India was indeed a major player in the negotiations. The United States, China, the United Kingdom, and France saw India and Pakistan as the major "prizes" that would make the CTBT's constraints on their own nuclear laboratories worthwhile. (That Israel's nuclear program did not figure prominently in the big powers' calculations only fueled the Indian and Arab feeling that the nonproliferation regime was fundamentally racist.) Thus, the nuclear-weapons states promoted a provision whereby the treaty would enter into force only if and when certain specified states including India, Pakistan, and Israel ratified it. For its part, India by 1996 had shifted its earlier position and now insisted that the CTBT must include a timebound framework for nuclear disarmament.

Many interests and perspectives lay behind these positions, but on the Indian side there was a growing majority in the strategic community that felt that India must keep its nuclear option open, and that this could not be done if testing were foreclosed. Debaters—retired military officers, nuclear scientists, former diplomats, think-tank analysts—differed on whether India actually needed to conduct nuclear tests. Almost all assumed and argued that India did not need thermonuclear weapons for deterrence. Thus the question was whether miniaturization of fission and boosted-fission weapons for delivery on missiles required tests.[46] Some argued that the 1974 test and subsequent major advances in computer-simulation capacity and laboratory testing provided enough know-how to obviate the need for full-scale explosive tests. Others differed. Yet, this argument occurred within a political atmosphere suffused with larger issues of identity, race, sovereignty, and even manliness.[47]

Top Clinton administration officials did little to improve the deliberations, though they tried. By July 1996 it was clear that India would not sign the treaty and was inclined to use the consensual decision-making rules of the Conference on Disarmament to prevent the rest of the world from adopting it. Thus, Secretary of State Warren Christopher communicated by phone and letter with Foreign Minister Inder Gujral to reassure India that the United

States and others would not sanction or otherwise punish India for not sign-ing the treaty, if only India would not block the Conference on Disarmament from concluding the treaty for others to sign. Dispassionate commentators in India recognized that this was a concession worth taking, especially because India's veto in Geneva would not block alternate routes to completing the treaty.[48] American officials, too, thought India would pocket Washington's promise of non-coercion and then not sign the treaty. However, such views neglected the role of personalities and tone in U. S.-Indian relations and non-proliferation policy. Foreign Minister Gujral was a proud, talented veteran of the independence movement, and he felt that the nonproliferation regime, including the CTBT, was a colonial project. Moreover, Gujral felt that Secretary of State Warren Christopher had treated him patronizingly.[49] The stubborn foreign minister put politics, pride, and principle ahead of pragma-tism and refused to agree not to block the treaty in Geneva, even though the move would be ineffective. For their part, American officials should have known that their rather hegemonic approach to India in the CTBT negotia-tions was destined to backfire.

India blocked the treaty in Geneva on August 14. As predicted, the rest of the international community took a detour and passed the treaty through the UN General Assembly where it won support by a 158 to 3 margin. India was joined only by Bhutan and Libya in voting "no." A thick thread of a national security strategy ran through India's handling of the CTBT since 1993, but the larger fabric revealed cross-cutting patterns of anticolonial passion, partisan politics, competing visions of India's normative mission, and confusion.

To many people's surprise, however, India's international isolation was rather short lived. The United States moved quickly to say that Indo-American relations were much broader than disputes on nuclear policy. More impor-tantly, in November 1996, Jiang Zemin became the first Chinese president to visit India. The two states agreed to further the withdrawal of forces along the disputed Sino-Indian border. More importantly, Jiang sent the message that China wanted to deepen ties with India and recognized that it must take a more evenhanded approach between Pakistan and India. Jiang dismayed his Pakistani hosts by declaring that Beijing no longer viewed Kashmir as "an international issue, notwithstanding UN resolutions."[50] He conveyed that Pakistan should put Kashmir on the back burner and strive to stabilize rela-tions with India. This was a strategically important shift. Notwithstanding recent Chinese support to Pakistan's missile and nuclear programs, China was reassessing its interests in South Asia and in global nonproliferation, and the trends were moving India's way. India gained further international respect and recognition in 1997, thanks to Inder Gujral's energetic and magnanimous con-duct of foreign policy, first as foreign minister, then, after April 1997, as prime minister.

However, fractious internal politics soon doomed the Gujral government, showing once again the relative unimportance of foreign policy in the Indian polity (as in others). Indian parties began campaigning once again for national elections, now scheduled for February–March 1998. Despite later conventional wisdom in the United States that the BJP made clear in this campaign that it would conduct nuclear tests if put in office, party officials sent decidedly mixed signals. The BJP manifesto said that the party would "re-evaluate the country's nuclear policy and exercise the option to induct nuclear weapons," but this language and other points surrounding it actually represented "a significant easing of the party's nuclear stand," as the journalist Raja Mohan noted.[51] On the specific question of nuclear tests, some party officials said they would be necessary or might be necessary, while others, including heavyweight L. K. Advani suggested that they would not be. (These ruminations would not have occurred if the Indian public had known that the top BJP leaders had decided to test in 1996.)

Upon being sworn in, Prime Minister Vajpayee and Defense Minister George Fernandes declared reasonably that there was no time frame for inducting nuclear weapons and that such decisions would await the conduct of India's first ever "strategic defense review."[52] This plan made obvious strategic sense: One should develop a rigorously analyzed national defense strategy before deciding how to proceed with nuclear weapons. Moreover, the BJP had criticized all past governments precisely for not having a clear national security strategy. Yet, in reality the BJP was not going to proceed so strategically. Within hours after receiving a vote of confidence on March 28, Prime Minister Vajpayee once again gave Chidambaram, Kalam, and their team the go ahead for conducing nuclear tests.

As before, this momentous decision was made by only a handful of top political leaders and scientists—Vajpayee, Principal Secretary Brajesh Mishra, Deputy Chairman of the Planning Commission Jaswant Singh, Chidambaram, Kalam, and perhaps a few others. Military leaders were excluded. There were no fully briefed independent scientists or national security specialists who could have been consulted even if the decision-makers had wanted to. By the government's own admission, the decision was not dictated by a national security strategy, because there was none. Nor was the decision to test precipitated by Pakistan's April 6 Ghauri test as many commentators have suggested.[53] BJP leaders had made up their minds in 1996 and again in 1998, before April 6. Pakistan's advancing missile program deepened the conviction that India must respond to its growing strategic might, but the Indian tests were meant to serve larger purposes.

In explaining the tests to a shocked world, India at first said that national security considerations emanating from its relations with China were the principal cause. Yet, many of India's most knowledgeable strategists and analysts before and after the tests said that China did not pose an actual military threat to India. India could readily defend the disputed northeastern border with conventional forces. Scenarios under which China would plausibly initiate nuclear conflict with India were extremely hard to conceive. China's internal challenges and problematic relationships with Taiwan, Japan, and the United States are so much more important than "winning" any dispute with India that the notion of Chinese aggression in this direction was untenable. This is not to say that India has no reason to want a just-in-case deterrent against possible Chinese aggression or bullying, but rather that much more is involved in motivating India's nuclear policies.

More than a Chinese national security threat to India, the most telling motivation for the Pokhran tests was broader and more political-psychological. Foreign Minister Jaswant Singh said it very well: "All that we have done is give ourselves a degree of strategic autonomy by acquiring those symbols of power which have universal currency."[54] The tests manifested the BJP's belief that India must be more assertive to achieve its international due and end any vestiges of colonialism. "We cannot have a situation in which some countries say, 'We have a permanent right to these symbols of deterrence and of power, all of the rest of you do not have that right,'" Singh explained.

Beyond repudiating colonialistic disrespect and disregard for India, the tests were meant to lead India on a shortcut to catch up with China in the race to be the major power of Asia. Indian officials such as Narasimha Rao, Inder Gujral, and now Vajpayee and Singh recognized that in the post–Cold War world, economic strength was the key to global standing and security. These enlightened men understood that economic growth rates and markets are what "earned" China more global deference than India received. Yes, China has nuclear weapons and a permanent seat on the UN Security Council, but so do the United Kingdom and France, and they are not regarded as major powers like China. Yet, ironically, the fact that India is a democracy unlike China, poses a handicap to achieving the economic growth that catapulted China ahead of India. The economic route to great powerdom looked too distant in 1998 to satisfy a new BJP government's need to make an immediate difference in India's international status. On the other hand, nuclear weapons could be exploded in weeks, allowing India to insist that it now receive the international respect and deference it deserved as a great power. In other words, China was a motivating factor, but less for reasons of national military security than for reasons of national identity, standing, and respect.

These grand motivations for conducting tests matched more parochial but still important considerations emanating from the nuclear establishment. As noted above, the top scientists argued that testing was necessary for technical reasons and to improve morale and recruitment in the defense and nuclear laboratories. Top political leaders had no way of evaluating the scientists' claims and no independent sources of expertise to consult. The potency and driving role of the scientists throughout India's nuclear history was reflected perhaps most clearly in the "decision" to detonate a thermonuclear device. There was no national security strategy that called for H-bombs; even the informed and long-standing strategic analysis community did not argue that India needed these superweapons. Yet, the big news on May 11 was that India now possessed a hydrogen bomb. The best explanation for this was that the top scientists, especially R. Chidambaram, wanted to prove to themselves, the nation, and the world that they were as brilliant and talented as the nuclear weapon designers in the more "advanced" world. Rugged fission weapons may have been enough for deterrence, but hydrogen bombs were better for symbolizing prowess and power.

Finally, the United States in several ways helped motivate India's decision to test in 1998. For 50 years the United States (and others) ignored or denigrated India's moralistic urgings in international affairs. This became most acute in nuclear policy during and after the negotiations of the NPT, when India made moral arguments in behalf of nuclear disarmament, and the United States and others belittled them. United States officials and academics generally did not recognize that India's self-restraint from 1974 through the late 1990s was at least partially due to normative commitments, and that if India's vision for ridding the world of nuclear weapons was decisively rejected, India would adopt other norms. Similarly, Western models of realist international relations theory and discourse and of nuclear deterrence held that India's self-restrained approach to nuclear weapons made no sense and deserved no respect. Indians who sought recognition and respect in the global international security "community" eventually decided that they must conform to these models. Partially by coincidence, and partially by causation, the BJP had long held views of nuclear weapons more like those of American and Chinese realists, rejecting the Gandhian-Nehruvian perspective. Thus, by the mid-1990s, India's unique approach to nuclear weapons was caught in a pincer attack from the BJP on one side and the dominant school of international security discourse on the other.

Events of 1999

The Indian and Pakistani nuclear tests of 1998 changed the nuclear situation in South Asia in ways that will not be clear for years to come. However, several developments did occur between May 1998 and late 1999 that reinforced some of the major lines of analyses offered above.

Immediately after both states' nuclear tests, Indian and Pakistani leaders proclaimed that they would not engage in a nuclear arms race.[55] Indian leaders were particularly emphatic on this point and on the related contention that they had learned from the excesses of the U. S.-Soviet nuclear arms race and would not repeat the same mistakes.

The downplaying of arms race tendencies derived in part from the contention that India did not see Pakistan as a primary threat or determinant of India's nuclear strategy. "Our nuclear posture and strategy are not directed toward Pakistan," said one prominent Indian strategist/pundit. "We can handle them *en passant* with whatever forces we deem necessary to deploy for other reasons."[56] Such assertions reflected how Indian strategists and politicians resented the outside world's tendency to lump India together with Pakistan, ignoring India's relative greatness and its focus on China. Still, the fact remained that Pakistan and the Indo-Pak relationship posed the most material international security threat to India.

Indian advocates of nuclear weapons responded that nuclear deterrence would stabilize both the Indo-Pak and Sino-Indian security relationships. This view echoed some refrains of Cold War deterrence theory and was accepted by a number of Western analysts as well.

In February 1999, Prime Minister Vajpayee took an historic bus trip to Lahore and joined with Prime Minister Nawaz Sharif in an inspiring summit meeting. The Lahore summit buttressed the contention that nuclear weapons somehow would bring out the best in India and Pakistan. "Despite what you Americans say, the bomb gives us the confidence to make peace," a former leader of India's nuclear establishment declared over drinks just weeks after the Lahore meeting.[57]

Unfortunately, four major events that followed in 1999 undermined such sanguine assertions and analyses. In April and May, Pakistan-backed forces infiltrated into Indian-controlled Kashmir precipitating an intense conflict that left many hundreds dead.[58] The conflict constituted a major crisis that shattered illusions that overt nuclear weapon capabilities necessarily would promote stability. It also exposed nuclear dangers that Indian and Pakistani strategists had preferred to overlook.

Most broadly, as the French writer Raymond Aron noted decades ago, nuclear deterrence can have the perverse effect of encouraging conflict at levels below which antagonists assume nuclear weapons would be unleashed. With nuclear weapons providing a firebreak against escalation, an aggressor can believe that it can "get away" with low-level military operations that the victim will not counter decisively for fear of triggering nuclear exchanges. This dynamic is dangerous in at least two ways. First, the belligerents may not properly assess the threshold above which each side would be willing to risk use of nuclear weapons. Second, the potential for misperception is dangerously exacerbated in cases where the belligerents lack the real-time intelligence gathering capabilities necessary to know whether and when the other side is preparing to escalate to nuclear use. The Cold War antagonists eventually acquired—at enormous expense—the means to monitor each other's nuclear arsenals and command and control operations. This reduced the risks of mistaken or uninformed actions and reactions. However, India and Pakistan lack these real-time monitoring capabilities. This leaves them vulnerable to faulty intelligence or guesses that one side or the other is preparing to launch nuclear weapons, which could in turn prompt military escalation and use of nuclear weapons to avoid massive losses under faultily assumed attack. Care should be taken not to exaggerate the difficulties Indian and Pakistani leaders would face in managing future conflicts or to underestimate both sides' awareness of the need for caution. Yet, to inspire confidence and protect against awful dangers, India and Pakistan must overcome their irresponsible reluctance to establish explicit "rules for the road."

The shadow of nuclear capability clearly emboldened Pakistani leaders to encroach significantly across the Line of Control into Indian-controlled territory. As the Kargil conflict escalated, Indian officials did not know whether and how Pakistan was managing its nuclear capabilities. New Delhi therefore could not assess how its military actions to remove the infiltrators were affecting Pakistan's calculation of the escalation process. For example, as pressure mounted to launch air or ground attacks on Pakistani supply lines and forces beyond the Line of Control, Indian officials did not know how Pakistan would react, including the remote possibility that Pakistan would prepare to retaliate with nuclear weapons. This was an exceedingly uncomfortable and dangerous situation that clearly was not anticipated during the euphoria following the Pokhran tests. In the event, of course, Indian officials demonstrated states-manlike restraint and avoided steps that might have escalated the conflict. This self-deterrence was consciously expressed by Principal Secretary Brajesh Mishra who said that India's restraint "will drive home the point that a nuclear India can and does act in a responsible manner."[59]

The Kargil episode, then, demonstrated several new realities on the sub-continent. Daring and aggressive Pakistani leaders were emboldened by the overt nuclear shield to undertake provocative military action against India. Indian and Pakistani leaders experienced the discomfort and risks of lacking adequate intelligence about each other, especially the dispensation of nuclear forces and the threshold of their possible use. And, more hopefully, both gov-ernments recognized the need to halt the conflict before it escalated. Among other things, these phenomena showed that the people that advocated nuclear weaponization in India did so without a full prior analysis of the strategic and operational implications. To the extent that sound national security policy requires such analysis, the Pokhran tests and the tendency they represented were less strategically informed than many realists claimed. At a minimum, the strategic folly of India's status-driven determination to downplay the equation with Pakistan was exposed. On the other hand, the bloody conflict was con-tained before it got out of control.

The second major "event" of 1999 was the National Security Advisory Board's Draft Report on Indian Nuclear Doctrine. This board was established to advise the newly created National Security Council. It was comprised of former officials, strategic analysts, and pundits, many of whom had been lead-ing advocates of a more hawkish nuclear policy for decades. Neither the board nor the draft doctrine represented official Government of India policy, but the document's release by National Security Advisor Brajesh Mishra did give it an official patina.

Issued on August 17, the document called for "a doctrine of credible mini-mum nuclear deterrence" under which nuclear weapons would be used for "retaliation only."[60] A "triad of aircraft, mobile land-based missiles and sea-based assets" would be built and deployed to carry the deterrent force that was to be "fully employable in the shortest possible time." A "robust command and control system" and "effective intelligence and early warning capabilities," including space-based assets, were envisioned to manage the force. The document emphasized the Indian tradition of civilian control over nuclear policy by stating that "the authority to release nuclear weapons for use resides in the person of the Prime Minister of India, or the designated successor(s)." The latter clause implied the need to revise the Indian Constitution or otherwise formalize a chain of command that had not been specified in existing Indian law.

The draft doctrine bore many marks of prestige-seeking, rhetorical posturing, bureaucratic politics, and strategic uncertainty. It was the product of a large group of disparate people and may have suffered from the need to find agreed lowest common denominators. Former Prime Minister Inder K. Gujral called the draft doctrine "childish." Others charged that the document was released to affect the national election campaign. Though the harshness of some commentators reflected political partisanship, much of the criticism was defensible.

For example, the "necessity" of a triad (land- air- and sea-based nuclear forces) was not explained. From a prestige standpoint, a triad would equate India with the United States and Russia. But strategic and economic cases could be made that a triad is unnecessary. After all, France and the United Kingdom now do without triads and are moving towards purely sea-based nuclear forces. Many serious officials and commentators in the United States believe that its land-based nuclear forces are unnecessary and are retained because of bureaucratic and political inertia. In calculating the requirements of a deterrent force survivability is a key criterion. Yet survivability can be achieved in several ways. Retaliatory forces can be dispersed and hidden, denying an opponent knowledge of targets that need to be destroyed to remove the possibility of a second-strike and/or creating a high enough number of targets to exhaust an opponents offensive assets. China has followed this strategy, and there is reason to think this strategy would serve India, especially against Pakistan. Yet, with few exceptions Indian analysts have not questioned the problematic assumption that a submarine-based force was both necessary and sufficient to ensure survivability of the deterrent.[61] Nor have advocates of a submarine-based deterrent addressed the fact that submarines cannot stay at sea forever, and that several would be needed to rotate between patrol, and port-time repair, maintenance, and crew relief. Moreover, submarines are not necessarily undetectable even on oceanic patrol. Would India's future nuclear-weapons carrying submarines be quiet enough to avoid anti-submarine capabilities of China, the United States and others? Would a state with any doubt about the survivability of its submarine force rely on, say, just one nuclear weapon carrying submarine on patrol during crisis periods? Would not, then, the quest for survivability drive requirements toward three or more strategic submarines? All of these vital questions were ignored by the draft doctrine.

The advisory board's call for a triad also offered no realistic assessment of when the envisioned weapon platforms could be built and at what cost. If strategic submarines are the ultimate element of a credible deterrent, when would they be built and deployed, and in what quantities at what cost? This and other sections of the document resembled claims by the Atomic Energy Commission in the 1950s, 60s, 70s, and 80s that nuclear reactors would supply tens of thousands of megawatts of electricity to India, when in fact the output in 1999 was less than 2,000 megawatts. Grandiosity and technical optimism were not balanced by realistic analysis.

The document stated that India would "not resort to the use or threat of use of nuclear weapons against States which do not possess nuclear weapons, or are not aligned with nuclear weapon powers."[62] This formula would leave Japan as a potential target of Indian nuclear weapons, insofar as it is aligned with the United States. When this was pointed out to one of the drafters—a prominent nuclear hawk—he could offer no response. Perhaps the authors meant to say that a state aligned with nuclear weapon powers *in aggression* against India would not be spared, but the omission suggested that the document was vetted less for its international security effect than for its domestic impact.

The draft nuclear doctrine did not designate states that were deemed targets of India's deterrent—such as Pakistan and China—but it did say that "the system" would contain "an integrated operational plan." This language invoked the sort of operational planning practiced by the United States and the Soviet Union, wherein weapons from air-based, land-based and sea-based nuclear forces were designated for particular targets in an elaborate preordained sequence. Such sequences were determined, for example, by the need to have missiles clear paths through air defenses, enabling bombers to proceed to targets unimpeded by defenses and free from the blast effects of the earlier arriving weapons. Among the liabilities of such plans is there resistance to political fine-tuning and control once nuclear operations begin. This led to the sort of massive overkill that alarmed political leaders such as President John F. Kennedy, National Security Advisor Henry Kissinger, and subsequent American political leaders.[63] The point here is that the notion of an integrated operational plan did not comport with the document's nonspecification of targets, nor with Indian capabilities, and the tradition of prime ministerial control. But it sounded robust.

The draft nuclear doctrine departed most dangerously from traditional Indian thinking about nuclear weapons when it emphasized repeatedly the need for rapid nuclear strike capability. Previously, prominent Indian strategists and politicians had argued that rapidity was unnecessary and destabilizing. Insofar as India would not be the first to use nuclear weapons, it would place a premium on retaliation that did not have to be rushed. As long as retaliatory forces could be dispersed and otherwise protected from preemptive destruction, India could take time to analyze the situation, determine the source and nature of incoming nuclear strikes, and launch a particularly suitable response. This would reduce risks of rushing into nuclear use based on faulty intelligence, accident or inadvertence. The wariness of rapidity stemmed in part from trenchant awareness that the United States and the Soviet Union led themselves into a dangerous, accident-prone and crisis destabilizing stand off of hair-triggered forces because they preoccupied themselves with ensuring nuclear-force survivability through rapid launch capabilities.

The National Security Advisory Board's advocacy of rapidity threatened to heighten insecurity vis-à-vis Pakistan and China. In operating nuclear forces there is an inescapable choice to be made between premiums on arsenal survivability versus protection against accident or unauthorized nuclear use. The United States and Russia, for example, chose force survivability, which led them to build huge, redundant arsenals on hair-triggered alert with delegated command and control systems. China thus far has eschewed maintenance of launch-ready strategic forces and put more emphasis on dispersal, opacity, and political control. To date, China's nuclear warheads are kept separate from delivery systems and the overall deterrent is not on ready alert. This may change as China modernizes its nuclear arsenal and seeks greater assurance that its deterrent can not be negated by U. S. offensive and defense capabilities. Indian moves to deploy launch-ready nuclear forces would invite China to develop more robust capacities and plans to try to find and destroy India's nuclear forces and command and control systems at the earliest stage of conflict. This is inherently destabilizing.

The launch-readiness of Pakistan's nuclear arsenal is now unknown, but the goal of crisis stability should motivate both India and Pakistan to try to maintain buffers of time between conflict outbreak and launch readiness. The more time it takes to launch nuclear weapons, the more opportunity to pursue diplomatic and political means of stopping conflict short of nuclear exchange. Time, rather than launch-rapidity, should be sought to assess events and the scale of a possible enemy attack before determining what if any nuclear riposte should be launched. If India were to move to rapid launch capability, Pakistan would respond in kind, meaning that from the onset of crisis leaders on both sides would fear that the other is about to use nuclear weapons. This heightens incentives to "go first" in order to destroy at least some of the adversary's nuclear capability before it can be used against one. India's political leaders and wisest strategists thus far have recognized astutely the strategic benefits of avoiding rhetoric and force developments suggestive of an "itchy" trigger finger. Yet in true political-military crises political and psychological pressures may make it difficult to maintain the rational calm implied by a strict no-first-use doctrine.

The authors of the draft nuclear doctrine seem to assume that India's commitment not to "initiate" nuclear strikes should persuade potential adversaries from adopting hair-trigger postures toward India. Yet, if India moves to deploy launch-ready nuclear forces, will adversaries take India's no-first-use claim seriously, especially in the absence of negotiated nuclear confidence-building measures between India and Pakistan and India and China?[64] Semantics as well as worst-case strategic planning would support such positions: What does it mean to "initiate" a nuclear strike? If India had intelligence that Pakistan was readying Ghauri missiles for launch against India, could not Indian leaders argue that Pakistan was in fact initiating a nuclear conflict, and India could respond by trying to destroy the Pakistani forces on the ground first? The point is that nuclear forces that are deployed to allow full employability "in the shortest possible time" seriously undermine the salutary effects of no-first-use pledges and erode crisis stability.

The draft nuclear doctrine, like much in Indian nuclear policy that came before it, reflected the aspirations, symbolic import, and influence of the Atomic Energy Commission and Defense Research and Development Organization. The document declared starkly that "India should step up efforts in research and development [and] will not accept any restraints on building its R & D capability." It was unclear whether the declared moratorium on further nuclear tests represents a restraint on R & D capability, but the statement suggested a strong bias towards giving the scientists carte blanche wherever possible. The revered leaders of the AEC and DRDO, Rajagopala Chidambaram and Abdul Kalam, communicated regularly with leading members of the advisory board, so there was every reason to think the document reflected their preferences. Interviews with knowledgeable Indian officials suggested that responsible political leaders found the scientists' interventions frustrating.[65]

The draft doctrine also reflected the historical inwardness of Indian nuclear policy and rhetoric, and the neglect of how they will affect outsiders (much like the United States Senate's vote on the Comprehensive Test Ban Treaty). Like the Pokhran test of 1974, the draft nuclear doctrine sought to give Indian audiences a feeling of strength, technological prowess, great-power know-how, and defiance, with little awareness of the document's effects on outsiders. Pakistan, for example, interpreted India to be declaring its intention for an open-ended, aggressive nuclear and missile arms race. China in all likelihood assumed the same. U. S. officials noted the absence of mention of China and Pakistan and inferred that the authors mean to develop a nuclear arsenal geared to deterring the United States. In each case, the result was to increase wariness about Indian intentions rather then inspire confidence in building a constructive relationship with it. These potential consequences would be somewhat less unfortunate for India if it were more prepared to implement the measures called for in the doctrine. But, as in 1974, India was unprepared for the response its declarations may engender.

In fairness, authors of the draft doctrine acknowledged under questioning that it was "perfunctory," and a vision for a "thirty-year course of activity."[66] Outsiders should not read too much into it. Moreover, the draft doctrine was only that—a draft. Plenty of time existed for correction and refinement. Yet, the draft did reflect the earlier-cited sources of Indian nuclear policy. It demonstrated to the Indian people and the world that India has arrived, that it is in the big leagues of the established nuclear powers. Sadly, the world's two largest nuclear powers—the United States and Russia—have done little in recent years to reduce the temptation for India, China, and perhaps others to measure their global standing in terms other than nuclear weaponry.

The third important development in 1999 was the U. S.-led NATO military campaign against Serbia in defense of Kosovar Albanians. India, like other

Asian and Third World states, viewed the NATO action much differently than did Western states. Marquette University scholar Raju Thomas aptly summarized the Indian perspective: "An expanding NATO now looms as an all-white colonial-type imperial expeditionary force determined to enforce its political diktats and moral standards on the rest of the world."[67] Little noticed in the West, some of India's prominent commentators on strategic affairs argued that the NATO action deepened India's rationale for acquiring nuclear weapons.[68] K. Subrahmanyam, the convenor of the National Security Advisory Board, suggested that only nuclear weapons could protect India from such Western pressures. "Is it not accidental," he wrote, "that the only countries voicing strong protests against the bombing in Yugoslavia happen to be Russia, China, and India, all nuclear weapon powers?"[69] Other Indian elites echoed this view in public and private, saying that India needed nuclear weapons to keep the United States from doing to India over Kashmir what it did to Serbia over Kosovo.

The Indian reaction to the NATO attacks on Serbia manifested longstanding underlying factors in the state's nuclear policy. First, once again nuclear weapons were seen in the context of the ongoing colonial struggle, now emblematic in the nuclear nonproliferation regime and U.S-NATO out-of-area exertions. Second, the actual military "targets" and security threats against which India's nuclear weapons were justified continue to shift. In the 1980s, Pakistan was the principal threat. In the 1998 decision to conduct nuclear tests, China was named the precipitating security threat. Only a year later, China and India were on the same side arguing that the threat of U. S.-NATO intervention necessitated nuclear weapons. Each of these threat perceptions could be justified, but no effort was made to describe operationally how India's nuclear capability would alter Chinese and U. S. behavior. Nor did Indian analysts provide evidence for thinking that China or the United States would seriously undertake military aggression against India in the foreseeable future.

Astute strategic thinkers such as Raja Mohan lamented this latest expression of the "deepest anxieties in the Indian mind about the current domination of the world by the sole superpower and the urge for defiance." Mohan and others found this gestalt antiquated and self-diminishing. Yet it did betray the lingering influence of anti-colonialism in Indian thinking about nuclear policy.[70] For their part, American officials privately complained that Indian statements about needing nuclear weapons to deter the U. S. betrayed immaturity and unreality. On the one hand, in the post–Cold War period it was impossible to imagine the United States using military force against India absent a precipitating Indian threat against the United States. On the other hand, if the United States were so inclined, India's prospective nuclear capabilities would do little to stop it. The Indian perspective of nuclear weapons as political symbols clashed with the over-militarized American perception of nuclear issues, as it had for decades.

The fourth major event bearing on Indian nuclear policy was the October 1999 coup in Pakistan. The Indian (and global) interest in preventing a nuclear/missile arms race in the subcontinent and the risk of escalating military conflict requires productive dialogue between Islamabad and New Delhi. Many Indian strategists still preferred to downplay the Pakistan problem while shifting attention to the China threat (even as some argued that India should join China and Russia in an entente against the United States). Yet, it is Pakistan that poses the threats that drive India's defense spending and force deployments, that cause Indian casualties, and that can lead to nuclear conflict. A Pakistan led overtly by the military could have the political maneuverability to resolve outstanding issues with India, but is unlikely to have this intention. As one Pakistani put it, "at least Nawaz Sharif was conflicted about negotiating with India; the military congenitally believe that India will only take advantage of Pakistan and that conflict cannot be abated."[71] If this is true and the military-controlled Pakistani government will not pursue accommodations with India, then the professed Indian desire to avoid an arms race will be extremely difficult to fulfil.

Conclusion

Since 1947, India's approach to nuclear weapons has been fraught with great tensions between competing values and interests. Many of these values and interests were domestic, having to do with national moral purpose, self-identity, competing personalities and parties, diverse institutional perspectives and aspirations, caste, and so forth. Tension also existed between India and the values and interests of the major external powers and the international system. This has been most evident in discussions and negotiations over nonproliferation. The international politics and diplomacy over nonproliferation then fed back into India's domestic political-psychological system in a replay of colonial struggle.

One of the most remarkable things about India has been its refusal to think about nuclear weapons as the Western nuclear powers have. To the dismay of the small circle of Western-focused hawks in New Delhi, Indian leaders for decades saw nuclear weapons more as political-psychological symbols than as military weapons. This perspective on nuclear weapons helped keep India from investing huge resources in a nuclear arsenal and falling onto the slippery slope toward active, hair-triggered deployments of nuclear weapons, with all of the attendant risks.

However, as the foregoing brief history has suggested, by the end of 1999 a small number of strategists, scientists and key decision makers had drawn India much closer to the U. S.-created model for understanding and managing nuclear weapons. A gradual convergence was underway as the logic of adversarial nuclear weapon development and deployments was putting India and therefore Pakistan on a slope heading toward an unregulated standoff between actively deployed nuclear arsenals. Indian and Pakistani officials and strategists continued to insist that they would not fall into the arms race trap, but they adopted no measures to manifest this rhetoric. Technical and financial limitations might limit their nuclear and missile competition to a crawl rather than a sprint, but even crawlers can cover enough ground to get into danger fairly quickly. The danger was exacerbated by the tendency of Indian pundits and officials to deny that Pakistan should be their principal concern and that there were risks of destabilizing nuclear and missile activities that had to be managed cooperatively. National self-regard required that India direct attention to relations with China and the United States, while downplaying Pakistan, but this only delayed the exertions needed to minimize nuclear dangers that India for years had managed to avoid.

Perhaps the most telling casualty in India's slide toward nuclear weapon deployments was the nation's long-standing ambivalence about these weapons. For decades Indian leaders and citizens genuinely expressed moral and existential doubts about possessing nuclear weapons, even as the capability to do so was in hand. This distinguished India from the six earlier nuclear-weapons states, all of whom developed and deployed nuclear weapons as soon as they physically could with no moral pause. India was different, and this difference reflected well on humanity's capacity for moral reasoning, for resistance to temptation, for moderation and forbearance. To be sure, some American leaders also displayed ambivalence about nuclear weapons—most prominently Jimmy Carter and Ronald Reagan—but such ambivalence waned by the 1990s. This was ironic: For decades it was said that the Cold War necessitated nuclear weapons, and if this overarching conflict could be resolved, these weapons of mass destruction would not be needed. When the Cold War did end, the nuclear weapons remained. What seemed to disappear was the feeling of moral ambivalence about possessing them under the rubric of plans for their large-scale use.[72]

Sadly, the waning of India's nuclear ambivalence brought it into alignment with the long-jaded American perspective on nuclear weapons. Would India be as lucky as the earlier nuclear-weapons states had been in surviving the dangers of active, adversarial deployments of nuclear arsenals?

Notes

1. Bradley Thayer, "The Causes of Nuclear Proliferation and the Utility of the Nuclear Nonproliferation Regime," *Security Studies* 4, no. 3 (Spring 1995): pp. 491-492.
2. Office of the Secretary of Defense, *Proliferation: Threat and Response* (Washington, D. C.: U. S. Government Printing Office, 1996), p. 36.
3. "Phaseology" is a somewhat arbitrary process. Other writers such as Sumit Ganguly divide this history into other phases, in his case five. His second phase begins with the Chinese nuclear test in 1964 but doesn't have an end point. His third phase has no beginning point but "comprises the buildup and execution of

India's first nuclear test, in 1974." Sumit Ganguly, "India's Pathway to Pokhran II: The Prospects and Sources of New Delhi's Nuclear Weapons Program," *International Security*, vol. 23, no. 4 (Spring 1999), p. 149. The historical evidence suggests that there were ups and downs in the 1964–1974 period but that a basic trend existed. Indeed, the basic trajectory towards the 1974 PNE was set from 1948.

4. This section draws from George Perkovich, *India's Nuclear Bomb* (Berkeley: University of California Press, 1999), chapter 1.

5. Ibid., p. 20, 34-35.

6. Ibid., p. 29.

7. Ibid., p. 34-36.

8. Ibid., p. 46.

9. Ibid.

10. Ibid., pp. 67, 73-74.

11. U. M. Trivedi, Lok Sabha Debates, November 24, 1964, in ibid., p. 79.

12. Inder Malhotra, in ibid., p. 65.

13. M. R. Masani, Lok Sabha Debates, November 23, 1964, in ibid., p. 80.

14. Almost all literature on the Indian nuclear program misses this "event." For example, Ashok Kapur, *India's Nuclear Option* (New York: Praeger, 1976), p. 194, and Sumit Ganguly, "India's Pathway to Pokhran II," p. 155, write that the authorization to work on a peaceful nuclear explosive came around 1966.

15. See Perkovich, pp. 90-91.

16. Ibid., pp. 121-122.

17. Ibid., p. 138.

18. Ibid., p. 143.

19. Ibid., p. 159.

20. "India's Pathway to Pokhran II," op. cit., p. 159.

21. Perkovich, p. 182.

22. Jones interview with Indira Gandhi, quoted in ibid., p. 175.

23. Perkovich, p. 201.

24. Ibid., p. 224.

25. Ibid., p. 244.

26. Matthew Evangelista, *Unarmed Forces* (Ithaca: Cornell University Press, 1999), p. 26.

27. Perkovich, pp. 282-288.

28. Ibid., p. 286.

29. Ibid., pp. 296-297.

30. Ibid., pp. 304-305.

31. Ibid., p. 313.

32. Ibid., pp. 365-66, 370.

33. Ibid., p. 346.

34. Ibid., pp. 340-344.

35. Ibid., p. 344.

36. Ibid.

37. Raj Chengappa, *Weapons of Peace* (New Delhi: HarperCollins India, 2000), pp. 382-384.

38. Perkovich, p. 365.

39. Ibid., p. 365.

40. Ibid., p. 366.
41. Tim Weiner, *New York Times*, December 15, 1995, p. 1.
42. Perkovich, p. 370.
43. Ibid., p. 363.
44. Ibid., p. 374.
45. Ibid., p. 383.
46. Ibid., pp. 384-386
47. Ibid., p. 457-458.
48. Ibid., p. 382.
49. Ibid., p. 383.
50. Ibid., p. 387.
51. Ibid., p. 407.
52. Ibid. p. 408.
53. See for example Sumit Ganguly, "India's Pathway to Pokhran II," p. 170.
54. Ibid., p. 441.
55. Prime Minister Atal Bihari Vajpayee, Suo Moto Statement in Parliament, May 27, 1998.
56. Indian strategist, remarks at Institute on Global Conflict and Cooperation, La Jolla, California, September 7, 1999.
57. Interview, March 8, 1999.
58. The exact Pakistani and *mujahideen* casualty figures have not been revealed. Indian sources reported 474 Indian dead and 1109 wounded. K. Subrahmanyam chair, Kargil Review Committee Report (New Delhi) p. 7.
59. Quoted in Dileep Padgaonkar, "Policy of restraint to keep Pak under global pressure," *Times of India*, June 26, 1999.
60. This, and subsequent quotations, from Draft Report of National Security Advisory Board on Indian Nuclear Doctrine, released by Embassy of India, Washington, DC, August 17, 1999.
61. G. Balachandran, *The Hindu*, September 10, 1999, is the best exception. Balachandran astutely argues that India could achieve greater survivability sooner and at lower cost by increasing procurement of mobile land-based missiles than by investing speculatively in a submarine-based force.
62. Ibid., paragraph 2.5.
63. See Jane E. Nolan, *Guardians of the Arsenal* (New York: A New Republic Book, 1989).
64. This is one reason why Rear Admiral (ret.) Raja Menon has called for India to initiate bilateral nuclear dialogues with Pakistan and China. Menon, *A Nuclear Strategy for India* (New Delhi: Sage Publications, 2000) pp. 191-92.
65. Author interviews, June 1998, March 1999.
66. Discussions with contributor to the draft doctrine, La Jolla, California, September 7, 1999.
67. Raju G. C. Thomas, "India's Nuclear and Missile Programs: Power, Intentions, Capabilities, in Raju G. C. Thomas and Amit Gupta, Editors, *India's Nuclear Security*, Boulder, Colorado: Lynne Reinner Publishers, 2000, pp. 97-102. See also Thomas's chapter in this volume.
68. Muchkund Dubey, "The NATO Juggernaut: Logic of an Indian Defence Deterrent," *Times of India*, April 8, 1999. Cited in Raju Thomas, "India's Nuclear and Missile Programs," op.cit., p. 100.

69. K. Subrahmanyam, "Clear and Present Danger: US Path to Unipolar Hegemony," *Times of India*, May 3, 1999. Cited in Raju Thomas, "India's Nuclear and Missile Programs," op.cit., p. 100. See also Subrahmanyam's chapter in this volume.

70. Raja Mohan, "Foreign Policy Transition," *Hindu*, September 2, 1999.

71. Conversation with author, October 13, 1999.

72. This was seen during the United States Senate's debate on the Comprehensive Test Ban Treaty when no one questioned or regretted that the United States. would retain nuclear weapons forever; the only question was whether the weapons would need to be tested forever to ensure their reliability.

Part II

Strategic Dimensions

CHAPTER THREE

India and the International Nuclear Order

K. Subrahmanyam

Summary

The analysis here first notes the nature and consequences of asymmetric power in the post–Cold War decade and its relevance for India's nuclear policy and security posture. Although "nuclear apartheid" between "haves" and "have-nots" prevailed during the Cold War, this discrimination has taken on increased importance in the new world characterized by a sole superpower, an unrivaled and expanding NATO alliance, and Western hegemony. The continued possession of nuclear weapons by the five permanent members of the United Nations Security Council has legitimized the role of nuclear weapons in the new international order. Under these circumstances, other states facing similar or greater threats to their security, carry the right to possess nuclear weapons. The chapter notes the drawbacks and limitations in the deployment and use of nuclear weapons, but these are problems faced also by the five formal nuclear-weapons states. The Indian security experience over the last five decades, including the ultimatum from China, and the entry of the American nuclear-powered carrier into the Bay of Bengal during the Indo-Pakistani war of 1971, makes the exercise of the nuclear weapons option imperative.

Asymmetric Power, NATO Doctrine, and the Autonomy of Nations

Interstate violence becomes more frequent when vast asymmetries develop in weapons capabilities of nations and there is no balance of power. In the era after World War II, peace prevailed in Europe because there was a balance of power due to bipolarity. The arms race ensured that there was no gross asymmetry in weapons capabilities between the two sides of the European divide. However, wars were fought in Asia where the aggressor had the advantage of superior weapons capability. There were also proxy wars in Africa between the two super powers. However, a new situation developed when the international system became unipolar and serious imbalances developed in the weapons capabilities between NATO and the rest of the world. The consequence of this asymmetry in the global military balance was demonstrated when the United States was able to wage a war devastating the infrastructure of Yugoslavia without itself suffering any combat casualties.

The type of war waged against Yugoslavia is specifically tailored to subdue countries that have reached a certain stage of industrialization. Vietnam did not have any industry, its people did not depend too much on power, piped water supply and telephone connections. Their transportation infrastructure was primitive. Therefore, Vietnamese could not be bombed into submission. But Yugoslavia was at a different stage of development and was, therefore, particularly vulnerable to the new kind of weapons technology—the accurate stand-off weapons incorporating modern information technology. The war was against the whole of the Yugoslav nation to cripple its infrastructure, its power and water supply, its industries and to pollute extensively air, soil and water. The destruction of oil refineries, oil storages, chemical plants, and other industries, and the setting ablaze of buildings with a lot of synthetic materials producing pyrotoxins, added an ecocidal dimension to this war. The ability of three nuclear weapons states, the United States, Britain, and France to devastate a nonnuclear-weapons state, Yugoslavia, while the other two nuclear-weapons states, Russia and China, could do nothing to stop it, reinforces the Indian case for pursuing a credible minimum nuclear deterrent.

Accompanying this high-technology campaign against a defenseless state in the name of some hypocritical universal morality, was the shrill international propaganda war conducted through the international media to project a world of good versus evil. While the suffering of refugees was extensively portrayed, not much was shown on the effects of thousands of bombs rained on Yugoslavia. This bombing was a monumental blunder arising out of the hegemonistic arrogance and appalling politico-military incompetence at the highest level of NATO decision-making. At the end of 78 days of bombing, with the exception of an exceedingly small number of dissidents, the bulk of the politico-military establishment, media, and academia in the Western countries did not raise some fundamental questions regarding NATO's unrestrained use of force, in violation of the UN Charter, against a sovereign independent state that had not used force beyond the disputed territories of the former Yugoslavia. The like-mindedness and strong conditioning of people's minds in NATO countries that their leadership is omniscient and omnipotent are as stifling of free independent thinking as President Milosevic's censorship. The lessons of the Vietnam experience appear to have been forgotten.

George Orwell's doublespeak and Aldous Huxley's conditioning are today practiced with a vengeance. Information is shaped and used to have maximum psychological impact to mislead both one's own and the adversary populations. Carefully doctored images portrayed on TV have a powerful effect on popular opinion. Having manipulated public opinion, the politico-strategic establishments cite that to justify their predetermined aggression.

With dominance over new military technology and information war techniques, it is logical to attempt to utilize the enormous power conferred by them for economic advantage. The industrial countries of Europe, Japan, Australia, and New Zealand tow the U. S. line on all-global trade and economic issues. Propaganda techniques are used to create nontariff barriers by raising issues like child labor, environmental damage, and low wages. If there is no autonomy in security for a major nation, it cannot exercise any autonomy in the economic sphere as well because of its one-way security dependence. Japan and Germany, in spite of their economic might, are unable to assert themselves internationally because they are small fry in the field of security. Whatever noises they may make, ultimately they have to fall in line when the United States cracks the whip. Let us look at the pitiable plight of German Greens, Communists in France, Italy and Poland and Japanese antinuclear activists meekly accepting the NATO doctrine on nuclear deterrence.

The NATO document spells out that nuclear weapons are essential political instruments and their role is to create uncertainty in the minds of aggressors and demonstrate that aggression of any kind is not a rational option. If that is their purpose, what is wrong in India creating uncertainties in the minds of potential aggressors and persuading them that aggression of any kind is not a rational option. That kind of insurance has become all the more imperative in the light of the widening gap in the sophisticated conventional technology of war using accurate long-range missiles.

The issue before India is whether it wants to preserve its sovereignty won after a long freedom struggle, and whether it should try to develop one sixth of mankind economically, socially, politically, and technologically according to the democratic wishes of the Indian people without the threat of foreign intervention of the type we saw in Yugoslavia. There were a number of Indians who considered Gandhi as a violator of British law and order, and they were content to enjoy the benefits of the British rule. That was not acceptable to the Indian population as a whole.

Nuclear weapons are a way of guaranteeing the sovereignty and territorial integrity of India against overt threats of humanitarian intervention in its internal wars and subtle threats stemming from nuclear weapons deployment in the present-day world. The five permanent members of the Security Council have legitimized nuclear weapons through the continuing deployment of their own independent nuclear deterrents. Despite the end of the Cold War, France and Britain have not given up their nuclear deterrents in a world without countervailing power. Even the Chinese are coming round to appreciate the need for India, Russia, and China taking a common stand against the dangers of unipolarity as demonstrated in NATO's aggression against Yugoslavia. Those who talked about international trends towards disarmament should explain the thundering NATO document asserting the centrality of nuclear weapons and why an ecocidal war against Yugoslavia was waged with hardly any protest from the peace movements. The international security environment has never been more threatening to the rule of law and autonomy of nations. The Indian credible minimum deterrent should be perceived as insurance for our autonomous development in a hegemonistic unipolar world.

Legitimization of Nuclear Weapons

The international community does not appear to be clear in its mind whether nuclear weapons are legitimate weapons of war or weapons of mass destruction that should be outlawed and eliminated. A UN General Assembly resolution had categorized nuclear weapons along with biological, chemical, and radiological weapons and urged the international community to move towards eliminating all of them. Biological and chemical weapons have been outlawed through international conventions. Chemical weapons are to be eliminated under an international verification system. In respect of biological weapons the lack of a verification system is being remedied and it is expected that the institution of such a verification system will be discussed and adopted in the near future.

Radiological and nuclear weapons are closely related since both of them generate radiation. There were expectations till 1995 that nuclear weapons would also be outlawed and eliminated as was done in the case of biological and chemical weapons. There was basis for this expectation since under Article 4 of the Non-Proliferation Treaty (NPT) all state parties to the treaty had undertaken to negotiate in good faith the cessation of nuclear arms race at an early date and nuclear disarmament and on a treaty on general and complete disarmament under strict and effective international control.

The NPT was an arms control treaty of the Cold War era meant initially for a period of 25 years. Before that 25-year period for the treaty expired, the Cold War ended. The nuclear-weapons powers were no longer adversaries of each other. Therefore there was adequate justification to expect that, as the NPT came up for its fifth review and extension, steps would be initiated to move towards delegitimization, prohibition, and elimination of nuclear weapons on a step-by-step basis. This was all the more necessary because the parties to the NPT found they could not agree that obligations under Articles 1 and 2 of the treaty had been faithfully fulfilled by the nuclear-weapons and nonnuclear-weapons states respectively.

What happened at the NPT Review and Extension Conference on May 12, 1995 jolted India. The NPT was extended unconditionally and indefinitely. This meant that the nuclear weapons in the hands of five nuclear-weapons powers were legitimized forever and so also their use. The rest of the international community was perpetually subjected to a nuclear apartheid in which five nuclear-weapons powers had the right to possess and use nuclear weapons while the rest of the international community was prohibited from exercising the same right. The three decisions adopted in the Review and Extension Conference of May 12, 1995 converted a Cold War arms control treaty of 25 years duration into a perpetual nuclear apartheid treaty.

Nuclear Apartheid

This nuclear apartheid regime categorized the world into five categories of nations. The first category consisted of five nuclear-weapons powers who are also the wielders of the veto power and permanent members of the Security Council. The NPT extension conference reconfirmed the status of these five powers under the Yalta-Potsdam order and attempted to ensure that this status quo would not be challenged. The bulk of the nations of the world (the Latin, the black and brown nations) were grouped into nuclear protectorates, called nuclear-weapon-free zones. They were extended security assurances on not being attacked with nuclear weapons in exchange for their undertaking not to acquire, possess, or introduce nuclear weapons on their soils. This assurance and the nuclear-weapon-free zone arrangement are reminiscent of protectorate status extended to native rulers during the imperial era. These nuclear protectorate arrangements were only restricted to nonwhite nations of the world. All the white industrial nations and the former republics of the Soviet Union came under a different security framework—the Organization of Security and Cooperation in Europe (OSCE)—that extended from Vancouver to Vladivostock. They were either members of the NATO alliance or Partners for Peace. They were under the security umbrella of four nuclear-weapon states—the United States, Russia, Britain, and France. The nuclear security also extended to Japan, Australia, New Zealand, and South Korea under bilateral security treaty arrangements. The fourth category of nations was those under the jurisdiction of U. S. Central Command and U. S. Fifth Fleet. In the last category were India and its neighbors, who were not covered by the nuclear security paradigm that enveloped the rest of the world.

It was quite clear that nuclear-weapons powers had no intention of moving towards nuclear disarmament and delegitimization of nuclear weapons. The nonnuclear-weapons states with four exceptions, Israel, Pakistan, India and Cuba, had been brought under nuclearized global security order through the indefinite and unconditional extension of the NPT. They had accepted an order dominated and regulated by five nuclear-weapons powers who were also the veto wielding permanent members of the Security Council.

The negative security assurances given by nuclear weapon states, on a careful analysis, raise serious cause for concern for India. For instance the U. S.

security assurance, which is almost the same as that given by the United Kingdom, France, and Russia, states: "The U. S. reaffirms that it will not use nuclear weapons against nonnuclear weapon states parties to the Treaty on the Non-proliferation of Nuclear weapons except in case of an invasion or any other attack on the United States, its territories, its armed forces or other troops, its allies or on a state towards which it has a security commitment, carried out or sustained by a non nuclear weapon state in association or alliance with a nuclear weapon state." India is not a party to the NPT and even carried out a nuclear test in 1974. Therefore none of the so-called security assurances would cover India.

Legality of Nuclear Weapons

When the issue of legality of use of nuclear weapons was referred to the International Court of Justice some of the nuclear-weapons states argued in favor of legal use of nuclear weapons. This is of great significance in the light of the unconditional and indefinite extension of the NPT. The International Court of Justice (ICJ) in its advisory opinion decided unanimously that the customary or conventional international law did not provide specific authorization for the threat or use of nuclear weapons. *It also decided by an 11-3 vote that customary or conventional international law did not contain any universal prohibition on the threat or use of nuclear weapons.* (Italics added.) The ICJ also was of the view that a threat or use of force with nuclear weapons was contrary to Article 2(4) of the UN Charter. Such an act, which failed to meet the requirements of Article 51 of the Charter, would be unlawful. The ICJ also concluded that the threat or use of nuclear weapons should be compatible with international law applicable to armed conflicts including principles and rules of international humanitarian law. The ICJ was unable to conclude definitely whether the threat or use of nuclear weapons would be lawful or unlawful in an extreme circumstance of self-defense, in which the very survival of a state would be at stake. The ICJ, however, affirmed unanimously that there existed an obligation to pursue in good faith and bring to a conclusion negotiations leading to nuclear disarmament in all its aspects under strict and effective international control.

When the endorsement of the ICJ opinion was considered in the form of a resolution in the UN General Assembly session Russia argued that the ICJ had found no comprehensive and universal prohibition against the threat or use of nuclear weapons. France and the United Kingdom stressed that the ICJ had not reached a definitive conclusion regarding the legality of such threat or use in circumstance of self-defense. (But these countries would not extend that right to other nations as per the NPT). Besides the four nuclear-weapons countries (the United Kingdom, France, Russia, and the United States) 16 European countries voted against the resolution, while 24 other members of OSCE abstained.

Impact on India

After May 1995, the nuclear-weapons powers not only had their weapons legitimized, as evident from their views on the opinions of the International Court of Justice (ICJ), four of them maintain they have a legitimate right to use those weapons and deny that right to other nations. They also refused to discuss nuclear disarmament in the Conference on Disarmament and argued that this must be left to nuclear-weapons powers. While such a blatantly hegemonic stand could have been supported by the NATO nations and the Partners for Peace in the OSCE, this stand clearly was not acceptable to India, which had a long history of struggle against colonialism as well as apartheid. India had no intention of accepting a nuclear protectorate status, or acceding to nuclear apartheid dispensation promulgated by the NPT. India had sought nuclear security guarantees in the sixties but failed to get any. India had also faced nuclear intimidation when the *USS Enterprise* was dispatched into the Bay of Bengal in December 1971, towards the end of the liberation war of Bangladesh. President Nixon in an interview to *Time* magazine (July 29, 1985) said about the 1971 crisis: "The Chinese were climbing the walls. We were concerned that the Chinese might intervene to stop India. We didn't learn till later that they didn't have that kind of conventional capability. But if they did step in and the Soviets reacted what would we do? There was no question what we would have done." Nixon lists this as one of the three instances when he considered using nuclear weapons. During the Cold War era there was bipolarity and nuclear deterrence between the two sides, which exerted restraint on nuclear weapon powers considering the use of those weapons. In the post–Cold War era, in which the five nuclear weapons powers act as a collective hegemonic entity, the risks of use of nuclear weapons in asymmetric situations is much higher.

Unwinnable and Unfightable Nuclear War

President Reagan and General Secretary Gorbachev issued a joint declaration after their Geneva summit in November 1985 in which they agreed a nuclear war could not be won and therefore should not be initiated. That declaration was no doubt a reference to a possible war between two nuclear-weapons powers. Obviously that realization led to some of the nuclear-weapons powers reducing and rationalizing their nuclear arsenals. At the end of the Cold War, the nuclear-weapons powers were no longer adversaries. The firm realization now prevails that a nuclear war between two nuclear-weapons powers is not fightable and winnable. In which case, the compelling question is why do the five nuclear-weapons powers insist on keeping their arsenals? Why do they cajole and compel the international community to legitimize them and argue before the International Court that they have a legitimate right to use them but others do not? Further, the rest of the world also has to bear in mind that the five nuclear hegemonic powers have been involved in more wars than other nations. Some of them also have a strategic culture that accepts city-busting air attacks and infliction of massive civilian casualties as legitimate acts of war.

The signing of the Paris Accord of November 19, 1990, and the end of the Cold War, with drastic reduction of armaments, tended to prove that nuclear deterrence was effective. Those for whom city-busting raids on Hiroshima and Nagasaki were legitimate acts of war had to reckon with the possibility of others similarly armed states inflicting unacceptable damage on them. The probability of weapons of mass destruction being used is tremendously higher in situations of asymmetry than where mutual deterrence operates. Therefore the nuclear threat to nonnuclear-weapons countries that are not part of security frameworks involving nuclear weapons nations, and which are not part of nuclear protectorates, has increased since the end of the Cold War. Unlike in the Cold War era, when nuclear weapons were sought to be justified apologetically on the basis of compulsions of nuclear deterrence, in the post–Cold War period the legitimacy of use of nuclear weapons and assertion of the hegemonic right of five permanent members of Security Council are flaunted before the International Court of Justice and other international fora. It is this enhanced threat posed by the hegemonistic assertion of the legitimacy of the most horrendous weapon of mass destruction, and the arrogant double standards of preaching against weapons of mass destruction in the hands of others, while asserting their own right to use them, that India had to counter. Therefore in the wake of this infamous legitimization of nuclear weapons in May 1995, India started preparing for nuclear tests of its own. In December 1995, under U. S. pressure, the then government of India under Congress party prime minister Narasimha Rao, halted the scheduled tests.

Nuclear Hegemony

The hegemony of the nuclear-weapons powers was directly felt by India during the negotiations on the Comprehensive Test Ban Treaty (CTBT). Even while the negotiations were going on in the Conference on Disarmament they were totally marginalized by the parallel negotiations among the five nuclear weapons states. Secondly after the conclusion of the negotiations, India made it clear in its statement on June 20, 1996 that it would not sign the CTBT since it affected its national security interests adversely. However, India indicated that it had no objection to the treaty being adopted by others, the entry into force clause was amended at the last minute to include India in the list of 44 countries whose accession to the treaty was necessary to bring it into force. This was done at the instigation of some nuclear-weapons powers responsible for nuclear proliferation. It was obvious that the aim was to prevent India from becoming a nuclear-weapons state and subject it to full rigors of nuclear apartheid. This entry into force clause is in violation of the Vienna Convention of the law of the treaties that stipulates that a nation not being a party to a treaty cannot be subjected to the obligations thereof. In spite of such gross violation of international norms the treaty was adopted by the United Nations with the offending clause. This was a further warning to India on the hegemonic dominance of five nuclear-weapons powers which wanted to keep their own weapons of mass destruction but disarm the rest of the world.

Why Nuclear Weapons?

It is necessary to analyze why the five hegemonic powers behave in this roguish manner and attempt to impose on the world the legitimacy of weapons of mass destruction in their own hands and prohibition for others. It is obvious that such hegemonic behavior will generate enormous resentment and will lead to nonstate actors considering not only nuclear weapons but all weapons of mass destruction legitimate especially when aimed at nuclear hegemonic powers. Terrorist use of weapons of mass destruction can never be successfully tackled unless there is overwhelming popular support for the effort through societal verification. That will not be forthcoming if a few hegemonic powers assert their right to have nuclear weapons. Therefore the policy of nuclear apartheid increases the probability of nonstate actors resorting to terrorist use of nuclear devices and other weapons of mass destruction and reduces the likelihood of popular cooperation in all countries which is essential to mobilize societal verification of clandestine activities of nonstate actors. Nuclear weapons are instruments of terrorism and offensive nuclear strategic doctrines are terrorist ones. Therefore though the nuclear weapons powers may reduce their arsenals and rationalize them, their legitimization of nuclear weapons has led to enhancement of risks of terrorism by nonstate actors.

   This irrational behavior on the part of the five nuclear hegemonic powers appears to be rooted in their objective to sustain the Yalta-Potsdam dispensation, and their privileged position as permanent members of the Security Council based on the outcome of the World War II. Since then the international system has undergone radical changes. Germany and Japan have overtaken the United Kingdom, France and Russia in their economic and technological performance. The center of gravity of political and economic international interactions has shifted from Europe to Asia. Some 130 new nations have emerged from the debris of empires. The Soviet Union has dissolved. Therefore, the Yalta-Potsdam order is unviable. The only way of shoring up the collapsing structure is to make nuclear weapons the primary currency of power in the international system and sustain the privileged veto-wielding status of five nuclear hegemonic powers on that basis. Therefore Germany and Japan, even if they become permanent members of the Security Council, cannot have the veto power.

Without nuclear weapons Russia would not be given the status it has today in the international system. Britain and France will find themselves totally out-ranked by Germany in the European Union. China's nuclear-weapons power status and its growing economic clout will make it the Asian hegemony. Presumably, the United States feels that if China were to overtake it in terms of market size, advanced nuclear weaponry will help to sustain its status as the sole superpower of the world. Therefore all five nuclear hegemonic powers appear to share a vested interest in asserting the legitimacy of nuclear weapons in their own hands while denying them to other nations. The international nuclear nonproliferation regime, with legitimization of the most horrendous weapon of mass destruction in the hands of five permanent members of the Security Council, is therefore being used to reinforce and consolidate the Yalta-Postdam order. The five nuclear-weapons powers appear to be prepared to take all risks arising out of hegemonic legitimization of nuclear weapons to sustain the present status quo. This is the only plausible explanation for the roguish behavior of nations that insist on keeping nuclear weapons legitimate.

Nuclear Proliferation as Policy

What has been overlooked by four out of five powers with the exception of China, who are insisting on legitimizing the nuclear weapons and making them a currency of power is that it can be used in a sophisticated way to settle scores among themselves—not by fighting a nuclear war but by selective and con-trolled proliferation. The NPT has no verification provision to check that nuclear-weapons powers fulfill their obligations. Nor is there any way of penal-izing a nuclear-weapons power that breaches the Nonproliferation Treaty. The four Western powers who feel they have a high stake in the NPT did not get any commitments from China when it formally joined the treaty in 1992 that it would not breach the treaty though they were fully aware of China's large scale assistance to Pakistan to assemble its nuclear weapons. Nor was the issue resolved during the NPT Review and Extension conference though there was no agreement that the obligations of not proliferating had been faithfully ful-filled by nuclear-weapons powers, as per Article 1 of the NPT. Presumably the Western countries were afraid that bringing out this issue into the open would erode the credibility of the NPT and damage it. Further, in the case of China, the U. S. Administration appears to have felt that any findings adverse to that country on proliferation would automatically trigger mandated sanctions and that would come in the way of further expansion of U. S.-China trade.

China had developed major proliferation interests in South and Southwest Asia in the eighties. It carried out a simultaneous proliferation of nuclear weapon technology to Pakistan and long-range C-SS-2 missiles to Saudi Arabia. Pakistan and Saudi Arabia were both very close allies of the United States, had very strong bonds between them, and the latter had financed the

Pakistani nuclear weapon program and the Peshawar-based *mujahideen* insurgency in Afghanistan. Such Chinese proliferation moves to two Islamic countries in West and Southwest Asia signaled the extent of Chinese influence in an area of vital interest to the United States. That gave China a powerful leverage in dealing with the United States on other issues, particularly Taiwan. (Even if one may not fully subscribe to Professor Samuel Huntingdon's thesis of the clash of civilizations and the Sino-Islamic alliance against the West, the Chinese proliferation interests in Pakistan and Saudi Arabia and according to the U. S. perception, in Iran should give some credibility to that formulation). The helplessness of the present U. S. Administration to tackle this proliferation is highlighted by its inability to reach a finding on Chinese supply of M-11 missiles to Pakistan in 1993, even after seven years. This "fudge" on not reaching a finding is maintained even after Pakistan and China have confirmed the transaction. Understandably this record of the present U. S. Administration has lost it all credibility in India on its commitment to nonproliferation.

Nuclear Realities on the Ground

Both the peoples of India and the rest of the world would have a better appreciation of the compulsions on India to go nuclear and the enormous restraint this country had exercised if the nuclear developments in this region had been publicized by our prime ministers. The conventional wisdom is that India went nuclear in 1974, and thereafter Pakistan responded. This is not wholly true. Recently three distinguished Pakistanis who have had access to the nuclear secrets of Pakistan, Agha Shahi, a former foreign minister, Abdul Sattar, the former and present foreign minister, and Air Chief Marshal Zulfikar Ali Khan published an article, "Securing Nuclear Peace," on October 5, 1999, in *News International*. They have made several disclosures that set the record straight. Shahidur Rehman, a correspondent of Kyodo News Service of Japan in Pakistan claims his book, *Long Road to Chagai*, is the untold story of Pakistan's nuclear quest. He wrote the book after interviewing a large number of participants in the Pakistani nuclear weapons program—scientific personnel, military officers, and diplomats.

Shahi, Sattar, and Khan argue, "Concerned in the wake of the 1971 disaster when neither conventional military strength, alliances nor the United Nations proved equal to the task of preventing Indian aggression and intervention the object was solely to deter another Indian onslaught aimed at the territorial integrity of residual Pakistan." In fact the decision of Pakistan to go nuclear was taken on January 24, 1972 by President Zulfikar Ali Bhutto in a conference of scientists in Multan. This was some nine months before Indira Gandhi authorized the Indian scientists to go ahead with the Pokhran-I test. In that conference Bhutto asked for a fission weapon in three years. Unlike India, which was aiming at demonstrating its technological capability at Pohkran at that stage, Pakistan was going for the nuclear weapon from the very start. The book *Long Road to Chagai* reveals that Bhutto was pressing for Pakistani acquisition of nuclear weapons even in the sixties, but was frustrated in his ambition mainly because of the opposition from Pakistan's Finance Ministry and the Planning Commission.

While Agha Shahi and others justify the Pakistani nuclear program, in the wake of emergence of Bangladesh and India's support for its liberation, many in Pakistan believe that Bhutto had a large responsibility for the events of 1971 and he wanted Pakistan to break up since that was the only way he could become the ruler of residual Pakistan. In any case these disclosures establish that Pakistan's decision to go nuclear was not a followup of India's Pokhran-II test but was independent of it.

Three years after the Pohkran test when the Janata government under Morarji Desai assumed office, with Atal Bihari Vajapayee as his foreign minister, the former renounced all ambition for India to acquire nuclear weapons. In his address to the UN Special Session on Disarmament in June 1978, Desai reaffirmed his pledge "not to manufacture or acquire nuclear weapons even if the rest of the world did so" and added that India "abjured nuclear explosions even for peaceful purposes."

Even as India was renouncing nuclear weapons Pakistan had concluded a secret agreement with China for collaboration in nuclear weapon technology in June, 1976 and independently had launched its uranium enrichment program, using the centrifuge cascades, based on technology "illegally" derived from Holland. They even started digging tunnels, preparing the sites for nuclear tests. Pakistan was able to procure in Western European countries all equipment and materials needed for centrifuge operation and for making uranium hexafluoride gas. All these are described in detail in the chapter "Shopping for a Bomb" in the book *Long Road to Chagai*. By 1983 Pakistan had a few cores of weapon-grade enriched uranium and was ready to carry out "cold tests" of subsystems. On May 19, 1999, Samar Mubarakmund, the Pakistani weapon designer, confirmed in an interview to *Gulf Today*, that 1983 was the year when the first Pakistani atomic device was manufactured and tested.

It is under these circumstances that Indira Gandhi ordered a nuclear test in 1983 and initiated both nuclear-weapons and missile programs. Though the country was not told by the Chinese Government, the prime minister was fully aware of the China-Pakistan nuclear weapon technology relationship and the tacit U. S. connivance of Pakistan's nuclear-weapons program.

In 1980 the Pakistanis made clear to the noted American South Asian specialist, Professor Stephen Cohen, that the objective of their relentless pursuit of nuclear weapons was to neutralize both India's conventional superiority and nuclear capability, to reopen the Kashmir issue, and to liberate Kashmir in a bold and brash move when the Indian government was weak and vacillating. In 1981 during the negotiations with the United States on the framework of collaboration to sustain the proxy war in Afghanistan, through support to the *mujahideen* groups, Pakistan persuaded the United States to give its tacit consent to its nuclear weapons program, and the U. S. Secretary of State General Alexander Haig assured the Pakistani delegation—Agha Shabi and General K. M. Arif—that the nuclear issue would not be the lynchpin of US-Pakistan relations. This has been disclosed in General Arif's book *Working with Zia*. By 1983 the U. S. government had information that China had transferred the technology and design of its fourth nuclear test—a missile-borne fission warhead. This information is available in the State Department briefing paper "The Pakistani Nuclear program," (June 22, 1983), which is cited in the Joyce Battle "India and Pakistan: On the Nuclear Threshold," National Security Archive Electronic Briefing Book, 6.

The Pakistani authors Shahi, Sattar, and Zulfikhar Ali Khan claim that their country deterred India on three occasions, in 1984, 1987, and 1990, through its nuclear capability, and implying that threats were conveyed to India on the use of nuclear weapons, either explicitly on implicitly. In 1987 during the time of Brasstacks exercise conducted by the Indian Army, it is well known that A. Q. Khan told the Indian journalist Kuldip Nayyar about Pakistan having reached nuclear-weapons capability and the possibility of its use if India threatened Pakistan's sovereignty or territorial integrity. It is now well established that the CIA operative in Islamabad at that time, Richard Barlow, reported on Pakistan having assembled the nuclear weapon. (This has been confirmed by General Aslam Beg, in an article in *Defense Journal,* vol. XIX, no. 11-12 [December 1993]). Yet the U. S. Administration decided to certify to the U. S. Congress that Pakistan had not reached nuclear-explosive capability and continued its military assistance till October 1990, as the United States still needed Pakistan's support for the *mujahideen* campaign in Afghanistan.

Then came the 1990 threat. The Pakistani authors confirm it as a threat, and it was to defuse this threat that the United States President George Bush sent his deputy national security adviser, Robert Gates to Islamabad and Delhi in May, 1990. This incident has been covered in various U. S. writings. This was also the beginning of sustained proxy war in Kashmir. Presumably the intention of Pakistan was to implement the objective they set out for themselves in 1980—to deter Indian conventional superiority and nuclear capability and try to grab Kashmir. Having tied down the Indian Army in Kashmir militancy and relying on their nuclear deterrence, Pakistan tried out its bold brash move at Kargil in 1999.

While the Indian Prime Ministers did not share even with their cabinet colleagues the intelligence information on Pakistan's nuclear program—actively supported by China and tacitly connived at by U. S.—they initiated and pursued a nuclear weapon and missile program to safeguard the country's security. Nor did they tell the country about Pakistan's nuclear threats of 1987 and 1990. They tried to play down the nuclear issue even as Pakistani political leaders, Ghulam Ishaq Khan, Benazir Bhutto, Nawaz Sharif, military leaders like General Aslam Beg, and diplomats like foreign secretary Shahryar Khan and

Ambassador Abida Hussain openly flaunted the Pakistani nuclear weapon capability. The Pakistani nuclear weapons were under the control of the Army and that was no secret. In India the armed forces, bureaucracy, and even senior politicians were kept out of the decision-making loop. The prime ministers dealt directly with the chairman of the Atomic Energy Commission and the Scientific Adviser to the Defense Minister. Even defense ministers were kept out. This produced an anomalous situation: Pakistani armed forces knew they had a nuclear deterrent of a proven design given to them by China. The Indian Armed Forces did not have a similar assurance about the Indian nuclear capability. This placed them at a disadvantage psychologically. There were always risks of Pakistan, which had persuaded itself it deterred India successfully on three occasions, concluding that a proxy war, a limited war, and a nuclear threat can be combined to force India to yield on the Kashmir issue.

The noted columnist Altaf Gauhar wrote an article entitled "Four Wars and One Assumption" on September 5, 1999 in *Nation,* pointing out that Pakistan had always assumed that Indians—the Hindus—would never fight back, and therefore they had initiated wars against India again and again. One cannot rule out the possibility that without overt nuclear tests and overt nuclearization Pakistani leadership might have doubted Indian nuclear capability especially since they were convinced their nuclear deterrence worked successfully against India on three occasions. That was why it was necessary for India to conduct the tests and make it clear beyond all doubt what India was capable of. The Indian program was a weapons program from the beginning in the 1980s. In spite of what they said in public, no prime minister from Indira Gandhi onwards ever thought of just keeping the option open.

India's Nuclear Doctrine

The Indian nuclear doctrine formulated by the non-official National Security Advisory Board has attracted worldwide attention. While there is some tendency among sections of Indian bureaucracy to distance themselves from it by saying that it is only a draft and only one of several inputs into the government decision-making, the fact remains that it is the first step in India proclaiming a restrained and logical nuclear doctrine that will be a kind of model for all other nuclear-weapons powers. The doctrine has to be assessed with reference to its logic, basic principles, strategic approach to nuclear war and use of nuclear weapons, and its philosophy of restraint. Since the doctrine poses a challenge to all other nuclear-weapons powers, it is understandable that there is criticism from them and their docile camp followers, not on the contents of the doctrine themselves but on what they impute to them. The antinuclear lobby in India too has resorted to the same strategy. It will be interesting to wait and watch how much modification the government of India will be able to incorporate in the final version it will adopt after taking note of all domestic and international criticisms.

Contrary to the misperceptions in many quarters and misunderstandings generated at second-tier levels in political parties, the Indian nuclear-weapons program and the Indian nuclear doctrine represent the consensus among the Congress, Janata Dal, United Front, and the BJP governments. The BJP administration had perhaps the least role in the development of the weapons and evolution of nuclear-strategic thought. One of the best kept secrets in India is that the nuclear-weapons program was initiated by Indira Gandhi, continued by Rajiv Gandhi, and fully brought into operation by P. V. Narasimha Rao. The Janata Dal prime ministers, Messrs V. P. Singh and Chandrasekhar, and the United Front Prime Ministers Messrs Deve Gowda and I. K. Gujral lent their full support to the program. They all did it in utmost secrecy without sharing any information with their colleagues and party men. The nuclear weapon tests were never criticized by Narasimha Rao and were endorsed by V. P. Singh and I. K. Gujral. Therefore some of the criticisms of the nuclear tests and nuclear policies are based on inadequate appreciation of facts and mistaken perceptions that they were exclusively attributable to the BJP. At the same time, it is highly regrettable that the BJP has not given the credit due to the Congress, the Janata Dal, and the United Front for their contributions in making India, a nuclear-weapons state. It must be noted that the scientists at the end of the tests thanked all the previous governments.

The Indian nuclear doctrine rests on four pillars—the no-first-use, credible minimum deterrent, the civilian control of the weapons, and commitment to nuclear disarmament. In evolving this framework, India had the benefit of 50 years of experience of the nuclear era and its right lessons and grievous mistakes.

No-First-Use

No-first-use is derived from two factors: first is the commitment never to initiate the use of nuclear weapons. Second, it is predicated on the doctrine of deterrence that warns an aggressive potential adversary that his use of nuclear weapons will lead to his suffering unacceptable retaliatory damage. Neither of the two factors is unethical. Every state has an ethical obligation to protect its citizens from the use and threat of use of nuclear weapons. What is a better way of doing it than to pledge no-first-use and demonstrate a credible retaliatory capability to deter those who flaunt their weapons in an intimidatory manner implying its first deliberate use even in nonnuclear context? The problem is the existence of nuclear weapons and doctrines of powers who do not rule out its first use and who flaunt the weapons as a currency of power.

Some in India have criticized no-first-use on the ground that it means that this country would accept the first hit and that declaration would encourage adventurism on the part of a potential aggressor. Some of the foreign critics are skeptical of no-first-use on the ground that it is unverifiable and is liable to be altered without any prior notice. Both these criticisms are somewhat superficial and do not take into account the ground realities. There is no way in which a first strike by an adversary can be averted or forestalled with the present state of technology. An aggressor who wants to strike first will always be able to get some of his weapons through even if the victim adopts policies of preemption or launch on warning or launch under attack. Such postures will involve much higher costs in terms of safety of weapons, command, and control. It would also mean a higher level of tension. Yet the real effectiveness of deterrence is a function of the anticipation of an aggressor of the adversary's capability to retaliate after a first strike and the unacceptability of the damage it would cause. For instance in the case of Pakistan the deterrence is not in terms of fear of India hitting a target or two in the first strike to face a retaliation of equivalent number of strikes or more, but due to the certainty that if they ever strike a single target in India most of their cities and high dams are within the ranges of Indian missiles. Therefore not having a no-first-use policy does not give any advantage in terms of deterrence. The policy of first-use is meaningful only when a country thinks of fighting a tactical nuclear war or use nuclear weapons against a nonnuclear country.

In 1961 the United States had 5,100 nuclear warheads while the Soviet Union had only 300. The United States made plans for a total disarming strike on the Soviet Union. But the plans were abandoned when the U. S. Chiefs of Staff could not assure that no Soviet weapons would get through. Deterrence is in terms of what damage a country is prepared to accept to achieve its aim. If Pakistan is not in a position to accept the damage that will be inflicted on it in terms of retaliation then it will be effectively deterred. Given the vulnerability of Pakistani cities and high dams, the damage Pakistan will suffer in any retaliatory strike will be totally unacceptable to it. Therefore India is in a position to adopt a no-first-use policy vis-à-vis Pakistan. That country is to be considered as the most provocative and least responsible. What applies to Pakistan can easily be extended to other cases.

Credible Minimum Deterrent

During the Cold War era the United States and USSR treated nuclear weapons as though they were conventional weapons, and therefore it was felt that the larger stockpile assured more of a chance of victory. It took some 40 years for the Western strategic establishment to realize that a nuclear war could not be won and therefore should not be initiated. There is a vital difference between the conventional war and nuclear war. In the former case, the country or the side with the superior capability defeats the country or the side with inferior capability and then tries to inflict damage unacceptable to it by occupying its territory and subjecting its people to hardships of different kinds. There have been cases like World War II in which one side—Germany in the West and Japan in the East—was initially victorious and inflicted unacceptable costs on the adversaries. Subsequently the tide turned, and the Allies developed adequate capabilities to defeat Germany and Japan militarily and occupy their territories.

In the case of a nuclear war it is not necessary for a country to be militarily defeated to be imposed unacceptable damage. Because of the reach of the missiles, the speed with which the damage can be inflicted, and the enormity of the damage that will be caused, both sides will suffer unacceptable damage. The fact that one side may suffer more damage is no consolation to the other for which the damage suffered may not be worth the stake it has in the outcome of the conflict. It is in those circumstances the two leaders of the United States and USSR felt that a nuclear war cannot be won. It is perhaps this factor that sustained deterrence between the two super powers and they finally agreed to scale down their armaments and conclude peace without fighting a war after four decades of eyeball-to-eyeball confrontation. This was a unique event in history and has no precedent.

There are also scientific hypotheses about nuclear winter and ecological damage that would follow a nuclear exchange of hundreds of weapons. A former U. S. National Security Adviser, McGeorge Bundy declared in 1968 that one H-bomb on one city was unacceptable damage. Therefore unlike in the Cold War era, today strategic establishments all over the world do not envisage nuclear exchanges involving even scores of weapons let alone hundreds and thousands as they used to do. The U. S. leadership has indicated that they would like to negotiate a START III agreement reducing the arsenals of the United States and Russia further downwards. Many U. S. strategists believe that one thousand weapons would be adequate for their global deterrence. Others have argued that even 200 would be enough. The United Kingdom has announced that its arsenal would be 200 deployed weapons and another 200 in reserve.

Therefore in India's case the deterrent force need not be in four figures. The debate is about whether it should be a low three figure or a medium three figure somewhat on the levels the United Kingdom and France have. No doubt the size of the arsenal will be determined by its survivability against a potential adversary's first strike and will be an inverse function of the survivability factor. The greater the survivability the lesser will be the requirement for a credible minimum deterrent. All the major nuclear powers have distributed their arsenals over a strategic triad, namely aircraft, land-based mobile missiles, and submarine-based systems, to maximize the survivability of the arsenal. The Indian nuclear doctrine also proposes that this country should follow the same strategy. Both foreign and domestic observers have criticized this on the ground that this goes beyond the requirements of a minimum deterrent.

This criticism overlooks the enormous advances in satellite surveillance and accuracy in missile guidance. Recently the Federation of American Scientists announced that they would be publishing the satellite imageries of nuclear missile sites of all nuclear-weapons states. Therefore the vulnerability of land-based systems has increased significantly. This is the reason why the United States and France relies heavily on sea-based deterrents. It is also not possible to rule out the possibility of nuclear submarines proliferating and coming into the market. Since the Indian nuclear doctrine lays down principles for long-term strategic posture, it provides for sea-based deployment also. Therefore, the critics will have to explain why they have ignored the world-wide trends of deterrents moving to the sea.

The credibility of deterrent is not based on a mere numbers game but essentially on its survivability. No nuclear aggressor, however powerful the nation may be can be absolutely certain that his first strike would eliminate all the weapons of the opponent, and there will be no risks of the latter's nuclear weapons getting through and causing unacceptable damage to the aggressor. This uncertainty is at the heart of deterrence concept.

In these circumstances, it has been argued, in the West by strategists like professor Kenneth Waltz, and in India by late General Sundarji that, because such uncertainty is at the heart of deterrence it is enough to have a minimum force to generate and sustain the uncertainty to project deterrence and there is no need to waste more money on a larger arsenal when a lesser one could be adequately effective. However efforts will have to be made to impress on the potential nuclear aggressor that there will be certain and punitive retaliation and the country has necessary capability for the purpose.

Civilian Control over Nuclear Weapons

Nuclear weapons are not weapons of war. This was recognized even in the early years of the nuclear era when the noted U. S. strategist Bernard Brodie said that with the emergence of the absolute weapon the role of armed forces was no longer to fight and win wars but to prevent wars from breaking out. Therefore these weapons should not be in the standard stockpiles of the armed forces deployed in forward areas. Given the nature of their destructive power the decision to use them should be taken at the highest possible level. If a country does not envisage the use of such weapons for war fighting but only for retaliation then it is all the more logical that the weapon be used under the strict orders of the highest political executive, namely the prime minister in India. This is what the Indian nuclear doctrine provides. The release of nuclear weapons can be authorized only by the prime minister or his designated successors. This last provision is necessary to provide for contingencies in which a first strike may be used by an adversary to eliminate the top leadership.

In the United States while in the immediate wake of the development of the nuclear weapons, the U. S. president had the weapons under his control, in the fifties, in the light of strategic doctrines developed about fighting wars with tactical nuclear weapons, powers were delegated to the commanders to use the weapons on their own in certain circumstances. Since, in those days neither of the two sides adopted a no-first-use policy the weapons were kept on hair trigger alert. When people talk of risk of accidental and unauthorized use they have in mind those situations. The Cuban missile crisis was a dangerous crisis because the commanders on both sides had delegated powers to use weapons.

Then came in the sixties the technology of locking the weapons through electronic permissive action links. These operated only up to the point when immediate hostilities were anticipated. At that stage the weapons were

unlocked and issued to the launching formations. Then again the commanders were on their own in respect of use of weapons. Those who worry about
the accidental and unauthorized use of weapons in the case of India must bear
in mind that such risks are not there when the power to use the weapon is not
delegated, there are no plans for nuclear war fighting and the country has a
no-first-use policy. The Armed Forces however have to be trained to implement the retaliatory strikes. They have to be involved in surveillance, protection of the weapons, target selection, and advice to the prime minister on
appropriate response and damage assessment. They will be integral part of
command and control system.

Commitment to Disarmament

Though India was compelled to declare itself a nuclear-weapons state as a
result of Pakistani acquisition of nuclear weapons with the Chinese support
and tacit U. S. connivance, India is still committed to nuclear disarmament. The
world has outlawed the biological and chemical weapons, and there is no reason why nuclear weapons should not also be outlawed. Now that the Cold War
is over and democracy and market systems have been accepted all over the
world, there is no reason to fear the kind of global war which initially justified the nuclear weapons. The longer the period without use of nuclear
weapons greater will be the taboo against its use. India's no-first-use policy is
a step towards delegitimizing its first use. Delegitimization is a prerequisite for
ultimate elimination and outlawing of the weapon. The Geneva Protocol of
1925 was a no-first-use treaty in respect of chemical weapons. Thereafter
chemical weapons were not used except in cases of asymmetry where the
aggressor had the weapons and the victim did not. In 1993, 68 years after the
no-first-use treaty on chemical weapons, they were outlawed through the chemical weapons convention.

If only the Indian example of no-first-use is followed by all other nuclear
weapon powers the world will be on its way to disarmament. Therefore the
Indian nuclear doctrine has posed a challenge to all other nuclear powers. This
is perhaps one of the reasons why there is a lot of unjustified criticism of the
doctrine.

The Doctrine as an Impediment to Nuclear Arms Races

One of those unjustified criticisms is the doctrine would unleash an arms race
in the region. China has a variegated nuclear arsenal and most of it is usable
only in China's neighborhood, since it has only some 20 missiles that can reach
the United States. Therefore the incipient Indian nuclear arsenal cannot make
much of a difference to China. It is more than likely when the Chinese started
helping Pakistan to build up its nuclear arsenal they would have anticipated
the Indian reaction and provided adequate margin for it. Pakistan's nuclear and
missile programs are highly dependent on Chinese help which is extended to
Pakistan in clear violation of various international arms-control regimes. It is
now well established that Pakistan continues to receive assistance for its nuclear

and missile program from China, and the United States continues to look away. Therefore any arms race in the region is due to the breakdown of the nonproliferation norms and not due to the Indian nuclear doctrine. India tries to exercise utmost restraint in spite of these acts of commission and omission by major powers who preach nonproliferation but do not practice it.

The development of Indian nuclear weapons and missiles has been on a deliberately moderate pace, and India did not step up its budget for these programs following the tests. India is conscious of the fact that chances of a nuclear threat of use or actual use are low but for the unpredictable and irrational behavior of Pakistan. While the overwhelming majority of the Indian population favors Indian nuclear deterrents, there are very few in India who would urge defense expenditure higher than three percent of the gross domestic product. An arms race is characterized by the intensity of effort, and there are no indicators of such a development in the nuclear and missile fields in this India.

Threat of Nuclear War in the Region

India was compelled to go for nuclear armaments because of Chinese support to the Pakistani nuclear-weapons program and the tacit U. S. connivance of that effort. Pakistan's nuclear-weapons program was linked up with the Kashmir issue from the seventies. Pakistan is the revisionist state in the region and wants to grab Kashmir on the basis of the two-nation theory that religion determines nationality. That theory preceded the clash of civilizations thesis by five decades. Pakistan is the epicenter of Islamic extremist terrorism and one of the three major centers of narcotics generation. Pakistan's stand on Kashmir, its nuclear philosophy, and its support to extremist terrorism and linkages with narcotics are all rooted in the militarism in that state and its inability to develop a national identity of its own. Its military exploited the Cold War rivalry to acquire nuclear weapons. It has the unique distinction of putting its deposed prime minister, elected in a landslide electoral victory, on trial on charges of terrorism.

The Pakistanis, as pointed out earlier believe that they were able to deter India through nuclear threats, and they hope that by holding out the threat of nuclear escalation they will be able to compel the international community, particularly the United States, to intervene in the Kashmir dispute and settle it in their favor. The partisan attitude of the West towards Pakistan because of the Cold War and their permissiveness of Pakistani proliferation encouraged the Pakistani military to believe that nuclear blackmail would pay.

However the Kargil War and the stand taken by the United States and the Western countries should signal to Pakistan that the principles developed by the international community in the Helsinki Declaration of 1975, that there should be no alteration of line of control or borders through force or threat of force, would apply in Kashmir as well. This is what President Clinton demanded and obtained from Prime Minister Nawaz Sharif on July 4, 1999.

In his broadcast on July 12, 1999, the Pakistani Prime Minister said, "The directions of atomic missiles were also aimed towards us." Whether this is true or false, for the first time Pakistan admitted that nuclear deterrence worked against itself, unlike on the three earlier occasions when they boast their deterrence worked against India. Now that Pakistan has been told that it cannot attempt to alter the territorial status quo by force, overt or covert, and it understands with overt nuclearization it is subject to nuclear deterrence the prospect of stability in this region has increased. Pakistan today is an international security issue. An Economically failing state, driven by religious fundamentalism, unable to have a coherent national identity, incapable of developing democratic values, dominated by a military-clergy-feudal combine dealing with narcotics and processing nuclear weapons, Pakistan itself is a nuclear flash point that needs to be handled collectively by the international community. India's nuclear capability is a stabilizing and balancing factor in a dangerous situation created by the fallout of cold war and proliferation permissiveness of major nuclear weapon powers.

Conclusion

When in May 1998, India conducted the nuclear tests and justified them on the ground that the security environment had deteriorated, many in the world and in India raised the question as to what precisely had happened to arrive at that conclusion. Following NATO's 78-day full-scale assault against Yugoslavia from March to June 1999, it should be clear that the present international security environment has not improved much since the end of World War II. The UN has been rendered redundant since there is no balance of power in the world, and the entire industrial world, barring a ramshackle Russia, is under U. S. overlordship. It was not accidental that the only countries that voiced strong protests against the bombing of Yugoslavia happened to be Russia, China, and India, all nuclear-weapons powers.

The West has criticized India's draft nuclear doctrine as being full of dangerous flaws and wishful thinking. However, nuclear deterrent relationships among the existing nuclear powers were not perfect either during the Cold War. The core of deterrence, especially for a country that commits itself to no-first-use policy, is its ability to carry out punitive unacceptable retaliation. This is not Cold War language but the appropriate language to communicate to the nuclear warriors who believe in the use of nuclear weapons first. Unless one opts to allow his society and nation to be destroyed in a cold-blooded first strike by the adversary and not do anything to deter him, it is logical to make it clear to such nuclear adversaries the consequences of his resorting to a first strike. The word unacceptable damage does not carry today the connotations of the MAD (Mutual Assured Destruction) age of Robert McNamara and Zbigniew Brezinski. It is now recognized that one bomb on one city is unacceptable. Therefore, those who believe in wielding nuclear weapons to intimidate other nations and in the first-use of nuclear weapons have to be deterred by spelling out the consequences of their actions.

The Indian nuclear doctrine rejects the western approach to nuclear theology, as is evident from the preamble and the last section that reiterates Indian commitment to disarmament. India was compelled to go nuclear because of the obduracy of nuclear-weapons powers, the legitimization of nuclear weapons by the international community, and the rising trend in interventionism by the industrialized nations in the affairs of the developing world. It became necessary to protect the autonomy of decision making in the developmental process and in strategic matters that are inalienable democratic rights of one sixth of mankind living in India. The Indian nuclear doctrine aims at providing India a credible minimum deterrent at an affordable pace of expenditure to create uncertainty in the minds of would-be nuclear intimidators, aggressors and interventionists that those actions against India's sovereignty and territorial integrity would not be rational options.

CHAPTER FOUR

India, the International System, and Nuclear Weapons

T. V. Paul[1]

Summary

Most explanations for India's nuclear behavior, especially the open tests in May 1998 emphasize one or more of three factors: the regional rivalries that India has with China and Pakistan, domestic politics, or the predispositions of individual decision makers. This chapter argues that although domestic factors may be associated with the timing of the 1998 tests, the overarching cause of India's nuclear behavior needs to be located in systemic factors. Although India couches its challenge to the nonproliferation regime in normative and idealistic terms, these rationales mask the real Indian concern: Namely, the nonproliferation regime privileges the five declared nuclear weapon powers and perpetuates their dominance, while keeping India as an underdog in the global power hierarchy. The tests should be seen in the larger context of global power politics involving the great powers and India, especially the fact that the former remain unwilling to accept the latter to their ranks.

Introduction

India's nuclear tests in May 1998 inflicted a powerful shock on the global nonproliferation regime. Since the end of the Cold War, the regime had become stronger with several former opponents acceding to it. Why did India take the drastic step of challenging the regime in an open manner by conducting five nuclear tests in the Rajasthan desert? Explanations for the nuclear behavior of

India largely rest on the nature of the regional rivalry between India and Pakistan and between India and China, domestic politics, and the predispositions of individual decision-makers.[2] This chapter looks specifically at the nuclear behavior of India and argues that domestic factors may be associated with the timing of the 1998 tests, but that the tests are the culmination of long-term systemic and subsystemic processes that began most prominently in the 1960s. The tests should be seen in the larger context of global power politics involving the great powers and India, the latter with aspirations to become a major power in the twenty-first century and the former unwilling to accept India into their ranks.

The chapter also presents a larger problem inherent in the current nonproliferation regime. Despite its success with a number of countries, the regime has-not been able to arrest nuclear proliferation completely, because it disregards the long-term political and military processes taking place in the international system, especially relating to global and regional balance of power.[3] A significant problem with the Non-proliferation Treaty (NPT) is that it contains no room for rising powers to acquire nuclear weapons. More concretely, the NPT was extended in perpetuity assuming that power relations in the international system will remain the same for the foreseeable future and that no new great powers will arise in the twenty-first century. This runs contrary to the logic of rise and fall of great powers and power transitions among them, as evident in the history of 500 year-old modern international system.[4] India, with aspirations to become a major power, finds the regime discriminatory because of systemic reasons. The efforts by the great powers to arrest India's advancement in the nuclear and missile technology areas are also largely driven by systemic imperatives.

India's opposition to the global nonproliferation regime is long-standing. This opposition springs from systemic considerations more than ideological or domestic politics, even though the latter two are not completely irrelevant. India often couches its challenge to the nonproliferation regime in normative and idealistic terms, such as sovereign equality of states and global disarmament, but they mask the real Indian concern; namely, the nonproliferation regime privileges the five declared nuclear-weapons states and perpetuates their dominance, while keeping India as an underdog in the global power hierarchy. In this sense, the strengthening of the regime, especially since the end of the Cold War in 1991, had a negative effect on India, forcing India to come out of the closet and declare itself a nuclear weapon state.

In the following pages, I first present the systemic foundations of India's opposition to the regime, especially in view of the discrepancy between India's ascribed status in the international system and its aspiration for a major power role. In this context, I discuss India's position on the nonproliferation instruments and the reasons for its strident opposition (stronger than by any other member of the international community) to the regime. This is followed by a discussion of the 1998 tests. I argue that the tests were a particular manifestation of these aspirations, as well as an effort to correct a perceived deterioration in the immediate geostrategic security environment of South Asia, largely the result of the behavior of India's long-term regional adversary, Pakistan, and of established nuclear powers, China and the United States.

A Systemic Framework

Robert Jervis has identified three characteristics of a systemic approach that are relevant here: First, outcomes cannot be inferred from attributes of actors because the international system can produce consequences that are not necessarily what the actors intended. Second, units are interconnected, that is, changes in some parts of the system produce changes in others. And third, relations between any two actors are conditioned in part by the relations between each of them and other actors in the system.[5] All these systemic characteristics have relevance to the Indian case.

In this chapter, I use the term "system" to refer to the larger international system, especially the power relationships among major power actors and between them and all the other actors. A systemic approach to understanding a state's nuclear policy would contend that the security behavior of a state needs to be explained in view of its position in the international system and how it is affected by the interactions between it and the major power actors. A subsystemic analysis would focus mainly on interactions and power relationships among the most prominent actors within a region.[6] The systemic approach I propose posits that different states placed differently in the international system have diverse security concerns and interests. Great powers tend to have global interests, while the security concerns and interests of most middle powers and small powers are concentrated in a given region. Aspiring great powers also would perceive their security as being tied to the larger balance-of-power processes occurring in the international system, involving established great powers. Since 1945, nuclear weapons have played a significant role in the power relationships among great powers and between great powers and smaller powers. As an aspiring major power, India has been the most affected by the nuclear politics involving great powers. From the Indian point of view, it has the most to lose in the perpetuation of the nuclear monopoly of the five great powers. Therefore, India's nuclear behavior, especially its approach towards the global nonproliferation regime, can be understood better by using a systemic approach than by any other prevailing frameworks.

With China and Pakistan as its nuclear adversaries and with aspirations to achieve a larger global role, India has both systemic and subsystemic concerns, with the latter driving India's attitude towards the global nonproliferation regime most prominently. The divergences in India's and Pakistan's strategic aims (the latter confined to the region) show that power balances in the larger international system matter more to rising powers with major power ambitions than to smaller actors.[7] In India's case, domestic factors are less salient because governments belonging to all political parties since 1988—in fact six of them—had maintained nuclear weapons ready to be tested. They differ mostly on the pace and extent of the program rather than the goals of it. True, it took the audacity of the BJP government led by Atal Bihari Vajpayee (with its stridently nationalistic position) to make the final decision to conduct the actual tests.

India's Systemic Compulsions

Submerged in the Indian position on the global nuclear order, and not discussed much in scholarship or the media, is the unique position of India in the international system. India's conduct represents the classic behavior of an emerging major power that finds the doors closed by the existing powers, which want to block the entry of any new states to their status in the international hierarchy. Conclusion of unequal disarmament treaties with the intent to arrest the rising state has been a path that major powers have undertaken in the past.[8] The interwar naval disarmament treaties between the United States, Britain, and Japan, which would have maintained the permanent inferiority of Japan, are a case in point. The Japanese perceived this as a grave injustice and began to violate the treaty even before the ink on it had dried.[9] The present-day nuclear states have been making efforts to contain India and keep it at its current middle-power rank because of the advantages that the monopoly of systemic leadership brings to them.

Among the developing states, India seems to be the key state in line for achieving major power status in the twenty-first century. Its closest parallel, Brazil, is situated in a geographically and strategically isolated region and has accepted a trading strategy within the ambit of U. S. hegemony.[10] Brazil's estimated 166 million population is dwarfed by India's 1 billion (in 2001). Other regional states, such as Indonesia, Nigeria, South Africa, and Pakistan, are all only more or less one-fifth of India's population or economic size. Moreover, few other countries in the world face two adversarial nuclear neighbors simultaneously, one of them a member of the nuclear club, China, and the other, a new nuclear state, Pakistan, yet have no nuclear ally to protect them. India, with its nuclear capability (as attested by the 1998 tests), missile capability (one of the most advanced in the developing world), fairly modern army, and rapidly increasing economic strength, is likely to emerge as a powerful actor in the twenty-first century. With the test firing of the 2,010-kilometer Intermediate-Range Ballistic Missile (IRBM), Agni, India can now reach many vital centers of its adversaries. India is also working on an advanced version of the Agni that could hit targets in Beijing and Shanghai. In a decade or so, India is expected to possess the capacity for ICBMs. India is also emerging as a leading state in space technology. Several indigenously built satellites have been launched during the past two decades. In May 1999, India reached a major milestone in commercial space technology when its Polar Satellite

Launch Vehicle, PSLV-C2, successfully launched a Korean and a German satellite into the space.[11] These achievements in space have increased India's potential for developing commercial-launch vehicles as well as advanced missiles.

Since its economic liberalization began in 1991, India has maintained an average 5-7 percent annual economic growth. If India can sustain this growth and at the same time alleviate the key problems facing the country, it could become a major economic power by the second decade of the twenty-first century. According to the World Bank's purchasing power parity based estimates, the Indian economy already ranks approximately fifth in the world.[12] The mobilizational capacity of the Indian government, despite all the problems associated with a soft state, has been steadily increasing as more and more Indians are joining the ranks of the middle class. This does not mean that formidable challenges in the realms of poverty, illiteracy, corruption, weak infrastructure, uneven economic growth of different parts of the country, and internal divisions do not exist in India. But, from the Indian point of view, when China achieved its major power status it was somewhat similar to India in the economic indicators of development. Today's Russia is economically a weak actor as well. The Indian elite rightly or wrongly believes that even if India gains economic might, without hard military-power resources, including nuclear capability, its proclamations for disarmament will not be taken seriously by the existing nuclear powers and it will not gain a foothold in the global power hierarchy.[13]

India still faces a number of hurdles before entering the major power league. Historically, war has been the main source of the rise and fall of great powers. The current members of the great power club or the P-5 were the winners of World War II. Unfortunately for India, when the world war came to an end, it was still under colonial rule. China gained the great power status due to the intervention of the Unites States, and China's willingness to ally with the Unites States against the USSR beginning in 1971 allowed it to regain its UN Security Council seat. China reinforced its major power status by acquiring nuclear capability before the Non Proliferation Treaty came into being in 1970, and since 1978, the liberalization of the economy has allowed Beijing to maintain a healthy level of economic growth.

India took over a decade longer to inaugurate economic liberalization, which began only in 1991. This liberalization allowed speeding up of economic growth, but fundamental problems still remain in the Indian economy, especially in terms of human resource development indicators. The dithering in acquiring nuclear and missile technology after the initial demonstrations of the capability also meant some loss of time for India. Waiting 24 years after the 1974 test made India susceptible to pressures by the nuclear-weapons states, especially the Unites States. Moreover, the nuclear powers have been able to unify their position on the issue, which meant increased pressure on India to rescind its nuclear program.

From the Indian perspective, its legitimate place in the international pecking order is denied because the current system leaders have no intention of integrating India by giving it a leadership role. At the political level, they oppose the induction of India as a permanent member of the UN Security Council, despite the fact that India is home to one sixth of humanity and is expected to be the most populous nation by the second decade of the twenty-first century. They are hopeful that international pressures will force India to scale down or abandon its search for major power status. Attempts to freeze India out have only increased New Delhi's resolve to accelerate indigenous development of its nuclear, missile, and other technological elements necessary for a modern, self-reliant defense force. The nonproliferation regime, aimed at arresting proliferation, has in fact increased the pressure on India to come out in the open and exhibit a capability that was held in the basement for 24 years.[14] No other regional power has shown such a continued opposition to the regime, demonstrating that India's exceptional position in the international system has something to do with this.

Nuclear weapons serve some key functions for a rising power. They provide protection against large-scale overt military intervention, such as preventive attacks by the existing major powers. They offer protection of the border from large-scale direct attacks by neighboring countries, although they have proven to be a weak source of compellent power.[15] The Indian leaders seemed to have convinced themselves of these functions of nuclear weapons as evident in their code-naming of the testing program, "Shakti," which means "power" in Hindi. Since 1971, India has not fought a war with its neighbors, and some believe that to a large extent, it is nuclear deterrence that is preventing interstate war in South Asia.[16] India's arch-rival, Pakistan, had to devise other coercive means such as stepped-up covert support for Kashmiri militants waging a guerrilla struggle for independence. The Kargil conflict of 1999 was the largest of these operations by Pakistan, yet it did not lead to an all-out war between the two states. Moreover, nuclear weapons also could provide a hedge against major technological breakthroughs in conventional capability. As a rising power, India seems to be concerned about the revolution in military affairs that is currently taking place, which may affect its long-term security, and potentially increase the hegemony of the established powers.

India's strategic environment is also unique in the developing world. India is engaged in enduring rivalries with two nuclear states, China and Pakistan, and it has no protective umbrella of a nuclear ally. These states initiated three of the four wars they fought with India. Moreover, China has colluded with Pakistan to build its nuclear forces. Beijing has joined the other nuclear powers to contain India and maintain its own preponderance in Asia. India could serve as the basis of an effective regional counterweight to China, which Beijing wants to avoid. The Indian experience with the Unites States has also been one ranging from adversarial to apathetic, despite improvements in economic relations since 1991. The arrival of the USS Enterprise during the Bangladesh War of 1971 was a wake-up call for India that without sufficient deterrent and defensive capabilities it could be the target of hegemonic intervention. There are strong indications that Indira Gandhi's decision in 1974 to conduct the nuclear test was partially a response to this perceived challenge by the United States. None of this is to suggest that India holds no responsibility for the conflict with its neighbors. But, as long as the conflicts continue, nuclear capability may remain a key element of security relations in South Asia.

The end of the Cold War has put India's earlier global strategy in jeopardy. It lost its key superpower supporter, the Soviet Union, following the latter's collapse as a state. Despite the fact that nonalignment was a response to Cold War rivalry, as a policy posture it lost much of its meaning when the Cold War ended. India's main adversary China, despite initial opposition by the West and its continued adherence to Communist ideology, has become well accepted as a major power. The Unites States, despite its increased trade and investment relations with India, still sees New Delhi through the Cold War prism. Unwilling to understand or appreciate the Indian security dilemma arising from systemic and subsystemic challenges, especially the nuclear activities of China and Pakistan, the United States and its allies have solidified their position on the nonproliferation regime. Their stance is that nuclear weapons are meant for major powers only and that no new nuclear power will be allowed to emerge. India's wavering after the tests in 1974 cost it dearly, because it gave the impression that India could be coerced into folding up its nuclear ambitions. The BJP, holding strident nationalistic views, is the most likely political party to reassert India's position vis-à-vis declared nuclear powers, although almost all other parties agree with them about the ends if not the means, such as, open testing without substantial direct provocation such as economic sanctions for not signing the Comprehensive Test Ban Treaty (CTBT).

The Indian opposition to the global nuclear order has been evolving since the 1950s. This opposition became solidified overtime as the nonproliferation regime became more embedded in international security relations. At this point, a brief historical discussion of India's approach towards the nonproliferation regime is necessary to elucidate the systemic arguments further.

India and the Global Nonproliferation Regime

At independence from Britain in 1947, India became a staunch proponent of nuclear disarmament. India's first Prime Minister, Jawaharlal Nehru, made several proposals for nuclear disarmament at the United Nations and other international forums. India was an active member of the United Nations Eighteen Nation Disarmament Committee that negotiated nuclear and conventional disarmament before the superpowers began bilateral arms-control process.[17] The proposals India made included a standstill agreement on nuclear testing (the precursor to today's CTBT) and a nondiscriminatory, nonproliferation treaty. India signed the 1963 Partial Test Ban Treaty in the hope that the treaty would lead to further nuclear disarmament. Nehru articulated pro-disarmament policies in different world forums, as he believed that the nuclear arms race between the superpowers was heading towards a global war.[18]

With China's nuclear test in 1964, the Indian position on nuclear weapons changed dramatically. Although China was acquiring nuclear weapons to obtain major power status and to prevent nuclear coercion, for India, the Chinese action altered its immediate strategic environment profoundly. This was because China had defeated India just two years earlier in the 1962 Himalayan border war. India claimed that China occupied 14,000 square kilometers of disputed territory. When the Chinese test occurred, India's Prime Minister was Lal Bahadur Shastri, who after failing to obtain nuclear guarantees from the major powers, authorized a limited peaceful nuclear explosion program that could be converted into a military program if the situation warranted.[19] Shastri's successor, Indira Gandhi, after initial reluctance, continued the program.

Following the Chinese nuclear testing, the nuclear powers began negotiations on the NPT. India was favorable to the conclusion of a nondiscriminatory treaty, but later became a strong opponent of the NPT, realizing that the nuclear powers wished to maintain their monopoly and that the treaty was primarily aimed at curtailing the nuclear aspirations of nonnuclear-weapons states. During the negotiations leading to the treaty, the Indian leaders vehemently opposed it and this opposition was out of systemic considerations. The major concern was that the treaty created two classes of states: those that had tested a nuclear device before January 1967 and those that had not done so by that date. The treaty would not only legitimize the nuclear capabilities of the five states that conducted such tests, including China's, but would prevent India from developing nuclear weapon capability even in the face of a major nuclear threat arising. Prime Minister Gandhi stated in the Indian Parliament that India refused to sign the NPT on the basis of "enlightened self-interest and considerations of national security . . . Nuclear weapon powers insist on their right to continue to manufacture more nuclear weapons. This is a situation that cannot be viewed with equanimity by non-nuclear countries, especially as they are called upon to undertake not to manufacture or acquire nuclear weapons for their own defense."[20] Although India cited the norm of sovereign equality of all states while arguing against the treaty, self-interest deriving from the treaty's constraining of its own nuclear options was the paramount reason for the opposition. The Indian opposition to the Treaty had solidified after 1971 when, during the final days of the Bangladesh War, the Nixon Administration sent the USS Enterprise into the Bay of Bengal, hoping to force a cease-fire.

The most compelling evidence of India's opposition to the NPT came in May 1974 when it tested a nuclear device in Pokhran in Rajasthan, the same test range where the 1998 tests were conducted. Indians dubbed the test as a peaceful nuclear explosion (PNE), although there is hardly any difference between a PNE and a militarily useful weapon. The Indian test galvanized international efforts at nonproliferation. According to one UN official involved in NPT negotiations, "it breached the walls of the 'nuclear club' and once again raised the specter of the Nth country problem."[21] India continued to maintain its opposition to the NPT all through the 1970s and 1980s while keeping its own nuclear weapons option open. However, available reports point out that New Delhi did not develop a nuclear weapons arsenal until late 1980s despite having proven its capability in 1974. The decision to build a weapon force occurred after two developments: Pakistan's success in the acquisition of uranium-enrichment capability and subsequently a weapons capability (announced by A. Q. Khan in January 1987), and the failure of Prime Minister Rajiv Gandhi's 1988 Action Plan aimed at convincing the nuclear-weapons states to achieve nuclear disarmament in a time-bound fashion.[22] There was also evidence that the Reagan administration was turning a blind eye to nuclear-weapons-related activities of Pakistan in order to continue using the country as a conduit to supply military and economic aid to the Afghan *mujahideen* forces fighting the Soviet Union.[23] Indian intelligence agencies reportedly received evidence of increased Pakistan-China nuclear collaboration. It was Rajiv Gandhi who authorized the weaponization project, despite his anti-nuclear orientation.[24] Open nuclear testing was still not in the cards, however, until further international and regional developments took place that affected India's security concerns and until the nationalistic-oriented BJP came to power.

The NPT Extension and the CTBT Negotiations

Two events in the second half of the 1990s, related to the nonproliferation regime, aggravated the Indian sense of grievance against the world nuclear order. The first was the extension of the NPT in perpetuity by a United Nations conference in May 1995, largely as a result of the pressures exerted by the United States and its allies. The efforts by signatories of the Treaty belonging to the nonaligned group for rolling extensions of 25-year periods, with further renewals subject to progress in nuclear disarmament did not carry the day.[25] This treaty outcome gave every indication to India that the Nuclear Weapons States (NWS) were keen to maintain their monopoly rights for a long period to come. From the Indian point of view, "disarming the unarmed" had become the main value of the NPT rather than genuine global nuclear disarmament.[26]

In 1996, India was almost alone in opposing the CTBT.[27] Although the seasoned Indian diplomat Arundhati Ghose forcefully presented New Delhi's case before the Geneva negotiating forum, the Indian decision to veto the draft CTBT and then not to sign the UN approved treaty received broad international condemnation. The stated Indian objections centered on two issues: (a) the proposed treaty was not linked to a timebound elimination of nuclear weapons as a key goal, and (b) it allowed laboratory type tests or subcritical tests, which meant that the five nuclear powers would be free to continue building their arsenals. The inclusion of the entry-into-force provision at the insistence of the United Kingdom, France, Russia, China, and Pakistan was also viewed by India as a clever way to tie its hands. This provision stated that the treaty would come into force only when all 44 states with at least one nuclear power reactor, especially the three threshold states, India, Israel, and Pakistan, had signed and ratified it. This, according to India, would open up pressures on New Delhi to sign away its sovereign right to keep its nuclear options open and thereby increase the possibilities for future coercive sanctions by the United States or the UN if India did not comply.[28] From the Indian perspective, the treaty was forced upon the nonnuclear-weapons states more as a nonproliferation tool than as a disarmament measure. Notably, Israel has expressed its willingness to sign the treaty, while Pakistan has agreed to do so if India signed it, which shows that among the new nuclear states only India was most concerned about the systemic implications of the treaty. The Indian fear was that once it signed the treaty it would not be able to conduct a test forever and thus not verify its nuclear capability, especially the reliability of its thermo-nuclear weapon. Although cold tests could provide much of the information, hot tests were perceived to be necessary for confirming the accuracy of the weapon capability.[29] India also wanted the five nuclear-weapons states to declare a timetable for elimination of nuclear weapons before it committed to a nuclear test ban since, as once it signed the treaty, it would lose a bargaining chip to influence the disarmament policies of the nuclear-weapons states.

The 1998 Tests

The coalition government under the leadership of Vajpayee came to power in the March 1998 parliamentary elections. The BJP had been a long-standing proponent of India acquiring nuclear weapons. Under its previous incarnation, Jana Sangh, the party had declared its intention to make India nuclear since the 1964 Chinese nuclear tests.[30] But until 1996, it was always in the opposition, except for a short interregnum as a coalition partner in the Janata party government of Morarji Desai from 1977 till 1979. When Vajpayee was prime minister for 13 days in 1996, he had ordered nuclear tests, but his government did not last long enough to carry through the decision. In 1998, the BJP had in its electoral platform a strong pro-nuclear message, and it called for India to exercise the weapons option if the national interests warranted doing so. The BJP has also been a strong advocate of India achieving a major power role in world politics, and the acquisition of a nuclear capability has a special meaning in that context. There is an element of truth in the argument that the BJP also saw the nuclear arena as a place where it could assert its nationalistic credentials well, and it seemed to have calculated possible electoral support for such a move.

However, the BJP could not have prepared a nuclear testing program from scratch barely seven weeks after gaining power. In fact the order for nuclear tests was given on April 10, 1998, 22 days after the 14-member coalition government came into power. The tests occurred on May 11 and 13, only one month after the government gave the green signal. Thus, the BJP seemed to have completed a program for which previous governments had prepared the way. Reports suggested that successive Indian governments since 1988 had maintained a nuclear bomb and the testing range in Pokhran in order to conduct a test on short notice. There have been six governments headed by various political parties since the time of Rajiv Gandhi. They were led by: V. P. Singh, Chandra Shekhar, P. V. Narasimha Rao, H. D. Deve Gowda, I. K. Gujral, and A. B. Vajpayee. India was on the verge of testing a device in December 1995 under Rao's Congress government, but the test was called off at the last minute after pressures from the United States. Frank Wisner, the U. S. ambassador to India "showed the [satellite] photographs to stop Indian officials in a successful effort to persuade them not to test."[31] Rao, however, left instructions with the scientists to be ready for tests within one month's notice. His successors, Deve Gowda and Gujral, did not change this state of readiness.[32] Thus the testing idea was never completely given up. Non-Congress coalition governments under the premierships of Gowda and Gujral had continued the plans for testing and were waiting for the opportune moment. Gujral in interviews after the tests said that since Rao's time the nuclear "file was on our table all the time."[33]

Why did the BJP government show such urgency in conducting nuclear tests? Systemic and subsystemic considerations were paramount, and domestic considerations were secondary, even though the latter are not totally irrelevant. Although almost all political parties desire to make India a major power, it is the BJP that holds such views most dearly and consistently. The party has also been a strong advocate of the nuclear deterrent, for its conceptions of security strongly uphold military instruments of power. A major provocation of the BJP was the extension of the NPT in perpetuity and the possibility of the CTBT coming into force in 1999. As one Indian commentator puts it, till the NPT extension in 1995 and the conclusion of the CTBT in 1996, Indian policymakers assumed that it was possible to guarantee "national security by keeping the *n*-option notionally open and simultaneously pressing for global disarmament . . . " However, after the NPT was extended in perpetuity, it was apparent that the big powers had no intention of shedding their nuclear arsenal. The moralizing tone of India's stand on disarmament may have held currency earlier but became meaningless after 1995. To compound this irrelevance, the CTBT tacitly sought to make the nuclear club a pre-entry, closed shop."[34] The two treaty developments convinced the BJP leaders that the nuclear-weapons states have formed a cartel and are determined to improving their nuclear capabilities while preventing new members from getting into the club.[35] According to Jaswant Singh, a senior foreign policy advisor to Prime Minister Vajpayee, who later became India's foreign minister, with its indefinite and unconditional extension, the NPT has now become "unamendable." This meant the "legitimization of nuclear weapons" was also "irreversible." "India could have lived with a nuclear option but without overt weaponization in a world where nuclear weapons had not been formally legitimized. That course was no longer viable in the post-1995 world of legitimized nuclear weapons."[36]

The post–Cold War security management by the UN Security Council and the unwillingness of the five permanent members of the Security Council (P-5) to induct India as a permanent member of the council also resulted in a perception that India needed to achieve hard power resources, such as nuclear weapons, in order to obtain respect from the members of the nuclear club. A former chief of the Indian Air Force articulated this desperation on India's part: "We're not being recognized by world powers. A lot of advanced countries are not backing a seat for India in the Security Council, even though India deserves it in every way. We are a democracy, we have economic strength, and we contribute resources and peace keepers all over the world to help the UN."[37] From the Indian perspective, the CTBT was further evidence of the nuclear-weapons states' interest in keeping their capability in perpetuity as it allowed laboratory-level tests and miniaturization of weapon systems. The adding of a clause that all countries with at least one nuclear reactor should sign the treaty before it came into force also gave the impression that the NWS wanted to constrain India from testing and developing the weapons as a paramount goal of the treaty. It was perceived that the Western powers would impose sanctions in any case in September 1999 when the CTBT review conference was expected to take place. According to K. C. Pant, the head of a task force set up by the BJP government to look into the functions of a proposed National Security Council, "our hope that the NPT Review meeting would concentrate on accelerating nuclear disarmament did not materialize. In fact this conference ensured that the nuclear weapon states retained their arsenals while unleashing nuclear apartheid on the rest of the world. The CTBT further reinforced this trend. These factors made it necessary for us to take a closer look at exercising our nuclear option."[38]

The BJP was also deeply concerned about the Pakistan-China nuclear and missile collaboration. Despite its adherence to the NPT and obligations not to transfer weapons and materials to nonsignatories, China since the 1980s had been steadily helping to build up Pakistan's nuclear and missile capabilities. This assistance included components for a uranium-enrichment plant, M-11 missiles, and other missile parts.[39] On April 6, 1998, Pakistan test-fired the Ghauri IRBM that could reach most major Indian cities. The missile is reportedly based on a North Korean design, but China might have helped in transferring technology and materials as well. China's purpose has been clearly to contain India and to perpetuate the India-Pakistan conflict relationship so that India's main adversary will remain Pakistan. The BJP-led government seemed to understand the larger Chinese containment efforts and has come to see China as India's number one potential threat in the twenty-first century.[40]

China's about-turn on nuclear issues has been ironic, because all the arguments about international inequity that China used in the 1960s to test its nuclear weapons are what India now is repeating. But China has become an accepted nuclear-weapons state, and for self-interest reasons China does not want to see India emerging with nuclear weapons and achieving the capability to target key Chinese cities. China has been one of the most strident critics of Indian nuclear behavior even when China has been partially responsible for that behavior: nuclear buildup since 1964, deployment of missiles in Tibet, and continued support to Pakistan's nuclear and missile capabilities. As one Indian analyst puts it: The pressure by China on India to sign the "NPT marks the assertion of China's status as the sole recognized nuclear weapon power in Asia. It opens the door for expanded cooperation with the United States on non-proliferation issues. And finally, the international reaction to the South Asian nuclear tests may have given China the opportunity to gain a long-term say in the management of South Asian affairs."[41] Moreover, the Clinton Administration's deep engagement with China gave a powerful signal to New Delhi of an impending strategic realignment involving its regional adversary and the hegemonic power.[42] Although the United States has been attempting to engage and integrate China with the hope of avoiding another Cold War, from the perspective of India, any realignment involving China and the United States would dramatically affect the balance of power in the region, which could adversely affect India's security calculations. This, again, underlines the fact that systemic changes involving great power relations affect the choices of aspiring great powers as well as middle powers that are not on friendly terms with the great powers.

In the wake of the Indian tests, a spate of newspaper articles raised the question: Does China pose a military threat to India? Some argue that the China-India border is stable along the line of control, established after the 1962 war and that China does not include India in its defense planning.[43] During the 1980s both China and India had made serious efforts to improve bilateral relations. A number of top-ranking official visits by both countries, a relaxation in the military situation on the border, and increased economic ties between the two countries have improved Sino-Indian relations to some extent. But, even when relations were improving, China accelerated its nuclear cooperation with Pakistan in an effort to contain India. Thus the Chinese policy towards India could be characterized as simultaneous engagement and containment. According to Indian defense analyst K. Subrahmanyam, the Chinese threat to India is at present not direct but indirect:

India as a neighbor of China is bound to be affected by the inevitable turbulent transition accompanying the emergence of China as a global power in the twenty-first century . . . Sun Tzu's advice—the best victory was one gained without fighting a war—may be what Chinese leadership is following vis-à-vis India. If China can transfer nuclear and missile technologies to Pakistan and thereby countervail India, there is no need for China to pose a threat to India. China can continue to be friendly with India, but at the same time lock India in a nuclear standoff with Pakistan. It can also treat both Pakistan and India in the same category as regional powers, not in the same class as China, which is a global player ... China's ambition is to replace the U. S. as the primary hegemonic power in Asia and in that perspective China looks at India as a regional player to be offset by Pakistan. This is a very sophisticated Chinese challenge to India and not a crude military threat.[44]

Thus, the Chinese threat to India is perceived in New Delhi as of both systemic and subsystemic nature. In the subsystemic sense, it is the changing balance of power in Asia, favoring China that is causing concern to India. India sees China as the model to catch up with and a potential and actual threat, while China sees India as a potential challenger that can be contained through aligning with its regional rival, Pakistan. China's elevation by the United States as the key state for obtaining nuclear nonproliferation in South Asia, has increased India's security fears as Indians view Chinese foreign policy as part of the problem and not the solution.[45]

Implications for the Future

In the wake of the nuclear tests in South Asia, the P-5 nations had accelerated their efforts to maintain their monopoly rights. In meetings in Geneva and London, following the Indian and Pakistani nuclear tests, they declared that "India and Pakistan do not have the status of NWS according to the NPT." Their effort was to see India roll back its capability and adhere to the discriminatory regimes it has so vehemently opposed.[46] This position of the great powers has largely been based on systemic considerations. Great powers tend to oppose the arrival of a new great power, until they are forced to do so through war or major diplomatic changes. They often follow polices of containment and "satellization" to stop regional powers from becoming too strong.[47] They tend to form concerts to prevent the emergence of rising powers. They are especially uncomfortable with middle-ranking powers acquiring nuclear weapons because such acquisitions would constrain their capacity to intervene militarily in regional theaters.[48] The acquisition of nuclear weapons by smaller powers would undermine the linkage between nuclear possession and great power status. But unlike the past, when war was an acceptable method of statecraft, in the nuclear age, war has become an unacceptable means of system change. Economic coercion has become the preferred alternative. However, independent-minded regional powers will resist efforts to contain them. This is again a systemic imperative, as without autonomous capabilities, they are likely to be dominated, directly and indirectly by the existing great powers. A state that perceives its potential power status is most adamant when it comes to resisting treaties that are meant to arrest its progress toward that goal.

The nuclear powers are likely to continue demanding India's unconditional adherence to all the treaties and arrangements designed to maintain their superiority. But India's nuclear capability is a fait accompli, which it is unlikely to give up without a substantial global move towards disarmament. The present major power attempt to contain and isolate India is unlikely to work. These efforts may slow down the Indian drive, but they will simultaneously increase India's resolve to achieve self-sufficiency in military capability. No disarmament treaty or regimes that fails to take into account the security interests of the great powers or rising great powers has functioned effectively.[49] The five hundred years of the modern international system powerfully attests to the fact that new great power states emerge periodically and see that the system has closed its doors against them. India is on the threshold of such a situation. The best course for the major powers is to make efforts to take into account India's perceived security interests and to integrate it into the international order before it becomes a thoroughly dissatisfied state and a system challenger.[50] Now that it has tested nuclear weapons, India has expressed its willingness to join the CTBT and the proposed Fissile Material Cut-off Treaty (FMCT) if certain conditions are met. This Indian willingness is an indication that, similar to its predecessors in the nuclear club, once a state obtains its nuclear capability, it is willing to stop others from acquiring the capability.

India's challenge is mostly directed against the global nuclear regime, especially its chief component, the NPT. The NPT, as structured currently, is likely to fail in the long run, because it attempts to freeze power relations in international politics indefinitely. This runs contrary to the forces of change that are characteristic of the modern international system. The fault line thus lies in the very structure of the treaty. At the global level, the treaty offers no room for new great powers emerging with nuclear weapons.[51] At the regional level, the treaty attempts to forestall regional powers from gaining nuclear weapons. Medium-sized states in high-conflict zones are likely to realize the value of deterrence and the great equalizer role that nuclear possession provides. Any threat of use of nuclear weapons by the present nuclear-weapons states will only increase the perceived need for nuclear possession by nonnuclear states. The NPT's future may lie in finding a way to accommodate a rising power such as India in its fold as a declared weapon state.

Notes

1. This chapter is a modified version of T. V. Paul's, "The Systemic Bases of India's Challenge to the World Nuclear Order," *Nonproliferation Review*, vol. no. 5(1) (Fall 1998) pp.1-11. Copyright MonteTrey Institute of International Studies. I thank Jeffrey Knopf and Baldev Raj Nayar for their useful comments.

2. For a domestic politics explanation, see Scott D. Sagan, "Why Do States Build Nuclear Weapons? Three Models in Search of a Bomb," *International Security,*

vol. 21 (Winter 1996/97), pp. 54-86; For a decision-maker type explanation, see Peter Lavoy, "Nuclear Myths and the Causes of Nuclear Proliferation," *Security Studies,* vol. 2 (Spring/Summer 1993), pp. 192-212.

3. Further, states involved in enduring rivalries and protracted conflicts find the possession of nuclear weapons advantageous. Without simultaneous efforts to resolve long-standing conflicts, especially among those states without a great power ally, have made the regime ineffective in arresting their nuclear ambitions. Some states like Iraq and North Korea have signed the NPT, but are continuing efforts to acquire nuclear weapons.

4. For an elaboration of these arguments, see T. V. Paul, "The NPT and Power Transitions in the International System," in Raju G. C. Thomas, ed., *The Nuclear Non-proliferation Regime: Prospects for the 21st Century,* (Houndmills, UK: Macmillan, 1998), pp. 56-74.

5. Robert Jervis, "Systems Theories and Diplomatic History," in Paul Gordon Lauren, ed., *Diplomacy* (New York: Free Press, 1979), pp. 212-44. See also, Robert Jervis, *System Effects: Complexity in Political and Social Life* (Princeton: Princeton University Press, 1992). Waltz reinforces the point, "we cannot understand system by summing up the characteristics of the parts or the bilateral relations between pairs of them." Kenneth Waltz, *Theory of International Politics* (Reading, MA: Addison-Wesley, 1979), p. 64.

6. A regional subsystem emerges as a result of regular interactions among two or more proximate states in a given region. William R. Thompson, "The Regional Subsystem: A Conceptual Explication and a Propositional Inventory," *International Studies Quarterly,* vol. 17 (March 1973), pp. 89-117. See also, David Lake, "Regional Security Complexes: A System Approach," in David Lake and Patrick M. Morgan, eds., *Regional Orders* (University Park: The Pennsylvania State University Press, 1997), pp. 45-67.

7. There are some crucial differences between the Indian and Pakistani objectives in the acquisition of nuclear weapons. For Pakistan, nuclear weapons are a great equalizer with India, which is four times bigger in terms of territory, seven times in terms of population, and six times in terms of gross domestic product. In 1996, the population of India was 967 million to Pakistan's 137 million. India's GDP was estimated at $371 billion to Pakistan's $64 billion. *The Military Balance,* (London: The International Institute for Strategic Studies, 1997), pp. 153, 159. Pakistan's aim to achieve nuclear parity with India was the reason why the tests were authorized by Prime Minister Nawaz Sharif, despite the promise by Western governments of substantial economic carrots and the threat of sanctions if Islamabad went ahead with the tests. Following the nuclear tests on May 29, 1998, Sharif stated: "Today, we have evened the score with India." John F. Burns, "Pakistan, Answering India Carries out Nuclear Tests," *New York Times,* May 29, 1998, p.1. Pakistan also seemed to have calculated that the moribund Kashmir issue could be revitalized and brought to international attention by pointing it out as the source of conflict and nuclear proliferation in South Asia. Pakistan subsequently rejected India's offer to conclude a no-first-use agreement in view of India's "overwhelming conventional superiority." Amit Baruah, "Pakistan Rejects Offer of No-First-Use Pact," *The Hindu,* July 19, 1998, p.1. In the summer of 1999, Pakistan engaged in an active guerrilla operation in the Kargil area of Indian Kashmir. The Indian armed forces reacted vigorously and succeeded in ejecting the intruders from several areas. The crisis came to an end

following diplomatic efforts by the United States. During the "warlike situation" some Pakistani politicians and generals raised the nuclear threat in an effort to deter India from expanding the war to other areas.

8. On this, see T. V. Paul, "Great Equalizers or Agents of Chaos? Weapons of Mass Destruction and the Emerging International Order," in T. V. Paul and John A. Hall, eds., *International Order and the Future of World Politics* (New York: Cambridge University Press, 1999), pp. 373-392.

9. On a comparison between inter-war naval treaties and the NPT, see Paul, "The NPT and Power Transitions in the International System."

10. A natural question arises why India has not adopted a trading state strategy similar to Japan and Germany. The major difference between the two defeated powers of World War II and India is that the United States, especially through the nuclear umbrella, guarantees their security, while India has no serious ally to rely on. Following their defeat, Germany and Japan were also forced to adopt a low-profile security policy by the victors, that is, the allied powers. Had there been no alliance support, it is conceivable that Japan and Germany might have gone nuclear and would have been forced to acquire more military capability than they have done so far. India initially followed a low-profile military policy, but the conflicts with Pakistan and China, especially the defeat in the 1962 Sino-Indian War, changed the Indian defense policy to a more assertive one. India chose a non-aligned policy and an autarkic economic policy largely for systemic reasons. Often the Indian leaders present these in ideological terms, but the underlying desire is to maintain as much autonomy as possible in the international system that they generally view as unequal and adversarial. For an excellent account of India's strategic dilemma, see Ashok Kapur, "Indian Strategy: The Dilemmas about Enmities, the Nature of Power and the Pattern of Relations," in Yogendra K. Malik and Ashok Kapur, eds., *India: Fifty Years of Democracy and Development*, (New Delhi: APH Publishing, 1998), pp. 341-371.

11. *The Indian Express*, May 27, 1999, p. 1.

12. For estimates based on purchase power parity, see World Bank, *World Development Report*, (New York: Oxford University Press, 1996), p. 188.

13. On India's power considerations, see Jaswant Singh, "Against Nuclear Apartheid," *Foreign Affairs*, vol. 77 (September/October 1998), pp. 41-52.

14. "In the last three decades, the global nuclear order kept punishing India through an ever expanding regimen of sanctions and technology denial, because it was considered a proliferation risk. Unwilling to make up its mind about nuclear weapons and clearly define its status, India had to relentlessly oppose every single international nuclear arms-control agreement." C. Raja Mohan, "Nuclear Politics-III: Signalling Nuclear Moderation," *The Hindu*, May 27, 1998, p. 13.

15. On the limitations of nuclear weapons as a source of power see, T. V. Paul, "Power, Influence and Nuclear Weapons: A Reassessment," in T. V. Paul, Richard J. Harknett and James J. Wirtz, eds., *The Absolute Weapon Revisited: Nuclear Arms and the Emerging International Order* (Ann Arbor: The University of Michigan Press, 1988), pp. 19-46. The Kargil crisis in 1999 points out that nuclear weapons are no effective deterrents in preventing guerilla-type operations. However, nuclear deterrence seems to be one of the reasons why the conflict did not escalate beyond the Kargil theater.

16. Former Indian Army Chief General K. Sundarji was a strong advocate of the viability of nuclear deterrence in India-Pakistan relationship. See his "India's

Nuclear Weapons Policy," in Jorn Gjelstad and Olav Njolstad, eds., *Nuclear Rivalry and International Order* (London: Sage Publications, 1996), pp. 176-81; See also, Devin T. Hagerty, "Nuclear Deterrence in South Asia: The 1990 Indo-Pakistani Crisis," *International Security,* vol. 20 (Winter 1995/96), pp. 79-114.; See also, Kapur, "Indian Strategy" p. 343.

17. On these, see Alva Myrdal, *The Game of Disarmament,* (New York: Pantheon Books, 1982).

18. On India's early disarmament efforts, see J. P. Jain, *India and Disarmament: Nehru Era,* vol. I (New Delhi, Radiant Publishers, 1974). Nehru made the proposal for a standstill agreement in 1954 in reaction to the Bikini Atoll atmospheric tests by the United States. In a statement made in the Indian parliament, he proposed such an agreement for halting nuclear explosions, "even if agreements about the discontinuance of production and stock-piling must await more substantial agreements amongst those principally concerned." Speech by Jawaharlal Nehru, Lok Sabha, New Delhi, April 2, 1954, Reprinted in *India and Disarmament: An Anthology of Selected Writings and Speeches* (New Delhi, Ministry of External Affairs, 1988), p. 36.

19. Shyam Bhatia, *India's Nuclear Bomb* (Sahibabad: Vikas, 1979), pp. 54-69. For the early nuclear debate, see also Ashok Kapur, *India's Nuclear Option: Atomic Diplomacy and Decisionmaking* (New York: Praeger, 1976); T. T. Poulose, ed., *Perspectives of India's Nuclear Policy* (New Delhi: Young Asia, 1978).

20. *A Debate on Foreign Affairs,* Lok Sabha, New Delhi, April 5, 1968, Reprinted in *India and Disarmament,* pp. 176-177.

21. William Epstein, *The Last Chance: Nuclear Proliferation and Arms Control* (New York: The Free Press, 1976), p. 285.

22. The plan called on nuclear weapon states to cease the production of nuclear weapons and weapon-grade fissile materials, the conclusion of CTBT, and a convention outlawing the use and threat of use of nuclear weapons, in addition to stopping transfers of weapons, delivery systems, and weapon-grade fissionable materials. In return, nonnuclear-weapons states would promise not to acquire nuclear weapons. Further, multilateral negotiations were to be initiated for the conclusion of a new treaty that would eliminate all nuclear weapons within a time period of 22 years. Rajiv Gandhi, "A World Free of Nuclear Weapons," Proposal Presented at the UN General Assembly, Third Special Session on Disarmament (New York, June 9, 1988), reprinted in *India and Disarmament,* pp. 280-294.

23. See T. V. Paul, "Influence Through Arms Transfers: Lessons from the US-Pakistani Relationship," *Asian Survey,* vol. 32 (December 1992), pp. 1078-1092.

24. K. Subrahmanyam, "Politics of Shakti: New Wine in an Old Bomb," *Times of India,* May 26, 1998, p. 4.

25. On the negotiations, see Tariq Rauf and Rebecca Johnson, "After the NPT's Indefinite Extension: The Future of the Global Non-Proliferation Regime," *Nonproliferation Review,* vol. 3 (Fall 1995), pp. 28-41; Joseph F. Pilat and Charles W. Nakhleh, "A Treaty Reborn? The NPT after Extension," in Raju G. C. Thomas, ed., *The Nuclear Non-Proliferation Regime: Prospects for the 21st Century,* (Houndmills, UK: Macmillan Press, 1998), pp. 41-55.

26. "It was not just the indefinite extension of an unequal treaty that troubled India, but also the fact that no real balance was stuck to bind the nuclear weapon states in the way the non-nuclear weapon states were bound . . . More serious was the

international reaction to the NPT extension: anger on the part of many leading non-aligned countries and the obvious triumphalism of some of the nuclear weapon states, which appeared to believe that the conference had secured their positions in power for the foreseeable future," cited in Arundhati Ghose, "Negotiating the CTBT: India's Security Concerns and Nuclear Disarmament," *Journal of International Affairs*, vol. 51 (Summer 1997), pp. 247-248.

27. For a comprehensive discussion, see T. T. Poulose, *The CTBT and the Rise of Nuclear Nationalism in India* (New Delhi: Lancers Books, 1996).

28. On the Indian objections to the Treaty, see Ghose, "Negotiating the CTBT," pp 239-61.

29. According to Indian analysts, the 1974 tests produced only limited data and further tests were necessary to prove beyond doubt the reliability of the nuclear weapons force. Amitabh Mattoo, "Enough Scientific Reasons Seen for Conducting Tests," *India Abroad*, May 15, 1998, p. 10.

30. Vajpayee, who was a member of the upper house of the Indian Parliament, Rajya Sabha, had declared in 1964: "The answer to an atom bomb is an atom bomb; nothing else." Quoted in Manoj Joshi, "Nuclear Shock Wave," *India Today*, May 25, 1998, p.14.

31. *New York Times*, May 25, 1998, p. A3.

32. Raj Chengappa, "The Bomb Makers," *India Today Webpage*, June 22, 1998 (http://www.india-today.com/itoday/22061998/cover.html).

33. Quoted in *India Abroad*, May 22, 1998, p. 10. The nuclear testing was approved by an overwhelming majority of the Indian public. In a public opinion poll after the first round of tests on May 11, 91 percent of those polled in cities supported the tests while 82 percent expressed support for India building a nuclear weapon force. *Washington Post*, May 18, 1998, p. A13. Interestingly, despite the high level of public support, the BJP could not capitalize on it on the electoral front, as in several by-elections in assembly seats spread around 13 states in less than a month after the tests, it did not make any major gain, but in fact lost its advantage in some states. "Tests Fail to Boost BJP's Poll Fortunes, *The Hindu*, June 7, 1998, p. 9.

34. Manoj Joshi, "Nuclear Shockwave," *India Today*, May 25, 1998, p. 16.

35. In a written statement before the Indian parliament on May 27, 1998, Vajpayee put "the onus of India's nuclear tests on the nuclear haves who had over the decades stubbornly refused to negotiate any treaty to dismantle the nuclear weapon stockpiles." To Vajpayee, India exercised restraint but during the 1980s and 1990s "a gradual deterioration of our security environment occurred as a result of nuclear/missile proliferation." *The Hindu*, May 28, 1998, p. 1.

36. Singh, "Against Nuclear Apartheid," pp. 44-45.

37. Quoted in Indira A. R. Lakshmanan, "New Delhi's View: A Push for Respect," *The Boston Globe*, May 13, 1998, p. A1.

38. The *Times of India*, June 6, 1998, p. 13.

39. Tim Weiner, "U. S. And China Helped Pakistan Build Its Bomb," *The New York Times,* June 1, 1998, p. A6.

40. Defense Minister George Fernandes in an interview in May 1998 contended that China's activities in Burma's Coco Islands off the cost of India and expansion of military airfields in Tibet as evidence of the emerging treat. Manoj Joshi, "George in the China Shop," *India Today International*, May 18, 1998, p. 12.

41. C. Raja Mohan, "China Takes the Hard Line," *The Hindu*, June 4, 1998, p. 11.

42. In response to the statement by the P-5 in Geneva on June 4, 1998, asking Indian and Pakistan to forgo their nuclear weapons, an Indian Foreign Ministry statement said that the five nations "are not unaware that one of the most serious threats to our security has arisen because of the non-observance of the obligations they have undertaken under the NPT," and they have declined to take any action to address a serious "violation of a treaty provision to which all of them were a party." Kenneth J. Cooper, "India Accuses Powers of Nuclear Transfers," *Washington Post*, June 6, 1998, p. A14.

43. Kenneth J. Cooper and Steve Mufson, "Nuclear Cloud is Cast Over India's Relations with China," *Washington Post*, June 1, 1998, p. A14.

44. K. Subhramanyam, "Understanding China: Sun Tzu and Shakti," *The Times of India*, June 5, 1998, p. 7.

45. Since the nuclear tests in May 1998, India has been on a course of mending relations with the great powers. It has engaged in several rounds of talks with the United States, initiated strategic dialogues with France and Russia, and begun resumption of bilateral talks with China on border and other issues. During the Kargil conflict of 1999, the great powers, especially the United States, sided with India and thereby further improving their mutual relations.

46. For the resolutions of these meetings, see Craig R. Whitney, "Top UN Members Urge India and Pakistan to End Arms Race," The *New York Times*, June 5, 1998, p. A8. At the Geneva meeting on June 4, 1998, foreign ministers of the five permanent members demanded India and Pakistan to end all further tests, adhere to CTBT unconditionally, negotiate the FCMT, and not to weaponize or deploy nuclear weapons and missiles. Text on India, Pakistan Statement, *The Associated Press*, June 4, 1998.

47. On this, see George Liska, "The Third World: Regional Systems and Global Order," in Robert E. Osgood et al., eds., *Retreat From Empire?* (Baltimore: Johns Hopkins University Press, 1973), p. 226; Baldev Raj Nayar, "A World Role: The Dialectics of Purpose and Power," in John W. Mellor, ed., *India: A Rising Middle Power* (Boulder: Westview Press, 1979), p. 119.

48. On the great power interests in this regard, see Hedley Bull, *The Anarchical Society* (New York: Columbia University Press, 1977), p. 50; Paul, "Great Equalizers or Agents of Chaos?"; Ashok Kapur, "New Nuclear States and the International Nuclear Order," in T. V. Paul, Richard J. Harknett, and James J. Wirtz, eds., *The Absolute Weapon Revisited: Nuclear Arms and the Emerging International Order* (Ann Arbor: The University of Michigan Press, 1998), pp. 237-61.

49. As Robert Jervis contends security regimes tend to emerge and persist only if the great powers want them. "Security Regimes," in Stephen D. Krasner, ed., *International Regimes* (Ithaca: Cornell University Press, 1983), p. 176.

50. According to Baldev Raj Nayar, India can already be characterized as a semi-challenger to the international order. "India: A Limited Challenger?" in T. V. Paul and John A. Hall, eds., *International Order and the Future of World Politics* (Cambridge: Cambridge University Press, 1999), pp. 213-234.

51. On this subject, see Paul, "The NPT and Power Transitions in the International System."

CHAPTER FIVE

India's Force Planning Imperative: The Thermonuclear Option

Bharat Karnad

Summary

In the wake of the nuclear tests in May 1998, and the public release by the Indian Government of the nuclear draft doctrine in August 1999, the country's force structuring intentions seem less clear than the ending of the system of non-weaponized-deterrence in South Asia. This chapter makes the case for India developing an all-azimuth nuclear deterrent with megaton thermonuclear punch and intercontinental ballistic missile reach, an option encompassed in the very elastic draft doctrine, even if it means the country withdrawing from its voluntary ban on testing.

The rejection by the nuclear-weapons states in 1988 of Rajiv Gandhi's plan for phased elimination of all nuclear weapons by 2010 led to the sanctioning of an accelerated program of nuclear weaponization by the Indian government. This policy thrust was justified over the years by two other developments: first, the disturbing nuclear geography in the offing of potentially two "failed" nuclear-weapons states, Pakistan and China, on its three sides; and second, the interventionist policies of the United States and its Western allies as manifested in the operation in Kosovo. The value of nuclear weapons as means to deter use or threat of use of nuclear weapons from any quarter as well as conventional military thrust by any big, out-of-area power is, therefore, obvious. A quantity- and quality-wise meaningful nuclear force, moreover, will also endow India with regional and international political heft and preserve the country's strategic independence.

The Indian designed and manufactured nuclear powered submarine (SSN/SSBN), able to fire indigenous nuclear war-headed sea-launched ballistic missiles (SLBM), will eventually be the centerpiece of a triad-based deterrent recommended by the draft doctrine, which will also include a host of ballistic missiles—short-range (Prithvi), intermediate-range (Agni), and the intercontinental-range variety derived from rockets and technologies incorporated in the proven and tested Polar Satellite Launch Vehicle and the soon to be available Geostationary Satellite Launch Vehicle. An Indian nuclear force of some 300-500 warheads matching the size of the deterrents possessed by the second-tier nuclear powers, is advisable for reasons other than purely political, not the least of which is "survivability" of the force emphasized by the Indian draft doctrine. There is the very real danger that a small number of nuclear weapons may invite a disarming conventional or nuclear first strike, which the United States, for instance, is presently capable of mounting.

Besides, a 400 plus warheads-strong Indian nuclear force is eminently affordable, with the costs worked out at Rs 89,920 ($18 billion at the current value of the rupee) over three decades. This total cost figure is put in perspective when seen as less than 0.1 percent of the Indian GNP in 2030, assuming an annual growth rate for the country of a doable seven percent. Or, when juxtaposed against some Rs 900,000 crores the country is likely to spend as per its traditional military expenditure pattern in just 20 years (2000–2020) on its armored and mechanized forces to fight outmoded wars that are unlikely to be replayed.

The Problem and Its Implications

Some two-odd years after the five nuclear weapons tests on May 11 and 13, 1998, and the subsequent test-firing of the indigenously developed two-stage, solid fuel-propelled Agni-II intermediate-range ballistic missile (IRBM), with a range of 2,500 kilometers, and in the wake of the disclosure by the Indian government in August 1999 of the nuclear draft doctrine, the country's force structuring intentions seem less clear than the ending of the system of non-weaponized deterrence prevailing in the subcontinent from the late 1980s onwards. This chapter makes the case for an all-azimuth Indian nuclear force with megaton thermonuclear punch and intercontinental ballistic missile reach, which capabilities, incidentally, are encompassed in the flexible draft doctrine.

To complement the development of the hardware, Prime Minister Atal Bihari Vajpayee outlined India's nascent nuclear policy. In a speech to Parliament, he voiced the resolve of the Bharatiya Janata Party coalition government "to maintain" a "minimum, credible, nuclear deterrent" whose size and quality, he said, somewhat pointedly, will be determined by "our own assessment of the security environment" and of the country's "requirements." Highlighting the "defensive" nature of the nuclear buildup, he emphasized the twin principles embedded in Indian strategic thinking—no-first-use (NFU) and non-use against nonnuclear-weapons states as well as those states not aligned with nuclear weapons-owning countries. The Prime Minister also sought to reassure the international community and the neighborhood, in particular that, India would not enter into a nuclear arms race with any one.[1] (It is another matter that this did not prevent Pakistan from setting off nuclear explosions of its own a scant fortnight after the Indian tests and launching the clandestinely-acquired Ghauri and Shaheen IRBMs—the ex-North Korean Nadong and the ex-Chinese M-9 missiles respectively—a few days after Agni-II's flight on April 11, 1999, from the Inner Wheeler Island base off the Orissa coast and its splashdown in the southern Indian Ocean.)

The Prime Minister's speech did not, of course, amount to a nuclear doctrine, but it did indicate that New Delhi was not unaware of the dangers to national security in the long-term of subscribing to nuclear scenarios that are limited in scope and of configuring a nuclear force with a purely South Asian orientation. Thus, depending on the nature of emerging threats and the likely future contingencies, the minimum, credible, deterrent-concept, for instance, is elastic enough to encompass a weapons/warheads strength in high three figures and with no limitations on the quality of weapons that the Indian atomic energy establishment may be able to muster.

In the context, moreover, of increasing U. S./NATO or Western-led UN military interventionism in the post–Cold War world, as happened in Iraq, Kosovo, and, more recently, in East Timor, influential sections of the Indian Government are generally wary and share the view expressed by the then Chief of Army Staff, General V. P. Malik, who, alluding to the vulnerability of multiethnic states, said that India had "to be strong to face any contingency in a strategic environment which is fluid."[2] The deterrent in the Indian definition is, therefore, minimum, relative only to the existing American and Russian inventories, each numbering in tens of thousands of nuclear armaments. And there seems to be an open mind in considering force structures that will ensure India's security even if these do not meet the current standards of political correctness articulated, ironically, by the five nuclear-weapons powers and those states enjoying the protection of the P-5.

Indeed, the catholicity of the prevailing official mindset, for instance, aided the National Security Advisory Board of the National Security Council in drafting the nuclear doctrine. The Board was afforded a virtual *carte blanche* to consider diverse deterrence concepts, mull over the often-contradictory experiences of nuclear-weapons states in the first 50 years of the nuclear age, and to recommend appropriate India-centric deterrence guidelines.

But perhaps the government of India took its Catholic attitude too far when, going against the official habit for secrecy, it made the nuclear doctrine paper public without first seeking the advice of even the group within National Security Advisory Board that drafted it. The Vajpayee government, in the event, seemed rattled by the largely negative reactions worldwide to the contents of the doctrine, but it also discovered that it had opened itself up to pressure from diverse quarters. The United States and the other P-5 countries, motivated in the main by the desire to perpetuate a comfortable international nuclear

correlation of forces, excoriated the supposed ambitiousness of the draft doctrine and worried that the Indian nuclear build-up would destabilize the immediate region. The nonnuclear Western states, including Japan and Australia,
shouted louder than everybody else and demanded a halt to the weaponization
process. That their protestations on behalf of the nonproliferation cause were
suspect owing to the security provided them by the American nuclear umbrella
notwithstanding, they joined Washington in imposing various economic sanctions. That the sanctions had little effect and ultimately each of these countries
separately sought a security dialogue with India suggests that a desire for a
modus vivendi overrode such reservations as they had. The outcome of all these
contretemps was that New Delhi has, perhaps, learned a lesson. India is
unlikely to be very forthcoming on nuclear weapons issues in the future.
Indeed, it will be a great surprise if it even announces the acceptance or otherwise of the doctrine.

The Indian Armed Services in the meantime has tried to understand the
doctrinal implications of the draft paper for nuclear war fighting.
Simultaneously, they have also embarked upon an intensive process of defining and rough-costing their nuclear force requirements. The planning direc-
torates in the three Service Head Quarters, for instance, are involved in drawing up detailed schemes for inducting a variety of nuclear armaments and
ancillary and support equipment in their orders-of-battle. And, they are flesh-
ing out on paper appropriate command and control frameworks. A reflection
of the urgency and the determination quickly to acquire a consequential deterrent is the priority accorded the nuclear-powered submarine project that had
until recently proceeded at a somnolent pace. The most experienced serving
submariner, Vice Admiral R. V. Ganesh who, uniquely for a naval person, has
commanded both an aircraft carrier (INS Vikrant) and the Charlie-II class SSN
(INS Chakra) leased from the Soviet Union in the mid-1980s, has been given
charge of the program. He is expected to bring the 'Advanced Technology
Vehicle' to sea trials by 2006.[3]

Why Nuclear Weapons and Why Now?

The beginning of India's more realistic appreciation of the politico-military
value of nuclear weapons and of relative disillusionment with the concept of
general disarmament can be dated precisely: June 9, 1988, when Prime
Minister Rajiv Gandhi enunciated his action plan for a nuclear-weapons-free
and nonviolent world in the Third Special Session on Disarmament of the UN
General Assembly. This plan envisaged the phased elimination of all nuclear
weapons by 2010 and, as interim measure proposed, among other things, that
the strategic arsenals of the five recognized nuclear-weapons states be cut by
half and that these states undertake radical changes in their nuclear doctrines,
policies, and institutions.[4] It was a last-ditch good-faith effort by Rajiv to avoid

Indian nuclear weaponization and to stay on the disarmament course championed by his grandfather, Prime Minister Jawaharlal Nehru in the fifties, and advanced with lesser conviction by his mother, Indira Gandhi, during her 17 years in office as head of government. The urgency was because by then New Delhi had hard evidence, what Rajiv Gandhi called "physical information,"[5] of Pakistan's having reached, or being on the point of reaching, nuclear-weapons status with no little help from China. Rajiv Gandhi's plan was ignored by the Nuclear Five. It prompted a disillusioned Indian Prime Minister, on his return home, to sanction an accelerated program of nuclear weaponization.[6]

The other major concern motivating change in the Indian policy was the worrying prospect of the emerging nuclear geography in the region. Potentially, there are now two "failed" nuclear-weapons states, Pakistan and China, on its three sides. It is difficult to argue which one is farther along the self-destruct road, but the difference would appear to be one of degree, about when, not if, the two polities are going to fall apart.

The military *coup d'etat* by the Chief of Army Staff, General Pervez Musharraf on October 12, 1999, juxtaposed against a popularly elected government in India being sworn in around the same time, has added to the misgivings about Pakistan's democratic system not maturing fast enough to withstand the diverse strains of dealing with the rising aspirations of the people, the socio-cultural fragmentation seeded by sectarian and inter-ethnic violence, the inability of a still remittance economy to deliver broad-based prosperity, and the stranglehold exercised by the bureaucratic-military nexus. Taken together with the paranoia of influential sections of the armed forces about "Hindu India" laced with the aggressive extremist Islamic impulses spawned in rightwing fundamentalist quarters, one can espy Pakistan's rulers being left with little else but the "Holy War tradition in Islam"[7] to fall back on as a means of keeping that country united and some how surviving as a nation-state, with what consequences for war or peace in the subcontinent can only be speculated.[8]

China, on the other two sides, continues to be in the throes of the post-Deng transition process. The crunch will come when the engine of Chinese power—its economy—slows down, as is already happening[9] and the vested interests in the bureaucratized state work to ensure their continued dominance even if this derails the program of economic reforms underway.[10] Then all bets are off. Unbridled ambitions, prompted by its undoubted conventional and nuclear military might, may turn out to be just the instrument a beleaguered autocratic Chinese leadership needs to start a "war on its periphery,"[11] as per its military strategy, to distract the people with and thus to put off the collapse of the authoritarian state it presides over. The Deng Xiao Ping-initiated policy of "socialism with a capitalist face," under the circumstances, will not merely describe the uncertain progress of China towards political freedom and free market, but also be the vehicle for conflict and disorder in the region and the world. These are worst case-scenarios. But in matters of nuclear weapons, it is best to plan forces on dire assumptions because it amounts to less of a liability than in the conventional military realm.[12]

Determining Deterrence

The Indian official nuclear threat fixation on Pakistan is not merely counter-productive, but downright dangerous. It at once validates the Pakistani nuclear/military apprehensions about India and the Pakistani armed forces' nuclear doctrine, that is keyed on early use of nuclear weapons should conventional military hostilities settle down on a losing note, as is bound to happen given India's considerable advantages.[13] And it complicates the problem of creating a wide enough firebreak between conventional and nuclear military operations as a margin for safety against errors and accidents. It results, moreover, in India's strategic focus being restricted to South Asia—a *denouement* that will be welcomed by Islamabad as much as it will be by China and the United States, all of whom fear the repercussions on their security of Indian nuclear weapons.[14]

China is more credible as adversary, but the lessons learned after the May 1998 tests when Beijing reacted with dramatic alarm is that it may not be politic to advertise this fact, and that adopting Beijing's rhetoric of opposing unnamed international nuclear hegemonists, is a better policy tact because this phrase covers the danger emanating from that source. It provides ample political rationale for the development of an effective deterrent both against China and even larger, more potent, and less obvious, threats.

The military rationale for nuclear weapons is that they primarily provide absolute security to the country in that they deter use or threat of use of nuclear weapons. Realpolitik-wise, they are instruments of strategic independence and constitute a diplomatic shield behind which national interests can be pursued more aggressively. A substantial nuclear force will also endow India with international political heft and status as a power of consequence.

Curiously, however, the theory of subdeterrent deterrence, variously described in the literature as "non-weaponized," "recessed," "existential," "opaque," and "virtual,"[15] continues to find support in an influential section of the Indian strategic community even after India has openly acknowledged possession of nuclear weapons. The only difference now is that the weaponization thrust is sought to be contained within the classical minimum deterrence theory exhaustively researched in the United States in the 1950s and 1960s.

This school of thought in India is represented mainly by K. Subrahmanyam, a former secretary to the government for defense production. He advocates Indian attachment to disarmament and morally responsible international behavior, and favors a low-risk, low-cost, minimal deterrent comprising a two digit-force strength of nuclear weapons, which, he maintains, will be adequate for the purposes of a credible retaliatory strike and for use as leverage to advance the cause of nuclear disarmament that India has always promoted.[16] Such advocates of minimum deterrence assumed, for example, that India need not and will not go beyond the simple fission-weapons stage because fission-weapons capability was thought of as sufficient for the purposes of deterrence. With this as premise, it was argued, that the one-off test in 1974 was adequate in and of itself to create a small nuclear weapons inventory, militarily service-able enough to obtain minimum deterrence and that further testing, therefore, was unnecessary.[17]

It was a short step from this position to advocating that India sign the hugely flawed Comprehensive Test Ban Treaty (CTBT) and supports the equally iniq-uitous Fissile Material Cut-off Treaty (FMCT) on the anvil.[18] The logic to commit to these accords was presumably that doing so would not in any way disturb or endanger the 1974 level fission weapons deterrent the country "vir-tually" possessed. The possibility that this capability would be further honed and developed to produce advanced fission and fusion weapons (as evidenced in the May 1998 tests) and that significant strategic benefits would accrue by doing this was never considered.

Such thinking, it turns out, was wrong in its essentials, a fact pointed out well before the 1998 tests,[19] and which was subsequently iterated by the lead-ing lights in the Indian nuclear program who considered additional testing "absolutely necessary" to realize any kind of a practical deterrent.[20] Such min-imalist thinking was and is opposed by the nuclear establishment in the mat-ter of signing the CTBT and FMCT as well. The well-founded fear is that acceding to the former will put a stop to testing and hence not only restrict the country to just kiloton-yield weapons but prevent the continuous upgrading of the quality of nuclear weapons already in the inventory.[21] Further, that ending production of fissile material any time soon, apart from gravely hurting national sovereignty (owing to the extremely intrusive verification provisions, et cetera) will mean letting the full-scope safeguards regime affect entry by the back door.[22]

Fortunately, the fact that thermonuclear armaments constitute a many times more effective strategic deterrent was better grasped by political leaders than by many Indian strategic writers who, ironically, rue the lack of knowledge of politicians on military/security issues![23] When he made the formal decision in 1985 to weaponize, Prime Minister Rajiv Gandhi expressly approved, for example, the development of thermonuclear devices, whence the successful fusion test of May 11,1998.[24] In the public debate, however, other than in stray writings,[25] the case for thermonuclear weaponization has received scarce atten-tion. Even writings by ex-military men, on the subject, for reasons unknown, have kept strictly to the "Subrahmanyam-limits,"[26] and talked mainly in terms of fission weapons in a minimum deterrent stance.[27]

According to Dr R. Chidambaram, chairman of the Indian Atomic Energy Commission (AEC), all that the lone thermonuclear test has done is enabled India to perhaps upscale the design and to produce a 200 kiloton fusion weapon.[28] This may be four times as big as the 43-45 kiloton (KT) hydrogen bomb exploded on May 11, 1998, but it is far from being a genuine megaton item. And, in any case, there is no unanimity of views on the subject. A for-mer chairman of the AEC, P. K. Iyengar, who headed the physics division at the time of the first Indian test in 1974, for example, believes strongly that test-ing is necessary to validate every new weapon type.[29] Moreover, while it is technically possible to have large yields with "boosted" fission weapons of the kind tested in May 1998,[30] megatonnage is most effectively and economically secured by developing hydrogen weapons. In any event, that additional tests will be required to prove the efficacy of newer thermonuclear weapons designs of various weight-to-yield ratios.

In the larger context, for the deterrent to be safe and credible, the country will need far greater numbers of fission/fusion weapons and warheads than is envisaged by those wedded to the notion of minimum deterrence.[31] The dilemma India faces is captured by an Israeli proverb: "Quality is more important than quantity—but is best in large numbers."[32] What that "large number" is to be and of what quality—fission or fusion—is the crux of the matter. At this early stage in the country's weaponization process, prudence dictates that India's sovereign right to the range of nuclear policy and force structuring options be zealously protected and that diplomatic and doctrinal protection be provided for intensive research and testing eventually to attain at least *notional parity*, both in qualitative and quantitative terms, with the three second-tier nuclear-weapons states—the United Kingdom, France and China.[33] Why a rough parity? Because a military balance is what facilitated political detente in the East-West context during the Cold War[34] and is most likely to beget an equitable peace with China and equal treatment with the other four nuclear-weapons powers.

This requires India to build-up to nothing less than 350-500 warheads, with the capping of the stockpile at this level being made conditional on the time-bound American and Russian draw-downs of their nuclear inventories to around 1,000 weapons/warheads each, and the French, British and Chinese, to stabilize theirs around the 350-500 mark. This reasonable and pragmatic approach, displaying abundant caution was, alas, weakened by India's moratorium on testing announced by Prime Minister Vajpayee after the May 1998 tests. But the moratorium was a voluntary act and can as easily be abrogated.

More troubling still, he offered to negotiate entry into the CTBT-FMCT net in return for what seems to be a small change—unhindered access to U. S. advanced dual-use technology. This deal has been the grist for the series of meetings between the Indian Minister for External Affairs, Jaswant Singh, and the U. S. Deputy Secretary of State, Strobe Talbott. It is another matter that the proposed bargain flies in the face of the long held Indian position of linking its acceptance of the CTBT and the FMCT to the total elimination of nuclear weapons by the five established nuclear-weapons powers. This was the Indian stance at the Commission on Disarmament (CD) in Geneva that failed to produce a draft CTBT.[35] Thereupon, the P-5, in an act of bad faith, made an end run around the Indian veto by using the procedural stratagem of having the Australian draft treaty, which was favorable to their interests, masquerade as the "National Text" of Belgium and presenting this to the UN General Assembly for vote.[36]

The draft nuclear doctrine produced by the NSAB and released for "public debate" by the government was mindful of the P-5 games being played in Geneva and at other international fora to see to it that only they enjoyed the security of nuclear weapons indefinitely into the future. The Board, therefore, attempted to reconcile the hoary Indian positions on nuclear weapons and disarmament with the actual demands of deterrence now that the country has acquired nuclear weapons and the attendant wherewithal. And, it managed to encompass the divergent ideas associated with the concepts of minimum and maximal deterrence. This was accomplished in the draft doctrine by showcasing the substantive differences between these positions as only facets of the two most desirable characteristics of any nuclear deterrent, namely, credibility and survivability.

Take the most glaring anomaly. The doctrine in enunciating "principles . . . central to India's nuclear deterrent" talks, for example, of the survivability of forces being ensured simultaneously by the capability for "rapid punitive response" and by their ability "to endure repetitive attrition attempts."[37] But both prompt response, which is antithetical to the NFU-principle and subscribed to by the Doctrine, and the forces' ability to absorb a series of nuclear strikes—however unrealistic this may be—which the draft Indian Nuclear Doctrine (IND) works out as a consequence of an NFU-policy, would require the country to have significantly larger forces than advocated by the champions of minimum deterrence.[38] This dual nature of some of the seminal deterrence concepts contained in the IND helped both the so-called minimalists and the maximalists in the NSAB to agree on a draft doctrine.

Whatever else it may or may not have achieved, the draft IND succeeded in protecting the hard-won strategic independence of the country by ensuring that that there was no doctrinal curtailment of any conceivable nuclear policies, strategies, and weapons-mix options by building up such capabilities as may become necessary in the uncertain future. Moreover, by permitting the Government the maximum feasible latitude to structure India's nuclear forces in the most efficacious way and to deploy them for the maximum deterrent effect against both the obvious and the not so obvious threats,[39] it did all that any military doctrine can be called upon to do. It safeguarded the country's freedom of policy choices, including the possibility of India's going megaton thermonuclear.

Why Thermonuclear Weapons?

Sir Solly Zuckerman, a former Science Adviser to the British Prime Minister, has noted: "There is built into nuclear weapons greater destructive power than is necessary for military purposes, and their secondary, non-military effects overshadow those which relate specifically to their military use."[40] The higher the yield of the weapon, the larger is the gap between its military purpose and the weapon's non-military effects and greater, in turn, it would seem, is its deterrent value. Because there is, as Donald Brennan and Morton Halperin have written, no "plausible strategy for limited nuclear war that would be unlikely to involve a mass destruction of the populace and of the industry of the country being defended,"[41] for the defender with limited resources, the crucial question is how to get the biggest bang for the buck in order to deter total war successfully?

The theoretical upper limits for yields of a fission device is 9 kilotons (KT) of TNT per pound of fissile material and for a fusion weapon (depending on the particular thermonuclear reaction) as much as 30 KT per pound. But because the weapons assembly begins to fall apart with explosive force before all the material undergoes fission, the ongoing fission or fusion reaction is cut short and the actual yields in detonated atom or hydrogen bombs are only a tenth of the theoretical maximum yields.[42]

According to the data collected by the U. S. Congressional Research Service, by the year 2000 India will have an annual production rate of 127 kg of unsafeguarded fissile material and an accrued total of some 1,607 kg of the same, which is sufficient to fashion 400 warheads.[43] (This data, circa the early '80s, is a bit dated. But it will do for the indicative purposes of this chapter.) Using the actual weapons yield figures, were all this material to be turned into fission (nuclear) weapons, the cumulative yield of the prospective Indian arsenal by the end of the century would be 3,095 KT or a little over three megatons, while the total destructive power if this amount of material were exclusively fusioned, would be over three times as much at 10,317 KT or nearly ten and a half million tons or megatons (MT) of TNT.

There is hardly any doubt that fusion weapons offer more destructive power and, hence, greater deterrence for the money. Though the Indian scientists are confident that they have mastered the two-stage, twin assembly, thermonuclear explosion technique[44] fission fuse to fire the fusion reaction, there are good reasons not to abjure further testing. More than a single test for any type of weapon is required before the explosion physics and other problems (materials, engineering) are mastered and weaponizing kinks worked out[45] to enable the assembling of a hydrogen weapons arsenal. France was offered simulation software and data relating to thermonuclear explosions by the United States to India in return for a cessation of tests. While highly unlikely, if a similar deal were to be worked out with New Delhi, India will still need to conduct more tests both to verify the American simulation package and to mesh indigenous test data with it.

While some 2,000 tactical nuclear weapons each with a couple of kiloton yields in theater use can take out 25 frontline army divisions,[46] the psychological, and therefore, the deterrent effect[47] of this is as nothing compared to thermonuclear weapons devastating whole cities—the repositories of the bulk of national wealth, or flattening high value hardened military-industrial complexes. The threat of instant destruction on this scale will more credibly deter the potential large adversary than 200 kiloton weapons with their more limited destructive power against the same targets.[48] And, in any case, if the nuclear weapons inventory is a relatively small one, megaton thermonuclear weapons stock will, *ipso facto,* have greater deterrent value than a small nuclear force equipped with kiloton devices. Further, for a small n-force to be credible, it will be forced to adopt a mainly a counter-cities or counter-value nuclear bombardment strategy and large yield thermonuclear weapons are the obvious vehicle for this strategy.

Without a force of 3-5 MT weapons available at the earliest to match those in the stockpiles of the P-5, India's negotiating position is weak and in crisis or war the other nuclear-weapons states, especially China, will enjoy political and military "escalation dominance," which, the nuclear war theorist Herman Kahn described as "the effect of the competing capabilities."[49] A country aware of a comparatively large differential in the yields of weapons in the adversary's arsenal will be under greater psychological pressure to cede ground if continuing differences snowball into actual conflict. More real than the military escalation dominance exercised by the country with the larger, more lethal nuclear arsenal in war is the political escalation dominance it can wield in periods of peace or non-war. India's policy of appeasement of China,[50] of accepting in 1996 a number of confidence building measures—injurious to Indian militarily posture in the disputed areas—proposed by Beijing without first delineating the border, is an instance of political escalation dominance at work. Those who pooh-pooh the coercive potential of huge numbers of weapons[51] disregard the basic fact of nuclear life that *deterrence is ultimately a mind game* played as much in peace time to cajole and compel obedience as during war to achieve the desired result.

The best evidence of this was provided by the Chinese who stared down American nuclear threats in the immediate past with great resoluteness.[52] India has mostly chickened out when the going got tough, especially in its dealings with Beijing. The political escalation dominance established by the better articulated Chinese nuclear arsenal has subliminally tilted the negotiating scales against India in a bilateral forum such as the Joint Working Group, where India, apparently, felt compelled to accept the formulation of "equal" rather than "equitable" security, which last would have served India's interests better.[53] In this context, the 3.3 megaton bulk strategic weapon with the Chinese Peoples Liberation Army's Second Artillery Corps, for example, will loom larger on the Indian mind than India's at most 200 KT weapon will on Beijing's mind in any future crisis or contingency.

There is a third set of reasons to favor a mostly thermonuclear force and it has to do with the "usability paradox" attending on nuclear weapons. In the mid-80s, the Harvard Nuclear Study Group, in a comprehensive study of the politics of nuclear weapons, described the paradox thus: "Nuclear weapons can prevent aggression only if there is a possibility that they will be used," but they should not be made "so usable that anyone is tempted to use one."[54] The decision to launch city-busting hydrogen bombs and thermonuclear warheaded ICBMs in a direct attack on the enemy homeland would, on the face of it, be more onerous and far-reaching and, hence, will be more difficult to make than, say, a decision to loose off a theater nuclear weapon or a tactical nuclear salvo on a peripheral target. And for this reason, thermonuclear weapons would, logically speaking, be under tighter command and control and will more easily help stabilize the security situation vis-à-vis a bigger nuclear power.

Any new member of the nuclear-weapons club faces a situation that the Soviet Union and China found themselves in when they first forced their entry. Unable to match the technological lead, like in warhead miniaturization and in the development of navigation and terminal guidance systems that obtained for the United States ever more lethal, accurate and versatile nuclear armaments, Moscow and later Beijing reacted mainly by increasing the throw-weight of their missiles, that is, by greatly raising the thermonuclear yields of their arsenals to multi-megaton levels. This is a proven method to compensate for inferior weapons technology.[55]

India will similarly have to contend with the range of weapons from the extremely advanced held by the United States to the relatively effective in the Chinese inventory. Their very sophistication and destructive power serves an intimidatory purpose. Caution dictates that the high-yield thermonuclear weapons are the only means available to India now and in the foreseeable future to balance the array of qualitatively advanced nuclear armaments owned by some of the potentially hostile P-5 states. Indeed, with Washington pressing India to translate its moratorium on testing into signature on the Comprehensive Test Ban Treaty, New Delhi may be left, pragmatically speaking, with only the megaton thermonuclear route to weaponization.[56]

Fusion weapons, promising unparalleled destruction spread over an unimaginably wide area, act as a very superior deterrent besides compensating for low accuracy of land-based and submarine-fired missiles and for weaknesses, like navigational errors in targeting, by nuclear ordnance laden long range bomber aircraft. Due to its large CEP (Circular Error Probable)—a measure of missile accuracy that denotes the distance from the point of impact to the location of the intended target as the radius of the circle within which 50 percent of the shots/missile strikes will fall—and problems with terminal guidance, an Indian IRBM (intermediate range ballistic missile) set on its course, say, for the center of an enemy city, may actually land in a distant suburb. But that would not matter very much, as much of the metropolitan hub along with a good part of the countryside in a 150 square mile area would be rendered uninhabitable by a 5 MT bomb[57]

Moreover, the extent of the threatened devastation is so spread out, horrendous and undiscriminating, that the technological sophistication of the delivery system or of the warhead design, and of on-board electronics, et cetera, are rendered irrelevant, because they add only marginally to the deterrent value. Indeed, a nuclear force planned with an eye on its perceived potency makes a very real difference to whether the deterrent will work.[58]

And, finally, the clinching argument: It is more cost-effective. It costs about as much to produce fission weapons as multi megaton thermonuclear weapons; most of the expense being in producing the fissionable bomb in the one case, and the fissionable material for the purposes of a trigger in the other.[59] In the event, it makes no sense to stick to the simpler fission variety of weapons when the fusion types promise so much "more bang for the buck" and palpably more deterrence value.

The CTBT and a Dud N-arsenal

The question now is whether India can go credibly thermonuclear without conducting further tests. The freedom afforded by the draft Indian nuclear doctrine and the absolute security consequent upon owning hydrogen weapons is at risk if the ruling Bharatiya Janata Party, having been frustrated the first time, decides to cobble together another "consensus" to sign the Comprehensive Test Ban Treaty, which the five nuclear-weapons powers, with the United States in the van, have been pressuring New Delhi to do.

It is unfortunately a characteristic of the Indian strategic culture or, perhaps, a character-flaw in Indian rulers that advantage is usually frittered away from a position of strength. CTBT is a case in point. The traditional Indian weakness—the Indian government's inability or unwillingness to know just what the vital national interests are, let alone how to protect them—did not seem to apply to the BJP. Alone among major political parties, it had made its aim to acquire nuclear weapons clear.[60] And, far from deviating from this goal, once in office it promptly ordered the series of nuclear tests in May 1998. On the cusp of redefining Indian power, however, it faltered. By declaring a moratorium on testing, the nuclear weaponization process was made hostage to the abstractions and make-believe of computer simulation.

The Indian expert view is divided between the many, including Chidambaram and A. P. J. Abdul Kalam, recently elevated to the post of Principal Science Advisor to the Government (with the rank of Cabinet Minister), who claim that high speed computers able to simulate nuclear/thermonuclear explosions can adequately replace physical tests, and the many more led by Iyengar, head of the Bhabha Atomic Research Center, at the time of Pokharan-I, who are convinced that, because reliable performance of weapons is the key to nuclear deterrence, testing is essential for every new type or genus of weapon.[61] This is the view also of nuclear weapons designers in the United States and elsewhere.[62] Testing is considered necessary, moreover, for proving the safety of the key components of weapons systems/warheads and of the weapons designs.[63] This is the avowed premise of the American nuclear stockpile "stewardship program."

A computer can simulate from an already existing database. Thus, were a military need to be evinced for a warhead only marginally different from any of the ones already tested, then drawing up an explosion physics simulation program may not be difficult. If, on the other hand, a software program has to be created to simulate, say, a megaton thermonuclear explosion or a 100 kiloton warhead of miniaturized design specifications to fit a submarine-launched ballistic missile, to name just two types of weapons that could be featured in the Indian nuclear force of the future, then the unrehearsed and inherently unknown, unknowable and, therefore, unprogrammable data not factored into the software simulation could skew the weapon design. The result could be a slew of nonfunctioning warheads.

In any case, there will be no way to know whether these weapons actually work except when it comes to using them in war, and then it will be too late. The severely limited test data in the bag, in effect, raises the frightening prospect of the country ending up having an entirely dud arsenal of the supposedly more advanced and "decisive" types of weapons. Indeed, one of the prime objectives of the CTBT, as senior U. S. government officials candidly have been saying, is to prevent the realization of genuine high-yield nuclear clout by newly weaponized countries. Putting a stop to tests will end up, as U. S. Secretary of State Madeleine Albright said, "locking in the technological status quo that is highly favorable to us."[64]

Even with the database generated by some thousand-odd atmospheric and underground tests, Americans fear that the CTBT will imperil weapons performance, hence the U. S. deterrent posture in the future. These, in any case, were the reasons why, the Clinton Administration's best efforts notwithstanding, the U. S. Senate failed to ratify that treaty. With just six tests under our belt, the Indian science and technology establishment is apparently confident of matching the P-5 in the ability to research, develop, and produce newer nuclear weapons designs using cost-prohibitive techniques such as subcritical tests, inertial confinement fusion, high-powered lasers, et cetera, which require an elaborate technological infrastructure the country does not currently possess.[65] It is either an instance of bravado masquerading as confidence or of confidence outpacing capabilities as well as common sense.

External Affairs Minister Jaswant Singh, has written sensibly "that the country's national security, in a world of nuclear proliferation, lies either in global disarmament or in exercise of the principle of equal and legitimate security."[66] But, how does signing the CTBT—which, incidentally, is opaque about what exactly it is supposed to be banning—help either the cause of disarmament or that of equal and legitimate security? And, considering the realities of power, why does anybody in government think that it would?[67] The fact is, it is imprudent for India not to utilize the hiatus between now and when CTBT is finally sealed and ratified by all parties to resume nuclear testing and to proceed apace with designing a variety of at once safe and powerful nuclear weapons.

But there is an apprehension in the minds of Indian policymakers that were they to renew nuclear testing and justify the decision in terms of credible weaponization, national security, and vital national interests, it would isolate the country internationally and lose it not merely the alleged goodwill and leverage in its dealings with the United States and the West afforded by its show of nuclear "restraint" during the Kargil crisis,[68] but affect India's larger image as a responsible world power. This line of reasoning is suspect considering that it is meant to go down well with the ones who, from under the protective cover of a nuclear umbrella or a nuclear arsenal, advocate and appreciate restrained behavior in others. Also, suggestions first made by the lame-duck Clinton Administration in Washington, Japan, et al, that New Delhi acquiesce in CTBT in some way—"sign, but don't ratify" or "ratify, but don't deposit the instruments"[69] be revived by the Republican Party Administration, once the war against global terrorism in Afghanistan is out of the way,[70] notwithstanding George W. Bush's branding the CTBT an "unwise" treaty.[71]

China is respected and allowed every consideration. India is badgered and asked to behave because Washington is convinced that the threat of punitive actions—trade embargos, credit cutoffs, technology denial regimes—is enough to turn Indian resolve to jelly. Or, it is tempted by offers of freer access to high technology or whatever else New Delhi puts a policy premium on, because it is believed that India (and Indians) can be bought off or won over with blandishments. That is the principal difference in the American attitude towards China and India.

When India's security imperatives and the strategic logic fuelling them are explained in the realpolitik context and the determination to proceed along a certain path dictated by Indian security concerns is communicated to them, American Government officials and Washington think-tanks alike quickly get round to adopting a more realistic attitude.[72] But realism also requires that the Indian government define just what the strategic end is and to be clear about the means at hand. Often, in Indian policymaking, that is where the disconnect is. Conforming to U. S. Government diktat on testing and nuclear weapons is not going to assure India technological advancement and accompanying economic prosperity, it will only damage Indian security and prestige beyond repair.

Rather, the solution lies in separating the security and economic spheres and, by inviting them to build up their stake in India, let the American multinationals influence and mold Washington's India policy. This is the Chinese model for productive relations with the United States and something India ought to emulate.[73] American business, in turn, will be motivated to invest when they find that the accelerating pace of economic reforms, the dismantling of the state-owned public sector, and of de-bureaucratization measures, will help them make big profits. American capital and U. S. high technology companies, always alive to the potential of a big emerging market,[74] will stream in unbidden. And this will happen regardless of what the American government wants. Once the economic transformation is genuinely underway—something the now millennial Prime Minister Atal Bihari Vajpayee has promised[75]—strategic accommodation with the United States on more equable terms, will follow naturally in its train.

India's bargaining position is far stronger than many of its leaders reckon. What is absent is a vision of India as a great and consequential state. And central to that vision and to the country's freedom of action in a dangerous world are nuclear weapons, which remain the prime currency of power.

Maximizing Strategic Forces

Until now, Indian analysts engaged in thinking about an appropriate nuclear force labored under the triple disadvantage of not knowing whether the government would at all exercise the nuclear option, what the purpose of the immanent nuclear force would be, and who the perceived threats were against. Lacking such basic directives and information from the government, Indian analysts and war-planners limited themselves to giving ballpark figures in line with the requirements of minimum deterrence for the warheads for the Indian inventory. The numbers, ranging from 60 to 150 weapons, were accepted as having a quasi-official sanction.[76]

Curiously, nobody spelled out the reasons for this or that level of N-arms inventory or detailed the force structure they had in mind.[77] With the government now more purposive in its outlook and pronouncements and the draft doctrine providing guidelines, force-structuring alternatives can be discussed more substantively. For a start it was officially stated that Indian nuclear weapons are for strategic deterrence, not for tactical use.[78] This preempts the residual security concerns regarding Pakistan from messing up a rationally constructed nuclear force. Pakistan is not too weighty a nuclear threat any way and there is unlikely to be a nuclear war in South Asia, whatever the Western prognostications on the subject.[79]

Shared culture and innumerable organic linkages have ensured that the subcontinental wars are severely controlled affairs, with both India and Pakistan habitually pulling their punches and refraining from striking at cities.[80] If the two countries fought conventional wars with unmatched restraint, it is hard to imagine their lobbing nuclear bombs at each other in a war, which could annihilate one and gravely damage the other.

In the South Asian context, any use of nuclear weapons is tactical use, which the Indian Government has wisely foresworn. So, there is no question of shaping a Pakistan-specific nuclear force. But with nuclear armaments on both sides of the border, the larger and more powerful country, India, will have to win Pakistan's confidence.[81] The Indian offer of no-first-use—notwithstanding the qualifier to the NFU-principle in the draft Indian Nuclear Doctrine (IND)—should persist. It will go a long way in making Islamabad rethink its demonology and should be strictly adhered to. More convincing proof that India is not gearing up for a preemptive nuclear strike could be provided by a unilateral Indian decision not to deploy the nuclearized short range Prithvi surface-to-surface missile on the western border, removing presently forward deployed short-range SSMs from the border with Pakistan, and by supplying verifiable evidence—like satellite data—to Islamabad on an ongoing basis, to show that these unilateral measures are not being clandestinely reversed. In time, these measures cannot but adequately reassure Pakistan and bring about stability.

These unilateral measures, based on the strategic ("out of the area") rationale undergirding the new Indian thinking on nuclear weapons, should be communicated formally to Pakistan. It will psychologically disarm that country, afford Islamabad the political room for maneuver, and motivate it to negotiate a mutually beneficial set of understandings in the nuclear realm. Additionally, India's taking the lead to stabilize the nuclear situation will create a groundswell of favorable opinion abroad and quiet the shrill and generally uninformed criticism emanating from within India[82] and the West about brinksmanship in South Asia.[83] And, it will dampen Washington's apprehensions of an indirect threat to American interests in Pakistan posed by a menacing India.[84]

Not pre-positioning the nuclear warheaded Prithvi on the western front makes ample military sense as well. It widens the firebreak between conventional and nuclear-use weapons and eases the "balance of terror" that Mushahid Hussain, the ousted Pakistan Prime Minister Nawaz Sharif's confidante and Information Minister, said existed.[85] In a hot border situation (like, in Kashmir), this will be a priceless development as it will remove the prospect of an unrecallable short range ballistic missile, accidentally or inadvertently, starting a nuclear conflagration. This, however, goes against the force structuring ideas entertained, among others by Subrahmanyam and former Army Chief, the late General K. Sundarji.[86] But short of putting the region on a nuclear hair-trigger, keeping the nuclear Prithvis out of the Punjab, Rajasthan, and Kashmir sectors, becomes unavoidable.

Going Ballistic

The discussion so far has pointed out that one main foundation stone for a full and robust nuclear deterrent is predominantly thermonuclear weapons stores. The second is reliable long-range missiles able to carry hydrogen-bomb loads. Missiles are at once the most economical, effective and symbolically potent delivery systems available today. Their military advantages, as an American study on Small Nuclear Forces (SNF) points out, are many. Missiles (1) need no expensive "fixed facilities" like air bases and runways and, therefore, are mobile and harder to target when dispersed in wartime, (2) have "certitude of penetration," which in the absence of an effective antiballistic missile system even threatens the big powers[87] and explains the strong missile technology denial tilt of American policies, (3) can be instantly launched, and (4) function best as specialized and dedicated second strike weapons.[88] This last, moreover, meshes with the emphasis laid in the Indian Nuclear Doctrine (IND) on the mainly retaliatory role of the nuclear deterrent.

The third main element to make the force edifice stable is the so-called C4I2—Command, Control, Communications, Computers, Intelligence, and Information—networks cobbled together into a "system of systems." This is the most critical aspect of a stable nuclear deterrent. Crafting a relatively simple, hardy, reliable, and appropriately responsive C4I2 system will be the great challenge. But suffice to say here that the unfolding advances in computer technology, like in molecular electronics, extra high-speed computing and fiber optics, make a short leash, relatively fail-proof, nuclear command and control system, perhaps, easier to configure than in the past.

At present, neither the Prithvi nor the 1,200-km Agni I and the 2,500-km range Agni II, evoke any great fear. The reasons for this are not far to seek. Based on mathematical modeling for missile accuracy, kill capabilities, target resistance, and damage parameters, a recent study conducted at the Massachusetts Institute of Technology, for instance, concluded that both these missile systems are, in the conventional military sense, useless.[89] Whether or not such conclusions about the Prithvi are merited—the Indian Army is impressed by its accuracy, and is configured to carry a 20 KT nuclear payload. In any case, missile accuracy is perhaps not as important when it comes to nuclear and especially thermonuclear warheads, but the range of the missile is crucial.

But this still leaves India with a big void where reliable, moderately accurate, long-range missile capability should be. It would be natural for the Integrated Guided Missile Development Program (IGMDP), initially headed by A. P. J. Abdul Kalam, to progress from IRBMs to acquiring expertise in intercontinental ballistic missiles (ICBMs). For many years now India has had in, latent form, an intercontinental weapons reach owing to its PSLV (Polar Satellite Launch Vehicle) capability. This conversion has not so far been attempted, but a partially militarized Indian Space Research Organization's (ISRO) space launch program will help facilitate distant deterrent capability. With ISRO having registered singular successes with its PSLV—Germany and South Korea used this rocket to put various payloads into orbit and, moreover, with the Geo-stationary Satellite Launch Vehicle (GSLV) being readied for launch in February 2001,[90] a choice of ICBM technologies is, in effect, already operational. All that is required is to down-weight the system by removing a stage from the PSLV/GSLV structure and to replace the satellite payload with a megaton nuclear/thermonuclear warhead atop the ISRO rockets.[91]

The skills and technologies needed to put multi-purpose satellites in precise orbits over the pole requires the rockets to keep to equally precise trajectories. The inertial guidance system—available in the strap down-mode for the Prithvi SSM, the in-flight control and impact-end guidance technologies, the carbon-carbon composite for the heat shield, and the mix of Ammonium Perchlorate and Hydroxy Terminated Poly Butedine as solid fuel propellant are all locally produced and proven technologies. Suitably amended, these technologies could speedily help confer Indian nuclear weapons with strategic reach in a way that no country anywhere can afford not to be deterred by.[92] This will necessitate a reverse flow of technology from ISRO to the IGMDP and other agencies of the Defense Research & Development Organization (DR&DO) working on military-use systems and to realize greater efficiencies, perhaps, even integration of the IGMDP with some parts of ISRO. With this infrastructure in place, the accuracy of Agni I and II intermediate range ballistic missiles and of the longer-ranged surface-to-surface variant, the Prithvi SSM 250 commanded by the Indian Air Force, could be improved.

For too long has synergy been sacrificed in order to keep the military and the so-called civilian sensitive technology programs artificially separated. This was an inherently bad policy to begin with but was, perhaps, unavoidable in an era when the U. S.-inspired missile technology control regime (MTCR) still caused some anxiety. Today there is no such excuse. In any case, the sooner it is, the quicker the country will derive substantive security benefits from the sizeable national investments over the past five decades in the dual-use space sector.

Nuclear Force Structure

Western analysts, in the main, have pondered the likely nuclear force design for a middle power like India and concluded that, taking into account its various resources and threats, what will finally accrue will be on par with that of China, the United Kingdom and France. Many of these exercises, however, are based on the unlikeliest of contingencies—an Indo-Pak nuclear fracas and have stressed nuclear strike aircraft and nuclear tipped short-range surface-to-surface missiles.[93] This sort of thing somewhat limits their relevance for India, whose strategic and threat compass includes lots more besides Pakistan.

Further, following the Western lead, Indian efforts in this direction have suffered from a mainly South Asia-bound "tactical" perspective. The force plan articulated in some detail by General Sundarji, for example, talks sensibly of obtaining a nuclear deterrent in three phases in an open-ended sort of way. But a potentially strategic-use weapons system, referred to as Agni Mark 2, does not make its entry into the proposed force structure until the very last phase. He relies on "road and rail-mobile" long-range missiles, and like a good foot soldier, entirely misses out on a possible role for the Navy.[94]

Most fatally, however, there is no mention in it or in the Subrahmanyam scheme for that matter of Atomic Demolition Munitions (ADMs) that are featured in nuclear force structuring exercises done even by Western analysts.[95] ADMs are ideal weapons for use in the mountains because they are designed to cause land slides and block possible attack routes through the Himalayan Passes that the Tibet-based Chinese Integrated Group Armies may seek to force. Vectoring SSMs to inflict the greatest damage in that terrain will be difficult. Aircraft carrying nuclear gravity or glide bombs (NGBs) too may be handicapped in the Indian northeast, notwithstanding the latest avionics onboard, by bad weather and other routine problems as hamper weapons aiming and release in mountain operations. So ADMs, providing sure but "passive deterrence," are a must against a China even remotely contemplating a conventional offensive in the high Himalayas.

Subrahmanyam, like Sundarji, has not chalked out in any great detail an Indian deterrent except to indicate that 60 nuclear weapons/warheads mounted atop some 20 Prithvi missiles and a like number of Agni missiles, and carried by strike aircraft, would do. Surprisingly, he is equivocal about equipping submarines with IRBMs/ICBMs, doubting whether a submarine-launched missile will be available any time soon.[96] Moreover, he thinks that such an Indian force will not worry Pakistan. A more recent analysis by a former head of the Army's Air Defense Artillery Directorate concludes that a force strength of around 186 nuclear weapons/warheads may do the job of deterrence.[97]

The Indian designed and manufactured nuclear powered submarine (SSBN), able to fire an indigenous nuclear war-headed ballistic missile (SLBM), will come on stream faster than many analysts, including Subrahmanyam, expect it to.[98] In any case, this boat, fitted with 12 ballistic missile tubes, is an Indian Navy priority and should enter the lists definitely by 2010. It will provide this country with an invulnerable second-strike capability that no mix of aircraft, land-based, and air-launched missiles will be able to obtain. If the Indian Navy follows the British Royal Navy standard, then to keep one submarine, and in an emergency two vessels, always on station, the country will have to have a minimum SSBN fleet of four vessels.[99]

In light of the discussion so far, a nuclear force architecture begins to crystallize. The Sukhoi-30 MKI fighter-bomber will serve as the manned platform for the delivery of nuclear ordnance on tactical missions over intermediate ranges, and is a reliable, primary, system in the force makeup before a follow-on Agni III IRBM with a range of 4,000-5,000 kms is obtained. The Su-30MKI and the extended-range Agni in tandem enhance the deterrent by increasing offensive/preemptive strike and retaliatory strike capabilities. A small portion of the Jaguar low level strike aircraft fleet and of the multi-role Mirage 2000 air-attack/air-superiority squadrons are convertible for immediate use on nuclear bombardment missions for ranges of up to 400 miles and, serviced by aerial refuelers the Indian Air Force is acquiring, can extend their operational radius by another 300-400 miles.

But that still leaves a big hole in the Indian nuclear order-of-battle for a genuinely long range strategic bomber able to operate independent of in-flight refueling that, among other things, complicates sortie routing and renders the tasked aircraft more vulnerable. A perception of this void may have impelled the Indian Navy's decision to lease four Russian Tu-22M strategic bombers,[100] ostensibly for maritime surveillance but meant for long-range nuclear missions. Leasing is cheaper than buying small numbers of this Tupolev aircraft. It provides a ready solution for distant strikes with nuclear weapons and, depending on the aircraft's performance and over all utility, in larger numbers this (NATO code name: Backfire) bomber, can become part of a more lasting deterrence order as well.

Targeting Policy

Targeting doctrines of the established nuclear-weapons states reflect a tortuous evolution in their thinking over the years. Of course, considering the 33,000-odd warheads owned by the United States and Russia, any discrete targeting philosophy is rendered moot because with an over-sufficiency of weapons, the whole range of mix and match counter-force and counter-value force profiles become practicable. Lesser powers have to be more selective given the limited numbers of nuclear armaments in their possession. The United Kingdom, France and China played it safe and exclusively targeted big cities during the Cold War.[101] The limitations of numbers and options available, in a sense, simplifies the choice of targets. India is in the same boat as these three countries found themselves in the East-West, Sino-Soviet and the Sino-U. S. versus Soviet Union confrontations during the Cold War. Its nuclear ordnance will have to be aimed to take out large enemy cities and main wealth-producing economic centers. A too ambitious and, equally, a too nuanced targeting philosophy may in fact be inimical to achieving the objective of strategic deterrence.[102]

To deter China, for instance, Beijing and the commercial and industrial concentrations—in the arc Shanghai-Hainan Island on the southeastern and southern seaboards, and including Hong Kong (accounting for over a third of China's trade), suggest themselves as obvious targets.[103] A secondary list should include prominent Chinese military and weapons complexes, among them, the North West Nuclear Weapons Research and Development Academy (the so-called Ninth Academy) inclusive of the testing site at Lop Nor in Xinjiang, the various aircraft production complexes in Sichuan and Yunan, which are provinces adjoining India, and specifically the regional military command in Chengdu, the naval base on Hainan Island and the Bohai shipyard in Huludao, Laoning province, constructed with Soviet help to manufacture nuclear submarines.[104]

A targeting philosophy to make deterrence credible, and ensure that it works in all circumstances, requires that the nuclear stockpile be large enough to provide redundancy and that it should be perceived by potential adversaries as capable of being delivered on target. Assuming that there are some 100 locations identified in the comprehensive Indian primary and secondary target lists, to ensure the certainty of destruction, at least initially when the accuracy of delivery may be suspect, requires, by one expert reckoning, that as many as four nuclear weapons of whatever mix be directed at each of these targets. Why four missiles/bombs on single high-value targets? Herman Kahn used probability theory and a matrix mapping survival of ICBMs against their yield to postulate that the efficiency of a ballistic missile is the square of its accuracy as represented by CEP. Assuming that with a one-mile CEP, the kill probability is 100 percent, for a two-mile CEP four missiles will be required to achieve the same kill probability. Were the CEP to be half a mile, it would take only one-fourth as many missiles.[105]

The logic of this formulation is that, short of pin-point accuracy, which the United States may now have attained, a city-busting weapon per target may not, in every situation, deter an adversary who, playing the averages, can bank on that single missile being wide off its mark. But were four nuclear weapons, each with a two-mile CEP at extreme range be aimed at a major target, the risk of even one or two hitting a metropolis would prove too daunting a prospect for the putative enemy to ignore.

Multi-weapons targeting on single points may also be necessitated by the anticipated advances in antiballistic missile technology. The physics and feasibility of an ABM remains doubtful. But this has not kept the United States and even China from making huge investments in R&D. Should such technologies beat the legal[106] and technological odds and fructify into regional Theater Missile Defense and later, National Missile Defense of the kind the U. S. government is currently debating, then a single shot-on-single target-policy may become infructuous, and Kahn's early Cold War recommendation of at least four nuclear weapons on a well-defended and valued target may once again be relevant. This still leaves open the possibility that with progressive improvements in missile accuracy and concurrent lack of progress in ABM systems, the number of weapons aimed at any one target will decrease, freeing ever larger numbers of missiles in the force for possible use on additional, value targets.

A nuclear force strength in the 350-500 range is advisable for another reason. There is the very real danger that a small, number of nuclear weapons may invite a disarming conventional or nuclear first strike, which the United States, for example, can presently mount.[107] But it also reveals the essence of the problem facing India in structuring, at least in the foreseeable future, a small nuclear force based principally on missiles of perhaps questionable accuracy.

Force architecture

The shape and size of an affordable nuclear force ought to be such as to eventuate into a "balanced deterrent,"[108] for the very good reason that inordinately to favor any particular nuclear delivery mode would be to skew the force and make it more vulnerable and less effective. The proposed force structure is detailed in Table 5.1 as is the rough time frame in which the various force levels can be expected to be attained.

The nuclear weapons in the operational category, according to this proposed scheme, will by the end of 2030, at a steady rate of production number some 293 mainly thermonuclear weapons/warheads. The Atomic Demolition Munitions will take care of the rest of the inventory of some 318 weapons/warheads. Another 100 weapons of various yields-to-weight ratios would require to be held as deployable reserves. The resulting ratio of weapons deployed to weapons held in stock for contingencies, to achieve the overarching goal of full and robust deterrence, seems far from excessive.

Costs of a Full and Robust Deterrent

Additional burdens on the public exchequer are always hard to justify. But in the wake of the Indian Government's getting serious about procuring a nuclear

Table 5.1 Nuclear Force Structure

Time Frame	Strategic	Tactical
2000 - 2010	1 x SSBN (D)	40 x Su - 30 (D)
	12 x SLBM (NWS)	20 x Jaguar (D)
	5 x ICBM (NWS)	10 x Mirage 2000 (D)
	20 x IRBM (NWS)	30 x NGB
	10 x Tu - 22M (D)	20 x SSM 250 (NWS)
	20 x NGB	10 x SSM 150 (NWS)
		5 x ADM (NWS)
	57 x NWS/NGB	65 x NWS/NGB
Total	122 x NWS/NGB	
	11 x D	70 x D
Total	81 x D	
2010 - 2020	3 x SSBN (D)	40 x Su - 30 MKI (D)
	36 x SLBM (NWS)	10 x Mirage 2000
	20 x Tu- 22M (D)	50 x NGB (NWS)
	15 x ICBM (NWS)	30 x SSM 250 (NWS)
	25 x IRBM (D)	20 x SSM 150 (NWS)
	30 x NGB (NWS)	15 x ADM (NWS)
	106 x NWS/NGB	115 x NWS/NGB
Total	221 x NWS/NGB	
	23 x D	50 x D
Total	73 x D	
2020 - 2030	4 x SSBN (D)	40 x Su MKI (D)
	48 x SLBM (NWS)	20 x Mirage 2000 (D)
	25 x ICBMs (NWS)	60 x NGB
	40 x IRBMs (NWS)	40 x SSM 250 (NWS)
	20 x Tu - 22M (D)	30 x SSM 150 (NWS)
	40 x NGB	25 x ADM (NWS)
	153 x NWS/NGB	155 x NWS/NGB
Total	308 x NWS/NGB	
	44 x D	60 x D
Total	104 x D	
	Contingency Reserves	100 x NWS/NGB
	Grand Total of Warheads	408 x NWS, NGB, ADM
	Grand Total of Delivery Platform	

Legend:
NWS = Nuclear Weapons Systems   D = Nuclear Delivery Platforms
NGB = Nuclear Gravity/Glide Bomb   ADM = Atomic Demolition Munitions
ICBM = Intercontinental Ballistic Missile   IRBM = Intermediate Range Ballistic Missile
SSM = Surface-to-Surface Missile
SSBN = Ballistic Missile – firing, Nuclear powered Submarine

deterrent force and the draft nuclear doctrine emphasizing the "triad," the costs of constructing a national nuclear force must be borne. Many estimates have been made about the likely cost.

It was lately revealed that a task force headed by the former Army Chief General Sundarji assessed the cost at the 1985 value of the rupee for a balanced minimum deterrent at Rs 7,000 crores over ten years.[109] At mid-1998 market value, this amount is nearly Rs 11,500 crores. But writing in 1994 and referring, perhaps, to this same study, Subrahmanyam mentioned Rs 5,000 crores as the estimated cost "at 1986-87 prices."[110] It is difficult to reconcile the two figures, unless he pared the force structure or adjusted the costs downward in some fashion and for reasons best known to him. However, no force details or a breakdown of the costs have been made public.

In the latter exercise, however, Subrahmanyam, estimated the total cost of constructing a minimum deterrent, including the production costs of 20 Prithvis and 20 Agnis, the deployment cost of these in the mobile mode, the fabrication costs of 60 warheads, and of command and control and safety measures as Rs 10,000 crores in 1994 rupees.[111] This figure would appear to be on the low side. The estimation of the likely costs for the full and robust deterrent (see Table 5.2), however, errs deliberately on the high side. Senior nuclear scientists strongly refute the contention that making nuclear weapons will cost a packet. They point out that the bulk of the costs of producing weapons is part of the "sunk costs" that have already been borne by the tax payer and, in the event, the country might as well get value for its money and go ahead and secure a nuclear arsenal.

Retired Chief of Naval Staff Admiral L. Ramdas concurs on this last point. He thinks that while the country may end up spending Rs 40,000 crores over the next ten years for a minimum deterrent, only five percent of this figure constitutes the cost of the nuclear devices, and that approximately 70 percent of the expenditure will have to be on "fire control, delivery, command and control systems, and on modernizing and refurbishing our nuclear capable war planes" with the "balance [being spent] on nuclear waste management." His predecessor in office, Admiral J. G. Nadkarni, is of the view that a deterrent comprising 50 warheads will cost Rs 10,000 crores.[112] But, like Subrahmanyam and General Sundarji, neither of the retired Chiefs of Naval Staff have articulated a nuclear orbit nor offered any details of their costing schemes. It must be cautioned that the costs calculated in this chapter are essentially guesstimates, extrapolated from the known/reported costs of nuclear weapons and delivery systems in India,[113] but within the context of the typical costs-scheme for similar systems that may be found abroad. These were computed and tabulated for the constituent elements as well as for the total force shown in Table 5.2. A charge of 40 percent of the total cost of the nuclear weapons systems is calculated as the price tag for a fairly extensive, relatively fail-proof, Command, Control, Communication, Computers, Intelligence and Information (C4I2) system. An additional Rs 30,000 crores are set aside for increasing the survivability of the force, i.e., for "hardening" the most critical deterrent ele-

Table 5.2   Costs (in crores of Rupees at current prices) of a Robust
Nuclear deterrent, operational by 2030

Service	Weopans	Unit System	Numbers	System Acquisition Cost
Navy	SSBN	5,000	4	20,000
	SLBM (NWS)	50	48	2,400
ARMY	ICBM (NWS)	40	25	1,000
	IRBM (NWS)	35	40	1,400
	SSM 150 (NWS)	20	30	600
	ADM (NWS)	10	25	250
Air Force	Tu - 22M (D)	50	20	1,000
	Su - 30 MKI (D)	150	40	6,000
	Mirage 2000 (D)	150	20	3,000
	Jaguar (D)	80	20	1,600
	SSM 250 (NWS)	25	70	1,750
	NGB	20	90	1,800
Contingency Rserves Warheads	NGB	20	100	2,000

Total Cost of 408 x NWS/NGB and 104 x D	Rs 42,800
C412	Rs 17,120
Force Hardening, Dispersal & Concealments	Rs 30,000
Grand Total Costs	Rs 89,920

ments (like the Tu-22M and Su-30 MKI pens and ICBM/IRBM silos) to at least 100 psi (pounds per square inch) overpressure to withstand nuclear kiloton strikes (though not direct hits), making land-based missiles mobile, and for their dispersed deployment and concealment.

Economists worry about the costs of economic sanctions, of lost business, trade, and investment and of denial of sophisticated technologies, owing to the G-8 countries turning the screw on India. But as the collapse of the sanctions regime imposed by the United States in the wake of the 1998 tests has shown, it is counterproductive and is unlikely again to be used.

There are two ways of putting the cost of India's nuclear arsenal in perspective. First, by considering it as a proportion of the Gross National Product. The total cost of the proposed nuclear force equals only 0.79 percent of India's GNP in 1996-97 of Rs 113,54,000 crores. The Indian GNP is increasing, moreover, at an annual rate of seven percent and can be expected to reach Rs 1058,800,000 crores in 2029–2030. In which case, the cost of this nuclear force build-up will amount to only 0.085 percent of GNP in 2030.

The other way to contextualize the above costs is to compare this figure with, say, the monies that are likely to be spent on the Indian Army's armored and mechanized forces alone just in the period 2000–2020, if the allocatory pattern in defense expenditure of the last thirty years continues into the future as it is expected to. This latter outlay is estimated as Rs 900,000 crores and that too for strengthening a military capability which, with the advent of nuclear weapons, has become redundant in any future war scenario on the subcontinent. Any which way one looks at it, the costs of the country's acquiring a muscular thermonuclear deterrent is eminently affordable, considering that such national nuclear forces will enable India to avail of "absolute" security from external threats and, as important, external pressures, perhaps, for the first time in its recorded history.

Conclusion

The nuclear endgame is a hard one to play because there are no rules, except those imposed by countries with the will to acquire the necessary instruments of power any which way possible and to exercise power they are thus endowed with. India has to stand fast to its stake in a full and versatile nuclear/thermonuclear deterrent with the clout and the distant reach of ICBMs. It will cement India's strategic independence.

Since the irreducible minimum demand for treatment as a nuclear-weapons state, on par with the United Kingdom, France and China, has not been met, it would be sensible for Delhi to disengage. An India, conducting all the necessary thermonuclear and missile tests, weaponizing to the extent required and, otherwise, holding all the powerful cards, will only strengthen its bargaining position by not being seen as too eager for a settlement other than on its terms.

If, however, New Delhi musters nothing more than its usual propensity for moderation when it is not warranted and for morality where it is inappropriate and irrelevant and negotiates away its sovereign right to thermonuclear security as defined by this country, then the odds are that India in the twenty-first century will subside gently to the position of a minor power.

Notes

1. Prime Minister's Statement in Parliament, "Bilateral Talks with United States," December 15, 1998.
2. Gaurav C. Sawant, "Missile Testing is not Pak-centric: Malik," *Indian Express*, April 15, 1999.

3. Srinivas Laxman, "India's N-sub plan gets priority," *Times of India* (Mumbai), October 28, 2000.

4. The Action Plan is reproduced in *Rajiv Gandhi: Speeches and Writings*, (Publications Division, Ministry of Information and Broadcasting, government of India, 1988), pp. 331-341.

5. Prime Minister Rajiv Gandhi's interview to *USA Today*, *ibid.*, p.447.

6. David Albright, "The Shots Heard Round the World," *Bulletin of Atomic Scientists*, (July/August 1998). Albright dates the Rajiv Gandhi decision to 1985. P. K. Iyengar, former chairman of the atomic energy commission, recalls 1987-88 as the year that serious weaponization started. (Interview with author)

7. Emmanuel Sivan, "The Holy War Tradition in Islam," *Orbis*, Spring 1998.

8. For an assessment of the internal dynamics of Pakistan, see A. K. Verma "Pakistan's Quest for Complete Nationhood: Implications and Possibilities," *Indian Defense Review*, Jan-Mar 1999. Verma formerly headed the country's external Intelligence organization, Research and Analysis Wing (RAW). Also see the Kewal Singh Memorial Lecture delivered by Najam Sethi, editor of *Friday Times*, Lahore, at the India International Center on 30 April 1999, wherein he analyzed the reasons for Pakistan turning into a "failed" state.

9. See *Strategic Comments* by the International Institute of Strategic Studies (IISS), London, reproduced as "The end of China's era of growth," in *Hindu*, April 9, 1999. On similar lines, see James Harding, "End of the China goldrush," *Financial Times*, April 25, 1999.

10. See John Pomfret, "Has Lack of Vision Left China Adrift?" *International Herald Tribune*, October 29, 1999.

11. See the fictionalized but very convincing future war scenario based on these same premises in Humphrey Hawksley and Simon Holberton, *Dragonstrike: The Millennium War*, London: Pan Books, 1997.

12. Raymond L. Garthoff, "Worst-case Assumptions: Uses, Abuses and Consequences," in Gwyn Prins, ed. *Nuclear Crisis Reader*, New York, Vintage Books, 1984.

13. The manner in which the Pakistan Army may initiate use of nuclear weapons has been discussed by serving officers writing in Pakistani military journals. Even an "escalation ladder" has been conceptualized. For a summary of these views, see Stephen P. Cohen, *The Pakistan Army*, 1998 edition, Karachi, Oxford University Press, pp. 177-179.

14. In fact, there is an insidious game afoot to frighten India into restricting its threat focus to Pakistan by equating the two countries and by "building up" Pakistan's nuclear capabilities. This is stock American effort. See Strobe Talbott "Dealing with the Bomb in South Asia" in *Foreign Affairs*, March/April 1999. For obvious reasons, Pakistan supports such attempts. See the Pakistan Foreign Secretary Shamshad Ahmad's response, "The Nuclear Subcontinent" in *Foreign Affairs*, July/August 1999 in which he seeks to extend the seeming parity in the nuclear realm to the conventional military sphere as well. Other American analysts, have followed Talbott's lead. Thus, George Perkovich of the Alton Jones Foundation, for instance, used the launch of his book—*India's Nuclear Bomb*—to warn New Delhi about the supposed "nightmares" it ought to be having about the Pakistani nuclear strength. See Press Trust of India report "Pak Boosting N-power to Challenge India," in *Pioneer*, November 18, 1999.

15. These various sub-deterrent deterrence concepts have been placed on the rungs of a "deterrence ladder" by Air Commodore Jasjit Singh. See his "A Nuclear Strategy for India," in Jasjit Singh, ed. *Nuclear India*, New Delhi, Knowledge World, p. 310.

16. Such thinking is critiqued in Bharat Karnad, "A Thermonuclear Deterrent," in Amitabh Mattoo, ed. *India's Nuclear Deterrent: Pokharan II and Beyond*, New Delhi, Har-Anand Publishers, 1998.

17. The flaws in this and the larger argument against renewal of testing made by Subrahmanyam and Air Commodore (retd.) Jasjit Singh, director of the Institute for Defense Studies and Analyses, were pointed out much before the May 1998 tests. See Bharat Karnad, "Cooking our goose," *Seminar*, Annual, January 1997.

18. This aspect scrutinized in Bharat Karnad, "The Quality of 'Expert' Advice," *Seminar*, August 1996.

19. *Ibid.*

20. See the interview of Dr Anil Kakodkar, director, Bhabha Atomic Research Center, and one of those centrally involved in the weaponization project in *Times of India*, July 30, 1998.

21. The freezing of the threshold countries' nuclear weapons capabilities on the "learning curve" is one of the professed aims of the Clinton Administration in pushing CTBT. It was so stated in Congressional testimony by director of the US Arms Control and Disarmament Agency. Interview with Ambassador Arundhati Ghose.

22. Soumyajit Pattnaik, "FMCT May Force India to Adopt Full-Scope Safeguards," *Pioneer*, August 14, 1998.

23. See, for instance, K. Subrahmanyam "Indian Politics and Vulnerability," *Economic Times*, June 25,1998.

24. David Albright, "The Shots Heard 'Round the World," *Bulletin of Atomic Scientists*, July/August 1998, p. 23.

25. See my "Cooking our goose," op.cit. and "A Thermonuclear Deterrent," op.cit., and "Going Thermonuclear: Why, With What Forces, At What Cost?" *United Services Institute Journal*, July-September 1998.

26. For a fuller examination of these "limits", see my "Going Thermonuclear . . . ," *ibid*.

27. The most conspicuous example of this may be found in the writings of Subrahmanyam's successor as director, IDSA, Air Commodore (retd.) Jasjit Singh. Former Army Chief General K. Sundarji makes no mention of H-weapons anywhere in his writings, not in his book (*The Blind Men of Hindoostan: Indo-Pak Nuclear War*, New Delhi, etc., UBS Publishers' Distributers Ltd., 3rd reprint, 1996) or in his monographs nor in his many press columns to date. Another senior Army officer known for serious interest in the subject likewise wrote a full sized book on the subject without once referring to the thermonuclear option. See Brigadier (retd.) Vijai K. Nair, *Nuclear India*, New Delhi, Lancer International, 1992. An indirect mention may be found in this book but only in a Table (no.9.9, p. 181) on force structure where he mentions 1 MT (megaton) warheads. But, there is no elaboration in the text of whether the source of the 1 MT yield is a "boosted fission" or fusion weapon.

28. "India Can Produce N-bomb of 200 Kiloton: Chidambaram," *Times of India*, May 23, 1998.

29. Interview with P. K. Iyengar. For an analysis of the danger of developing an Indian deterrent simply on the basis of computer simulation, see Bharat Karnad "Policy on CTBT," *Hindustan Times*, November 4, 1999.

30. Alexander De Volpi, "Technological Misinformation: Fission and Fusion Weapons," in David Carlton and Carlo Schaerf (Eds.), *The Arms Race in the 1980s*, The Macmillan Press Ltd., London and Basingstoke, 1982, p. 138. De Volpi is a physicist at the Argonne National Laboratory, Illinois.

31. I developed this thesis in various published studies immediately after the May 1998 tests. See my "Going Thermonuclear . . . " op.cit., "A Thermonuclear Deterrent," op.cit.

32. Michael I. Handel, "Numbers Do Count: The Question of Quality Versus Quantity" in Samuel P. Huntington (Ed.) *The Strategic Imperative: New Policies for American Security*, Cambridge, Massachusetts, Ballinger Publishing Company, 1982.

33. For a definition of the "second tier" and analyses about the nuclear policies of the states constituting this tier, see John C. Hopkins and Weixing Hu, eds. *Strategic Views from the Second Tier*, New Brunswick and London, Transaction Publishers, 1995.

34. See Walter Slocombe, *The Political Implications of Strategic Parity*, Adelphi Paper No. 77, 1971, and max Schmidt, "Military Parity, Political and Military Détente," in *The Arms Race in the 1980s*, op. cit. Schmidt was a then senior East German academic.

35. For the Indian position at the CD in Geneva, refer *Statements by India on Comprehensive Test Ban Treaty (CTBT), 1993–1996*, published by the Ministry of External Affairs, New Delhi.

36. Source: Ambassador Arundhati Ghose, Indian Representative at the CD in Geneva during the CBT negotiations.

37. *Indian Nuclear Doctrine*, National Security Advisory Board, p. 4.

38. For a case that the draft IND is the result of compromises affected between the "rejectionists," "pragmatists," and "maximalists" within the NSAB, see Kanti Bajpai "The Great Indian Nuclear Debate," *Hindu*, November 12, 1999.

39. Writes the Clinton Administration's chief of the Counterproliferation Office in the Pentagon, Peter R. Lavoy: "the United States is now the world's strongest military power, it probably is the most likely candidate to engage in future preventive attacks against some emerging nuclear state . . . Washington has a long experience of planning military preventive strikes." See his "The Strategic Consequences of Nuclear Proliferation: A Review Essay," in *Strategic Studies*, Summer 1995, p. 725.

40. Solly Zuckerman, *Nuclear Illusion and Reality*, New York, Vintage Books, 1882, p. 69.

41. Donald G. Brennan and Morton H. Halperin "Policy Considerations of a Nuclear Test Ban" in Donald G. Brennan (Ed.) *Arms Control, Disarmament and National Security*, New York, George Braziller, 1961, p. 237.

42. Brennan and Halperin, "Policy Considerations of a Nuclear Test Ban," pp. 247-248.

43. Rodney W. Jones, *Small Nuclear Forces*, The Washington Papers, No. 103, New York, Praeger, 1984, pp. 16-17. For the fissile production rate and accrued totals, see Table 5.1.

44. "Matters of Technology", *Frontline*, July 17 1998, p. 84.

45. See Theodore B. Taylor, "Nuclear Tests and Nuclear Weapons" in Benjamin Frankel, ed. *Opaque Nuclear Proliferation: Methodological and Policy Implications*, London, Frank Cass, 1991. Taylor is one of the leading American nuclear weapons designers.

46. Brennan and Halperin, "Policy Considerations of a Nuclear Test Ban," p. 254.

47. Robert Jervis, Richard Ned Lebow and Janice Gross Stein, *Psychology and Deterrence*, Baltimore and London, the Johns Hopkins University Press, 1985.

48. Typically Subrahmanyam thinks small, recommending the international standard warhead of 125 KT size. See his "Nuclear Force Design and Minimum Deterrence Strategy," in Bharat Karnad, ed. *Future Imperiled: India's Security in the 1990s and Beyond*, New Delhi, Viking, 1994, p. 190.

49. This concept, originally Herman Kahn's, was of pivotal importance to his theory of "the escalation ladder". See his *On Escalation: Metaphors and Scenarios*, New York, Washington and London, Frederick A. Praeger Publishers, 1965, p. 290. For an informed commentary on this concept, refer Lawrence Freedman, *The Evolution of Nuclear Strategy*, New York, St. Martin's Press, 1983, pp. 218-221.

50. See Bharat Karnad, "Getting Tough with China: Negotiating Equitable not 'Equal' Security," in *Indian Defense Review*, Oct-Dec 1997. This is an updated version of an article with the same title published in *Strategic Analysis*, January 1998. (The original version published in Strategic Analysis was, however, submitted earlier.)

51. Subrahmanyam thinks that 60 weapons would deter even a 100 weapons strong thermonuclear Pakistani arsenal, and rejects the escalation dominance aspect as flowing from "the conventional nuclear strategic thought which is based on warfighting." See his "Nuclear Force Design and Minimum Deterrence Strategy for India," p. 190.

52. The most recent example of this was in the 1996 Taiwan Straits crisis when the Chinese missile forces refused to be cowed by the US Seventh Fleet aircraft carrier task forces ingressing into the proximal waters. It was a textbook case of nuclear "standoff." See Barton Gellman "New US-China Ties Are the Fruit of '96 Shift in Policy," Washington Post Service, *International Herald Tribune*, June 23, 1998.

53. See Bharat Karnad, "Getting Tough with China."

54. The Harvard Nuclear Study Group: Albert Carnesale, Paul Doty, Stanley Hoffmann, Samuel P. Huntington, Joseph S. Nye, Jr., and Scott Sagan, *Living with Nuclear Weapons*, New York, Bantam Books, 1983, p. 34.

55. See David Holloway, *Stalin and the Bomb: The Soviet Union and Atomic Energy 1939-1956*, New Haven and London, Yale University Press, 1994, and John W. Lewis and Xue Litai, *China Builds the Bomb,* Stanford, CA, Stanford University Press, 1988.

56. According to the US Secretary of State, Madeleine Albright, "Would-be proliferators . . . must test if they are to develop the kind of advanced compact nuclear weapons that are most threatening." See her interview to *Time*, November 29, 1999.

57. The most comprehensive data source on the effects of nuclear weapons is Samuel Gladstone, ed. *The Effects of Nuclear Weapons*, Rev. ed., U. S. Atomic Energy Commission, Washington, DC, 1964.

58. Philip A. Sabin, *Shadow or Substance: Perceptions and Symbolism in Nuclear Force Planning*, Adelphi Paper No. 222, London, IISS, Summer 1987.
59. Brennan and Halperin, "Policy Considerations of a Nuclear Test Ban," p. 252.
60. The Bharatiya Janata Party's 1998 General Elections Manifesto—"Vote for a Stable Government and an Able Prime Minister" stated forthrightly (p. 31) that once in power it would "Reevaluate the country's nuclear policy and exercise the option to induct nuclear weapons."
61. Interview with author.
62. Refer Theodore Taylor "Nuclear Tests and Nuclear Weapons," op.cit.
63. See Avner Cohen and Benjamin Frankel "Opaque Nuclear Proliferation" in *Opaque Nuclear Proliferation*, op. cit., pp. 14-44.
64. For the particular quote in full, see footnote no. 66.
65. Plainly, the United States is unimpressed with the capacity of any other country to match American nuclear capabilities. See the Albright interview, op. cit.
66. Jaswant Singh, *Defending India*, Basingstoke and London, Macmillan, 1999, p. 330.
67. How hypocritical and self-serving the U. S. policy on nonproliferation/counterproliferation is may be gauged from Secretary Albright's interview, op.cit. She says "Under the CTBT, America would gain the security benefits of outlawing nuclear tests by others, while locking in the technological status quo that is highly favorable to us."
68. For an analysis of the nuclear signaling that took place during the military operations in Kargil in May-June 1999, see my "A New Strategy for LoC," *Faultlines*, Vol. II, August 1999.
69. Jyoti Malhotra, "Sign CTBT, its ratification can wait: Tokyo to Delhi," *Indian Express*, November 22, 1999. This advice by the Japanese Ambassador given on the eve of the Indian External Affairs Minister, Jaswant Singh's visit to Japan, was repeated by the Japanese Prime Minister.
70. Frank Bruni and Eric Schmitt "Crash Course: Bush Crams For Foreign Policy Tests," *International Herald Tribune*, November 20-21, 1999.
71. Gov. Bush, in his first major foreign policy speech in Washington said: "We can fight the spread of nuclear weapons but we cannot wish them away with unwise treaties." See "Bush Jr. praises India's role in Asia," *Times of India*, November 21, 1999.
72. This is what I discovered in my meetings with, among others, Assistant Secretary of State for South Asia, Karl Inderfurth, and Assistant Secretary of State-designate for Nonproliferation, Robert Einhorn, and in discussions at the Brookings Institution and the Heritage Foundation, during a trip to Washington in early September 1999.
73. According to David E. Springer, a Washington lobbyist for Indian causes, the U. S.-China Business Council has over 150 American MNC members. The U. S.-India Business Council has only 40 such members. The difference in the strengths of the two Councils, he implies, reflects the difference between the treatment accorded Beijing and New Delhi. Springer is of the view that were all the necessary policies implemented to "free" the Indian market and otherwise to liberalize the economy, the Government of India's target of $10 billion a year in foreign investment will be easily surpassed.

74. According to a major American investment and banking firm, India today ranks along side of Singapore and South Korea, as a preferred investment location. See S. Muralidhar, "India to be Favorite Market in Asia: Morgan Stanley," *Indian Express*, November 15, 1999.

75. Interview of Prime Minister Vajpayee in the Delhi Times section of *Times of India*, November 12, 1999.

76. The 60 weapons figure was offered by K. Subrahmanyam. See his "Nuclear Force Design and Minimum Deterrence Strategy for India." The 150 figure is General Sundarji's. See his "Imperatives of Indian Minimum Deterrence," in *Agni: Studies in International Strategic Issues*, May 1996, p. 21.

77. Gen. K. Sundarji has written about a nearly all missile deterrent force. See his "India's Nuclear Weapons Policy" and "Imperatives of Indian Minimum Deterrence" in Jorn Gjelstad and Olav Njolstad, ed. *Nuclear Rivalry and International Order*, International Peace Research Institute, Oslo, and London, Thousand Oaks & New Delhi, Sage Publications, 1996. Subrahmanyam, likewise, has talked only of a mixed force of aircraft and missiles, see his "Nuclear Force Design and Minimum Deterrence Strategy for India." There has been little detailed analysis in either of their writings.

78. Interview by Defense Minister George Fernandes to *Jane's Defence Weekly*, July 1, 1998.

79. An India-Pakistan nuclear imbroglio is a staple Western fear. For recent samples of such scare scenarios, in the popular literature, see Col. Trevor N. Dupuy, *Future Wars: The World's Most Dangerous Flashpoints*, New York, Warner Books, 1992, chapter 2; and in the specialist field, see Ashley Tellis, *Stability in South Asia*, Documented Briefing, RAND Corporation, 1997.

80. For an analysis in some depth about the organic linkages between the two countries and of their mutual non-hurting and "non-violent" war fighting methods, see Bharat Karnad "Key to Peace in South Asia: fostering 'social' links between the armies of India and Pakistan," *Round Table, The Commonwealth Journal of International Affairs*, April 1996. A version of it—"Key to Confidence building in South Asia: Fostering Military-to-Military Links"—was published in *USI Journal*, April-June 1996.

81. Much of the sabre-rattling—it was only tongue rattling, really—by Pakistani officials and ministers in the period before and after the nuclear tests, was driven by fear. This is evident, for instance, in the then foreign minister Gohar Ayub Khan's interview to *Outlook*, June 1, 1998.

82. For a sample of the over-wrought school of writing on the issues by a couple of disarmers—at-all-cost, see Praful Bidwai and Achin Vanaik, *South Asia on a Short Fuse: Nuclear Politics and the Future of Global Disarmament*, New Delhi, Oxford University Press, 1999.

83. On fears of nuclear instability see Neil Joeck, *Maintaining Nuclear Stability in South Asia*, Adephli Paper No. 312, IISS, London, 1997.

84. Eric Arnett, earlier of SIPRI and now serving in the U. S. State Department, has made this point. See his "Choosing Nuclear Arsenals," in *Opaque Nuclear Proliferation*, p. 169.

85. "Sanctions May Not Stop Arms Race: Celeste" *Hindu*, July 20, 1998.

86. Both Subrahmanyam and Sundarji are for nuclearizing the Prithvi missile. See the former's "Nuclear Force Design and Minimum Deterrence Strategy for India," pp. 185-191; and the latter's "India's Nuclear Weapons Policy," p. 181.

87. The "threat" from third world states, among them India's long-range ballistic missiles, is a stock fear in U. S. official circles. See the unclassified 'Executive Summary' of the *Commission to Assess the Ballistic Missile Threat to the United States* headed by former U. S. Secretary of Defense, Donald H. Rumsfeld (Internet). For a more general treatment of the subject, Jane E. Nolan, *Trappings of Power: Ballistic Missiles in the Third World*, Washington, DC, The Brookings Institution, 1991.

88. Rodney Jones, *Small Nuclear Forces*, pp. 34-35.

89. Z. Mian, A. H. Nayyar and M. V. Ramana, "Bringing Prithvi Down to Earth: The Capabilities and Potential Effectiveness of India's Prithvi Missile." From the Internet.

90. "India Set to Launch GSLV-D1 in Feb." *Asian Age*, November 4, 2000.

91. For several years now, ISRO officials have been aware of the potential and confident that, if called upon to do so, the Polar Satellite Launch Vehicle could quickly be converted into an ICBM able to carry a five-ton warhead. See Raj Chengappa "Joining the Big Boys" *India Today*, April 15, 1993.

92. The head of the Central Intelligence Agency, R. James Woolsey, in U. S. Congressional testimony stated some five years back that "India has already demonstrated the ability to build guidance sets and warheads, the two key ingredients to convert the SLV into a ballistic missile." See C. Raja Mohan, "CIA Assessment of India's N-Program," *Hindu*, October 15, 1993.

93. For the most recent example of such thinking, see Eric Arnett, "Test of Endurance," *Newsline*, Islamabad, June 1998. See his earlier attempt roughly along the same lines, "Choosing Nuclear Arsenals."

94. Gen. K. Sundarji "India's Nuclear Weapons Policy," pp. 181-186. op.cit.

95. Jones, *Small Nuclear Forces*, p. 22; Arnett "Choosing Nuclear Arsenals," pp. 156-157.

96. Subrahmanyam, "Nuclear Force Design and Minimum Deterrence Strategy for India," pp. 189-190, 193.

97. See Lieutenant General (ret'd.) P. K. Pahwa. *Organisation and Concept of Employment of Strategic Rocket Forces*, National Security Paper, United Service Institution of India, draft manuscripts.

98. According to the *Jane's Defence Weekly* the indigenous Indian nuclear submarine will join service by 2007. See "India's N-sub by 2007," *Hindustan Times*, June 24, 1998.

99. Alexander Nicoll, "The Disappearing Act," *Financial Times*, May 23-24, 1998.

100. "Russia to Lease Long Range Bombers to India," *Economic Times*, October 18, 1999.

101. Hopkins and Hu, eds., *Strategic Views from the Second Tier*.

102. See Desmond Ball, *Targeting for Strategic Deterrence*, Adelphi Paper No. 185, London, IISS, 1983.

103. Useful if a bit dated information about potential Chinese targets may be found in Geoffrey Kemp, IISS Adelphi Paper, which information is reproduced in Brigadier Nair, *Nuclear India*, op.cit, pp. 149-151.

104. The names and locations of the major Chinese nuclear and conventional arms production centers may be found in John Wilson Lewis and Xue Litai, *China's Strategic Sea Power: The Politics of Force Modernization in the Nuclear Age*, Stanford, California, Stanford University Press, 1994, pp. 80-81, 103.

105. Kahn, *On Thermonuclear War*, pp. 482-483.

106. The United States seems to be trying desperately to wriggle out of the 1972 ABM Treaty obligations signed with the erstwhile USSR. See the speech by Dr Stanley Riveless of the U. S. Arms Control and Disarmament Agency (ACDA) to the 11th Annual Multilateral Conference on Theater Missile Defense held in Monterey, California, June 1, 1998. (Internet)

107. Washington think tanks make this point about the likely dangers to small Indian and Pakistani nuclear arsenals from each other. See Steven Erlanger, "The New Cold War in South Asia," *New York Times Service, International Herald Tribune,* July 13, 1998. But the fact is the danger to these arsenals is more from the United States and other established nuclear-weapons states. See footnote no. 106.

108. In the mid to late-80s The Rajiv Gandhi government apparently had in mind "a balanced minimum deterrent." See Subrahmanyam "Politics of Shakti: New Whine in Old Bomb," *Times of India,* May 26, 1998.

109. Subrahmanyam, "Politics of Shakti." More recently, Gen. Sundarji has scaled down the costing figure drastically to Rs 2,760 crores for 150 weapons for a Prithvi-Agni missile force. See his "Imperatives of Indian Minimum Deterrence," p. 21.

110. Subrahmanyam, "Nuclear Force Design and Minimum Deterrence Strategy for India," p. 193.

111. Subrahmanyam "Nuclear Force Design," p. 193.

112. Sarosh Bana, "India's Nuclear Enigma," *Business India,* March 22–April 4, 1999.

113. The unit cost of a nuclear device has been authoritatively given as Rupees one crore by former chairman, IAEC, P. K. Iyengar. See "N-arms Cheaper than Conventional Weapons," *Hindu,* May 19, 1998. Rs 3 crores is estimated as the cost, for instance, of a Prithvi SSM. See "India to Test New Prithvi," *Aviation Week & Space Technology,* June 29, 1998. But the cost computation in this chapter owes most to the extrapolations from the $6.4 million figure at 1975 rupee value for design and manufacture of a single plutonium weapon worked out by Narasimhiah Seshagiri. See his *The Bomb! Fallout of India's Nuclear Explosion,* Delhi, Vikas, 1975, p. 69.

CHAPTER SIX

Why Do States Acquire Nuclear Weapons? Comparing the Cases of India and France

Jacques E. C. Hymans

Summary

Why did India suddenly decide to acquire an overt, weaponized nuclear deterrent in 1998 after resisting that temptation for so many years? The best way to investigate this question is to look at the Indian case in comparative context. In particular, much insight can be gained by drawing from the history of another nuclear weapons state: France. Using information gleaned from in-depth field research conducted in both India and France, it can be demonstrated that hypotheses for nuclear proliferation based on the objective security situation, the quest for international prestige or bureaucratic politics fall short. Rather, "oppositional nationalist" understandings of national identity were at the root of the bomb decisions in both the France of the mid-1950s and the India of the late 1990s. An oppositional nationalist identity combines a great antagonism toward an external enemy of the nation and an exaltation of the actual or potential strength of the nation. This type of identity produces a mix of fear and pride—an explosive psychological cocktail.

Introduction[1]

The Indian nuclear tests of May 1998 were a major surprise to the strategic communities in Washington and Delhi alike. Why did India suddenly choose to acquire an overt, weaponized nuclear deterrent after years of remaining on the other side of the nuclear threshold? An obvious hypothesis is that the tests were an expression of the newly installed Bharatiya Janata Party (BJP) government's most deeply held understandings of Indian identity—in particular its deep-seated fears of the Pakistani "other" combined with its fervent belief in India's capacity to prevail in that struggle. Surprisingly, the by now voluminous scholarly literature on the Indian tests has tended to soft-pedal the BJP's distinctiveness in favor of a teleological view that sooner or later this step was bound to come.[2] Indeed, the "BJP hypothesis" has become a straw man that the analyst sets up before going on to explain the supposedly "deeper" causes of the tests, which are said to be found in the objective security situation, in India's (not just the BJP's) desire for international prestige, and/or in the activities of India's scientific-bureaucratic "strategic enclave."[3] Those few who have given great weight to the "BJP hypothesis"[4] have found themselves tarred as "arms chair strategists" who know nothing about India.[5] But the fact that a hypothesis is obvious does not necessarily mean that it is wrong. In this chapter, I contend that while the BJP's unique understanding of Indian national identity is certainly not the explanation for why India was physically ready to test A–and H-bombs on such short notice in May 1998, it is by far the most powerful explanation for the decision to cross the threshold and become a nuclear weapons state.

I make this case using two basic methodological tactics. The first is a close analysis of the Indian case—the importance of doing this goes without saying. The other is a structured, focused comparison between the Indian case and that of France. Indian thought about nuclear weapons and the tortuous path of Indian nuclear history are in many respects undoubtedly unique. But the similar way in which India and France wrestled with the issue of acquiring nuclear weapons provides a substantial basis for separating mere local color from variables of true explanatory power.

The rest of this chapter is organized as follows. I first explain why the France-India comparison is of particular relevance for sorting out the relative strength of various hypotheses. I then consider the arguments that bureaucratic politics drove the French and Indian decisions for the bomb or that the quest for international prestige did so. Then I shift gears and explain my national identity framework as it applies to the choice to acquire nuclear weapons, and I follow this theoretical exposition with an empirical application of the framework to the French and Indian cases. I conclude by summarizing my empirical and theoretical findings and suggest what these findings may mean for predicting the future of nuclear proliferation.

A Comparison of the Indian and French
Decisions to Acquire Nuclear Weapons

Why compare France and India? Besides the fact that France and India are major powers and intrinsically worthy of study, a number of theoretical considerations drive this choice. First, both cases are clear anomalies for traditional realist theories of nuclear proliferation, as has notably been highlighted by Professor Scott Sagan.[6] Objective power and threat analyses simply do very poorly at explaining the nuclear histories of these two countries. Second, France and India are the only two nuclear states whose nuclear programs did not originate as military-driven bomb programs, and this fact undoubtedly created special dynamics in their nuclear proliferation decisions. Third, the proposed symmetry between a Western charter member of the nuclear club and an Asian developing country avoids the typical charge that analyses of nuclear proliferation tend to display a Western cultural bias against the nuclear aspirations of emerging regional powers.[7]

The empirical evidence is drawn in the main from my field research in both France and India, and I also benefited from archival sources in the United States and United Kingdom. In the French case, I undertook an exhaustive study of hundreds of previously classified documents on nuclear and security policies, in addition to interviewing several key decision makers from the crucial 1950s period. In the Indian case, the paucity of available internal Indian government documents led me to do a much greater number of in-depth interviews, over three dozen in total, with major players in the nuclear and security policy-making arenas. I followed up these interviews with letters in which I requested confirmation or further clarification of the statements that I had recorded.

I structure my account of the two cases around three plausible explanatory models. I first look at the two most popular explanations for each case: bureaucratic politics and the quest for prestige. I then turn to my own identity framework. All three models appear to have some justification in the historical record, but the evidence from these two cases above all confirms the identity approach.

Bureaucratic Politics and the French and Indian Decisions for the Bomb

Because of the seeming lack of explanatory value of objective external power and security variables for explaining the Indian and French nuclear decisions (and especially their timing), several scholars of each case have attempted to build explanations based on internal political factors. The "bureaucratic politics" literature on the French case, notably the major study by Professor Lawrence Scheinman, focuses attention on the atomic energy bureaucracy's manipulation of incentives for politicians, through political alliances and through the creation of technological momentum toward the bomb.[8] Similarly, in the case of India, a number of scholars contend that the Indian bomb was a product of an empire-building, politically popular atomic bureaucracy that had its way with weak-willed politicians.[9] Paying attention to these variables can certainly help us to understand why India and France began developing various nuclear capacities that could eventually have military applications. But do they explain why particular governments in the two countries finally decided to acquire nuclear arsenals? I argue that the answer is no.

Discussion of the case for domestic politics-based explanations

The idea that atomic bureaucracies want to build the bomb is highly questionable.[10] In both India and France, in fact, bureaucratic actors did *not* exhibit a clear consensus over time in favor of going in for a nuclear bomb. For instance, the French *Commissariat à l'Energie Atomique* (CEA) of the 1950s was the scene of a great debate between its two chiefs; while the scientific chief was opposed to building the bomb, the administrative chief supported the idea.[11] This is quite reminiscent of the Indian story. After Homi Bhabha's death, the Atomic Energy Commission (AEC) can hardly be said to have spoken with one voice. Many of its top physicists, such as Raja Ramanna and P. K. Iyengar, may have been in favor of developing the military side, but there were brilliant exceptions such as Vikram Sarabhai; meanwhile, many of its engineers, such as M. R. Srinivasan, were quite opposed to that trajectory.[12]

Second, the idea that atomic bureaucracies can create technical momentum or offer technical opinions to cause political decision makers to decide for the acquisition of nuclear weapons is also quite dubious.[13] In France, Pierre Mendès France decided for nuclear weapons even though he had clear information that there was no technical urgency to make such a choice.[14] In the case of India, which initiated a study of nuclear explosions in the mid-1960s, then dropped it, then came back to it in the early 1970s, then dropped it again for several years before returning to it again in the 1980s, it is simply incredible to argue that the scientists were operating with a free hand. Moreover, the AEC tended to downplay the degree of advancement of the Pakistani nuclear program through the 1970s and 1980s, which goes against the idea that it was willing to use its position of technical expertise to promote its supposedly pro-bomb agenda.[15]

Third, the idea that cocky atomic bureaucracies can bully weak politicians into bomb decisions is also not supported by either case. In both India and France the bomb decisions to test were taken not by weak politicians trying desperately to cling to power, but rather by relatively strong leaders who were generally recognized to know what they wanted and to have the political courage to take risks. The father of the French bomb program, Prime Minister Pierre Mendès France, was the strongest prime minister of the French Fourth Republic, a man who in spite of an unstable weak coalition took bold political risks in every area of foreign and domestic policy.[16] Similarly, it was Atal Behari Vajpayee, a strong prime minister and someone who had been explicitly calling for this step for years, who ordered the Indian nuclear tests immediately upon coming to power in 1998. The bureaucratic politics hypothesis would presumably have expected one of the series of weak prime ministers who preceded him to be pushed into going for the tests.

In sum, while any policy is subject to the pushes and pulls of internal struggles, the French and Indian decisions to acquire nuclear weapons were essentially top-down decisions that can hardly be explained as an outcome of these bureaucratic battles. Clearly the bureaucratic politics story, while colorful and interesting, is of secondary causal importance.

The Desire for Prestige and the French and Indian Decisions for the Bomb

States' desire for international prestige is another proposed explanation for nuclear proliferation that has garnered much scholarly support. Scott Sagan argues that France's choice to develop its independent nuclear arsenal was primarily due to the desire to avoid the fate of being relegated to minor power status—a fate inconsistent with its understanding of its historical rank and role.[17] For the case of India, scholars such as Stephen Cohen point to India's deepest identity as a "frustrated great state" as being the ultimate reason why it drove towards nuclear weapons.[18] In a shorter-term time frame, many writers see the 1998 tests as the result of an intensification of India's frustration through the 1990s, a frustration brought to boiling by American diplomatic high-handedness in the Comprehensive Test Ban Treaty (CTBT) negotiations.[19]

Discussion of the case for prestige-based explanations
There is clearly ample evidence that for both of these countries, the quest for international prestige is a central motivation for their overall foreign policies. But although India and France are clearly "prestige-seekers," this hardly makes the quest for prestige an adequate *explanation* for their decisions to acquire nuclear arsenals. India and France have always pursued international prestige, yet their nuclear weapons policies shifted from abstinence to acquisition at a certain moment in time. A constant cannot explain a variable.

In the French case, a whole series of dramatic events in the first postwar decade—Hiroshima, the Russian bomb, the Russian and American H-bombs, the British bomb—did not spark the French decision to acquire nuclear weapons. Indeed, most French state elites in the early 1950s argued that the country's international prestige and diplomatic power would be most enhanced by development of a purely civilian nuclear program, combined with the maintenance of the legal option to acquire nuclear weapons at a later date.[20] This abstinence is hard to explain if we accept the view that nuclear weapons were desired by the French because they were "obviously" essential for maintenance of French great power status. So what happened in mid–to late-1954 to make some French decision makers suddenly feel the need to increase the country's international prestige, and why did they suddenly feel that nuclear weapons would do that for it? Clearly more than the mere desire for international prestige is needed to explain this shift.[21]

For the case of India, a similar story can be told. It is true that the Chinese bomb test of 1964 led to the creation of the Indian bomb lobby, a lobby that was evidently motivated by concerns for Indian international prestige or rank.[22] But Indian leaders before 1998 had consistently rejected the lobby's views, maintaining instead that steering clear of full weaponization was best not only for India's security but also for India's international standing.[23] Moreover, worldwide the prestige value of acquiring nuclear weapons had been fast declining for a decade and more.[24] And while it is certainly true that the United States put India in a tight diplomatic spot on the question of CTBT, the fact that successive prime ministers considered *and then shelved* the nuclear test option is hardly evidence that the supposed CTBT "window" made the tests inevitable—it is rather evidence to the contrary.[25] As with the case of France, the Indian decision to acquire nuclear weapons, while not a 180-degree shift, represented a dramatic turnabout in policy that cannot be explained without a comprehension of the particular mindset of those in power at the time.

Summary: The limits of traditional explanatory variables

The purpose of this analysis has not been to argue against any impact of objective security conditions, bureaucratic interests, and the desire for prestige on the overall shape and direction of Indian and French nuclear policies. Rather, it has been to argue that these factors were not determinant in the political decisions to acquire nuclear weapons. Such decisions, whether they come six years before the first test (as in the case of France) or 24 years after it (as in the case of India) are never mere ratifications of technical developments. India may have taken a decades-long "pathway to Pokhran II," but the final destination of that path was never predetermined until the BJP government chose it. Estimates of technical capability can never substitute for estimates of political intentions.

It is my hypothesis that we should locate the political choice for the bomb in particular state leaders' *subjective perceptions* of the nation's international situation. And in order to understand what led *these* people to *these* perceptions of their nation's security position and options, we must investigate their deepest understandings of national identity. We must equally investigate the understandings of those who did *not* draw the conclusion that the bomb was necessary. Such comparative analysis is the best method of discovering what factors were most crucial in pushing actors in one direction or another.

Oppositional Nationalism and Decisions to Acquire Nuclear Weapons

I begin by making my case on the theoretical plane.[26] What ideal-typical understanding of national identity could produce the cognitive and emotional basis for a leader to decide to acquire nuclear weapons? I call it "oppositional nationalism." Oppositional nationalism is a combination of "oppositional" and "nationalist" understandings of national identity. I define opposition as a national self-definition versus an external enemy that is thought to be fundamentally threatening to the nation's security and values.[27] Opposition leads to a feeling of fear in interactions with that enemy. I define nationalism as a national self-definition of having a natural or essential right to independence from, and influence over, others in the world. Nationalism leads to a feeling of pride in interactions with those other nations. Opposition and nationalism can be fused into a single understanding of national identity that I term "oppositional nationalism." Oppositional nationalism produces a strong predisposition to feel both emotions of fear and pride in interactions with the enemy. The principal theoretical argument I make is that it is the combination of fear of one's enemy plus pride in oneself that creates a uniquely explosive psychological cocktail.

One level on which the combination of fear and pride promotes the decision to acquire nuclear weapons is through biased perceptions of threat and capacity. Assume that a reasonably technically competent state A is faced with a state B that has the capacity and the intention to destroy it, and with whom an explicit or tacit compromise is impossible. If state A can find no credible third-party protection against this threat, and if a counter-threat of nuclear retaliation could well lead state B to back down, then state A is likely to decide to acquire nuclear weapons. Now, assuming that the real situation does *not* unambiguously merit state A's perception, the fear and pride felt by leaders under the influence of oppositional nationalism will cause them to *think* that the situation clearly does merit it. The nuclear bomb decision flows naturally from this belief.

The perceptual dimension is important, but fear and pride also affect the oppositional nationalist's decision making on a deeper level. Fear and pride are emotions, and these emotions can lead people to seek *symbols* of power whose practical utility may be doubtful, but which temporarily assuage the dread of imminent annihilation.[28] For leaders of one national group wracked by fear of another, a nuclear bomb can appear to be the ultimate power totem. Getting "the bomb," perhaps even just one bomb, is thus perceived as a general solution to the problem of the enemy menace.[29] The emotional basis for the decision means that it tends to be made without a clear idea of the particular scenarios in which the bomb might be applied politically or militarily, and certainly without a full consciousness of the likelihood of future developments that could trigger an arms race or even nuclear war.

Oppositional nationalism is not a mere synonym for nationalism. A nation can be proud, self-assertive, and desire to stand tall in the world even in the absence of a feared enemy; this is what I call "nonoppositional" nationalism. Nonoppositional nationalists, I hypothesize, should generally be against acquiring nuclear weapons, because they will see no justification for paying the high security costs of doing so. These same people, on the other hand, may well want to build nuclear technology and resist the nonproliferation regime, viewing it as a discriminatory arrangement. Resistance to the regime has often been

assumed by the Western nonproliferation community to imply "nuclear ambitions," but in fact there is no logical reason to make this assumption, as Indian
diplomats long pointed out. Indeed, the mainstream Indian point of view for
many years was that of AEC chairman Vikram Sarabhai (as summarized by
his former colleague, Raja Ramanna): "Dr. Sarabhai did not believe in nuclear
weapons, but more than that, he did not believe in signing inequitable
treaties."[30] The distinction that I make between oppositional and nonoppositional nationalism provides the theoretical basis for disputing the facile idea of
many in the West that "anti-NPT equals pro-bomb."

Having outlined the basic theoretical underpinnings of my "identity" framework for understanding states' nuclear choices, I now turn to an evaluation of
the utility of this framework for the cases of France and India.

The French and Indian Decisions
to Acquire Nuclear Weapons

The parallel empirical stories told in this chapter are summarized in table 6.1.

France[31]

As previously noted, the French nuclear program began as a purely civilian
entity (indeed, one run by a Communist) in the early days after the country's
liberation from Germany. The main reason for this civilian focus was that
mainstream French strategic thinking in the decade after the end of World War
II tended to take a dim view of the potential utility of a French nuclear arsenal. French diplomats and military men also took the view that the country's
international position was best served by abstention from the pursuit of nuclear
weapons. Their rhetoric on the subject in the late 1940s and early 1950s bore
great similarity to that of pre-1998 India.[32] Then, in 1954, France suddenly
reversed course and embarked on a quest for the bomb.

On the basis of my intensive historical research on the French case, I can
affirm that the French decision to build nuclear weapons was born out of the
combination of the rise to power of an "oppositional nationalist" leader, the
Radical Pierre Mendès France, and an external political shock: The 1954 return
to sovereignty and rearmament of the "hereditary enemy," Germany. The
return of Germany—West Germany in particular—to the international power
game was viewed as a significant blow not only to French standing in the
Western alliance, but also to French security since the Germans were believed
to lust for war.[33] But if France was united in its fear of German rearmament,
it was far from united in believing that a nuclear arsenal was the right response.
As argued above, it is not fear alone, but fear plus nationalist pride that leads
to decisions to acquire nuclear weapons. In early-1950s France, there was division over that second element, nationalist pride. France in those days was split

Table 6.1

	France	India
Period of Abstinence	"Pro-Europeans" (oppositional, not nationalist) in power before 1954: No Bomb Decision Taken.	"Secularists" (nationalist, not oppositional) in power before 1998: No Bomb Decision Taken.
"Going Nuclear"	"Nationalists" (oppositional nationalist) in power from 1954: Bomb Decision Taken 1954.	"Hindu nationalists" (oppositional nationalist) in power from 1998: Bomb Decision Taken 1998.

by a newly emergent political cleavage—between those who believed in maintaining national sovereignty, and those who believed in "dissolving" France into the nascent European Community. This cleavage did not respect the traditional divisions of left and right, and even a relatively disciplined party such as the Socialists found itself riven in two by the issue.[34]

This "nationalist" versus "pro-European" cleavage showed itself most prominently in the parliamentary debates over the formation of a supranational European army, known as the European Defense Community (EDC), and it also was evident in the secret debate between state elites over the bomb.[35] The nationalists combined fear of Germany with self-assertive nationalism and can thus be categorized as oppositional nationalists. This group included such strange political bedfellows as the left-leaning Pierre Mendès France and the right-leaning General Charles de Gaulle.[36] When German rearmament became inevitable, their response was to seek the bomb. By contrast, while the pro-Europeans also feared Germany, they tended to draw from World War II the lesson that not only German but *all* nationalisms were outmoded. They were thus oppositional, but not nationalist. This was also a group of strange bedfellows, one that included for instance the socialist Guy Mollet and the businessman and European visionary Jean Monnet.[37] The pro-Europeans were opposed to a French nuclear deterrent because they feared that news of such an effort would lead to a renaissance of German nationalism, destroy the European project and cause a new spiral towards war.[38]

In a lively internal battle, the nationalists first defeated the pro-Europeans on the issue of EDC, and then they used their newly enhanced position to decide the question of the French bomb.[39] Certainly, given the weight of the Franco-German conflict over the previous 70 years, the nationalist argument was likely to prevail; but the fact that it did not come without a fight is significant for the explanation of the case. Not opposition alone, not nationalism alone, but rather oppositional nationalism led to the French bomb decision.

India

It is my contention that the BJP's coming to power is the single most important fact that explains the Indian decision to move beyond nuclear ambiguity
and acquire nuclear weapons. Of course, the BJP could not have made such
quick work of its decision to "go nuclear" in 1998 unless the way had been
prepared for such a decision. There is no question that India was closer to the
bomb in 1998 than it was in 1988 or in 1968. But the notion of being a certain number of weeks or months away from having the bomb assumes a certain technical teleology that the Indian case and many others clearly disprove.
In May 1998, India had been "two weeks from the bomb" for years, and few
observers saw any reason to believe that such a stance could not continue indefinitely. The surprising shift in India's nuclear weapons stance was due to a political decision by the newly elected BJP government. Why? What did the BJP
have or think that the other parties did not? I find the explanation for the 1998
Indian decision in the same place I found it for the 1954 French one: oppositional nationalism.

Why Indian leaders chose not to
acquire nuclear weapons before 1998

The history of India's relationship with nuclear weapons can be divided into
five distinct stages[40]:

- From independence to 1964, characterized by a clear desire to increase Indian
  mastery of nuclear technology but no sense of urgency for, indeed a strong
  moral revulsion to, anything that smacked of nuclear weapons development[41];
- From 1964 to 1972, characterized by a less moralistic view of the nuclear
  weapons option, but still a strong feeling that building the bomb would have
  significant negative consequences for Indian prestige and security;
- From 1972 to 1989, characterized by much more significant work on preparing the nuclear option, but a continued avoidance of weaponization in spite
  of Western doubts about this distinction;
- From 1989 to 1998, a period of true strategic ambiguity;
- From 1998 to the present, characterized by the clear decision to acquire a
  nuclear arsenal.

Here I begin the story in the late 1980s, when the move to strategic ambiguity took place.

In 1986, India's massive military exercises near the Pakistan border led to
the most serious military crisis in the subcontinent in more than decade. At the
end of the crisis, Pakistani scientist A. Q. Khan granted an interview to the
Indian journalist Kuldip Nayar and asserted that Pakistan had developed the
bomb.[42] This was generally interpreted in India, probably rightly, as a mix of
true revelation and nationalistic bombast.[43] Indian Prime Minister Rajiv
Gandhi had already considered and rejected the idea of acquiring nuclear
weapons in 1985, in large part due to American assurances that Pakistan's
nuclear program would be held in check.[44] But the 1987 Khan interview and

other information showed that these were hollow assurances. At the same time, Gandhi's cherished "Action Plan" for world nuclear disarmament fell on deaf ears. So in 1988 or 1989, Rajiv Gandhi did start proceeding with weaponization, and in this respect P. K. Iyengar of the AEC and V. S. Arunachalam from the Defense Research and Development Organization (DRDO) were to be key players.[45] The affair was so secret that even Rajiv Gandhi's closest associate on nuclear policy, the diplomat Muchkund Dubey, only learned of the plans because a scientist contacted him for an estimate of how long India would have to complete bomb assembly in a crisis, and also how many bombs it might need.[46]

The decision to move toward weaponizing India's nuclear capacities was a serious decision. It was not just a ratification of the work that had gone before. Weaponization, according to the AEC and DRDO, involved "design, testing and production of advanced detonators, ruggedized high volt trigger systems, interface engineering, systems engineering and systems integration" as well as various "contributions in aerodynamics, arming, fusing, safety interlocks, flight trials etc."[47] But in terms of weaponization Rajiv Gandhi gave Iyengar and Arunachalam not a green light but a flashing yellow one, requiring them to ask for permission for every forward step they took.[48] The idea was never to prepare a test series as soon as possible and thereafter to proceed to the "induction" of nuclear weapons into Indian military practice. Rather, as Dubey's statement indicates, the idea was rather to have everything ready in order to be able quickly to "go nuclear" in the full sense of the term *if circumstances changed*— the most likely scenario being a Pakistani nuclear breakout.

Until this ultimate decision to acquire nuclear weapons came, there was a limit to what the AEC and DRDO could do. India could not build reliable warheads unless it had more data than that gleaned from its 1974 "peaceful" test; it could not build reliable weapons systems unless it fitted missiles with the warheads and tested and trained with the ensemble; and it could not develop a safe and reliable deterrent unless it trained its military in the handling of the weapons.[49] The political leadership was well aware of these facts—indeed, how could it not be given the bomb lobby's incessant reminders?[50] Yet it stayed put. Through several governments of different political configurations, the final order required for India to become a nuclear-weapons state never came.

These governments' inaction was hardly due to a belief that India already had nuclear weapons. They well understood the vast difference between holding virtual and real nuclear arsenals.[51] Estimates that India had already stockpiled dozens of warheads by the late 1990s are simply fantastic.[52] They chose to remain shy of the nuclear-weapons threshold because believed that a South Asia without nuclear weapons was more secure than the alternative. India's stopping just short of the nuclear weapons threshold was the result neither of elite incompetence nor of Gandhian moralism. Indian leaders before 1998 believed that since India faced no clear and present nuclear threat, to acquire nuclear weapons would simply—in Indira Gandhi's words—"bring danger where there was none before."[53]

There has been much discussion of the 1995 consideration of nuclear testing by the government of P. V. Narasimha Rao. It is definitely true that
American satellites picked up suspicious activities underway at the Pokhran test
site.[54] But the idea that the American knowledge of test preparations forced
them to be scrapped is highly suspect.[55] In fact, a decision to test had not been
taken, and information that has come to light recently indicates that Rao—like
Indira Gandhi in the early 1980s—decided that the security and economic costs
of testing outweighed the political benefits.[56] In sum, the 1995 Indian non-test,
far from proving that an Indian nuclear breakout was inevitable in the late
1990s, demonstrates the continuing resilience of the policy of remaining just
shy of the nuclear threshold—a policy that India had already maintained for a
decade or even longer.[57]

Why Indian leaders chose to acquire nuclear weapons in 1998

In the spring of 1998 the BJP came to power and immediately, without waiting for the strategic review and without consulting its coalition partners or the
civil service, broke the nuclear equilibrium on the subcontinent. The BJP's tests
surprised not only American intelligence but all seasoned India observers, who
had not registered any change in the security situation and who could not
believe that the BJP was actually implementing what they considered to be its
"ridiculous rhetoric."[58] In his heavily researched inside story of India's nuclear
weapons program, the journalist Raj Chengappa has recounted how the new
Prime Minister cut off discussion and debate on the merits and the likely consequences of testing and simply ordered it done. According to Chengappa,
Vajpayee said, "There was no need for much thought. We just have to do it."[59]

The disarray of government spokesmen, including the prime minister, in the
wake of the tests indicated that more thought could have been useful. In the
days following the tests, Vajpayee and other top governmental officials argued
that such a step was necessary because of Pakistan's "covert" bomb and its
recent Ghauri missile test, Chinese encirclement, Western hypocrisy, India's
legitimate aspirations for great power status, and anything else they could think
of.[60] The public fishing for reasonable explanations makes it clear that the need
for nuclear weapons seemed so "obvious" to the new government that it had
not made any attempt to clarify its thinking beforehand. More than three years
after the tests, confusion about how nuclear weapons fit into India's foreign
policy goals remains rampant, and the continuing silence on strategic doctrine
and command and control is deafening.[61] Events since September 11 have
served to underscore how risky it was to break the non-weaponized deterrence
equilibrium without first resolving these problems.

In the decision to test, however, Vajpayee's thinking seems to have been
remarkably unclouded by such likely complications. Rather, Vajpayee permit-
ted a glimpse into his real motivation with the simple yet menacing statement,
"We have a big bomb now."[62] Vajpayee must never have felt so sure of any decision in his life; indeed he showed the same dead certainty twice, once in his
short-lived government of 1996 (which fell before the decision could be imple-

mented) and again when he returned to power in 1998. The combination of supreme confidence in the correctness of this decision and the inability to articulate a clear strategic rationale for it is a clear indication that the basis for the decision was emotional. It is not at all unusual for decisions to be based primarily on emotion; indeed, how could one ever hope to calculate with any degree of certainty all the likely consequences of such a revolutionary act as the acquisition of nuclear weapons?[63] The aim here is not to criticize Vajpayee for making an emotional decision; rather, the aim is to answer a simple empirical question: What made this decision so easy for him when it had been so hard for all his predecessors in power?

The answer is that it was Vajpayee and the BJP's oppositional nationalism that provided it with the emotional motivation to embrace what earlier governments had deferred or shunned. The Indian case shows the importance of differentiating between oppositional and non-oppositional forms of nationalism. The BJP does not have a monopoly on Indian nationalism. The Indian National Congress made Indian nationalism at home and abroad central to its appeal. But there is a major difference between the BJP and the secularist versions of Indian nationalism. Jawaharlal Nehru's nationalism, as exemplified by his book, *Discovery of India,* was an inclusive, nonoppositional nationalism that exalted communal diversity as the key to Indian greatness and did not envision any permanent enemies, not even Britain. By contrast, Hindu nationalism is oppositional, pitting Hindu against Muslim—and by extension India against Pakistan.[64] Indo-Pak relations have of course always been tense, but the BJP "difference" is that it places that tension at the very center of its narrative of Indian history and its vision of Indian destiny.[65] Professor Christophe Jaffrelot has shown the decades-long continuities in this distrust, fear and loathing of the Muslim "invaders"—a mindset he calls a "majority complex of inferiority."[66]

With such an understanding of Indian identity, it is no wonder that the BJP has perceived Pakistani nuclear achievements and intentions in the darkest possible colors, nor that the Pakistan question was at the heart of the BJP's desire for nuclear weapons.[67] The centrality of Pakistan in the BJP's nuclear calculations is often denied, but in fact the historical record is clear. The BJP's current interest in nuclear weapons dates specifically from July 1985, when in response to new reports about Pakistani nuclear progress, the party adopted a resolution in favor of an Indian nuclear bomb.[68] This resolution stated, "Reports from Pakistan indicate that the threat of a Pakistani nuclear bomb is real and an immediate response to this is necessary. The BJP, therefore, calls upon Government to take immediate steps to develop our own nuclear bomb."[69] No other developments in other countries were cited in justification of this shift in the BJP's position. The failure to mention China is particularly telling.

The singular focus on Pakistan in the 1985 resolution was hardly an anomaly for the BJP; it came as part of the party's dramatic post-1984 rhetorical escalation against Pakistan and Muslims.[70] The call for the bomb thus dovetailed with the BJP's overall political strategy, but it would be wrong to view the BJP's bomb as an electoral gimmick. If it was that, it failed miserably, as Indian voters in the first elections after the tests, the regional elections in December 1998, punished the BJP for the soaring price of onions and potatoes. But in fact the BJP can be given credit for greater political acumen than that. The BJP was well aware of the short-lived popularity that Indira Gandhi's blast had given her, and that foreign and security policies have historically been of minor electoral importance in India.[71] And indeed the government did not attempt to cash in politically as some of its supporters were recommending; for instance it scotched the idea of setting up a Hindu temple on the site of the blasts.[72] A more credible starting point than pure electoral politics is to see both the BJP's political strategy and its nuclear ambitions as two parallel consequences of a deep-seated fear of Pakistan and Indian Muslims combined with a strong sense of Indian (or Hindu) pride.

It is true that the BJP is not monolithic; within it "moderates" contend with "purists" for dominance.[73] Moreover, since the 1998 election victory, the "moderates" have seemingly been more firmly in the drivers' seat than ever before.[74] But the nuclear issue was one place where that internal political contest was less relevant. The dispute between "moderates" and "purists" is not over fundamental ideals but over tactics for gaining and holding power.[75] The nuclear issue was not on the front-burner of electoral politics, and it was not likely to upset the governmental coalition with minor and regionalist parties. So this issue held no cause for disagreement between the two wings of the BJP.

Whether "moderate" or not, BJP leaders wanted the bomb. This was nowhere more true than in the case of the BJP's chief "moderate," the Prime Minister himself. Ashis Nandy cites a poem by a young Vajpayee, which apart from explicit reference to (in Nandy's words) "the victimization of the Hindus in history" at the hands of the Muslims, offers a chilling reminder of the link between Vajpayee's long-standing oppositional nationalist sentiments and his bomb decision as prime minister:

This is the identity of the Hindu body, the Hindu soul and the Hindu life,
I am that rage of Shankar, which can destroy the earth and reduce it to ashes,
I am the devastating sound of his drum to which death dances,
I am the unquenched thirst of the goddess of war, I am the divine laughter of
    Durga,
I am the doomsday call of the god of death, the burning fire from the funeral
    pyre,
If with this fire raging inside me, I burn the earth,
And the water, earth, sky, soil go up in flames on their own, do not be sur-
    prised.[76]

Conclusion

In this chapter I have shown that the Indian decision to acquire nuclear weapons, like the French decision more than four decades before it, was fundamentally driven by the oppositional nationalism of the leaders who made it. Oppositional nationalism on the part of Atal Behari Vajpayee and Pierre Mendès France sparked an explosive emotional cocktail of fear and pride. It was this combination of fear and pride that produced the two decisions to acquire nuclear weapons.

What does the India-France parallel imply for the future of India's nuclear weapons policies? In fact, it would be wrong to impute too much continuity between the original motivations for nuclear weapons acquisition—the histories outlined here—and the eventual domestic and international uses to which the bomb is put. One of the reasons why both Indian and French leaders long abstained from acquiring the bomb was that they fully understood that it would have revolutionary implications that could not be predicted with any certainty before the deed was done. Now India is living in that whirlwind, and all that can be said is that it has yet to find its way in the new nuclear order in South Asia.[77]

What does the India-France parallel imply for the future of nuclear proliferation? One strong implication is that fears of runaway proliferation due to copycat testing in other regions of the world are unfounded.[78] No states will feel a pressing need to build nuclear weapons in order to keep pace in a status competition with India and Pakistan. The overall thrust of this chapter has been to argue that state leaders do not take nuclear weapons decisions lightly. It is the gravity of the choice to "go nuclear" that best explains why so few such decisions have been made. The oppositional nationalists studied in this chapter understood the gravity of the decision every bit as much as their predecessors in office. Their beliefs that nuclear weapons would benefit their countries' security may have been inchoate, but they were sincere. Not mere prestige-seeking, not bureaucratic politics, but a combination of fear and pride on the part of top leaders drives nuclear weapons decisions. The international norm of non-proliferation will continue, not primarily because of redoubled efforts by American diplomats, but because almost all states understand that nuclear weapons offer them limited military and political value.

Notes

1. I would like to thank the many dozens of scholars, archivists, and policymakers in France, India, the United Kingdom, and the United States who consented to share their information, recollections, and wisdom. Thanks also to all those who reviewed and commented on this and related papers, including Michael Barletta, Michael Desch, Bertrand Goldschmidt, Seung-Young Kim, Aaron Lobel, Jorge I.

Domínguez, Stanley Hoffmann, Alastair Iain Johnston, Devesh Kapur, Jeffrey Knopf, Thomas Lienhard, Dinshaw Mistry, Gilles Pécout, M. V. Ramana, Pramathesh Rath, Stephen Rosen, Scott Sagan, Albino Santos, Kenneth Scheve, Michael Tomz, Maurice Vaïsse, and Jim Walsh. Special thanks to Georges Ripka, president of the French Pugwash Association, to Eduardo Ortiz of Imperial College, London, and to Maurice Vaïsse of the *Centre d'Etudes d'Histoire de la Défense* (France) for inviting me to present my work before their groups. For research support I would like to thank the Krupp Foundation, the Institute for the Study of World Politics, the Harvard University Minda de Gunzburg Center for European Studies, and the Stanford University Center for International Security and Cooperation. It goes without saying that I accept all errors as my own.

2. Amitabh Mattoo neatly encapsulates the mainstream position: "While the BJP may have taken the decision to test . . . virtually every prime minister since Independence is implicated in the development of India's nuclear weapons programme." Amitabh Mattoo, "India's Nuclear Policy in an Anarchic World," in Mattoo, ed., *India's Nuclear Deterrent: Pokhran II and Beyond* (New Delhi: Har-Anand Publications Pvt. Ltd., 1999), p. 16.

3. Most authors offer some combination of these variables, while leaning toward one of them to explain the actual 1998 decision to test. The "objective situation" hypothesis is promoted most forcefully by Jasjit Singh, ed., *Nuclear India* (New Delhi: Knowledge World, 1998); T. V. Paul, "The Systemic Bases of India's Challenge to the Global Nuclear Order," *Non-Proliferation Review* Vol. 6, No. 1 (Fall 1998), pp. 1-11; and Ashok Kapur, "India and Multipolarity in the Asia-Pacific Regional Sub-System," paper delivered at the 1999 Annual Meeting of the American Political Science Association, Atlanta, September 1999. The international prestige element is placed in the foreground of explanation by Mattoo, "India's Nuclear Policy," and Pramit Pal Chaudhuri, "The Challenge for Indian Diplomacy" in Mattoo, ed., *India's Nuclear Deterrent*; Raj Chengappa, *Weapons of Peace: The Secret Story of India's Quest to be a Nuclear Power* (New Delhi: Harper Collins, 2000); and Sumit Ganguly, "India's Pathway to Pokhran II: The Prospects and Sources of New Delhi's Nuclear Weapons Program," *International Security*, Vol. 23, No. 4 (Spring 1999), pp. 148-177. "The "strategic enclave" hypothesis is highlighted by George Perkovich, *India's Nuclear Bomb: The Impact on Global Proliferation* (Berkeley: University of California Press, 1999); and Itty Abraham, *The Making of the Indian Atomic Bomb: Science, Secrecy and the Postcolonial State* (London: Zed Books, 1998). The most balanced statement is Stephen Cohen, "Nuclear Weapons and Conflict in South Asia," paper presented to the Harvard/MIT Transnational Security Project, November 1998 [viewed on the web at http://www.brook.edu/views/articles/cohens/1998TSP.htm].

4. Two who have argued for the "BJP hypothesis" are Achin Vanaik, "The Indian Nuclear Tests: Causes, Consequences, and Portents," *Comparative Studies of South Asia, Africa and the Middle East* vol. 18, No. 1 (1998), see esp. p. 54; and Dinshaw Mistry, "India and the Comprehensive Test Ban Treaty," *ACDIS Research Report*, September 1998, see esp. p. 47.

5. For instance, Ashok Kapur has written, "It is irresponsible for an arms chair strategist, who is far removed from the Indian Subcontinental zone of conflict, and whose judgement does not entail any risk-taking or decisionmaking concerning issues of war and peace in the region, to dismiss the strategic and pres-

tige aspects of Indian nuclear behavior. It is also illogical to locate the issue in BJP party politics and not Indian strategic policy when successive Indian governments have declined to join the NPT and have insisted on keeping their nuclear weapons option open." Kapur, "India and Multipolarity," p. 3.

6. Scott Sagan, "Why Do States Build Nuclear Weapons? Three Models in Search of a Bomb," *International Security*, Vol. 21, No. 3 (Winter 1996-97), pp. 54-86.

7. Martin Van Creveld, *Nuclear Proliferation and the Future of Conflict* (New York: the Free Press, 1993), esp. pp. 123-124.

8. Lawrence Scheinman, *Atomic Energy Policy in France under the Fourth Republic* (Princeton: Princeton University Press, 1965).

9. Apart from the authors listed in footnote 3, see the earlier work in this vein by Peter Lavoy, "Nuclear Myths and the Causes of Proliferation," in Zachary S. Davis and Benjamin Frankel, eds., *The Proliferation Puzzle*, special joint issue of *Security Studies* vol. 2, Nos. 3/4 (Spring-Summer 1993); Scott Sagan, "Why Do States Build Nuclear Weapons?"; and Dhirendra Sharma, *India's Nuclear Estate* (New Delhi: Lancers Publishers, 1983).

10. For more on this point, see Jacques E. C. Hymans, "The Strangelove Fallacy," *The Telegraph* (India), July 6, 2000.

11. In fact, there were two scientific chiefs in succession who opposed the bomb: Frédéric Joliot-Curie and Francis Perrin. The administrative chief was Pierre Guillaumat. See Dominique Mongin, *La bombe atomique française 1945–1958* (Bruxelles: Bruylant, 1997), pp. 294-307.

12. Even the engineer Homi Sethna, who as AEC chairman was deeply involved in the preparations for the first Pokhran blast in 1974, argued against more than a single symbolic test at that time. Homi Sethna, personal communication, Bombay, December 8, 1998.

13. For more on "epistemic communities," see Peter M. Haas, "Do Regimes Matter? Epistemic Communities and Mediterranean Pollution Control," *International Organization*, vol. 43, No. 3 (Summer 1989), pp. 377-403.

14. Mongin, *La bombe atomique française*, pp. 318-19.

15. Indeed, Indian technical experts such as Homi Sethna have remained to this day highly skeptical of Pakistan's nuclear achievements: "Based on information which I gathered while working with the Dept. of Atomic Energy, to reach high enrichment levels, the design of the [model for the Pakistani] centrifuge particularly its size has to be increased. I do not think that Pakistan has the wherewithal to develop that technology on its own. Therefore I have my reservations about the capability of Pakistan, in the area of the design of the device as well as in the area of the production of materials required for the device." Homi Sethna, "Nuclear Energy in the 21st Century," unpublished manuscript, December 1998, p. 3.

16. Jean Lacouture, *Pierre Mendès France*, translated by George Holoch (New York: Holmes and Meier, 1984).

17. Sagan, "Why Do States Build Nuclear Weapons?" Sagan has support in the historical literature. See especially Georges-Henri Soutou, "La politique nucléaire de Pierre Mendès France," *Relations Internationales*, No. 59 (Autumn 1989). The desire to remain influential in NATO is seen as important but not determinant by Maurice Vaïsse, "Le choix atomique de la France (1945-1958)," *Vingtième Siècle*, No. 36 (1992) and by Mongin, *La bombe atomique française*.

18. Cohen, "Nuclear Weapons and Conflict"; this argument is also quite explicit in Perkovich, *India's Nuclear Bomb.*

19. Ganguly, "India's Pathway," Kapur, "India and Multipolarity," and Mattoo, "Indian Nuclear Policy," all agree on the centrality of this variable. Jasjit Singh, "Why Nuclear Weapons?" in Singh, ed., *Nuclear India,* tries to give this hypothesis a "realistic" twist by contending that India had to test before September 1999 to avoid facing worldwide sanctions under the CTBT regime. But Mistry easily rebuts this argument, citing the numerous official statements that the September 1999 CTBT conference "would not entail sanctions against states not signing the CTBT." Mistry, "India and the Comprehensive Test Ban Treaty," p. 46.

20. Pierre Mendès France, verbatim transcript of interview conducted by Georgette Elgey, August 20, 1969, in the Fonds Elgey (archives privées), Archives Nationales, Paris.

21. One could argue that France before 1954 had not given the issue much thought because it was technically unready to build the bomb. But even in 1954, the first nuclear test was 6 years away. Indeed, this secret "too early" decision is in its own right a puzzle for the "international prestige" hypothesis.

22. Abraham, *The Making of the Indian Atomic Bomb,* p. 126.

23. The arguments for this position were succinctly stated in P. R. Chari, *Indo-Pak Nuclear Standoff: The Role of the United States* (New Delhi: Manohar, 1995), pp. 94-96.

24. Nina Tannenwald, "The Nuclear Taboo," *International Organization,* vol. 53, No. 3 (Summer 1999), pp. 433-68.

25. This is a point also made by Achin Vanaik, "The Indian Nuclear Tests," p. 54.

26. For a more extended discussion, see Chapter 2 of Jacques E. C. Hymans, "Pride, Prejudice, and Plutonium: Explaining Decisions to Acquire Nuclear Weapons," unpublished doctoral dissertation, Harvard University, September 2001.

27. Richard Cottam's similar conception of this enemy-based variety of nationalism is described in Daniel Druckman, "Social Psychological Aspects of Nationalism," in John L. Comaroff and Paul C. Stern, eds., *Perspectives on Nationalism and War* (Amsterdam: Overseas Publishers Association, 1995), pp. 47-98.

28. Donald Horowitz, *Ethnic Groups in Conflict* (Berkeley: University of California Press, 1985), esp. pp. 186-187.

29. This perception is often proven incorrect after the deed is done, which leads to a felt need for ever-increasing stockpiles of bombs.

30. Raja Ramanna (personal communication), New Delhi, November 19, 1998.

31. Here I can only provide the most bare bones skeleton argument of this case. For a fuller treatment see chapter 6 of Jacques E. C. Hymans, "Pride, Prejudice, and Plutonium."

32. See Jean-Christophe Sauvage, "La perception des questions nucléaires dans les premières années de l'Institut des Hautes Etudes de Défense Nationale 1948-1955," in Maurice Vaïsse, ed., *La France et l'Atome: Etudes d'histoire nucléaire* (Bruxelles: Bruylant, 1994), esp. pp. 77-78.

33. One can see this perception clearly in the debates over German rearmament that took place in the French Parliament. An extreme example is the speech by Adolphe Aumeran, *Journal Officiel de la République Française, Débats Parlementaires—Assemblée Nationale,* 2e Séance du 29 Août 1954, pp. 4436-4439.

34. Alfred Grosser, *La IVe république et sa politique extérieure* (Paris: Librairie Armand Colin, 1961), pp. 113-14.

35. The "nationalist" versus "pro-European" cleavage was not limited to the security sphere; it also showed itself in a range of other areas, such as economic integration. See Daniel Lerner and Raymond Aron, eds., *France Defeats EDC* (New York: F. A. Praeger, 1957).

36. The diplomat Jean-Marc Boegner recalls that the first time Mendès France privately declared his support for the bomb (in October 1954), the Prime Minister put it this way: "I know that General de Gaulle is in favor of making the atomic bomb, and he is entirely right." This was a rare doffing of the cap to a political opponent. Jean-Marc Boegner, personal communications, Paris, January 27 and 30, 1998; see also Mongin, *La bombe atomique française*, op. cit., p. 321.

37. François Duchêne, *Jean Monnet: The First Statesman of Interdependence* (New York: W. W. Norton and Co., 1994).

38. Pierre Guillen, "La France et la négociation du traité d'Euratom," in Michel Dumoulin, Pierre Guillen, Maurice Vaïsse, eds., *L'Energie Nucléaire en Europe: Des Origines à Euratom* (Bern: Peter Lang, 1994).

39. The key documents that reflected the victory of the pro-bomb forces are the internal memoranda *"Projet de Décision"* and *"Conceptions Stratégiques,"* both dated Dec. 26, 1954, in the *"Energie Atomique"* file of the Institut Pierre Mendès France, Paris, France.

40. I share with Sumit Ganguly the periodization of the first two stages, but I differ on the last three. Ganguly, "India's Pathway."

41. In this short chapter I am unable to explore fully this Indian particularity of moralism in foreign policy, but it is undoubtedly one of the key elements of a complete description of the Indian case.

42. A. Q. Khan interview in *The Observer*, cited in Sumita Kumar, "Pakistan's Nuclear Weapon Programme," in Jasjit Singh, ed., *Nuclear India*, p. 174.

43. K. Subrahmanyam argues that until May 1998, "China did not allow Pakistan an entirely autonomous capability. Pakistani nuclear weapons, therefore, were strictly not military weapons capable of being used against India." K. Subrahmanyam in "India's Nuclear Policy—An IIC Debate," June 8, 1998 on web at http://www.ipcs.org/issues/articles/113-ndi-banerjee.html. Subrahmanyam seems to have taken a more robust view of Pakistan's nuclear attainments before May 1998 in the Kargil Committee report, however.

44. K. Subrahmanyam, "Indian Nuclear Policy—1964–98," in Jasjit Singh, ed., *Nuclear India*.

45. P. K. Iyengar, personal communication, Bombay, December 8, 1998.

46. Muchkund Dubey, personal communication, New Delhi, December 15, 1998.

47. "Joint Statement by Department of Atomic Energy and Defence Research and Development Organisation," New Delhi, May 17, 1998, on web at http://www.indianembassy.org/pic/PR_1998/May98/prmay1798.htm.

48. Chengappa, *Weapons of Peace*, p. 335.

49. That the military had not been exposed to the weapons was a point strongly made to me by Gen. V. N. Sharma, personal communications, New Delhi, December 16, 1998, and in a follow-up letter of February 18, 1999. For a careful discussion of various concepts of weaponization, see Ashley J. Tellis, *India's Emerging Nuclear Posture: Between Recessed Deterrent and Ready Arsenal* (Santa Monica: The RAND Corporation, 2001).

50. One dramatic attempt to shake the political leadership into action was Army Head General K. Sundarji's polemic book, *Blind Men of Hindoostan* (New Delhi: UBS Publishers, 1993).

51. Michael J. Mazarr, *Nuclear Weapons in a Transformed World : The Challenge of Virtual Nuclear Arsenals* (New York : St. Martin's Press, 1997).

52. Given the need for additional tests on the bomb design, before May 1998 the AEC "would have considered it foolish to make 30 warheads, not knowing if it would work or not" (senior Indian nuclear engineer, name withheld upon request, personal communication, 2000. A recently publicized US estimate is that India even in early 2000 still had only about 5 warheads of dubious quality. Robert Windrem and Tammy Kupperman, "Pakistan Nukes Outstrip India's, Officials Say," MSNBC News report, June 6, 2000, available on web at http://www.msnbc.com/news/417106.asp?cp1=1. From February 2000, the Atomic Energy Regulatory Board no longer has oversight responsibility over weapons-related nuclear facilities. This is indicative of round-the-clock production of warheads since that time.

53. Indira Gandhi, interview with Rodney Jones, quoted in Perkovich, *India's Nuclear Bomb*, p. 178.

54. Andrew Koch, "Nuclear Testing in South Asia and the CTBT," *The Nonproliferation Review* vol. 3, no. 3 (Spring-Summer 1996).

55. "Even after India's national security establishment . . . was ready, a political decision was necessary. In 1995, testing was averted not so much by prompt US action as by the fact that Prime Minister Narasimha Rao was not fully convinced." Aaron Karp, "Indian Ambitions and the Limits of American Influence," *Arms Control Today*, May 1998.

56. George Perkovich gives a good summary of the earlier episode: Perkovich, *India's Nuclear Bomb*, pp. 242-244. The Rao episode was recounted to me by A. N. Varma and on the economic side by Manmohan Singh (personal communications, New Delhi, December 2 and 19, 1998) and was reinforced by the evidence in Chengappa, *Weapons of Peace*, p. 395.

57. This analysis is shared by Achin Vanaik: "That neither the Congress nor the UF went so far as to actually test also indicated, given their official position of ambiguity, that such a dramatic change of course could not easily be carried out without a minimum of political and ideological preparation by these political forces at least among their staunchest support bases." Achin Vanaik, "The Indian Nuclear Tests: Causes Consequences, and Portents," *Comparative Studies of South Asia, Africa and the Middle East* XVIII, No. 1 (1998), p. 54.

58. Sumit Ganguly in Henry L. Stimson Center, "Southern Asia Internet Forum V: Implications of a BJP-led Government in India" on web at http://www.stimson.org/cbm/saif/bjp.htm. See also Karp, "Indian Ambitions."

59. Raj Chengappa, *Weapons of Peace*, p. 49.

60. "Suo Moto Statement by Prime Minister Shri Atal Behari Vajpayee in Parliament on May 27, 1998" and "Evolution of India's Nuclear Policy," paper presented by A. B. Vajpayee to the House on May 27, 1998, available on web at http://www.indianembassy.org/pic/nuclearpolicy.htm.

61. "Apparently, neither the long road beyond the tests had been visualized nor was an action plan thought through." V. R. Raghavan, "Dangerous nuclear uncertainties," *The Hindu*, March 13, 2000.

62. George Perkovich notes that an embarrassed government retracted this statement after it was printed in *India Today*. Perkovich, *India's Nuclear Bomb*, p. 420.

63. One might have expected Pakistan to respond in kind; one would have to have been truly prescient to see that this would embolden the Pakistani military to launch the Kargil operation; but who would have been able to foresee that that fiasco's dénouement would prepare the ground for the 1999 military coup?

64. This is an example, in Theodore Wright's terminology, of the "interface of foreign and domestic conflict" in South Asia. See Theodore P. Wright, Jr., "The BJP/Shiv Sena Coalition and the Muslim Minority in Maharashtra: The Interface of Foreign and Domestic Conflict," *Journal of South Asian and Middle Eastern Studies* XXI, No. 2 (Winter 1998), pp. 41-50.

65. I demonstrate this claim through an intensive, qualitative and quantitative content analysis of speeches at the Red Fort on Indian Independence Day in Chapter 11 of Jacques E. C. Hymans, "Pride, Prejudice, and Plutonium."

66. Jaffrelot, *Les nationalistes hindous*. Stephen Cohen has written that a similar psychological dynamic to the one I describe as "oppositional nationalism" has been at work in both India and Pakistan ever since Independence (he calls it "paired minority psychologies"). Stephen P. Cohen, *The Structural Dimensions of Conflict in South Asia* (Colombo, Sri Lanka: Regional Centre for Strategic Studies, 1997). But there is surely at least a major difference in degree between the secular and BJP "minority psychologies."

67. Indeed, so strong was the "Pakistan threat" thesis that the cognitive dissonance produced by the delay in Pakistan's reply "unnerved the BJP government" (Chaudhuri, "The Challenge for Indian Diplomacy," p. 207). Its officials began practically to beg Pakistan to follow suit. When it finally did, a clearly relieved Vajpayee explained that Pakistan's tests "vindicated" the previous Indian tests that had caused them to happen. The subcontinent was clearly on the other side of the looking-glass. CNN staff, "India reconsidering its pledge not to test," on web at http://europe.cnn.com/WORLD/asiapcf/9805/28/pakistan.india.reax/index.html and viewed May 21, 2001.

68. The BJP and its predecessor party, the Jana Sangh, were long on record in favor of an Indian nuclear deterrent. But this call had shifted into the background and was not even included in the BJP's election manifesto of 1984.

69. BJP manifestoes and resolutions, as well as those of other major Indian parties, are reprinted in the annual series edited by A. Moin Zaidi, *Annual Register of Indian Political Parties* (New Delhi: India Institute of Applied Political Research, 1972-1991).

70. Christophe Jaffrelot, *Les nationalistes hindous. Idéologie, implantation et mobilisation des années 1920 aux années 1990* (Paris: Presses de Sciences Po, 1993), esp. pp. 403-540.

71. "Foreign policy, even national security, has never penetrated very far as an electoral issue." Philip Oldenburg, *The 13th election of India's Lok Sabha (House of the People)* (New York: The Asia Society, September 1999) on web at http://www.asiasociety.org/publications/indian_elections.13.html.

72. Kalpana Sharma, "The Hindu Bomb," *Bulletin of the Atomic Scientists*, Vol. 54, No. 4 (July/August 1998), available on web at http://www.bullatomsci.org/issues/1998/ja98/ja98sharma.html.

73. For an assessment of the forces behind BJP "moderation," see Thomas Blom Hansen and Christophe Jaffrelot, eds., *The BJP and the Compulsions of Politics*

in India (Delhi: Oxford University Press, 1996), and Ashutosh Varshney, *India's 12th National Elections* (New York: The Asia Society, February 1998), available on web at http://www.asiasociety.org/publications/update_indian_elections.html.

74. For instance, in the 1999 election manifesto, written in cooperation with the BJP's National Democratic Alliance partners, the Ram temple issue did not get top billing. National Democratic Alliance, "For a Proud, Prosperous India: An Agenda," available on web at http://www.bjp.org.

75. This is one of the main points made in Jaffrelot, *Les nationalistes hindous.*

76. Cited in Ashis Nandy et al., "Creating a Nationality: The Ramjanmabhumi Movement and Fear of the Self" in Ashis Nandy, *Exiled at Home* (Delhi: Oxford University Press, 1998), p. 55.

77. I have described this unstable period of searching in Jacques E. C. Hymans "Inside a Bomb Shell," *The Hindustan Times*, April 16, 2001.

78. Concerns about the effect of the South Asian tests on the global nonproliferation regime are ubiquitous. A clear-headed, representative analysis is George Bunn, "The status of norms against nuclear testing," *Nonproliferation Review* Vol. 6, No. 2 (Winter 1999), pp. 20-32.

CHAPTER SEVEN

The International Dynamics of a Nuclear India

Siddharth Varadarajan

Summary

Serious questions arise on the benefits to India of going overtly nuclear in May 1998. There had already existed a state of opaque or existential deterrence between India and its neighbors, China and Pakistan, and whether the 1998 nuclear tests make deterrence any more robust is questionable. Like the general concept of nuclear deterrence, India's declared policy of minimum deterrence remains a chimera. However, UN Security Council Resolution 1172 passed in June 1998 is unprecedented insofar as it urges India and Pakistan to sign the Nuclear Nonproliferation Treaty (NPT) and Comprehensive Test Ban Treaty (CTBT), a demand that cannot be supported by international law. If India's decision to go nuclear may lack strategic, political and economic benefits, there are even more serious flaws underlying the NPT and CTBT that have not been addressed. The U. S. policy of aggressively pursuing its missile defense program further complicates this international state of affairs. It is unfortunate that India, which earlier opposed the global arms race, has now come out in support of the U. S. program.

Going Nuclear

In analyzing the regional and international dynamics of India's decision to test five nuclear devices on May 11 and 13, 1998, it is important to bear in mind exactly what changed and what did not. The fact that India has nuclear weapons was already more or less an open secret. Though the country has had a civilian nuclear program since soon after Independence, it was only in 1964 that its potential military spin-off was officially acknowledged. In that year, Homi Bhabha made a statement—in response to parliamentary questions about China's first nuclear test at Lop Nor—that India could assemble a nuclear weapon in 18 months if the need should so arise.[1] In 1974, the Indira Gandhi government conducted a so-called peaceful nuclear implosion at Pokhran, in reality a simple fission bomb. While the decision to go nuclear was apparently held in abeyance after that, most foreign analysts and governments assumed India had embarked on a dedicated weapons program in 1987.[2] The open development of ballistic missiles like Prithvi and Agni—that have little military value other than as delivery systems for nuclear weapons—added to this sense of certainty about India's intentions. Thus, those governments with a vital interest in the regional and global proliferation of nuclear weapons— China, the United States, Russia, France, Japan, and, of course, Pakistan—had already begun to factor India's arsenal into their strategic calculations. Pokhran-II only served to validate these widely held beliefs.

Likewise, it has been an article of faith for India's strategic elites that Pakistan has had a full-fledged nuclear weapons program for more than two decades. Moreover, many Indian and Western analysts have assumed Pakistan has been in possession of fully assembled nuclear weapons for at least a decade. With the testing of Pakistani nuclear devices at Chagai some two weeks after Pokhran-II, this belief would also seem to be proven correct.

A Critique of India's Strategic Rationalization

Insofar as the stated rationale for nuclear weapons in both India and Pakistan is "minimum deterrence," it is reasonable to surmise that the same was already operating in the bilateral context since well before Pokhran-II and Chagai. Of course, the nonfalsifiable and circular logic of deterrence—the absence of nuclear conflict despite the possession of nuclear weapons by two adversaries is sufficient proof of the validity of the theory—would suggest Pokhran-II and Chagai cannot be explained with reference to that rationale alone. Moreover, since (according to the Indian government) Pakistan's nuclear capabilities have been created by China and, therefore, are fully known by it, Beijing would be extremely foolish to assume New Delhi did not possess a similar—if not more advanced—weapons capability. Thus, deterrence, such as it is, was already operating on the Sino-Indian plane as well, and the absence of nuclear conflict between India and China since 1964 (when China unveiled its nuclear weapons and India acknowledged its capability) or at least since 1974 is sufficient proof of that fact.

It is difficult logically to sustain the claim that Pokhran-II was necessary to make the already existing deterrence (or existential deterrence) more robust and, at the same time, cling to the doctrine of minimum deterrence. In fact, like the concept of deterrence itself, minimum deterrence is a chimera. For if qualitative weapon enhancement—which is what sets apart Pokhran-II from Pokhran-I—is a *sine qua non* of credible and dynamic deterrence, it is inevitable that governments will ceaselessly seek more precise, well-honed nuclear devices that are superior to those possessed by their adversaries and whose only utility would be as first-strike weapons. The experience of the Cold War arms race, the technological history of nuclear weapons, and the latest moves by the United States to develop a missile defense system clearly prove that deterrence is not stable or autonomous but requires continuous ratcheting-up. The draft Indian Nuclear Doctrine authored by the Vajpayee government's National Security Council Advisory Board—which speaks of a triad of aircraft-delivered bombs, land-based missiles and sea-based platforms, as well as space-based assets—also shows how elastic the concept of minimum deterrence really is.

This preliminary excursus on deterrence was necessary in order appreciate better the motives behind Pokhran-II. To sum up the argument so far, the stated passive rationale of wanting to deter Pakistani and Chinese nuclear weapons cannot fully account for the Indian government's decision to test. Rather, there must have been an active reason. New Delhi's decision openly to go nuclear might well have been fuelled by the ruling Bhartiya Janata Party's desire to do something spectacular in order to win popular support but it can only be understood in the context of the Indian ruling elites' international ambitions at a time when the world order is fluid and in transition.

The nuclear tests were a pro-active declaration of intent, the issuing of notice that India has every intention of emerging as a big power and will not confine its ambitions to the regional theater. They were an expression of the Indian state's rejection of a multipolar world that excludes India from the division of the spoils. At the same time, this does not mean India will be able to sustain such an ambition in economic terms, or even that it is unwilling to play along with this or that power in order to further its own interests regionally and globally. Indeed, the BJP-led government's initial pronouncements holding China responsible for its decision to test—articulated directly and in Prime Minister Atal Bihari Vajpayee's explanatory letter to U. S. President Bill Clinton—were intended to signal a willingness on its part to sign up for a loose international alliance against Beijing. In the event, the government seriously miscalculated, for despite the acrimonious debates in U. S. political and intelligence circles about the wisdom of President Clinton's China policy, the national consensus there favors the engagement of Beijing rather than its isolation or explicit containment. In the long-term, this view may change but for the present, U. S. capital is too committed to China to envisage the kind of rupture India would like to see in Sino-American relations.

As far as China is concerned, Pokhran-II has affected it at two interrelated levels. Not only has New Delhi's proclamation of nuclear status been read as a claim to a greater role in the world—this is something Beijing might have lived with—but the explicit identification of China as the "other" suggests this claim is being advanced at the expense of the Chinese. Thus, while Beijing's response to the first set of Indian nuclear tests on May 11 was rather muted, there was a marked difference in the tone and thrust of its official statement following the May 13 explosions. It is self-evident that the change was brought about by the revelation of the contents of Vajpayee's letter to Clinton—in which the Chinese threat was alluded to.

The issue of Chinese missile and nuclear proliferation to Pakistan deserves careful analysis and is not something that should be brushed under the carpet by critics of the Indian government's nuclear or China policy. As a big power with hegemonic regional and global ambitions, China's outlook and policy is not very different from, say, the United States. Proliferation to Pakistan serves several important objectives, especially in the post–Cold War world. First, it ensures the loyalty of Islamabad, desirable as an end in itself and as an entry-point for making inroads into Central Asia.[3] Second, it helps confine a potential rival like India to a narrow, South Asian context. Third, it provides crucial leverage in the strategically important region of West Asia, especially when taken together with its sales of M-9 missiles to Iran and CSS-2 missiles to Saudi Arabia.

Indian analysts often tend to forget that Pakistan sits astride the sea-lanes out of the Persian Gulf and that this fact of geography has played a vital role in U. S. calculations about Pakistan's strategic value.[4] For China, the same logic applies. In October 1991, President Yang Shangkun visited Iran—the first visit by a Chinese head of state—as well as Pakistan, in a tour that was seen by Western analysts as aimed at building a strategic consensus against the post-Desert Storm U. S. dominance of the Gulf. The Chinese side noted the similarity of views on many international and regional issues while President Hashemi Rafsanjani was quoted as saying Iran rejected the U. S.-dominated new world order and its attempts to "interfere in other countries internal affairs by simply accusing them of developing nuclear weapons."[5] As for Pakistan, Yang's visit was significant because it came so soon after Washington's decision, as mandated by the Pressler Amendment, to terminate military aid to Islamabad because of the latter's nuclear weapons program.

While it is doubtful China has provided nuclear-weapons technology to Iran—the latter is a signatory to the Nuclear Non-Proliferation Treaty (NPT), is subject to full-scope safeguards and has repeatedly been certified as weapon-free by the International Atomic Energy Agency (IAEA)—there is little doubt that it has proliferated technology and materials to Pakistan.[6] Most of this collaboration took place after Pokhran-I in 1974 and before China signed the NPT in 1992, but some transfers have taken place since. The United States has deliberately failed to make a determination to this effect mainly because of its inability to do anything about it. This display of U. S. powerlessness has obviously caused consternation and disbelief in Indian official circles. For India, however, there is little *strategic* difference between a wholly indigenous Pakistani nuclear weapon, a purloined one or a gifted one.

So long as Indian and Pakistani nuclear weapons were kept behind a veil of official denial or obfuscation, the United States did not fret too much. Even though the Comprehensive Test Ban Treaty (CTBT) marked a turning point in U. S. policy and suggested Washington's patience with nuclear hold-outs was running out (this point will be discussed at length below), there were no strident demands for the two countries to renounce their weapon option by signing the NPT. This situation changed in the immediate aftermath of the 1998 tests. Not only did the United States and the other four permanent members of the UN Security Council make this demand in a joint communiqué on June 4, 1998, but the full Security Council meeting the next day also passed a resolution to that effect (UNSCR 1172). While all indications are that Washington has today more or less reconciled itself to the fact that India and also Pakistan possess nuclear weapons, Resolution 1172 remains a precedent the United States can invoke to deal with other countries it accuses of developing weapons of mass destruction.

Resolution 1172 is the first explicit reflection of the Indian and Pakistani nuclear tests on the plane of international law and represents a disturbing watershed in at least two important senses. First, it is unprecedented insofar as it urges India and Pakistan to sign the CTBT and NPT. Adherence to the NPT has been raised before by the Security Council only in reference to Iraq (e.g. UNSCR 687, the Gulf War cease-fire resolution) but then Iraq has been a party to the treaty since 1968 and could be expected to conform to its obligations. The case of India and Pakistan, however, is different. It is a common precept in international law that countries cannot be forced to sign treaties they do not wish to and that the obligations of treaties cannot be applied to non-signatories. Apart from Article 34 of the Vienna Convention on the Law of Treaties (1969), which states that "a treaty does not create obligations or rights for a third State without its consent," Articles 2(4) and 2(7) of the UN Charter also guarantee non-coercion and non-intervention. Thus, there is a compelling case for considering the Security Council demand for India and Pakistan to accede to the two treaties to be *ultra vires*.

The second questionable aspect of Resolution 1172 is its linkage of the Indian and Pakistani tests to the omnibus notion of threats to peace and security. Thus, even though it is not enforceable, some of the language of the resolution is reminiscent of Chapter VII of the UN Charter and could conceivably serve as a guide for future enforcement action should a consensus or majority in the Security Council emerge. At any rate, this is the first time that a UN resolution has considered the proliferation of nuclear weapons (rather than their possession or use) to be a threat to international peace and security. The only precedent is the Security Council presidential statement issued after its summit-level meeting in January 1992, in which two paragraphs were devoted to the proliferation of weapons of mass destruction and, specifically, to nuclear proliferation. The context, of course, was the aftermath of the Gulf War against Iraq and the heightened sensitivity of the United States towards the possibility of nuclear, biological, and chemical weapons falling into the hands of an adversary.

That statement, which India also signed in its capacity as a nonpermanent, rotating member of the Security Council said: "The proliferation of all weapons of mass destruction constitutes a threat to international peace and security. The members of the Council commit themselves to working to prevent the spread of technology related to the research for or production of such weapons and to take appropriate action on that end."[7] Even though India lamely justified its acceptance of this sweeping and motivated assertion by making a distinction between vertical and horizontal proliferation[8] the real aim of the statement's instigators was never in any doubt. James Leonard, a former U. S. ambassador to the UN, has said that the Security Council statement is sufficient to give nonproliferation the status of a customary norm of international law, binding on all states whether or not they are signatories to the NPT. He said: "It could pretty well serve as the text of a Security Council resolution in which the Council would go on record as saying 'This is now a norm and we intend to enforce it.'"[9] Resolution 1172 of June 5, 1998 is a step in that direction. Certainly the United States, Britain and Japan would have liked some threat of enforcement but stopped short of this goal only because of the opposition of several nonpermanent members from the developing world, as well as Russia.

The Fallacies of the NPT and CTBT

As a regime, the NPT was a product of the bipolar era. At the same time, even though its drafters could not have anticipated the momentous changes ushered in by the end of the Cold War, its architecture has proved to be remarkably enduring and has continued to dominate the contours of the emerging world order. The purpose of the NPT as far as the United States, Soviet Union, and Britain were concerned was to make sure no more countries (other than France and China) went nuclear. It was an attempt to lock in place the balance of power as it existed on January 1, 1968, and make the emergence of new challengers to the seemingly stable bipolar division of the world that much more difficult.

As Eric Chauvistre has noted, "the NPT was originally aimed at West Germany and other Western states that were considering the acquisition of nuclear weapons. (Only later did) the focus shift to Third World countries."[10] On the same day that Germany acceded, the then British foreign secretary, Michael Stewart, conceded that the "whole future of the NPT (had been) dependent on the position of the Federal republic."[11] The German debate on the NPT was bitter and divisive, with Franz-Jozef Strauss, the defense minister from the ultraconservative Christian Social Union declaring in 1965 that the NPT would be the equivalent of "a new Versailles of cosmic dimensions." When in November 1969, Germany finally signed the NPT it made its accession conditional on a number of factors, such as the continued existence of NATO and its right to withdraw at extremely short notice in the case of an emergency, before even the mandatory three month waiting period.[12]

One of the legacies of this original aim of a non-nuclear Germany was the stipulation—inserted at the insistence of Bonn and Rome—that the NPT would last only 25 years, unless renewed. This legacy was overcome on May 12, 1995, when the state-parties to the NPT voted to extend the treaty indefinitely and unconditionally. This decision was taken even though the five nuclear weapon states had shown themselves to be manifestly disinterested in keeping their side of the NPT bargain, namely undertaking to disarm in accordance with Article VI of the Treaty.

Another legacy of the NPT's original aim is that INFCIRC/153, the document governing the IAEA's right to conduct inspections in nonnuclear-weapons states, is today considered by the United States to be too weak. The IAEA's rights had been limited so as to encourage West Germany, Japan, and Italy to sign the NPT, but Washington would now like to broaden the scope of inspections to make them more intrusive. Many countries fear this will make their sensitive military sites vulnerable to international (mainly U. S.) espionage. The 1993 controversy over the IAEA's demand for special inspections in North Korea based on alleged evidence collected by satellites and other National Technical Means of the United States was an attempt to retrofit the Agency with vastly expanded powers. Since the 1994 'Framework Agreement' between the United States and North Korea led to the IAEA ending its insistence on special inspections and Pyongyang suspending its notice of withdrawal from the NPT, a lid was put on the crisis without the issue of the IAEA's powers having been resolved. Nevertheless, the United States has succeeded in innovating a parallel inspection instrumentality—the UN Special Commission for Iraq (UNSCOM)—that reports directly to the Security Council and not to a more representative body like the IAEA Board of Governors. It has also managed to legitimize the use of National Technical Means, both in the case of Iraq and for purposes of verifying the adherence of state-parties to the CTBT.

If the indefinite and unconditional extension of the NPT legitimized in perpetuity the possession of nuclear weapons in the hands of five nuclear weapons states, the CTBT—which the United States alone out of the five has championed steadfastly since 1994, until, of course, the election of President George W. Bush—sought to build on that regime in two vital ways. First, by asking countries to forswear nuclear tests, it was a way of getting the nuclear holdouts (India, Pakistan, Israel and Cuba) to sign the NPT by the back door and make the latter treaty even more watertight. Second, by allowing for subcritical tests and computer simulation of new and improved fourth generation nuclear weapon designs—a field in which U. S. expertise was far ahead of any other country—it gave Washington an advantage in enhancing its arsenal. As Christopher Paine has argued: "A comprehensive test ban by itself will not prevent additional nations from acquiring a basic fission weapon in the 1 to 30 kiloton range (that goal can only be achieved by a worldwide ban on the production, acquisition and transfer of weapons-usable fissile material). But a test ban would severely limit the ability of current undeclared nuclear states, and future proliferant states, to develop optimized pure fission weapons, and compact boosted fission and two-stage thermonuclear weapons of vastly greater yield, for ballistic and cruise missile delivery. And depending on its scope, a CTB could inhibit further engineering development *by at least some nuclear powers* of a class of very-low-yield nuclear weapons specifically designed for tactical use in regional conflicts—the so-called 'mininukes'—deployment of which would be a major, perhaps fatal blow to nonproliferation" (emphasis added).[13]

The CTBT's scope, of course, was finally fixed at a zero yield and excluded so-called hydrodynamic tests. Only the United States, and arguably France, therefore, have the unambiguous capacity to refine their arsenals purely on the basis of computer codes and simulation. China reluctantly accepted the asymmetry this implied so long as it could lock in place the asymmetry on the Sino-Indian and Sino-Russian planes. As for the United States, Chinese doctrine continues to believe in the value of a limited deterrent, at least for the moment. A second line of defense for China was its insistence on the controversial Entry-into-Force clause—requiring India's accession despite its stated objections to the treaty—in order to delay the CTBT from coming into effect.

Washington's multi-billion dollar Stockpile Stewardship Program is aimed precisely at developing new nuclear weapons in the post-CTBT world. As Paine argues: "This is a program that goes beyond maintaining the six or seven proven weapon designs currently planned for retention in the enduring nuclear weapons stockpile under a CTB. The intent appears to be to preserve the "core" of the current nuclear-weapon-design capabilities of Los Alamos and Livermore through "an increased level of effort" in computer simulation and weapons physics research using a series of large-scale experimental facilities, most of which have yet to be constructed, and could ultimately entail an investment of several billion dollars. In the words of David Sharp, a Los Alamos weapons scientist, "we have to learn to design weapons on the basis of better computations, better modeling, and the testing of components." Some of these proposals come perilously close to what might be characterized by some as a deliberate program to offset, and thereby evade, the intended restrictive effect of a CTB on the ability to design and certify the performance of new nuclear weapons."[14] In a July 1998 report, the Washington-based Institute for Energy and Environmental Research has said that the United States is now focusing its attention on developing pure fusion weapons—which do not require fissile material or explosive testing outside the controlled environment of a laboratory. The institute's scientists argue that the research programs of the National Ignition Facility (under construction at Lawrence Livermore National Laboratory), the joint U. S.-Russian laser experiments at Los Alamos, and the wire-array z-pinch device at Sandia National Laboratory are solely weapon-oriented, as is France's Megajoule laser near Bordeaux.[15]

Regardless of what decision India takes on signing the CTBT in the post-Pokhran-II era—and there are compelling reasons on either side—it is important to realize that the CTBT has nothing to do with disarmament or with reducing the salience of nuclear weapons in the military strategy of the United States or any other nuclear weapon state. On the contrary, the NPT-CTBT apparatus is aimed at ensuring the perpetuation of these weapons as instruments of domination and terror. Both the Clinton administration's August 1993 report to Congress on its test ban policy as well as its sanitized Nuclear Posture Review released in 1994 continue to be couched in the Cold War discourse of extended deterrence. Other documents, declassified in recent years, speak of newer rationales for the use of nuclear weapons, especially "mininukes," "micronukes," and "tiny nukes" in battlefield situations or for deterring an adversary from using weapons of mass destruction against the United States or its allies in any part of the world. These include the United States military's *Doctrine for Joint Operations* and the United States Navy's *Stratplan 2010*.[16]

To summarize, by ensuring (1) the NPT's indefinite extension; (2) a CTBT with enough of a loophole for improving its own weapon designs; (3) an expanded scope for intrusive inspections; and (4) the treatment of non-proliferation as a customary norm of international law at the UN, the United States has assembled for itself a political and legal framework for making permanent its military-technological superiority over all other countries. Central to this is the retention and refinement of nuclear weapons and the centrality of nuclear blackmail as the last resort guarantor of hegemony. "Of all the potential weapons of mass destruction—nuclear, biological an chemical," writes Glenn C. Buchan in a RAND organization study, "nuclear weapons still remain the most militarily useful and the most spectacular as terror weapons. Thus, if weapons of mass destruction (WMDs) continue to proliferate in the world and possessing them has any value either as a deterrent or a war-fighting instrument, nuclear weapons are still the best choice, particularly for an 'established' nuclear power such as the United States."[17]

Problems With a U. S. Nonproliferation Policy

Of course, such a dispensation is guaranteed to be unstable. Because of the law of uneven development, this framework is bound to appear unreasonable and highly rigid to different countries at different points of time. Already multiple long-term challenges to U. S. power are emerging around the world, such as the establishment of the single European currency (which might eventually rival the dollar), the failure of 'dual containment' in the Persian Gulf, the growing clout of China and the possibility of Sino-Russian entente, and so on. The Bush administration's military response to the September 11, 2001, terrorist strikes in New York and Washington will also generate destabilizing dynamics. So long as economic and political rivalries remain dormant or below some threshold level, treaties like the NPT and CTBT present an illusion of stability, of the permanence of U. S. leadership. But when these contradictions cannot any more be contained within the old arrangements, they inevitably lead to tectonic shifts in the global balance of power.

The secret Pentagon strategy documents "Defense Planning Guidance Scenario Set" and "Defense Planning Guidance for Fiscal Years 1994–1999," leaked to the press in February and March 1992,[18] suggest the United States is not unaware of future challenges to its pre-eminence. Indeed, the threats factored in go far beyond the rogue doctrine propounded by the Bush Administration in the aftermath of Iraq's invasion of Kuwait. Thus, it was suggested that Germany and Japan, besides Russia and China, could emerge as potential superpowers and rival the United States in military terms. Though the two documents were disavowed and later replaced by sanitized versions in which all uncharitable allusions to potential rivals were expunged, it is obvious that the United States is planning for a world that is robustly and even antagonistically multipolar. And the key to managing such a world is to preserve, as far as possible, the basic architecture of the NPT, CTBT and the proposed Fissile Materials Cut-off Treaty, as well as developing, at a rapid pace, a missile defense system. Of course, to the extent to which U. S. weapons scientists and politicians feel they might have exaggerated the technological gap between their own arsenal and that of the Chinese—especially in the light of evidence that Beijing might have acquired U. S. weapons designs by clandestine means—the CTBT and FMCT are dispensable.

India's 1998 nuclear tests were initially seen by Washington as a dangerous challenge to the very relevance and rationale of the NPT. And so they were. Not only did Pokhran-II show the NPT to be obsolete and anachronistic—which was already known—but it was also an invitation for other countries to test the treaty's limits. Pakistan followed suit two weeks later and there the present phase of proliferation came to an end. Israel, the only other non-signatory to the NPT with an undeclared nuclear arsenal, has given no indication of wanting to move away from its long-standing policy of ambiguity (that is, "Israel will not be the first country to introduce nuclear weapons into the Middle East"). Nevertheless, it would be naive to think that Pokhran-II and Chagai will not have repercussions elsewhere. Countries that gave up their nuclear weapons option on the understanding that no others would develop them are bound to think again about the usefulness of their decision.

In the region, Iran might feel threatened by Pakistan's nuclear weapons and feel compelled to develop its own arsenal. Another scenario, though less likely, is for Pakistan to pass the nuclear baton–either officially or clandestinely—to Saudi Arabia, a scenario that was once the subject of some speculation in the international media. And in other regions too there are likely to be knock-on effects. In that sense, the Pakistani tests were seen by the United States as especially destabilizing. If there was a marked hardening of Security Council and G-8 attitudes after Chagai, this was mainly because the 'demonstration effect' of Pakistan's tests on nuclear threshold states in the region is considered to be much stronger than India's. The latter's image as a global player is, after all, not really in dispute. For the United States, the most worrisome scenario stemming from the Indian tests was the possibility that China might use them as an excuse to resume testing. That is why, even today, despite the Bush

Administration rejecting the CTBT and pursuing its missile defense program, it is keen for both India and Pakistan to sign the test ban treaty.

One U. S. analyst, Peter van Ham, has described a scenario where "an overt North Korean or Indian nuclear weapons program might also encourage other states in the Middle East and East Asia to pursue a nuclear option. Indeed, should several middle-ranking powers acquire nuclear status, countries such as Japan and Germany would feel real pressure at least to rethink their current policy of nuclear self-denial."[19] In many U. S. accounts, the nuclearization of Germany and Japan is the proliferation equivalent of doomsday, for it would, in some sense, mark the formal end of the post–World War II era. Yet, how real is this possibility?

Stephen Meyer has characterized the dynamics of the nuclear proliferation process as one of technological-motivational convergence. "On the whole," he argues, "the technological aspect of the process is fairly monotonic over time. It increases both quantitatively and qualitatively as time goes on." The nuclear motivation of a country, however, can rise or fall depending on "how the constellations of national and international events and politics develop. As a consequence, any given nation's nuclear propensity may bounce between various levels of weak, moderate and strong."[20]

In technological terms, both Japan and Germany (and several other countries) can go nuclear with virtually no lead-time. In motivational terms, the propensity for either country to go down that path would be directly proportional to the extent of global and regional proliferation and instability, and inversely proportional to the degree of U. S. commitment to extended deterrence via the U. S.-Japan Security Treaty and NATO. A major reason for the U. S. desperation to establish a new role for NATO after the Cold War is the understanding that the dissolution of NATO would be considered by Germany and some other European states as a sufficient compromise of its supreme national interests as to warrant withdrawal from the NPT. Likewise, Washington's reluctance to leave Asia to the Asians or to exclude Japan from its proposed missile defense shield is based on its assessment that Tokyo would then almost immediately nuclearize.

At any rate, important voices have been raised in both countries questioning the viability of the NPT in a changing world. Thus, Erwin Haeckel of the DGAP (the German Society for Foreign Affairs) has argued that "in the circle of the great powers . . . probably in the foreseeable future some actors (Japan, India, the European Community . . .) might come onto the stage who have neither the privileges of being permanent members of the UN Security Council nor enjoy being acknowledged as established nuclear-weapons states. . . . How to overcome this difference in status is not clear . . . but one should not put off considering the idea that some of these new great powers might contemplate making a legitimate claim to nuclear weapons. The NPT would be forced to face a terrible dilemma, a dilemma with apparently no way out."[21] In the academic literature, the possibility of German and Japanese "Gaullists" pushing for independent nuclear arsenals is increasingly being considered. But the real danger stems from missile defense and the inevitable reaction this will provoke from China, even if an economically weakened Russia agrees to scrap or modify the Anti-Ballistic Missile Treaty.

Deterring danger or dangerous deterrence?

If geo-strategic considerations and hegemonic ambitions are the main motivational factors for any country to acquire nuclear weapons, the myth that nuclear deterrence provides a perpetual guarantee against the danger of conflict is the most important ideological smoke screen that they can hide behind. As long as this myth is sustained by U. S. nuclear strategy and substantiated by its perpetual possession of nuclear weapons, other countries—especially those with global ambitions—will almost certainly see some utility in acquiring the same.

One of the imponderables that advocates of deterrence have to grapple with is that the logical conclusion of their doctrine must surely be that more is better and that proliferation of nuclear weapons (in a controlled and gradual manner) will actually help to prevent conflict throughout the world. Indeed, neorealists like Kenneth Waltz and John Mearsheimer have argued this seemingly absurd position with elegance if not persuasiveness.[22] Stephen J. Cimbala, a typical representative of the less is better school, on the other hand, argues that "the logic of 'more is better' applied to nuclear spread is mistaken because it assumes that the decision for or against nuclear war is a rational calculus based on a comparison of costs and benefits coolly evaluated. It is more likely that a decision for or against nuclear first use will be one of desperation or inadvertence, not one based on calculation and deliberation."[23] Of course, the use of nuclear weapons in desperation or inadvertence was as much of a danger for the Cold War adversaries as it is for any other possessor state. On several occasions, the accidental launching of nuclear weapons was averted at the nick of time. The paradox is that deterrence is actually predicated on the possibility of such accidents since, as Louis Beres has argued, "the implementation of ever more stringent measures to prevent the accidental use of nuclear weapons would in most cases impair the credibility of a country's nuclear deterrence position."[24]

On the whole, it is difficult to disagree with van Creveld's assessment that "much of the Western literature on proliferation appears to be distorted, ethnocentric and self-serving. It operates on the principle of *beati sunt possedentes* ('blessed are those who are in possession'); like the various treaties to which it has given rise, its real objective is to perpetuate the oligopoly of 'old' nuclear powers." Thus, he argues, "weapons and technologies that used to be presented as stabilizing when they were in the hands of the great powers were suddenly described as destabilizing when they spread to other countries."[25] In reality, these weapons were destabilizing even when possessed by the two superpowers, and the theology of deterrence their strategists peddled offered little succor to the millions of people around the world worried about the danger of nuclear holocaust.

Nuclear weapons are not acquired for deterrence but for the hegemonic value they confer as currencies of power. In the South Asian context, even if overt nuclearization combined with the doctrine of deterrence does not lead to atomic war, it is likely to delay indefinitely the prospects of normal state-to-state relations between India and Pakistan. It is hardly a coincidence that the Kargil conflict of 1999 occurred so soon after the overt nuclearization of South Asia. The explicit possession of nuclear weapons may act as a barrier to the escalation of Kargil-type situations but the fact is that they also make the occurrence of such situations that much more likely.

The interference of an external power like the United States can produce dangerous situations leading to deterrence breakdown. U. S. contingency plans to destroy or exfiltrate Pakistani nuclear weapons in the event of an Islamist coup against General Pervez Musharraf is a case in point. The journalist Seymour Hersh has written about the actual existence of this plan in the aftermath of the U. S. attack on Afghanistan in 2001. Any coup or regime change in Pakistan which prompts the United States to try and implement such a plan would also prompt the Indian armed forces to be placed on full alert. What would a Pakistani general do if confronted with evidence of an Indian build-up and an impending U. S. missile attack against his nuclear arsenal? He could either choose permanently to lose his weapons and thereby lay Pakistan open to an Indian nuclear strike, or he could choose to use his weapons against India while he still has them.

The premise of deterrence is the possibility that the worst-case scenario of a nuclear first strike might one day happen despite the irrationality of such a strike in military terms. But as Cori Dauber argues, "the problem is that worst-case analysis can lead to self-fulfilling prophecies regarding international relations . . . in which there is no real place for discourse. Even as summits, meetings, negotiations and other forms of discursive communication are increased, they are dominated by a perspective that believes these activities to be sideshows."[26] In other words, talk is cheap. It is only weapons that really matter. So long as Indian and Pakistani elites remain possessed by the deterrence mindset, they will be locked into a situation where negotiations on substantive issues are considered unimportant. And the same applies to Sino-Indian relations as well. What needs to be grasped is that it is friendly relations, and not nuclear weapons, that provide the most durable security.

A Faustian Bargain

Where does all this leave us? The 1998 Pokhran-II and Chagai nuclear tests heightened tension in South Asia. They have not served to enhance the national security interests of India and Pakistan, either in the broad sense of the well-being of the population or even in the narrow sense of state security. True, Pokhran-II did not lead to the kind of isolation of India the United States and

China had initially wanted to see internationally, mainly because of popular revulsion against the hypocrisy of the five nuclear weapon states. But nor have there been any expressions of solidarity with New Delhi. Nuclear weapons have been flaunted in order to assert a claim to a larger global role but it is not certain that the tests have given Indian elites the kind of clout they desire.

If India stands a chance of truly making its mark on the world stage, it can only do so by making a clean break with the big power mindset that has gripped since the days of Rajiv Gandhi or even earlier. The world is sick and tired of nuclear-armed, big powers throwing their weight around, intervening wherever they feel like and imposing their will on small countries. The world does not need another big power of this kind. If India simply wants recognition as a nuclear weapon state, it will be reviled in the world. If it challenges the unequal world system in order to make it genuinely democratic, it will win respect and adulation. Unfortunately, it is clear that New Delhi has not chosen the latter option. Unlike in the past, when the country formally stood against any manifestation of an international arms race, India is today one of the few vocal supporters of the U. S. missile defense program. The Vajpayee government has won the grudging acceptance of its nuclear status by the United States but it has done so by endorsing a program that is bound to undermine the security of not just the world but also specifically of South Asia and India as well.

Notes

1. See Itty Abraham, *The Making of the Indian Atomic Bomb: Science, Secrecy and the Postcolonial State* (New Delhi: Orient Longman, 1999) for a detailed account of the genealogy of Pokhran-II.

2. Virtually no mainstream advocate of the nuclear option in either India or Pakistan has developed maximalist rationales for the Bomb like the Cold War doctrines of mutually assured destruction (MAD) or pure warfighting. The fact that these have not openly been articulated in the South Asian context, however, does not mean they are totally absent. See James H. Lebovic, *Deadly Dilemmas: Deterrence in U. S. Nuclear Strategy* (New York: Columbia University Press, 1990) for an assessment of these doctrines.

3. The Central Asian consideration may not be as important as is commonly assumed given China's success in politically engaging several Central Asian republics via the 'Shanghai process' and the signing of a major oil deal with Kazakhstan by which China will start to access the region's energy resources by pipeline.

4. Recently, Hamza Alavi has reminded us of this point by tracing the origins of Washington's pro-Pakistan tilt in the Cold War to the uncertainty of Iran's reliability as an ally following Mossadegh's nationalization of oil in 1953. See ". . ." in *Economic and Political Weekly*, June 26, 1998.

5. See Lillian Craig Harris, *China Considers the Middle East* (London: I. B. Tauris, 1993), p. 258.

6. See William E. Burroughs and Robert Windrem, *Critical Mass: The Dangerous Race for Superweapons in a Fragmenting World* (New York: Simon and

Schuster, 1994), pp. 60-90, for a fairly credible account of Pakistan's nuclear weapons program.

7. UN Doc S/23500 of January 3, 1992.

8. UN Doc S/PV.3046.

9. Quoted in Siddharth Varadarajan, "Playing Monopoly: The Nuclear Club Wins NPT Extension," *Frontline*, June 2, 1995.

10. Eric Chauvistre, "The Future of Nuclear Inspections," *Arms Control*, Vol. 14, No. 2 (August 1993), p. 51.

11. Quoted in Matthias Kuntzel, *Bonn and the Bomb: German Politics and the Nuclear Option* (London: Pluto Press, 1995), p. 124.

12. See on this period Kuntzel, op cit., and Jeffrey Boutwell, *The German Nuclear Dilemma* (London: Brassey's, 1990).

13. Christopher E. Paine, "Issues in the Test Ban Negotiations," in *The United States, Japan and the Future of Nuclear Weapons* (Washington, D. C.: Carnegie Endowment, 1995), p. 101.

14. *ibid.*, p. 104.

15. Arjun Makhijani and Hisham Zarriffi, *Dangerous Thermonuclear Quest: The Potential of Explosive Fusion Research for the Development of Pure Fusion Weapons* (Takoma Park, MD: IEER, 1998).

16. See Hans M. Kristensen and Joshua Handler, *Changing Targets: Nuclear Doctrine from the Cold War to the Third World* (Washington, D. C.: Greenpeace International, 1995).

17. Glenn C. Buchan, *U. S. Nuclear Strategy for the Post-Cold War Era* (Santa Monica: RAND, 1994), x. He goes on to argue that submarine-launched ballistic missiles should be the core of the U. S. nuclear force, with bombers as back-up, while "the U. S. should be out of the ICBM business since they no longer offer any important advantages and they have distinct liabilities".

18. Patrick Tyler, "Pentagon Imagines New Enemies to Fight in Post-Cold War Era, *New York Times*, February 17, 1992, and "United States Strategy plan calls for insuring no rivals develop," *New York Times*, March 8, 1992, cited in Michael Klare, *Rogue States and Nuclear Outlaws: America's Search for a New Foreign Policy* (New York: Hill and Wang, 1995).

19. Peter van Ham, *Managing Non-Proliferation Regimes in the 1990s: Power, Politics and Policies* (New York: Council for Foreign Policy, 1993).

20. Stephen M Meyer, *The Dynamics of Nuclear Proliferation* (Chicago: University of Chicago Press, 1984), p. 112.

21. Quoted in Kuntzel, *op cit.*, p. 175.

22. See Scott Sagan and Kenneth N. Waltz, *The Spread of Nuclear Weapons: A Debate* (New York: Norton, 1995).

23. Stephen J. Cimbala, "Nuclear Weapons in the New World Order," *Journal of Strategic Studies*, Vol. 16, No. 2.

24. Louis Rene Beres, *Mimicking Sisyphus: America's Countervailing Nuclear Strategy* (Lexington: Lexington Books, 1982), p. 89.

25. Martin van Creveld, *Nuclear Proliferation and the Future of Conflict* (New York: Free Press, 1993).

26. Cori Elizabeth Dauber, *Cold War Analytical Structure and the Post Post-War World: A Critique of Deterrence Theory* (New York: Praeger, 1993), p. 182.

Part III

Technological and Military Dimensions

CHAPTER EIGHT

India's Nuclear Technology Policy: Capabilities and the Aftermath of Testing

Rajendran Raja[1]

Summary

This chapter examines the set of circumstances that led to the decision to test in 1998 and the technological capabilities India possesses to manufacture and deliver nuclear weapons. The question is posed as to whether going nuclear has India safer as a result or whether it has merely added to the instability in the region. Perhaps the history of foreign aggression against India over the ages and the partiality of the United States to China are two contributing factors to India going nuclear. The main fallout from nuclear testing has been the sanctions against India by the United States. These involved, among other measures, expelling scientists of Indian origin from the United States and banning Indian Scientists from participating in pure research in the United States at places such as Fermilab. It culminated in the United States denying travel funds to eight physicists to take part in a pure research conference held at the Tata Institute. The author was one such affected. The measures taken by the U.S High Energy Physics community to fight such sanctions is detailed. Finally the juxtaposition is made of the Indian heritage of Gandhian nonviolence and the current Indian capability to produce nuclear weapons. I argue that India has lost moral prestige as a result of the tests, something that is more significant than any gains made as a result of becoming a nuclear power.

Introduction

My interest in nuclear nonproliferation started in the early 1970s, when as a graduate student at the Cavendish Laboratory, I shared an office with Professor Otto Frisch, the father of nuclear fission, who had recently retired. We would argue at length as to whether it was necessary to actually drop the nuclear bomb on Japan to end World War II or whether a demonstration at sea of the weapon would have been sufficient. Frisch would hold that it was actually necessary to drop the bombs, since the Japanese were very belligerent. I would question then whether the second bomb was also necessary. Would not waiting an extra month not have ended the war? We never converged, but in the process of this discussion, we dwelled on several issues pertinent to nonproliferation.

In what follows, I will give a brief history of India's nuclear development, discuss the present nuclear capability and delivery systems and examine whether becoming a nuclear state has made India more secure. I will then give a historical review of aggression on the Indian subcontinent, beginning with the eleventh century A.D. and examine the pressures on India that led her to test nuclear weapons in May 1998. I will examine the impact of the tests on the Kashmir issue and examine the political fallout from the nuclear testing.

A Brief History of India's Nuclear Adventure

In 1945, when the first atomic bomb destroyed Hiroshima, Mahatma Gandhi uttered the following words: "I did not move a muscle, when I first heard that an atom bomb had wiped out Hiroshima. On the contrary, I said to myself, 'Unless now the world adopts nonviolence, it will spell certain suicide for mankind.'"[2]

Following Indian independence, the Tata Institute of Fundamental Research (TIFR) and Bhabha Atomic Research Center (BARC) were founded by Homi Bhabha with encouragement from the first prime minister of India, Pandit Jawaharlal Nehru, who also acted as his own minister of science. TIFR's function was solely to conduct pure research and BARC's explicit role was to harness nuclear energy to provide for the electric power needs of a post-independence industrial India. India in the early days managed to acquire nuclear reactor technology from a number of western countries such as Canada (CANDU reactors) and the United States (Tarapur).

The Gandhian edict against the use of nuclear energy for military ends managed to prevent the development of the Indian bomb well into the late 1960s. It was only after the Bangladesh War of 1971 that an India under Indira Gandhi, emboldened by the military victory against Pakistan, decided to test a nuclear device of its own. In 1971, she gave the order to go ahead with the test. It took two years to complete under top secrecy and was reportedly beset with problems with electronic detonators that force the nuclear material together. In 1974, India conducted its first test of a "peaceful nuclear device," the so-called "Smiling Buddha" detonation in the Rajasthan desert at Pokharan. Estimates of the yield vary but center around 12 kilotons of TNT, somewhat smaller than the Nagasaki bomb of 20 kilotons.

China, on the other hand, made remarkable progress in the 1960s in developing nuclear weapons. In a 32 month period, China successfully exploded its first atomic bomb (October 16, 1964), launched its first nuclear missile (October 25, 1966), and detonated its first hydrogen bomb (June 14, 1967).

After much hand-wringing by various governments, on May 11, 1998, India conducted 3 nuclear tests of a 12 kiloton conventional fission device (an improved version of its 1974 device), a 43 kiloton thermonuclear device and a device smaller than a kiloton. Enriched plutonium is the suspected fuel, although for the small devices, enriched uranium may have been used. This was followed days later by two small devices at a different site. In both cases, the devices concerned were exploded simultaneously. P. K. Iyengar, former chairman of the Indian Atomic Energy Commission (AEC) and a key player in the development of the 1974 device, said in an interview that the tests show that India has three categories of nuclear weapon design: a low-yield tactical weapon, a full-size fission weapon, and a thermonuclear weapon. He added that these three options should satisfy the military's interests.

Seismic tests analysts have disputed India's claim of the strength of the devices, but a New Scientist report supports the Indian claim, citing a University of Leeds seismic expert, Prof. Roger Clark, whose calculations tend to buttress the Indian claims of the yield.[3] Debate continued in the pages of Science Magazine on the strengths of the Indian tests and the ability of seismic monitoring to verify the CTBT. India continues to maintain that it exploded a hydrogen bomb. R. Chidambaram, the AEC chairman, has said that India can explode a 200 kiloton device, if it chooses to do so. Others in the west have cast doubt on this, speculating that what was exploded was a fusion-boosted fission device that is technologically less challenging.

Delivery Systems

India has developed missile systems named Prithvi with a range of 250 km and Agni with a range of 1500 km that are capable of delivering nuclear weapons. These could already be mass produced and are capable of reaching as far as the Chinese cities of Beijing and Shanghai. India is thus capable of conducting retaliatory strikes against nations that threaten it with nuclear power, although the Indian government has foresworn the first use of nuclear weapons. There is also not much evidence that India or Pakistan have begun nuclear missile deployments as of this date.

According to an article in *Jane's Defence Weekly*, Indian scientists are reportedly developing a longer version of the intermediate range ballistic missile Agni-

III with a 3,500 km reach: "Together with the just test-fired two stage solid fuel 2,000-km range Agni-II, designed to carry nuclear warhead, Agni-I, already test fired three times, and short range surface-to-surface missiles Prithvi I and II, surface-to-air Akash and Trishul missiles and to be acquired Russian-300V anti-tactical ballistic missile, the Agni-III, being developed now, will form India's minimum nuclear deterrent (MND)."[4] The defense journal claimed that along with land-based missiles, India was also on the threshold of deploying submarine launched ballistic missile Dhanush, which could later also be deployed on surface warships.

Does Being a Nuclear State Make India Safer?

India shares common borders with China and Pakistan who have been at war with India since independence, China once (1962) and Pakistan on three occasions. China and Pakistan are allies. The Soviet Union, which used to be aligned with New Delhi, is no more. Instead one has a weakened Russia that is hardly likely to want to come to India's defense in times of war. The United States looked the other way as Pakistani trained and supported insurgents wreaked havoc in Kashmir. This was the post–Cold War situation that successive Indian governments have found themselves in. It was clear that Indian defenses needed to be shored up. The question clearly is, do the last round of nuclear tests and the subsequent weaponization make India safer?

The answer may be found in the situation faced by Argentina during the Falklands War. Here was Argentina, a non-nuclear state, engaged in a full-fledged war with Great Britain, which possesses the H-bomb and the needed delivery systems. One can speculate whether Great Britain would have dared to use these weapons against Argentina, had the course of the war swung against Britain in Argentina's favor. The answer has to be clearly no. Margaret Thatcher did not have the nuclear option, since using the bomb to win the war would have forever damned her nation in the eyes of the world and would have invited economic retaliation from most of the world and in-kind retaliation at a future date from vengeful factions sympathetic to Argentina. The answer clearly has to be that first use of nuclear weapons even in the course of a war is highly destabilizing and is not an option for any civilized government. One can then ask what would have happened if Argentina faced not a civilized government, but a ruthless government that engages in terrorism? Such a government can sponsor terrorists to deliver nuclear weapons to its objects of terror much the same way as the embassy bombings in Nairobi. It does not need to go to war overtly. So war or no war, the threat would have been real. Possessing nuclear weapons does not necessarily deter a terrorist nuclear attack, since nuclear retaliation against a band of a hundred to a thousand people is difficult unless one can prove state-sponsorship of that terrorism beyond a reasonable doubt. The only possible justification for the use of nuclear weapons is when a nation and a people are faced with conquest and annihilation as a result of aggression by another nation.

A case can thus be made that the proliferation of nuclear weapons in the subcontinent has increased the likelihood of the extremist organizations in the region acquiring small nuclear weapons and using them covertly against their avowed enemies anywhere in the world. No missile defense technology can defend against a nuclear bomb delivered in a suitcase. One has thus to conclude that the recent spate of nuclear tests in the subcontinent has increased the tension and has made both nations less safe. The economic sanctions, if continued long enough, will also adversely affect the stability of the region, and India is less safe as a result.

The Impact of India's Historical Experience

Before condemning the Indian action as unwise, one should also look at political instability in the region over the course of history. It is true that since eleventh century, North India has seen a string of invasions: Ghazni (1026), Ghori(1192), Mongols (1221), Timur (1398), Mughals (1526), and Nadir Shah (1739). The last resulted in the loss of Shah Jehan's famous Peacock throne. India also suffered economic warfare at the hands of the European powers, especially the British East India Company that exploited the existing political instability at that time. These invasions have occurred at times when the central power and defenses in Delhi was weak, devastating Indian culture and economy. V. S. Naipaul wrote the book *India-A Wounded Civilization* to take note of this. It is only natural that the modern rulers in Delhi took a page out of India's long history and concluded, "Never again will we be weak." Subsequent events, however, have shown that this course of action has not made India any stronger or more secure.

The other factor that impelled the Indian government towards nuclearization has clearly to be the partial treatment successive U. S. governments have shown the communist dictatorship in Beijing. Until 1998, relations between the United States and China were cozy. Since then, allegations of Chinese spying at a U. S. nuclear weapons lab, and the NATO bombing of the Chinese Embassy in Belgrade, have put U. S.-China relations on a more difficult plane. For the greater part, however, since Nixon's opening to China in 1972, successive U. S. governments have shown a blind eye towards large-scale abuses of human rights in China and rewarded totalitarian behavior by giving China most-favored nation status, a permanent seat in the UN Security Council. Chinese heads of state visiting Washington are given the highest red-carpet welcomes. The UN privilege is enjoyed by all five members of the nuclear club. This partiality extends even to scientific cooperation ventures. The U. S. position is that the only way to wean China away from her Communist political system is to teach her capitalist economics and to engage her constructively.

India wonders whether it is the United States that is reforming China or whether it is China that is corrupting the United States. The Indian defense minister, George Fernandes even announced a few weeks before the 1998 Indian nuclear tests that it is China and not Pakistan that is India's "main threat", perhaps thereby signaling the coming nuclear tests.

The harsh U. S. reaction to the tests (sanctions, suspension of scientific collaborations, repatriation of Indian scientists visiting the United States who were unconnected to the nuclear issue, denial of visas to scientists wishing to visit the United States, and preventing U. S. scientists from attending conferences held in India) is clearly to be contrasted to the lack of reaction when China and France last conducted nuclear tests in violation of the Comprehensive Test Ban Treaty (CTBT), which neither had then signed.

It is clear that this puzzling asymmetry in U. S. behavior is to a great extent to blame in driving the Indian government to test. The United States also looks weak when it tries to persuade the nuclear have-nots to sign the CTBT while sitting on a nuclear arsenal of approximately 10,000 weapons. To gain credibility, a bona fide effort to reduce the number of weapons to an acceptable non-zero level (in the hundreds) will have to be made by all the nuclear powers.

An unfortunate and perhaps unforeseen effect of the current spate of tests by India and Pakistan is that the Kashmir issue, which was languishing on a bilateral backburner, has suddenly found "legs" and been elevated to a high-profile item in the international list of "problems to be solved." This clearly is not beneficial to the Indian position and may in the course of the next few years be seen to have been an unfortunate outcome of these tests. Current hostilities between India and Pakistan underscore this point.

Fallout from Nuclear Testing

On May 13, 1998 the U. S. government imposed sanctions on India, "in accordance with Section 102 of the Arms Export Control Act, also known as the Glenn amendment." This involved:

1. Termination of assistance under the Foreign Assistance Act of 1961, except for humanitarian assistance for food or other agricultural commodities;
2. Termination of sales of defense articles, defense services, or design and construction services under the Arms Export Control Act, and termination of licenses for the export of any item on the United States munitions list;
3. Termination of all foreign military financing under the Arms Export Control Act;
4. Denial of any credit, credit guarantees, or other financial assistance by any department, agency, or instrumentality of the U. S. government;
5. The United States opposition to the extension of any loan for financial or technical assistance by any international financial institution;

6. Prohibition of U. S. banks from making any loan or providing any credit to the Government of India, except for the purposes of purchasing food or other agricultural commodities; and

7. Prohibition of export of specific goods and technology subject to export licensing by the Commerce Department.

On May 28, Pakistan conducted tests and U. S. Sanctions were applied also. In July 1998, seven Indian scientists were expelled from the United States and a blacklist of 63 Indian and 5 Pakistani institutions was announced. The Tata Institute of Fundamental Research and the Bhabha Atomic Research Center were on that list.

The D0 experiment at the Tevatron collider at Fermilab, in which I participated, and which discovered the top quark in 1995, has collaborative efforts with a number of Indian institutions namely TIFR and the Universities of Panjab and Delhi. As a result of the sanctions, the Department of Energy (DoE) suspended the collaboration between D0 and TIFR. Two TIFR graduate students who were stationed at D0 left for India when their visas expired, while Fermilab sought clarification with the DoE on their status. No further scientists from TIFR were allowed to come to Fermilab. The Indian flag is one of several international flags flown at the front of the Fermilab high-rise building. The DoE ordered the Fermilab director to take the flag down, even though the sanctions were aimed at TIFR only and not at the other Indian collaborating institutions. TIFR had spent the equivalent of $500,000 in hardware contributions to the upgrade of the D0 detector. The hardware was delivered to D0, but the scientists could not visit Fermilab to install the hardware. In January 1999, TIFR held an international conference on High Energy Physics entitled the XIII Topical workshop on Hadron Collider Physics. It had major participants from the United States, Japan, and Europe, as well as scientists from India. Of the U. S. physicists participating in the conference, 21 were from U. S. universities and 8 from national laboratories run by the DoE (7 from Fermilab and 1 from Argonne National Laboratory). The DoE denied travel funds to those 8 physicists to attend the TIFR conference, while 21 physicists from U. S. Universities participated.

It should be pointed out that the high-energy physics research conducted at Fermilab and TIFR is totally open and has no national security implications. The results from the research are presented at open conferences and published in peer–reviewed journals. I was one of the invited speakers at the conference and one of the 8 physicists denied travel funds. I asked the Fermilab directorate whether it was all right to travel using my own funds to the conference and give the invited talk as a private citizen. I was told that there was nothing wrong with this, and I then proceeded to the conference using my own funds and gave the talk as planned.

A letter signed by the international participants of the conference was sent to Bill Richardson, the Secretary of the Department of Energy, deploring the unprecedented denial of travel funds to U. S. physicists. It said in part, "Restriction of access of U. S. national laboratory scientists to open conferences is antithetical to the spirit of scientific inquiry; is wholly unprecedented in basic research over the past 50 years; and is wholly irrelevant to national security concerns. We strongly urge that the restrictions on U. S.-Indian scientific collaborations by the U. S. Government be removed." This was followed by another letter to the DoE and the State Department from the D0 experiment signed by 195 people. Both of these letters were met with responses from the State Department that stated that the sanctions were "a regrettable consequence of India and Pakistan's decisions to conduct nuclear tests" and gave little encouragement for an early lifting of the restrictions.

It was only with the visit of President Clinton to India that the U. S. government relented and removed TIFR from the entities list. The ban on BARC is still in effect as of this writing. Currently, the TIFR physicists have resumed their collaboration in D0, and the Indian flag once again flies at Fermilab. As of this writing neither India nor the United States has signed the Comprehensive Test Ban Treaty (CTBT), though India has announced a voluntary moratorium on further testing. The sanctions presumably will remain in effect till India signs the CTBT or there is further warming of relations.

One can ask whether there was any measurable impact on the Indian economy due to the U. S. sanctions. The answer clearly has to be in the negative. The trade relations between the two countries were largely unaffected. The restrictions on exporting some items from the United States to India that could be deemed sensitive might have had some impact, but most of these restrictions could be circumvented by finding alternate vendors from other nation not participating in the sanctions. The effect due to restrictions on pure research, such as between TIFR and Fermilab, was felt personally and intensely by scientists who felt that it was wrong to conduct foreign policy in such a manner. The lifting of TIFR sanctions was a result of much lobbying by distinguished scientists and educators of U. S. origin.

Is Science to Blame?

It is perhaps easy to blame science and technology for the nuclear tension the world has lived through during the years following the World War II. It is sobering and instructive to look at the present situation from another perspective that also has largely been acquired through scientific endeavor during the same years. We now know more about our position as a planet and a species in the larger scheme of things. We know now that our sun is a middling star in one of the corners of the Milky Way Galaxy that contains approximately 300 billion stars. In the known Universe, there are hundreds of billions of such galaxies. A large hydrogen bomb that can wipe out a city is about 20 megatons of TNT in size. The sun puts out the equivalent of 76 billion megatons of

TNT energy every second! Nuclear fusion is very common in this Universe, and most of the time it is used constructively. However, there are phenomena in the Universe that are far more violent and destructive. A supernova occurs in a galaxy once every 100 years or so. In a few tenths of a second, when the star explodes as a supernova, it puts out so much energy in visible light that it will take the sun 8 billion years shining at its present rate to output an equivalent amount! The entire solar system of the supernova is destroyed, and the neutrinos from the supernova will kill life even in neighboring solar systems. Yet even the supernova, violent though it is, is essential for life, since all the heavy elements we see around us, including most of our bodies, are made in supernova explosions.

Nature, when it uses violence, does so for a purpose! Speaking in a personal scientific capacity, I would hypothesize that the Universe is teeming with life. No doubt, this is merely a statement of probability. However, there are billions of galaxies in the observable Universe. If certain inflationary scenarios of the Big Bang are correct, the observable Universe may only be a tiny fraction of the whole, which may even be infinite. There must be civilizations that have harnessed nuclear energy, similar to ours and some that have used it peacefully and others that have destroyed themselves because they could not see the larger picture. Both of these cases are "natural." The question is: "What is it going to be for the third planet in the solar system?" The bottom line is, when all is said and done, it is a small fragile planet, and we all have to share it peacefully during the small number of years we each inhabit it.

At the dawn of the nuclear era, a statement in Poona on July 1, 1946, by Mahatma Gandhi will illustrate the degree to which India has deviated from his wisdom: "It has been suggested by American friends that the atom bomb will bring Ahimsa (nonviolence) as nothing can. . . . So far as I can see, the atomic bomb has deadened the finest feeling that has sustained mankind for ages. There used to be the so-called laws of war that made it tolerable. Now, we see the naked truth. War knows no law except that of might. The atomic bomb brought an empty victory to the allied arms but it resulted for the time being in destroying the soul of Japan. What has happened to the soul of the destroying nation is yet too early to see."[5] This quote is directed in the Gandhian sense not just at America, but all nations that would use nuclear weapons, even in retaliation.

The events of September 11, 2001

The recent terrorist bombings of the World Trade Center buildings in New York have cast a horrific pall on the world stage. It has brought the whole world to the brink of prolonged war. The promise of peace that was the legacy of the end of the cold war seems to fade rapidly, to be replaced by uncertainty, distrust and strife. India and Pakistan with their nuclear arsenals have now to learn to cool their rhetoric and passions and not get into uncontrollable situations brought on by opportunism. While the situation in Afghanistan is being brought under control, utmost restraint has to be exercised by both the governments in India and Pakistan. After the Afghan situation has stabilized, the Kashmir problem can be tackled, once both sides agree to avoid the methods of terrorism to achieve their ends. It will then be realized that borders cannot be determined by religion and that the status quo is the only stable solution.

Conclusions

India and Pakistan are nuclear powers and the status quo has been altered, irrevocably. I have argued that going nuclear has not increased the security of the countries on the subcontinent, if anything quite the reverse. The great contribution that India has made to the world in the twentieth century is the use of active nonviolence to combat the forces of oppression. The greatest empire known to man, ceased to exist for all intents and purposes within a period of 20 years after the dawn of Indian independence. This is entirely due to the power of the method, pioneered by Gandhi, which also contributed to the peaceful transition to equal civil rights for all in the United States. This is testimony to the power of nonviolence. It is that legacy that India must preserve at all costs. The recent attempt to join the nuclear club has affected that heritage negatively. The events of September 11, 2001 and their aftermath have made the situation in the subcontinent even more precarious. Utmost restraint will have to be exercised by all sides in the coming days to avoid nuclear confrontations.

Notes

1. The views expressed in this paper are those of the author alone and do not represent that of any organization with which he is affiliated or associated.
2. Mahatma Gandhi, in a speech given at New Delhi, September 24, 1946, quoted in M. Gandhi, "Essential writings," published by Gandhi Peace Foundation, V. V. Ramana Murthy, ed.
3. Debora Mackenzie, article in *New Scientist,* June 13,1998.
4. *Jane's Defence Weekly,* May,1999.
5. Mahatma Gandhi, in a speech given at Poona, July 1, 1946, quoted in M. Gandhi, "Essential writings," published by Gandhi Peace Foundation, V. V. Ramana Murthy, ed.

CHAPTER NINE

Ballistic Missiles:
Complicating the Nuclear Quagmire

Ben Sheppard

Summary

Since the early 1990s India and Pakistan have been steadily moving their nuclear deterrence from aircraft based to ballistic missile based with potentially devastating results for the Indo-subcontinent's stability. The introduction of nuclear capable ballistic missiles on a significant scale adds to the negative variables that collectively raises the risk of an inadvertent nuclear war breaking out in a region that is unstable principally due to the Kashmir territorial dispute. The ongoing ballistic missile development signifies that the region is adopting a new and more precarious strategic dimension. India and Pakistan's missile developments are arguably a greater threat to South Asia's stability than the nuclear tests of 1998 that merely underlined they were nuclear powers. Despite signs of cooling relations between India and Pakistan highlighted by the Lahore Accord of February 1999, in practice very little has been achieved to stem the proliferation of nuclear weapons and ballistic missiles. Only two months after the much heralded Lahore Accord and bus diplomacy, the region witnessed the largest round of missile tests with India launching the 2,500 km Agni-II followed by Pakistan's flight test of the 2,000–2,300 km-range Ghauri-II/Hatf-VI and the Shaheen-I/Hatf-IV (750 km) within days of each other.

The effects of ballistic missiles on South Asia's stability must be viewed through a three-way perspective of Pakistan-India-China. This three-way relationship has been and will continue to be crucial to our understanding of ballistic-missile proliferation within the region. The implications missiles have for stability between India and Pakistan will be closely examined in this chapter followed by the changing strategic climate between New Delhi and Beijing.

Following this analysis, I will discuss how the conventional balance of power between Islamabad and New Delhi has been undermined by the procurement of missiles and the repercussions this has for avoiding a nuclear war. The chapter takes a long-term view at the possible implications of missile proliferation in the region as India and Pakistan look set to continue augmenting their capabilities. To understand the significance of India and Pakistan's ongoing transition from aircraft-based to missile-based deterrent, it is first necessary to outline their respective missile programs.

Missile Capabilities

A survey of the missile programs, acquisitions and capabilities in the region will indicate the nature of the problem. It is the nature, effectiveness, and credibility of delivery systems for nuclear weapons that will ultimately determine the nuclear military balance and the conditions of stability.

Pakistan

The Islamic nation has embarked on one of the most dramatic missile programs in the developing world in light of its present and emerging ballistic missile systems. The remarkable aspect is not so much in Pakistan's missile capabilities, but in the relatively short time it has taken for Islamabad to procure advance missiles through its extensive foreign connections, notably from China and North Korea. India's first test of the Agni-I missile in 1989, coupled with the U. S. blocking of the delivery of F-16 aircraft to Pakistan in 1990, led Islamabad to conclude that missiles were the most effective means to counter New Delhi's strategic buildup. At the time of India's Agni-I launch in 1989, Pakistan's missile arsenal, composed only of the Hatf-I (80 km) and Hatf-II (300 km) lacked guidance and control functions.[1] With a maximum warhead payload weight of 500 kg, the Hatf-I and Hatf-II are unlikely to have been nuclear capable considering first generation nuclear warheads tend to weigh 1,000 kg.

The Hatf-I has since been improved with the successful launch of the Hatf-IA in February 2000. With a range of 100 km, the Haft IA includes improved guidance systems and can deliver a greater payload. The Hatf-I and II sounding rocket technology based on the three decades of experience in this area provided Pakistan with the foundation to develop a credible nuclear force based on missiles to strike key Indian targets. However, this goal has only been achieved through significant foreign assistance. There are two main ballistic missile programs in Pakistan. First, the Chinese-based Shaheen systems (750 km-range Shaheen-I, 2,500-km range Shaheen-II, and possibly a 3,000 km-range Shaheen-III), second the North Korean based Ghauri missiles (1,500-km-range Ghauri-I, 2,300-km range Ghauri-II, and the 3,000 km-range Ghauri-III).

In 1992 Pakistan received from China around 30 M-11 (CSS-7/DF-11) missiles, which are capable of carrying a nuclear warhead to a range of 280 km.

The missiles are believed to be stored at Sargodha Air Force Base west of Lahore and can probably be deployed in the field within a matter of days of an order to become operational.[2] China is understood to have provided the technology for Pakistan's Shaheen-I/Hatf-IV and Shaheen-II missiles. The 750-km range Shaheen-I was successfully flight tested in April 1999 and was reported by *Jane's Defence Weekly* to have entered serial production in mid-1998.[3] If this missile did enter production before its maiden flight test, the solid-fuel Shaheen-I may be based on an existing design, probably China's solid-fuel 800-km range M-9 missile. It is unusual practice for new missiles to enter serial production before flight testing, unless they are based on an already-proven weapon system.

According to a U. S. intelligence draft report in August 1996 Pakistan was building a missile factory using blueprints and equipment supplied by China for serial production of what was then believed to be the M-11.[4] This facility may have since started to manufacture the Shaheen-I.[5] The Shaheen-II was first displayed at the Pakistan Day military parade in Islamabad in March 2000 and was exhibited alongside the Shaheen-I at the Pakistan defense exhibition in November 2000. Like the Shaheen-I, the Shaheen-II is also believed to be nuclear capable. In late 2000 the Shaheen-II was said to be ready for flight-testing.

China is not the only nation to play a significant role in Pakistan's missile programs—North Korea has been critical to the Islamic nation's development of a credible nuclear-tipped missile capability. In December 1993 then Prime Minister Benazir Bhutto visited Pyongyang to secure North Korea's help in developing ballistic missiles referred by Pakistan as the Ghauris. The Ghauri program offered Pakistan its first medium-range ballistic missiles and importantly the ability to deliver a nuclear warhead to the heart of Indian territory. There are three Ghauri variants: Ghauri-I/Hatf V (1,500 km) and Ghauri-II/Hatf VI (2,300 km) tested in April 1998 and 1999, and a longer-range variant called the Ghauri-III/Abdali with a range of 3,000 km. Pakistan successfully conducted a static engine test of its Ghauri-III in September 1999.[6] The propulsion system and general design for of the Ghauris are based on North Korean rocket technology. The introduction of North Korea into the missile equation enables Pakistan to procure missiles with greater range than the Chinese connection provides. Pyongyang's assistance provides Islamabad with a willing supplier of intercontinental ballistic missile (ICBM) technology. China, despite possessing ICBMs, is unlikely to export related technologies in view that such transfers would be an overresponse and counterproductive to Beijing's efforts to maintain a balance of power in its southern region. North Korea is less likely to hold such concerns.

On August 31 1998 North Korea launched a three-stage rocket referred to as the Taepodong in an attempt to place a satellite into the earth's orbit. Despite failing to place a satellite, North Korea called the Kwangmyongsong No. 1 into orbit. The essential truth is that all three stages of the rocket separated successfully. In December 1998 Donald Rumsfeld, prior to becoming Secretary of

Defense for President George W. Bush, informed *Jane's Intelligence Review* that "The 3 stage ballistic missile launched suggests that North Korea is only a relatively short step from a deployable ICBM capability."[7] The transfer of North Korea's 1,500-km range Nodong-1 technology to Pakistan for the Ghauri-I/Hatf-V raises the serious prospect of Islamabad acquiring Pyongyang's multistage Taepodong rocket technology. This would provide the foundation for Pakistan to develop ICBMs. Certainly Islamabad aims to induct missiles that could deliver a nuclear warhead to all of India, thus strengthening its nuclear deterrent.

The interception by Indian authorities in June 1999 of a ship carrying large amounts of missile technology from North Korea to Pakistan reaffirmed the importance of Pyongyang to Islamabad's missile program. Strategically Pakistan has no need to develop missiles with a range greater than the 3,000-km range Ghauri-III. The furthest distance from the most westerly points in Pakistan on the border with Iran and Afghanistan, and the far northwestern corner to the most southerly point of India is 3,000 km. In view of this Pakistan may be content with developing missiles with ranges no greater than 3,000 km. Having the option of deploying missiles at the furthest distance from the Indian border and still being able to target any part of India would enhance the survivability of Islamabad's nuclear-tipped missile force.

Although Pakistan has no need to procure a missile of intercontinental range, considering a missile of 3,000 km is sufficient to cover all of India, for prestige purposes Pakistan might feel compelled to demonstrate it can match India at the ranges India tests at. This may be done under the auspices of developing its own Satellite Launch Vehicle (SLV), a route North Korea has taken. SLV and ICBM rocket technologies are virtually indistinguishable. Islamabad is more than capable of developing a comprehensive nuclear-tipped missile force against India.

The drive behind Pakistan's missile program is not solely the need to counter India's strategic developments, but until April 2001 had been fuelled by fierce competition between the two heads of the missile programs: Abdul Qadeer Khan of the Kahuta Research Laboratories (KRL) and Samar Mubarak Mund of the National Development Complex (NDC).

Competition in Pakistan

Until Abdul Qadeer Khan's retirement in April 2001, the KRL (which develops the North Korean-based liquid-fuel Ghauris) was in fierce competition with Samar Mubarak Mund's NDC who are behind the Chinese based Shaheen missile systems. This competitiveness gave rise to two separate missile programs of similar ranges rather than concentrating Pakistan's scarce resources on a single program. The end result was the development of the KRL's 2,300 km range Ghauri-II and the NDC's 2,500 km range Shaheen-II and later the prospect of a 3,000 km range Ghauri-III and Shaheen-III (as of early 2001 there had been no official reports of a Shaheen-III program but the development of this missile cannot be ruled out). Although work on the Ghauri-III had already started prior to Khan's departure, the future of this missile program and the Ghauris in general was unclear in mid-2001. Javed Arshad Mirza took over from Khan as the new chairman of the KRL.

Umer Farooq, a defense analyst based in Islamabad, commented that the rivalry "came to surface after the May 1998 nuclear explosions [with] both claiming credit for the nuclear tests."[8] Prior to Khan's departure and Musharaf taking power, a well-placed source in Pakistan revealed, "There is a clear rift between Mund and Qadeer [Khan]. It became fairly embarrassing for the government, and sources say Nawaz [Sharif] himself intervened between the feuding scientists to ask them to not make their differences publicly."[9] He added, "while the government say the efforts [for the missile programs] have been converged and no one is working on cross-purposes, some people indicate privately that this is not the case. In fact, a certain degree of competition is perhaps being encouraged to get optimum results from both sides." So intense was the rivalry between the two that reportedly they refused to shake hands with each other.

It is understood that Pakistan's government first encouraged an element of rivalry in the missile programs to provide the nation with a credible missile capability, but this then got out of hand. There is speculation over the future of the KRL's role in developing ballistic missiles, and it may be that the NDC will be given preferential funding (particularly for R&D) to develop the favored solid-fuel Shaheen missiles over the North Korean-based liquid-fuel Ghauri systems that were probably procured as a stop-gap measure until the more reliable and flexible Shaheen's came on line. Compared to liquid-fuel missiles the solid-fuelled systems do not require a number of hours to prepare for launch and are easier to maintain once deployed in the field.[10] In addition solid-fuel missiles are relatively easy to move thus making them simpler to hide and shelter from an preemptive attack. The changes in the KRL are unlikely to mean the Ghauri-I and Ghauri-II will be taken out of service. With considerable resources already poured into this North Korean-based missile, Pakistan may allow the Ghauri-I and Ghauri-II to go through serial production and remain in service for their life span as originally planned.

India

India possesses one of the most advanced missile programs outside the original five declared nuclear states. With its sophisticated missile and space programs, New Delhi is technically capable of indigenously developing nuclear-tipped missiles comparison in range to the long-term members of the nuclear club India joined with its nuclear tests in April 1998. The Agni-II test in April 1999 heralded not only the resumption of the Agni program but more importantly signified India's intention of inducting missiles capable of striking deep inside China. There were no Agni launches between the 1994 and 1999 tests.

Research into ballistic missiles began in the 1960s under the Defense Research and Development Organization (DRDO). In July 1983 India created the Integrated Guided Missile Development Program (IGMDP) with the aim of developing an indigenous missile infrastructure. The IGMDP's first indige-nously-developed missile was the Prithvi (meaning "Earth") of which there are to be three variants: a support version for the Indian Army with a range of 150 km referred to as the SS-150; a medium-range missile of 250 km (SS-250) for the India Airforce; and a boosted-liquid propellant version with a range of 350 km (SS-350).[11] All versions of the Prithvi are nuclear capable.[12] As of early 2001 both the SS-150 and SS-250 are in service.

Of particular interest is the development of India's long-range Agni missiles of which there could be four variants with ranges of 1,500 km (Agni-I), 2,500 km (Agni-II), 3,500-4,000 km (Agni-III), 5,000 km (Agni-IV). The Agni pro-gram had its first launch in 1989 with Agni-I. The Agni series has been tested successfully on four occasions, most recently in January 2001, to a range of 1,500 km (not tested to its maximum range due to the limited size of India's flight test facilities). The induction of the Agni (meaning "fire") into India's nuclear doctrine was held up in the first half of the 1990s by successive gov-ernments' reluctance to order further tests of the missile. This attitude changed with the electoral victory of Atal Vajpayee and his BJP in 1998. The April 1999 launch of Agni-II heralded the resumption of the Agni program and was fol-lowed by the announcement that the Agni-II was ready to be mass-produced.[13] As of early 2001 the number of Agni-I and Agni-II missiles in service may be no more than a dozen in total.

Information on the Surya (meaning "sun") is limited and often contradic-tory. There are likely to be several Surya missile variants however reports over their ranges have varied. Flight-testing may not commence until after 2002. It seems clear that India intends to develop several versions of the Surya missile. Reported ranges have varied from 5,000 km to as much as 20,000 km. Initially there could be two Surya missiles: Surya-I (5,000–6,000 km) and Surya II (8,000–12,000 km), and possibly a Surya-III (20,000-km).[14] The Surya-I is sometimes referred to as the Agni-IV. Although it is not known for certain what range the Agni-III and Agni-IV and Suryas will be, India is technologically capable of developing missiles of at least 12,000 km over time. The Suryas are likely to benefit from India's satellite launch-vehicle program in the same way the Agni program has.

Throughout India's ballistic missile program, the country's developments in the space program are understood to provide valuable technology for a com-prehensive missile-based nuclear deterrent. India's SLV program, headed by the ISRO, has produced a series of SLVs. The second SLV-3 launch in July 1980 was the first successful launch by the ISRO placing a satellite into orbit. The first attempt in 1979 ended in failure. The SLV-3 was only launched on two other occasions in 1981 and 1983, to then be followed by the Augmented-SLV (ASLV). The first stage of the two-stage Agni launch of 1989 used a solid pro-pellant based on the SLV-3 and the second stage derived from the liquid-fuel

Prithvi.[15] The ASLV was tested on four occasions between 1987–1994 before being retired. Six of the ASLV boosters were later used for the new Polar Satellite Launch Vehicle (PSLV) program.[16] The PSLV could form the bases of the Agni-III. The Agni-III may therefore be a hybrid of the Agni-II and the PSLV—one stage liquid fuel and two stages solid.

According to Pravin Sawhney, South Asia Correspondent *for Jane's International Defense Review,* the diameter of Agni-II would need to be widened from 1 meter to 1.8 meters to incorporate the PSLV's propulsion system to develop the Agni-III. In light of the current PSLV solid-fuel rocket propellant possessing a diameter of 2.8 meters, India would need to convert this technology to the 1.8-meter specification set out for the Agni-III rocket motor.[17] The successful launch of the four-stage PSLV in May 1999 provided further information for developing the Agni-III propulsion system. Despite the complication in deciphering the extent of which SLV programs play in the present and emerging Agni variants, it is important to realize that the developments by the ISRO have a direct relation to the ongoing developments of the IGMDP. During the suspension of the Agni's flight-testing program from 1994 to 1998, the Agni may have gained technological support from the ISRO's activities that included the PSLV launch of March 1996.

The Agni-IV may utilize the same ISRO technology as the Surya ICBM program. The Agni-IV and the Surya ICBM series could be derived from either the successful conversion of the PSLV as a missile or incorporating the ISRO's ambitious rocket technology from the Geostationary Satellite Launch Vehicle (GSLV) program. The ISRO in 1993 concluded a contract with the Russian space company Glavkosmos to supply seven upper-booster rocket stages from 1998 to 2002 for India's GSLV program. According to Moscow's Khrunichev Space Center (KSC), the first of the seven upper stages were delivered in September 1998.[18] In addition the ISRO successfully tested in February 1998 an indigenously designed cryogenic engine as part of the GSLV project.[19] The transfer of Russian cryogenic rocket engines suggests that India may still have difficulty in developing this technology for a flight worthy GSLV. The GSLV as an ICBM could strike targets at a distance of 12,000–14,000 km. India successfully launched the GSLV in April 2001. An operational ICBM based on the GSLV would however be fairly cumbersome. The cryogenic rockets would take several hours to fuel up and therefore a GSLV-type missile would be unsuited for a rapid nuclear response. The solid-fuel Agni-II, on the other hand, could take around 20 minutes to prepare for launch. India's nuclear capability could transcend into a significant strategic force, comparable in range to the original five nuclear powers.

The DRDO's missile program does not stop at land-based systems: India is placing extensive resources towards the development of a submarine-launched cruise missile (SLCM). The Sagarika project is believed to have started in 1994, however there were reports of the project's cancellation in 1996. These may have referred to a realization that domestically turning a Unmanned Aerial Vehicle (UAV) into an SLCM presented insurmountable difficulties. However there is evidence that India still seeks a sea-based nuclear deterrence. An Indian SLCM (referred to as the Sagarika) is likely to be nuclear capable and would be carried by imported Russian Kilo-class submarines and indigenously constructed. Despite the lack of official information on the project, the Sagarika is, according to defense analyst T. S. Gopi Rethinaraj, "very much in existence."[20] According to Ian Synge, Coordinating Editor of *Jane's Sentinel,* the Sagarika may not be an indigenously developed program but a renamed Russian SLCM:

> It is possible that India's experience during the late 1980s and early 1990s with the leased Charlie class cruise missile nuclear submarine Chakra may have opened up Indian eyes to the possibilities presented by sea-launched cruise missiles. It is possible to judge that the 1996 announcement of project termination was correct. India may have discovered that the difficulties of modifying an existing UAV to function as a cruise missile, combined with the complexities of underwater-encapsulated launch from a 533-mm torpedo tube were insurmountable in the short term. However, submerged torpedo launch technology is comparatively widespread, systems being produced by the U. S., Israel, France, and India's long-term arms supplier, the Russian Federation. India's Kilo-class submarines have regularly returned to Russia to be refitted and in 1999 the Sinhuvir returned to Vishakapatanam from Zvyozdochka State Mechanical Engineering Enterprise in Severodvinsk for modernization including the fitting of 9M45E1 Club-S cruise missiles (NATO codename SS-N-27). These systems, with a range of 300 km, and which are also envisaged being employed aboard indigenously built Type 1500 submarines, fit closely with the Sagarika requirement. It is thus postulated that continued references to Sagarika refer not to an indigenous Indian program as is the case with Agni and Prithvi, but to a requirement that has been fulfilled by Russian submarine launched cruise missiles.[21]

Development of sea-based systems also include the 250–350-km range Dhanush, a naval version of the land-based Prithvi. This surface ship missile was first test launched in April 2000 in the Bay of Bengal of the Orissa coast with partial success according to the Defense Research and Development Organization (DRDO). An Indian defense ministry spokesman commented afterwards, "There are a number of qualitative requirements (QRs) in the flight test, [the] test met some of the QRs." The test was not that successful with the missile travelling only 20–25 kilometers before plunging into the sea. The Indian Navy is reported to view the 9-metre long and 4 tons Dhanush more as a technology demonstrator in view of its vulnerability to enemy anti-ship missiles and naval reconnaissance planes.

Greater survivability of India's and Pakistan's nuclear deterrent through the possession of mobile missiles may initially appear to be more stabilizing, but the procurement of ballistic missiles by both sides is increasing the prospect of nuclear confrontation. The change in India and Pakistan's nuclear posture presents a number of negative variables that have not been granted the attention they deserve.

A Dramatic Nuclear Change

Nuclear deterrence between India and Pakistan has been steadily changing from aircraft-borne counterbalance of terror to nuclear-tipped missiles. India and Pakistan may have possessed missiles capable of delivering a nuclear warhead several years before the May 1998 nuclear tests, but the declaration by both sides as members of the nuclear club coupled with the ongoing missile developments is resulting in greater reliance on missiles for nuclear deterrence. The previous form of deterrence, referred to as aircraft-borne counter-balance of terror based on nuclear ambiguity, was stabilizing to the Indo-subcontinent's security. Pakistan in particular viewed this form of deterrence at essential as its security. In March 1996 the then Pakistan Foreign Minister Ali Said asserted that India's lack of knowledge about the extent of Islamabad's nuclear capability gave Pakistan "security in ambiguity."[22] This was echoed by former President Zia of Pakistan who stated in 1988 that "the programs of India and Pakistan have a lot of ambiguities, and therefore in the eyes of each other, they have reached a particular level, and that level is good enough to create an impression of deterrence."[23]

Devin T. Hagerty, who assess the affects of nuclear weapons on South Asia, refers to aircraft-based nuclear deterrence as "opaque existential deterrence" whereby both sides pursue a policy of calculated nuclear ambiguity, mixing a public posture of restraint with covert development of nuclear weapons, or at least the option to build them quickly.[24] Hagerty adds that "since each side in an opaque nuclear arms competition has only limited information about the other side's nuclear forces, any deterrence derived from nuclear capabilities will logically be existential."[25]

Significantly pure aircraft-borne counterbalance of terror may have been crucial to maintaining stability between the two powers in times of crisis, serving as a counterbalance to the ingrained instability posed by the territorial dispute of Kashmir. The peaceful resolution of the 1990 Indo-Pakistani crisis was, according to Hagerty, attributed to the aforementioned nuclear stance.[26] War may have been averted because of "security in ambiguity." Pakistan's aircraft-based nuclear capability surrounded in ambiguity was an effective means of offsetting India's larger non-missile-based strategic arsenal, creating a stable nuclear balance–imbalance. This, however, is changing with greater reliance on missiles for deterrence, and with it a new form of deterrence is emerging.

Ambiguity and opacity may still persist, but in a different form through the lack of knowledge of either sides missile force and possible locations of where mobile ballistic missiles may be deployed in the event of a major crisis or conflict. However, due to missiles characteristics this new form of opacity may be highly destabilizing to the region's stability. The movement away from the stable opacity has been gradual as India and Pakistan continue to develop and induct missiles with no prospect in sight of either side stemming their programs. South Asia is unwittingly adopting a new form of opacity based on missile counterbalance of terror minus the stability aircraft-borne deterrence had brought to the Indo-Subcontinent. These negative variables include the fear of preemptive strike and the prospect of early warning failure. In the context of the Kashmir dispute, these factors collectively could create a precarious situation for maintaining stability and averting nuclear war.

Fear of Preemption

Psychologically ballistic missiles could make each side feel more insecure than before in the knowledge that the adversary's nuclear-tipped missiles could be kept safe from air attack and launched in anger with impunity. The perceived fear of either side considering and possibly carrying out a pre-emptive nuclear strike by using missiles could risk causing a fourth Indo-Pakistan war escalating to the nuclear level.

The prospect of either side launching a preemptive nuclear attack is aggravated by Pakistan's declaration that it will be the first to launch a nuclear strike if necessary. Islamabad's refusal to follow India's decision to adopt a policy of no-first-use is due to Pakistan's concerns that such a stance would restore Indian conventional superiority. Pakistan views its nuclear capability as a means to compensate the nation's conventional inferiority with India.[27] Were a scenario to arise where Indian troops crossed into Pakistan, New Delhi could face the prospect of Pakistan considering to launch a preemptive nuclear strike believing its national survival to be critically under threat.

Interestingly India has realized that Pakistan has adopted an unstable nuclear posture. As an indication of New Delhi's concern, then Defense Minister George Fernandes urged Pakistan in January 1999 for cooperative security and a firm commitment of a no-first-use policy to eliminate the risk of accidental and miscalculated use of nuclear weapons.[28] Islamabad's refusal to adopt no-first-use has placed India into a precarious security environment arguably of its own making. Had Vajpayee not authorized the nuclear tests in 1998, Pakistan may not have been compelled to reassess its security environment and led into thinking that up to 70 nuclear warheads are required to achieve a credible nuclear deterrent against India.[29]

A further burden placed on Islamabad and New Delhi is the realization that it would be extremely difficult to destroy their adversary's deployed missiles and their Transport Erector Launchers (TELs) that may be readied for a nuclear attack compared to attacking airbases at known fixed locations that may be used for readying aircraft for a nuclear strike. This could place tremendous strain on both sides, knowing that their adversary's nuclear forces are effectively immune to detection on the ground. All present and emerging land-based missile capabilities by India and Pakistan are based on mobile road/rail TELs. The 1991 Gulf War demonstrated that even with air supremacy and superior ground-attack aircraft, missile busting is an extremely difficult task: Not one Iraqi mobile Scud launcher was destroyed by allied aircraft during Desert Storm.[30] Added to this is the realization that missiles once launched can not be intercepted. At least with nuclear deterrence based on aircraft both sides would stand a realistic chance of intercepting incoming attack aircraft armed with nuclear weapons by either their own fighter interceptors of Surface to Air Missiles (SAMs) and importantly more time to react compared to a few minute warning of a missile attack.

Concern over False Early-Warning Alerts

The prospect of a false ballistic missile early-warning alert leading to an accidental launch needs to be considered when looking at the long-term development of ballistic-missile capabilities in the region. Neither India or Pakistan are understood to have devoted much discussion or resources towards developing reliable ballistic-missile early-warning systems. Although India's radar capabilities are probably more advance than Pakistan's, New Delhi may not be able to detect an incoming missile much more than a few blips on a screen. These antiquated early-warning capabilities could be more of a danger than having no early warning systems at all. This opens up the prospect of a false early-warning alert leading to the misunderstanding that a missile attack has commenced risking a retaliatory strike based on false data. Fortunately neither side has yet adopted a launch on warning strategy, although this could change over the years should their ballistic-missile-capabilities increase and greater reliance be placed on them for their nations' security. The immediate concern here is Pakistan's refusal to adopt a no-first-use strategy and how much pressure this could place on India's early-warning systems. It is probably more crucial for India to develop a credible early-warning system considering China's advance missile capabilities could pose considerable pressure for New Delhi should there be a major crisis with Beijing.

A possible approach to stem this problem is to develop an International Early Warning Center (IEWC) as part of a near global network covering other regions where missiles are prevalent (including Middle East, Northeast Asia, Europe, and the United States). The IEWC could be based on the U. S.-Russian Joint Data Exchange Center (JDEC). The agreement on establishing a joint center for the exchange of U. S.-Russian data from early-warning systems was signed by President Putin and then President Clinton in June 2000. The IEWC would require the construction of ground-based radar stations in South Asia possibly financed and built as part of a multinational effort to develop an IEWC. The aim would be to avoid the prospect of a false early warning alarm caused by a Satellite Launch Vehicle (SLV), missile test, or a technical/human failure leading to strike orders. There have been a number of well-documented cases over the last 50 years of Russian and American false early-warning alerts that almost led to missiles being launched. The IEWC could provide constant early-warning data to India and Pakistan including notification of all missile and SLV launches within the region to compensate for their lack of reliable early-warning systems.[31]

An IEWC would not be effective detecting short-range missiles like the Prithvi in view of the short flight-times. This possible long-term solution is designed for a long term problem as India and Pakistan place in service a greater number of long-range missiles like the Ghauris, Shaheens, and Agnis.

These longer-range missiles look set to become the main delivery vehicles for their nuclear weapons and form the backbone of both nations' nuclear deterrent. It is hard to say what the complications for the lack of early-warning systems could be for India and Pakistan and how their nuclear strategies will evolve, but there is a need to consider possible responses to the ongoing proliferation of ballistic missiles in the region.

Lessons from the Cold War

Comparisons with the age of nuclear hostility between Washington and Moscow during the Cold War provides valuable lessons and warnings that are particularly relevant to India and Pakistan's nuclear relationship. Although New Delhi and Islamabad attempt to exercise constraint, the superpower experience during the Cold War is testimony to how an accidental nuclear war could occur. Former U. S. Secretary of Defense Robert McNamara and former Special Assistant for National Security McGeorge Bundy have both commented that the superpower rivalry demonstrates it is not possible to predict with confidence the consequence of military action because of misjudgment, misinformation, and miscalculation.[32] James G. Blight and David A. Welch offer a similar warning to new and aspiring nuclear states in their analysis of the Cuban missile crisis concluding, "it now appears more plausible than ever that nuclear war really could have been the inadvertent result of a series of mistaken perceptions, judgements and decisions. Far from solving acute security dilemmas, nuclear weapons may only make them more serious."[33] In a similar tone former Secretary of Defense William Perry warned that although the superpowers avoided nuclear conflict during the Cold War "by good luck, I can only hope [India and Pakistan] will be as lucky as we were."[34] Clearly a fourth India-Pakistan war would raise the stakes of a nuclear war to a considerable degree. Comparison with the superpower experience during the Cold War offers a stark warning for the new nuclear adversaries when the Kashmir dispute is added to the equation: the key to the region's instability.

India and Pakistan's continuing territorial dispute over Jammu and Kashmir is arguably the greatest risk for causing a nuclear confrontation. The threat of nuclear war was far less apparent during the Cold War where the superpowers were essentially satisfied powers. This infers that our conception from the superpowers Cold War experience of missile based nuclear deterrence as a linchpin for stability can not be extended to South Asia.

Prominent analysts have argued that nuclear weapons were with hindsight not essential for keeping the peace during the Cold War. John Mueller wrote in 1988 that the post-war world might have turned out much the same in the absence of nuclear weapons. Without them, he argues, "world war would have been discouraged by the memory of World War II, by superpower contentment with the post-war status quo, by the nature of Soviet ideology, and by the fear of escalation."[35] Ned Lebow, Janice Stein, and Bundy argue along similar lines adding that successful coexistence between the East and West were possible because there was literally no sphere of influence where dominance was a truly vital interest to both superpowers at once.[36] Indeed Cold War nuclear strategies of compellance and deterrence only served to provoke, as much as to restrain, each other,[37] and the necessity of nuclear weapons for Cold War stability is questionable.

Satisfaction with the status quo is certainly one label that can not be given to India and Pakistan's relations. With two of the three wars fought between the two over Kashmir, this region continues to be viewed by Islamabad and New Delhi as essential to their national character.[38] Despite attempts by both sides to try resolve their differences over this region, Kashmir remains a flashpoint that could potentially lead to another conflict. Šumit Ganguly states that as the Kashmir "insurgency drags on, and border tensions persist, war may still ensue through a mix of misperceptions and inadvertence."[39] The Kargil conflict during 1999 served as a reminder to the continuing volatility of Kashmir. In light of this continuing territorial dispute, India and Pakistan are clearly far less satisfied with the status quo than NATO and the Warsaw pact were during the height of their tensions. With this in mind, the chances of a nuclear exchange occurring through uncontrolled crisis escalation exists greater on the Indo-subcontinent than during the superpower's era of mistrust. For these reasons, the induction of nuclear-tipped missiles by Islamabad and New Delhi is dramatically shifting their nuclear posture to a new and more dangerous era of strategic relationship.

Despite the dramatic change in the nuclear deterrence on the Indo-subcontinent, Hagerty still believes that opaque existential deterrence remains stable. Writing shortly after the Ghauri-I missile flight test and the nuclear underground explosions in 1998, Hagerty stated that he had "no reason to believe that nuclear deterrence in South Asia is any less robust than it was indeed it may be more so."[40] He even goes so far as to say that "missile deployments are unlikely to generate severe instabilities."[41] Just because the superpowers during the Cold War era escaped inadvertent nuclear war is no justification that other nuclear adversaries will be so fortuitous.[42] The changes in the strategic relationship in South Asia is not confined to events between India and Pakistan. China's role in the region's stability is equally pivotal and too raises ominous signs for the future.

A New Era of Strategic Rivalry

Throughout the 1990s the missile rivalry in South Asia had been largely contained to India and Pakistan. India's induction of the Agni missile against China threatens to herald the beginning of an ominous period of strategic rivalry with New Delhi locking itself into an arms competition with Beijing. In response this could lead to China increasing its assistance to Pakistan's missile and nuclear weapons program in an attempt to avert a destabilizing strategic imbalance materializing between New Delhi and Islamabad.

India's threat assessment of China has led New Delhi to believe it needs to procure missiles that can cover all of China. Raja Mohan, Strategic Affairs Editor of *The Hindu* newspaper revealed shortly after the first Agni-II test that "India has been dying to get this [Agni-II] capability vis-à-vis China. For India it is now being able to look at China in the eye to say we are equal now. The central element of this long-range missile for India is about gaining parity with the Chinese, parity not in numbers of missiles, but we have the ability to deliver nuclear weapons on to China and thereby gain a credible deterrence against China. That is the real political significance of Agni-II."[43]

India's insistence on inducting the various Agnis against China into the early part of the twenty first Century risks Beijing responding possibly with the deployment of nuclear forces in the Tibet region and other bordering provinces with India. This may in turn lead New Delhi to heighten its threat perception of China as the threat from the north becomes (in India's eyes) ever more real. While it is hard to gauge what Beijing's response will be to the targeting of the various Agnis against its country, it is difficult to conceive that Beijing would do nothing to counter India's nuclear buildup that is so overtly aimed towards China.[44] As with India's commitment to maintaining strategic superiority over Pakistan, China's similar goal towards India sets the region on a gradual arms race between all three countries that threatens to cause greater regional insecurity.

The induction of Agni against China may not only tempt Beijing to deploy nuclear forces in the Tibet region aimed at India, but could also lead to the additional transfer of Chinese nuclear- and missile-related technology to Pakistan. This may exacerbate another concern held by New Delhi of Chinese encirclement through Beijing's close political and military relationship with Islamabad. In April 1998 George Fernandes made clear his concern that: "Certainly there is the threat of Chinese encirclement of India."[45] China views bolstering Pakistan's nuclear capability as necessary to counter India's strategic buildup. By attempting to maintain a strategic balance between India and Pakistan, China hopes to maintain stability in its southern border region.[46]

In the process of New Delhi augmenting its nuclear capability to counter the perceived threat perceptions, India in the long term appears set to actually exacerbate the nation's security concerns of Pakistan's and China's nuclear capabilities together with the fear of Chinese encirclement. Stephen P. Cohen warns that "if Beijing takes the Indian actions as a threat, and moved to counter them, then the traditional misperceptions between these two countries (which far exceed those between India and Pakistan), could lead to a new and far more dangerous stage in nuclear and strategic developments."[47]

Besides the nuclear issues affecting stability in South Asia lies the additional negative factor of the conventional force balance of power. As mentioned earlier, Pakistan's inferior conventional capability to India's has led Islamabad to believe that possession of nuclear weapons and the option to strike first is the best means to compensate for its deficiencies in the conventional field. In light of this, the widening of the conventional balance gap between the two powers can only lead to even more reliance by Pakistan on the nation's nuclear weapons for security and with it further emphasis on inducting nuclear tipped missiles with all the risks that could ensue. Unfortunately the procurement of ballistic missiles by India is undermining the delicate conventional balance with its Western neighbor.

The Conventional balance–imbalance

The alteration of the conventional balance of power between India and Pakistan is yet another negative variable contributing to instability in South Asia. While the proliferation of ballistic missiles in the region is primarily discussed in the context of the nuclear dimension, observers must not omit the effects missiles are likely to have on the conventional-forces front. Stephen P. Cohen writing in 1992 stated that by "New Delhi's legitimate preparations against a hypothetical two front conflict with China and Pakistan, India has acquired the capabilities to defeat Pakistan. Pakistan's forces would be adequate to protect itself against an Indian attack, but not so large or modern that they threaten India."[48] Although Pakistan, India, and China each have varying military capabilities, their present conventional imbalance posture is adequate deterrent for their adversary. In the light of this, the premissile threshold was itself an arms control measure[49]; now it is breached with India's induction of the Prithvis, the result may be unpredictable consequences for regional stability.

In December 1998 India deployed for the first time in a major military exercise the conventional Prithvi SS-150,[50] signifying that New Delhi has fully inducted this missile into its military doctrine. Although the Prithvi SS-150 was not actually deployed for the maneuvers, the missile was factored into the exercise.[51] Code named Shakti, the Indian exercise was the largest since operation Brasstacks in 1987. This is the first of the IGDMP's missiles to become fully operational. In procuring the Prithvi SS-150, India has already undermined the conventional balance–imbalance that has existed between New Delhi and Islamabad. The prospect of the Prithvi SS-250 and SS-350 being brought into service threatens to exacerbate this further.

Indian military commanders view the Prithvi SS-150 as an extension of their artillery capability by increasing their range from 40 km to around 100–200 km, depending on the variant of Prithvi used[52] and introducing operational uncertainty into the Indo-Pakistani stand of thereby reducing the possibility of armed conflict.[53] In practice the procurement of this system threatens to drastically change Pakistan's time-tested war fighting doctrines like concentrations of mass, surprise and deception. According to Brigadier Naeem Ahmad Salik,

Director of Arms Control and Disarmament Affairs at the Joint Staff Headquarters, Pakistan, the induction of the Prithvi SS-250 will further exacerbate the Indian Airforce's five to one advantage over Pakistan's Airforce. Brigadier Ahmad Salik adds that the Prithvi SS-250 is able "to engage targets throughout the length and breadth of Pakistan." He goes onto say that, "Even if conventionally armed [the Prithvi SS-250] missile could prove to be a very effective weapon against PAF bases."[54]

When produced in large numbers, the Prithvi missile may well tilt the conventional arms balance between India and Pakistan decisively in favor of the former.[55] Even if the Prithvis are not deployed on Pakistan's border,[56] the mere fact that India has them and will in the future possess these missiles in large numbers may inject some uncertainty for Islamabad. Furthermore, a ballistic missiles penetration capability would make the Prithvi immune to Pakistan's air defense system thus adding a greater sense of vulnerability to Islamabad during a crisis.[57] The demise of the conventional balance–imbalance is compounded by India's ongoing modernization of its conventional forces. Pravin Sawhney, who served in the 333rd Missile Brigade comments:

> A few Prithvi, even when not used, however will add uncertainty for the attacking commander by forcing him to disperse reserves instead of concentrating them for a breakout through enemy linear defenses. Advancing commanders will have difficulty in shifting forces between contiguous corps, resulting in time-delays for crucial objectives. Irrespective of an assured tactical air support, the defending commander would have an ability to switch fire, at will, right to the enemy's depth and logistics support base. He will also have the ability to influence his flanks while he is defending large stretches. The command, control, coordination and cohesiveness of the enemy effort would most certainly be disrupted and dislocated by the presence of Prithvi and Hatf-II. In simple words, given the right surveillance, Prithvi or Hatf-II will help in harassing and forcing change of plans on a battlefield.[58]

The 300 km range Hatf-II and 280 km range M-11 are the closest Pakistan has come to the SS-150 Prithvi, although only a trickle have been indigenously developed. With a limited number of M-11s procured from China and few indigenously developed in Pakistan, these missiles are likely to be confined to the nuclear role. Until Pakistan significantly increases the production rate of these short-range missiles, Islamabad may lack a short-range missile force to counter the conventionally-armed Prithvi on the battlefield.

The Risks for the Future: Life After Kargil

The Kargil crisis in 1999 was a stark reminder of how a fourth Indo-Pakistani war could break out. There was the real threat of a repetition of the 1965 and

1971 wars, where Pakistani attempts to seize Kashmir prompted India to extend the war across the international frontiers in Punjab and Rajasthan and drive towards Lahore and Karachi. This strategy would have again compelled Pakistan to divert it forces to defend its territory in Punjab and Sindh, only this time it could have escalated to nuclear confrontation.[59]

The greatest risk for South Asia's security lies in the increasing number of negative variables that are detrimental to the region's security. Together they threaten to lead to an inadvertent nuclear war in the event of major crisis or future conflict escalating out of control. Leaving aside the ongoing missile developments, India and Pakistan's geostrategic environment is inherently unstable and looks set to remain so until there is a satisfactory solution to all sides over the disputed region of Kashmir. The sharing of a contiguous border itself leaves a very small margin for error to interpret intelligence correctly to what the adversaries intentions at any one moment might be.

Pakistan's refusal to follow India's line of adopting a policy of no first use of nuclear weapons is one factor that could prove to be decisive to whether nuclear weapons were to be used in the event of another conflict. It is generally recognized that Pakistan's conventional forces are inferior to those of India's. Should India decide a conflict necessitated crossing the Line of Control, Islamabad would unlikely be capable of repelling such an advance. Deeming its national security to be at risk, Islamabad might then be forced to consider launching a nuclear strike. Pakistan has already made clear it views on nuclear weapons viewing them as a means to compensate for its conventional inferiority with India.

In the months following September 11, 2001, attention focused on the control of Pakistan's nuclear and missile capabilities as Islamabad risked internal instability to assist the U. S. military campaign against the Taliban in Afghanistan. The protests led to concern over what could happen to Islamabad's strategic capability should Musharraf's government be toppled were the internal unrest to get out of hand. Fortunately the prospect of the Talibanisation or Islam fundamentalists taking power in Pakistan is not that great. Prior to the events of September 11, Anthony Davis, a leading commentator on Afghanistan and Pakistan wrote:

> Traditionally, political Islam in Pakistan has been neither united nor, in electoral terms at least, popular. Riven by doctrinal difference and personality squabbles, it covers a broad spectrum of belief from Sufi-influenced reverence for local saints to the harsh purism of sects espousing Wahhabi reformism from the Arabian peninsula. Since the death of thinker Abdul Ala Maududi in 1977, Pakistani Islamism has failed to produce any commanding leaders of the stature of Sudan's Hassan al-Turabi or Algeria's Abbasi Madani.[60]

With regards to the direct custody of Pakistan's strategic capability, the components of Islamabad's nuclear tipped ballistic missile capability are understood be kept at separate locations and under the close control of the Army. The capability is therefore not thought to be at risk of falling into the hands of the Taliban or similar organizations. On a separate issue, Pakistan and India have benefited from September 11 from the lifting of sanctions imposed following their nuclear tests in May 1998. Just days after the terrorist attacks on the U. S. World Trade Center and the Pentagon, President Bush announced that sanctions against India and Pakistan were "not in the national security interest of the United States." In the long term this is likely to be reflected in Washington cooling its pressure on India and Pakistan to stem their nuclear and missile programs in view that the United States needs to have India and particularly Pakistan on their side for the duration of the military campaign against the Taliban in Afghanistan.

As mentioned at the beginning, it is the ongoing ballistic-missile tests that poses the greatest threat to regional security as both sides augment their missile capabilities, as opposed to the nuclear tests of 1998. There is no serious prospect in sight of either India or Pakistan terminating their missile programs. Developing and possessing nuclear weapons is one matter (and is still significant), but possessing the means to deliver such a payload within a region that possess a number of key negative variables undermining the areas stability only increases the chance of nuclear weapon's being used. Primary among these negative variables is obviously Kashmir. Despite the optimism after the Lahore Accord in February 1999, the Kargil conflict of May–June 1999 underlined how both sides could slip into an all out war that could lead to a nuclear conflict. Nawaz Sharif speaking during the Kargil conflict rightly warned that "God forbid, a war breaks out, it would not be a conventional war but a nuclear war."[61] Sharif's warning was reiterated by former Pakistan Foreign Minister Agha Shahi who expressed fears that if Pakistan and India went to war, one of them could be tempted to use nuclear weapons.[62] It is of paramount importance for India and Pakistan to resolve their territorial disputes and not stop at symbolic agreements like the Lahore Accord. Failure to do so risks an inadvertent nuclear confrontation on the Indo-subcontinent. The superpowers during the Cold War on a number of occasions narrowly escaped nuclear war, often by chance. India and Pakistan may not be so fortunate. With a number of negative variables set to remain, the accumulative effect could prove to be catastrophic.

Notes

1. Cameron Binkley, "Pakistan's Ballistic Missile Development: The Sword of Islam," in William Potter and Harlen Jencks, eds., *The International Missile Bazaar: The New Suppliers' Network* (Boulder: Westview, 1994), p. 85.

2. R. Jeffrey Smith and David Ottaway, "Spy Photos Suggest China Missile Trade," *The Washington Post,* July 3, 1995, p. A.1.

3. Umer Farooq, "Pakistan needs up to 70 nuclear warheads," *Jane's Defence Weekly,* June 1998, p. 3. Dr. Mubrik told *Jane's Defence Weekly,* "The NDC has

started serial production of the 700 km range Shaheen-I missile although it has not been tested yet."

4. R. Jeffrey Smith, "Pakistan Is Building Missile Plant, U. S. Says," *Herald Tribune,* August 26, 1996, p. 1.
5. Ben Sheppard, "Pakistan tests 'Chinese/North Korean-based missiles,'" *Jane's Intelligence Review,* vol. 11 no. 5, May 1999, p. 3.
6. "Pakistan tests Ghauri-III engine," *Jane's Defence Weekly,* October 13, 1999, p. 6.
7. Ben Sheppard, "Ballistic missile proliferation and the geopolitics of terror," *Jane's Intelligence Review,* vol. 10 no. 12, December 1998, pp. 40-41.
8. Correspondence with the author, *Jane's Information Group,* Coulsdon, June 1999.
9. Correspondence with the author, *Jane's Information Group,* Coulsdon, June 1999. The interviewee wished to remain anonymous.
10. Ben Sheppard, "Regional rivalries are replayed as India and Pakistan renew ballistic missile tests," *Jane's International Defense Review,* vol. 32 no. 5, May 1999, p. 57.
11. Pravin Sawney, "Standing Alone: India's Nuclear Imperative," *Jane's International Defense Review,* November 1996, p. 28.
12. Ibid.
13. "Defence Official says Agni ballistic missiles can be mass produced," *BBC Survey of World Broadcasts,* May 19, 1999 (FE/3230 A3).
14. Vivek Raghuvanshi, "Indian Scientists Poised to Test-Launch Country's First ICBM," *Defense News,* April 30, 2001, p. 26. The report quoted a DRDO scientist as saying the Surya-II will have its range extended to 20,000 km.
15. Kathleen Bailey, *Doomsday Weapons in the Hands of Many,* (Urbana-Champaign: University of Illinois Press, 1991) p. 115.
16. Andrew Wilson, *Jane's Space Directory 1996–97,* (Coulsdon: Jane's Information Group, 1996) p. 226.
17. Interview with the author, Jane's Information Group, Coulsdon, May 1999.
18. "Russia sends India upper stage of booster rocket," *Reuters,* September 22, 1998. India's previous attempt to acquire Russian Cryogenic engines was blocked by the United States. in 1991 as it violated the Missile Technology Control Regime (MTCR). The current contract, which was concluded in 1993, does not include the transfer of blueprints to develop the technology itself.
19. "ISRO tests indigenous cryogenic engine," *The Hindu,* February 27, 1998, p. 11.
20. T. S. Gopi Rethinaraj, "Navalised Prithvi causes confusion," *Jane's Intelligence Review,* January 1999, vol. 11, no. 1, p. 4.
21. Interview with Ian Synge, Coordinating Editor of *Jane's Sentinel,* Jane's Information Group, Coulsdon, September 2000.
22. Christopher Thomas, "Pakistan keeps India guessing as stakes rise in game of nuclear bluff," *The Times,* March 8, 1996, p. 14.
23. Leonard Spector, *Nuclear Ambitions* (Boulder: Westview Press, 1990), p. 100.
24. Devin T. Hagerty, "The Power of Suggestion: Opaque Proliferation, Existential Deterrence, and the South Asian Nuclear Arms Competition," in Davis and Frankel, "Proliferation Puzzle," *Security Studies,* vol. 2 no. 3/4 (Spring/Summer, 1993), p. 257.
25. Devin T. Hagerty, "Nuclear Deterrence in South Asia: The Indo-Pakistani Crisis," *International Security,* vol. 20, no. 3 (Winter 1995–96), p. 88.
26. Ibid., p. 112.

27. Umer Farooq, "Islamabad rejects no-first-use pact for nuclear weapons," *Jane's Defence Weekly,* July 22, 1998, p. 15.

28. "Fernandes calls for no-first-use policy by Asia's N-states," *The Times of India,* January 28, 1999, http://www.timesofindia.com.

29. Umer Farooq, "Pakistan needs up to 70 nuclear warheads," p. 3.

30. Stewart M. Powell, "Scud War, Round Three," *Air Force Magazine,* October 1992, p. 33. According to Mark Miller of Johns Hopkins University, the Allied raids "did not destroy a single mobile launcher."

31. For a full discussion see Ben Sheppard, "The Risk Factor: An International Early Warning Center," *Jane's Defence Weekly,* February 2001, pp. 22-27.

32. Robert McNamara, *Out of the Cold* (London: Bloomsbury, 1990), p. 102 and McGeorge Bundy, Blundering into Disaster (New York: Pantheon Books, 1986), p. 140. Bundy comments that in a crisis situation it is inconceivable, with all its inevitable pressures, decisions regarding use of nuclear weapons would be unaffected by such factors.

33. James G. Blight and David A. Welch, "Risking 'The Destruction of Nations:' Lessons of the Cuban Missile Crisis for New and Aspiring Nuclear States," *Security Studies,* vol. 4, no. 4 (Summer, 1995) p. 824.

34. Harvey Stockwin, "Developed command, control procedures key to Asian security: Perry," *Times of India,* June 2000.

35. John Mueller, "The Essential Irrelevance of Nuclear Weapons," *International Security,* vol. 13, no. 13, (Fall 1988), p. 56.

36. Ned Lebow and Janice Stein, *We All Lost the Cold War* (Chichester: Princeton University Press, 1994), p. 357, and McGeorge Bundy, Danger and Survival (New York: Vintage Books, 1990), p. 598.

37. Lebow and Stein, *We All Lost the Cold War,* p. 4.

38. Mitchell Reiss, *Bridled Ambition: Why Countries Constrain their Nuclear Capabilities* (Washington, D. C.: Woodrow Wilson Center Press, 1995), p. 196.

39. Šumit Ganguly, "Explaining the Kashmir Insurgency," *International Security,* vol. 21, no. 2, (Fall 1996) p. 107.

40. Devin T. Hagerty, *The Consequences of Nuclear Proliferation: Lessons from South Asia,* (Cambridge: MIT Press, 1998) p. xvi.

41. Ibid. p. 193.

42. Ben Sheppard, "South Asia's Ballistic Ambitions," in Raju G. C. Thomas and Amit Gupta, eds., *India's Nuclear Security,* (Boulder: Lynne Rienner, 2000), p. 184.

43. Interview with Raja Mohan, Jane's Information Group, Coulsdon, April 1999.

44. Ben Sheppard, "South Asia Nears Nuclear Boiling Point," *Jane's Intelligence Review,* vol. 11 no. 7, July 1999, p. 32.

45. "China and Pakistan present a collaborated threat," *The Times of India,* April 12, 1998, http://www.timesofindia.com

46. Ben Sheppard, "South Asia Nears Nuclear Boiling Point," p. 33.

47. Correspondence with the author, Jane's Information Group, Coulsdon, April 1999.

48. Stephen P. Cohen, "Controlling Weapons of Mass Destruction in South Asia: An American Perspective," in S. A. Stahl and G. Kemp, eds., *Arms Control and Weapons Proliferation in the Middle East and South Asia* (New York: St Martin's Press, 1992), p. 204-205.

49. Devin T. Hagerty, "South Asia's Nuclear Balance," *Current History,* vol. 95, no. 600 (April 1996), p. 167.

50. Christopher Thomas, "Indian exercises stir border tension," *The Times*, December 3, 1998, p. 10. The nuclear variant of Prithvi was not simulated in the exercises.

51. Rezaul H Laskar, "New doctrine Army-IAF exercises in desert," *Asian Age*, December 3, 1998, p. 2. General Khana was quoted to have said on the military exercise, "we have given the 'enemy' a missile capability."

52. Interview with Pravin Sawney, *Royal United Services Institute*, February 1997.

53. "India's Missile Programme: Changing the Subcontinents Balance of Power?," *RUSI Newsbrief*, vol. 15, no. 11, November 1995, pp. 84-85.

54. Brigadier Naeem Ahmad Salik, *"Pakistan's Ballistic Missile Development Programme—Security Imperatives, Rationale and Objectives,"* paper presented at the Jane's Ballistic Missile Proliferation Conference, London, October 2000.

55. "India's Missile Programme: Changing the Subcontinents Balance of Power?" *RUSI Newsbrief*, Vol 15, No 11, November 1995, pp. 84-85. The report from a study undertaken at the Royal United Services Institute by Pravin Sawhney stated: "The Prithvi is ideal for battlefield interdiction: rail marshalling yards, logistic bases, and forward air bases. The Prithvi would be able to disrupt and dislocate Pakistan's C3 system. The Prithvi's conventional warhead will get the target to display a high degree of nervousness, which will eat into the vitals of the will of an enemy."

56. Greg J. Gerardi, "India's 333rd Prithvi Missile Group," *Jane's Intelligence Review*, vol. 7, no. 8, p. 362. India is introducing the Prithvi missile into its reserve forces and stationing it away from the border area with Pakistan. In this way, India's leaders can avoid international pressure by maintaining that they have not deployed the Prithvi system, but it can still be deployed when conflict is imminent.

57. Ben Sheppard, *"South Asia's Ballistic Ambitions,"* p. 180.

58. Pravin Sawhney, *"India, Pakistan, China: Need for a missile stabilization regime,"* paper given at the annual Jane's Ballistic Missile Proliferation Conference, London, October 1999.

59. Professor Raju Thomas, *Jane's Sentinel South Asia Security Assessment*, Online update, July 1999, http://janes.com

60. Anthony Davis, "Musharraf's Dilemma" *Jane's Intelligence Review*, vol. 13, no. 3, March 2001, p. 39.

61. "Pakistani leader says war with India would be nuclear," *BBC Survey of World Broadcasts*, June 2, 1999, FE/3550 A/4.

62. "Nuke Weapons may be used in case of war: Pak ex-Minister," *The Hindustan Times*, June 9, 1999. Shahi commented: "The ongoing situation on the Line of Control might take an ugly turn if one of them sees defeat. Despite possessing nuclear weapons, let us continue diplomacy of bilateral talks."

CHAPTER TEN

Nuclear Weapons and The Indian Armed Forces

Rajesh Kadian

Summary

Like much of the world, the Indian armed forces were taken by surprise by the five nuclear tests undertaken by the newly elected BJP Government on May 11 and 13, 1998. The subsequent Indian doctrine of minimum credible deterrence, too, was based on few inputs from the end-users—the Indian armed forces. At present the Indian Air Force has the most developed infrastructure, equipment, and trained forces to provide a limited deterrent. However, the most versatile deterrent is in the form of nuclear-powered submarines armed with ballistic missiles. Not unexpectedly, the Indian Navy has staked such a claim. On the other hand, the largest and most powerful of the three defense services, the Indian Army, too, has sought a significant role in nuclear war fighting. Ultimately, an integrated higher defense organization will be required to manage the competing claims and provide a rational cost-effective system of minimum credible nuclear deterrence. India has already taken some steps in this direction.

The Lotus Flower

On May 11, 1998 at 3:45 P.M. in the remote desert test site at Pokharan, the earth shook and a 350-foot plume of dust mixed with black and white smoke shot up in the cloudless sky. To eyewitnesses, the dust cloud "blossomed like a lotus flower." However, much of the rest of the world viewed it as a variant of a mushroom cloud, because, India had, after 24 years of self-imposed restraint, resumed nuclear testing. Three devices—a normal fission bomb, a sub-kiloton explosive and a thermonuclear device—were exploded in matter of five seconds with a total yield of about 60 kilotons.[1]

Around noon that day, three miles from the test site, the inhabitants of the village of Khetolai had been asked to move into open ground. From previous experience, old-timers guessed that a nuclear test was imminent. A couple of days before the villagers became privy to India's closely guarded secret, in far-away New Delhi, the three heads of the Indian armed forces were, for the first time, informed by the newly elected prime minister, Atal Bihari Vajpayee of the Bharatiya Janata Party (BJP), that India was going to test nuclear devices within the next 48 hours. Later, the writer, Amitav Ghosh, described his encounter with senior Indian military officers in late August 1998:

> I found myself sharing the table with several major generals and other senior offi-
> cers. I was interested to learn these senior officers' views of the nuclear tests, but
> I soon discovered that their curiosity exceeded mine. Did I know who was behind
> the decision to proceed with the tests? They asked. Who had issued the orders?
> Who had known in advance?
>   I could no more enlighten them than they could me. Only in India, I thought,
> could a writer and a tableful of generals ask each other questions like these. It
> was confirmation at any rate, that the armed forces' role in the tests had been
> limited.[2]

Ghosh was not alone in either his experience or in his conclusions. The role of the end-users of the weapons, the armed forces, appeared to be, indeed, limited both in the timing of the explosions and in the type of devices tested. In fact, the Indian military had never publicly articulated a preference either for or against the weaponization or testing of nuclear devices. Such silence was in keeping with the norms and traditions of the Indian armed forces, where most issues were not debated or discussed in public. However, after retirement, a number of military officers had publicly supported nuclearization. For instance, the blunt-speaking former chief of the Indian Army, General V. N. Sharma, stated so within two years of his retirement. In 1992, he wrote, "Our example of having the technology but not electing to develop nuclear weapons has not impressed anyone. . . . Strategically, we have no alternative to development of a minimum but effective nuclear deterrent capability as soon as we can."[3] Regardless of such pronouncements, inputs from the armed forces were plainly limited. This fact was further highlighted a few days later. On May 17, four days after two more sub kiloton nuclear devices had been successfully exploded, the armed forces were formally thanked for their narrow and restricted participation in the tests. In a joint statement the chairman of India's Atomic Energy Commission, R. Chidambaram, and the scientific advisor to the defense minister, A. P. J. Abdul Kalam, acknowledged, "The DAE (Department of Atomic Energy) and the DRDO (Defense Research and Development

Organization) would like to place on record their thanks to the Indian Army and the Indian Air Force for the excellent support to the campaign." Since the tests were conducted in the desert, the navy had not provided technical support, and, therefore, was not thanked.

By early August 1998, an Indian doctrine had been enunciated. Responding to the foreign policy debate in the Lok Sabha (the lower house of the Indian parliament), Vajpayee said, "India no longer requires to undertake nuclear explosions" and would not seek more than a "minimum, but credible, nuclear deterrent." The weapon inventory sufficient for such minimum deterrence was not quantified, though estimates ranged from 50 to 400 warheads. The Indian prime minister also reiterated a commitment made as long ago as May 1990: The then Minister of State for Defense, Raja Ramanna, had officially stated that India would never be the first to use its nuclear weapons. Vajpayee reaffirmed this no-first-use pledge. Over the next six months, other elements of the Indian strategic doctrine emerged. These included the following:

1. The warheads were to be kept in a non-mated, non-alert posture.
2. Nuclear devices were not to be considered as war fighting weapons but as instruments of last resort. Hence, tactical warheads were not required and the full triad of delivery systems—land-based rockets, submarine-launched missiles and manned bombers—was not needed. However, further refinement of the design of the bombs and the fabrication of additional warheads was to be continued as evidenced by an approximately 50 percent increase to $418 million in the 1999–2000 budget of the Department of Atomic Energy.
3. Missile development was to proceed, albeit at a slower pace, as suggested by the modest $58 million increase in the 1999–2000 budget of the Department of Space.

Neither the defense minister, George Fernandes, nor the three service chiefs made such public policy statements. They were clearly more like onlookers rather than participants in the unfolding drama.

The Onlookers

The process leading to the exclusion of the armed forces from decision making in matters of national security slowly evolved in the years following India's Independence. Prior to August 15, 1947, military power was the bedrock of the British paramountcy in India. Hence, close civil-military-political cooperation was a feature of British rule in the subcontinent. At Independence, the first governor-general was a British admiral and the exigencies of partition and of military action in three princely states (Junagadh, Hyderabad, and Kashmir) led to a close working relationship between Prime Minister Nehru's government and senior military officers. Therefore, within two months of Independence, the

Defense Committee of the Cabinet (DCC) was established as an apex body for making decisions pertaining to national security. It was initially presided over by the governor-general and all three service chiefs were members. As the prime minister was also in attendance, the military chiefs were able to give unfiltered advice directly to him. After India became a republic, the governor-general was replaced by a president as the head of state. The president was vested as the nominal supreme commander of the nation's armed forces, but, unlike his predecessors, the governor-general, was not the head of government and played no direct role in the decision making process.

As a consequence, the DCC was now presided over by the prime minister. Subsequently, this apex committee underwent a number of reorganizations, and ultimately became the Cabinet Committee of Political Affairs (CCPA) in 1971. It continued to be headed by the prime minister but was enlarged to include the Ministers of Defense, Home Affairs, Finance and External Affairs. The augmentation of the CCPA was accompanied by an enlargement of its role in the administration of the country. In the meantime, the Cabinet Committee on Defense was created to handle security related issues. In practical terms, the CCD was quite redundant as its composition was very similar to that of the CCPA. Inexplicably, the Cabinet Committee on Defense, too, excluded the three service chiefs. Only the Chairman of the Chiefs of Staff Committee (COSC), retained direct access to the defense minister and prime minister. The COSC is comprised of the three service chiefs under the chairmanship of the officer with the longest tenure. The Committee was supposed to coordinate broad military aims and strategies. Nonetheless, the COSC had no statutory authority and the civil servants in the ministry of defense processed its recommendations.

Military officers continued to have some participation in strategic policy issues through the Joint Intelligence Committee (JIC), which reported to the cabinet. It was chaired by an additional secretary in the Cabinet Secretariat and had representatives at the joint secretary level from the Ministries of Home, Defense and External Affairs, and, as the name implies, officers from the Research and Analysis Wing (RAW), the Intelligence Bureau (IB), and from the intelligence services of the three uniformed services. However, as RAW and IB reported directly to the prime minister, the two intelligence agencies did not treat the JIC as the true nodal agency for providing inputs to the government.

Working under the CCPA were several committees chaired by the defense minister. The names of most of these committees were self-explanatory: War Book Committee, Defense Minister's Appellate Committee on Pensions, et cetera. The highest level of interaction among the three military chiefs and the political leadership of the country were restricted to the Defense Minister's Committee (DMC). This committee, chaired by the defense minister, also included the Minister of State for Defense Production, the Secretaries of Defense, Defense Production, Defense R&D, and the Financial Advisor to the Defense Minister. In practical terms, this committee only functioned as the defense minister's weekly ("morning") meeting and had neither fixed agenda nor statutory powers to impact the deliberations of the CCPA.

Earlier, as a consequence of the disastrous border war with China in 1962, systematic management of national security was instituted by drawing up five-year defense plans. Accordingly, a planning cell was set up in the Ministry of Defense (MoD) in November 1965. This cell was intended as a liaison to integrate defense planning with the National Planning Commission and other ministries. Nonetheless, in private conversations, senior military officers aver that the Planning Cell was barely functional. Similarly, the Committee on Defense Planning (CDP), created in 1978, to periodically review national defense objectives, rarely met despite its high-powered membership. It was headed by the head of the Indian bureaucracy, the Cabinet Secretary. Its members were the three service chiefs and a number of high ranking civil servants—the Secretaries of Defense, Finance, External Affairs, Defense Production, Financial Advisor to the Defense Minister and the Secretary of the National Planning Commission. Likewise, the Defense Planning Staff (DPS), set up in 1986, remained moribund. It was constituted as a multidisciplinary body under a three-star military officer with representation from the three services, the Ministries of Defense, Finance and External Affairs, and the Defense Research and Development Organization (DRDO). The DPS was to provide inputs to the COSC on international and regional security affairs, defense policy, weapons and equipment, financial planning, and joint training, logistics and management. In practice, neither the Ministry of Defense nor the three service headquarters vested the DPS with clear or meaningful responsibilities. Consequently, its role remained marginal and military officers regarded it as a professionally wasted assignment. The outcome: Members of the armed forces do not head a committee or an organization with direct access to the prime minister and the three service chiefs are excluded from decision making processes at the highest level.

Nevertheless, despite the present marginalization of the armed forces, the military will have to be intimately involved in future planning. Mere possession of the bomb does not constitute deterrence. To be credible, it requires a military trained and equipped with a retaliatory or second-strike capability. In addition, the force structure should take into account the underlying circumstances that led to weaponization in the first place.

The Road back to Pokharan

The following international developments are likely to have taken India back to the Pokharan test site:

The Altered Security Environment

After the "peaceful nuclear explosion" in May 1974, Indian nuclear policy evolved into two undeclared doctrines: "recessed deterrence" (a term attributed to Air Commodore Jasjit Singh, the director of well-known Delhi-based think-tank Institute of Defense Studies and Analyses) and "nonweaponized deterrence" (a concept proposed by the American arms control expert George Perkovich). Recessed deterrence was based on the fabrication of warheads and delivery systems but not their induction into the armed forces. This concept of nonweaponized deterrence was derived from India's proven technological capability of producing nuclear weapons at short notice in the event of a significant or imminent military threat.

However, in 1988, Prime Minister Rajiv Gandhi reportedly sanctioned the development of nuclear weapons in response to remarks made by Abdul Qadeer Khan, the head of Pakistan's nuclear program. During an interview, conducted in 1987, Dr. Khan confirmed that Pakistan had successfully developed nuclear bombs.[4] Following Rajiv's directive, India's own nuclearization was apparently completed by 1990. Since then, successive Indian prime ministers have planned or considered nuclear testing. In April 1998, Pakistan test fired the first operational Intermediate Range Ballistic Missile (IRBM), the Ghauri, in South Asia. This dramatic and unexpected increase in Islamabad's strike reach presumably raised concerns in New Delhi. India has generally considered Pakistan a smaller, aggressive, and militaristic neighbor that had launched preemptive strikes in each of the three Indo-Pakistan wars. The first such war started in October 1947 when Pakistan aided and abetted a tribal invasion of Kashmir in a pre-emptive bid to seize the princely state before the Maharaja could accede to India. Similarly, in August 1965, Pakistan tried to upstage India's growing military might by dispatching armed infiltrators into Kashmir. Likewise, in December 1971, in response to increasing Indo-Bangladeshi military pressure in the East, Islamabad launched a series of surprise air attacks in the West as a prelude to ground and naval attacks against India. Since then, it is a commonly held belief in the civil-military-political circles in New Delhi that Islamabad remains determined to avenge its defeat in the 1971 war by destabilizing, and, if possible, fracturing India. In this vein, India considers the insurgency in Kashmir as a proxy war waged by Pakistan. Considering these factors, New Delhi is likely to regard Islamabad's nuclear-tipped IRBMs as the instruments of a potential preemptive strike in a future Indo-Pakistani war. Under these circumstances, India was impelled to test its nuclear devices and proceed with similar weaponization to deter Pakistani adventurism in the future.

However, India's major security concern remains China. Despite some warming of Sino-Indian ties since the resumption of full diplomatic relations in 1976, the underlying hostility, suspicion, rivalry, and territorial disputes remain unresolved. In addition, Beijing continues to remain the major supplier of both conventional and nuclear-related technology and weaponry to Pakistan. Chinese assistance is reportedly most marked in providing warhead designs, guidance systems, and missiles. Furthermore, China's phenomenal economic growth in the past decade led to greater spending on both the manufacturing and the purchasing of modern military hardware including 200 ultra sophisticated Suhkoi-27 ground attack fighters from Russia, Z-9A jet helicopters from France, and the indigenously developed 20 Dongfeng-31 mobile

Intercontinental Ballistic Missiles (ICBMs). This military buildup further altered the balance of power in China's favor. Moreover, despite considerable economic liberalization, the Chinese continued to pursue an aggressive and hostile foreign policy as evidenced by Beijing's refusal to recognize the legally impeccable accession of Sikkim to India or to carry out meaningful negotiations with the Dalai Lama and the 120,000 Tibetan refugees in India. In addition, New Delhi was presumably influenced by the Chinese perspective on nuclear strategy being based on Sun Zi's concept of "forcing the other party to resign to our will without fighting a battle." Under the threat of possible nuclear blackmail, New Delhi had little choice but to go nuclear.[5]

The Impact of Pernicious International Treaties

After the end of the Cold War, the nuclear-weapon states assiduously sought to prevent further proliferation of nuclear weapons while retaining and refining their own stockpiles. Accordingly, in 1995, the Nuclear Nonproliferation Treaty (NPT) was indefinitely and unconditionally extended. During the negotiations that led to the NPT, India had argued that either the nuclear-weapon states should guarantee not to use such arms against nonweapon-states or undertake to defend the latter, if attacked by a nuclear weapon state. In response, in 1968, the two super-powers jointly supported the Security Council Resolution 255 to 'assist' non-nuclear states threatened by nuclear attack. In the face of such a vague assurance, India sent a high level delegation to Moscow, London and Washington DC to seek explicit, binding guarantees in the event of a Chinese nuclear threat. None was forthcoming. The NPT was signed in 1970. Not unexpectedly, in the absence of international guarantees against nuclear attack, India refused to sign the treaty.

In 1996, a Comprehensive Test Ban Treaty (CTBT) was opened for signature. Like the NPT, this treaty, too, sought to ratify the existing nuclear status quo. From the Indian perspective, Article XIV (2) of the CTBT was particularly disturbing. Under this article, if the CTBT did not enter into force by September 1999, a conference of the subscribing countries would be convened to "consider and decide by consensus what measures consistent with international law may be undertaken to accelerate the ratification process." In this formulation, New Delhi saw the clear threat of universal sanctions being applied to important nonentrants, like India, into the CTBT. Hence, nuclear tests had to be conducted prior to September 1999.

The search for status

India shared this basic motivation for acquiring nuclear weapons with the other democracies, Britain and France that have significant standing in global affairs. As early as 1948, four years before the United Kingdom successfully tested a nuclear device, a British interservices subcommittee concluded that the type and number of weapons in Britain's projected nuclear arsenal were not important because the fundamental reason for acquiring atomic weapons was for political benefits that would supposedly accrue from such possession. Five years later, then British Prime Minister Winston Churchill rejected demands from his armed forces for tactical nuclear weapons. Churchill, with unparalleled experience in armed conflict, ranging from Victorian colonial skirmishes to the two world wars, considered nuclear devices as instruments of diplomacy, not as weapons of war. The French motivation for weaponization, too, was political. The decisive push towards nuclear weapons was made in 1954. Following the staggering military defeat at Dien Bien Phu (Vietnam) in May that year, Prime Minister Mendes-France told a French scientist that other permanent members of the Security Council of the United Nations were like gangsters with their bombs, but he had no bomb to talk about.[6] The bomb, therefore, was to reestablish France's international prestige. By October 1990, the French had distilled their nuclear doctrine into a purely political one by declaring, "The French nuclear deterrent is not directed against any one in particular. France has no designated enemy. Our deterrent is at the service of our independence."[7] The French have also refused to qualify or quantify their concept of deterrence. *Le Monde,* in an editorial succinctly summed it up as, "By revealing one's intentions to the adversary, one fails to maintain the famous uncertainty that is at the heart of all deterrence."[8] Leading Indian public figures are on record for stating as much. Therefore, New Delhi, probably shared the view that nuclear weapons were symbols of a nation's true sovereignty, hard-won independence and technological achievements. In addition, these weapons become a form of insurance coverage in a world in flux at the end of the Cold War and the associated demise of the Soviet Union. Some in New Delhi also hoped that the first tangible effect of becoming a nuclear power might be a permanent seat in a reorganized Security Council of the United Nations.

There were a number of domestic considerations as well. The predominant ones were the following:

Institutional pressures from within India.
It is likely that the armed forces were not the only institutions pressing for nuclear tests. Scientists from the Atomic Energy Commission and from the Defense Research and Development Organization (DRDO) had to test nuclear devices to obtain data for weaponization, computer simulation, and for subcritical tests in the future. The Indian scientific community may have further argued that without testing, the induction of nuclear warheads for the ballistic missiles under development could not be exercised with full confidence. Similarly, it could be reasoned that, if India did not go nuclear, then the investment in the development of supercomputers, ballistic missiles, nuclear submarines, etc., was pointless. Furthermore, nuclear tests were imperative for refining the hitherto unproved thermonuclear and sub kiloton bombs.

A new war-fighting paradigm
After the Gulf War, in a paper for the Los Alamos National Laboratory, Stephen Rosen hypothesized that a nuclear-armed Iraq could have deterred or interfered with U. S. military deployments in the gulf in two ways: (1) By coercing Saudi

Arabia and other neighboring countries into denying the United States access to their ports, airfields, etc., and (2) American field commanders would have had serious doubts about concentrating 500,000 U. S. service-personnel within range of Iraqi nuclear weapons.[9] A similar verdict was given by a former chief of the Indian Army, General K. Sundarji. His conclusions were widely quoted. India, having been exposed to a half-hearted attempt at nuclear blackmail by the United States during the 1971 war to liberate Bangladesh, was loath to suffer from such an experience again. Weaponization was the obvious answer.

Fulfilling a political commitment

On December 29, 1962, in the immediate aftermath of a humiliating defeat in a Sino-Indian border war, the Jana Sangh, became the first party in India to pass a resolution for the production of nuclear weapons as a part of the country's long-term defense effort against China. Not unexpectedly, the BJP, as the Jana Sangh's subsequent reincarnation, too, was committed to the acquisition of nuclear weapons. Accordingly, during an earlier stint as prime minister in 1996, Vajpayee had reportedly ordered the resumption of nuclear tests. However, his government fell in just 13 days and the nuclear tests were aborted. On returning to office in 1998, Vajpayee was determined to press ahead with the tests.

Domestic political pressures

In March 1998, Vajpayee returned to power at the head of a motley 17-party coalition. Though the BJP was by far the largest member of the coalition, Vajpayee had to make far-reaching concessions in order to put the alliance together. It is speculated that some party zealots, in turn, may have extracted nuclear tests as a price for their continued loyalty and support. It is more probable that Vajpayee felt that nuclear testing was likely to be immensely popular with the Indian voters. Therefore, after the tests, his personal popularity and prestige would soar, making him politically stronger and better able to keep his coalition partners in line.

The Road Ahead

The ethos of the Indian military is of a loyal and capable servant of the state. Since Independence, both the bureaucrat and the politician have nurtured such servitude. As a result, the armed forces probably lack the wherewithal and confidence to take up the leadership in defining the road ahead. Hence, the politician, the civil servant, the economist, and the scientist are likely to decide the mix and type of nuclear weapons for the military.

At the time of the tests, India had two delivery systems in place: a variety of aircraft and a missile—the Prithvi. The latter was a cumbersome, short-range, liquid-fueled, inaccurate missile of limited military capability. Despite these limitations, the Prithvi was in service in the Army, Navy and Air Force.

Accordingly, all three services were nuclear capable. On the other hand, the more versatile nuclear-capable warplanes were only with the Air Force. Therefore, the road ahead is likely to be marked by all three services presenting rationales for deploying nuclear weapons under their own individual commands. In this context, all three services can cite their experience and role in handling nuclear weapons. It is speculated that the largest service, the army, carried out exercises in a simulated nuclear battlefield in the 1980s. The scenarios presumably ranged from launching tactical nuclear strikes against an enemy to hitting the adversary with such weapons in terrain ranging from the deserts of Rajasthan to the snowy peaks of the Himalayas. The Air Force has supposedly acquired extensive experience in the toss-bombing of nuclear devices. The Navy's experience in the handling of a nuclear submarine is well known. However, the political decision has already been made: The Indian military will only be trained and equipped as a deterrent force. To credibly deter, a second strike or retaliatory capability is dependent on the following factors:

Survivability of forces
For maximum survival of a second strike retaliatory capability, there should be adequate dispersal of forces. The ultimate dispersal was reached by the United States and Russia. Both countries had developed, at great cost, a triad of forces, i.e., land based missiles in hardened silos, manned aircraft and submarine based ballistic missiles. The triad could be further refined by fitting multiple, independently targeted warheads on the weapon system as well as mounting the land-based missiles on mobile launchers. To a lesser extent two other powers, France and China, too, had developed a triad of nuclear forces. The fifth nuclear power, Britain, maintained only submarine-based missiles and some manned aircraft. Obviously, India could settle for one or two legs of the triad. If manned aircraft were a part of the force, then reinforced hangers and a number of secret, widely dispersed airbases would be required. To improve survivability, a number of early warning systems would have to be in place. Satellite and airborne reconnaissance and guidance systems as well as over the horizon radar capabilities would be required. In addition, in order to protect land based sites, defensive systems consisting of a substantial fleet of interceptor aircraft, Surface-to-Air missiles and Anti-missile Missiles would have to be in place. At this stage, other than manned aircraft, some interceptors and Surface-to-Air Missiles, India has to develop the remaining systems.

The adequacy of strike elements
The Indian Air Force has four different types of nuclear-capable strike aircraft, the SU-30, the Jaguar, the Mirage 2000, and the MiG-23/27. The maximum effective fighting range of any of these aircraft while flying in the typical 'high-low-high' or 'low-high-low' pattern in an attack mission is less than 700 miles. Mid-air refueling could extend the range but none of the aircraft have been so configured. Apparently, the IAF has practiced toss bombing using MiG-23/27 aircraft. There were two rationales behind the use of these older warplanes

with a smaller range. First, since nuclear bombs are not precision munitions but area bombs, the less sophisticated bomb-sights of the MiGs were considered adequate for area bombing. Second, the MiG, being a more ruggedly-built aircraft, was more likely to survive hits on the way to the target. At this stage, the air force requires improved Electronic Counter Measures (ECMs) to neutralize the enemy's defensive systems. On the other hand, it is the only service that has a ready-built organization that can be converted into a strategic command. The Central Air Command, headquartered at Allahabad, is well located, has no significant operational role at this stage, and has at least eight well-maintained airfields to station the designated nuclear-armed aircraft.

The Indian Navy acquired three years of experience in the handling of nuclear-powered boats during 1988-91 by leasing a Charlie-class submarine (INS *Chakra*) from the Soviet Union. The choice of a Charlie-class submarine was particularly canny: In the Soviet Navy these submarines had an anti-carrier primary role and the boats were also capable of launching cruise missiles. Presumably, similar submarines in the Indian Navy would not only deter an inimical carrier task force from threatening Indian interests but also launch missiles against targets on land. Later, the Navy plausibly claimed that, "In the history of no other nation's navy, the transition from a conventional to a nuclear capability has been completed in one generation. The Indian Navy has done it. INS *Chakra* was commissioned in the mid-1980s, well within twenty years of the first conventional submarine being inducted in 1968."[10] Following the threatened intervention by the United States in the 1971 war, the Indian government had decided to develop an Advanced Technology Vessel (ATV)—a nuclear-powered submarine. The construction of the ATV's hull was scheduled to begin in 1997. It was delayed. All the same, the Indian Navy still expects to have the first boat by 2005, with an eventual fleet of five submarines.[11] However, the ATV is not being designed as a submarine capable of launching ballistic missiles. Even after suitable modifications, it will only be able to launch nuclear-tipped cruise missiles. There appear to be no plans to develop diesel-powered SSBNs for the specific purpose of lurking in the Indian Ocean while maintaining a reasonable second-strike capacity in an ocean where the detection of submarines is particularly difficult. In the meantime, the Navy has reportedly suggested the deployment of the naval version of the Prithvi missile (named Dhanush) on selected surface ships. Some corvettes and three new frigates under construction in Russia are favored for such conversion.

Unlike the Air Force and the Navy, the Indian Army has had little to do with nuclearization though it was supposedly offered the option of developing tactical nuclear weapons in the aftermath of the Sino-Indian border war of 1962. The army leadership demurred, recognizing that the funds for nuclearization would largely come from money earmarked for the enlargement and modernization of conventional forces. Apparently, tactical atomic weapons were again considered in the 1980s after Pakistan had clearly acquired nuclear weapons. As mentioned earlier, there is widespread speculation that related exercises were conducted as well. However, no clear doctrine appears to have emerged for the use of such weapons, either along the Indo-Pakistan border or in the Himalayas against the Chinese. Notionally, the nuclear-tipped Prithvi could be used in the extended battlefield against either country. As a related step, the Indian Army has apparently trained approximately 120 men per year in NBC (Nuclear, Biological, and Chemical) warfare. Therefore, by 2001, two fully trained and equipped battalions may be in service in the army. These troops are vital for managing the damage caused by a nuclear explosion. Such an explosion may result from an attack, an accident, sabotage, or a natural calamity. The army will also have to hold the ground or advance in an area struck by a nuclear explosive.

All three services have considerable experience in the use of short-range guided missiles. As far as ballistic missiles are concerned, India created the Integrated Guided Missile Development Program (IGMDP) in 1983. The program undertook to develop five different guided rockets including two surface-to-surface ballistic missiles, the Prithvi and the Agni. At present, the only operational missile is the liquid fueled Prithvi. It comes in three variants, based on the principle of range-payload tradeoff. Hence, the missile with the longest range (225 miles) has the smallest payload (500 pounds), the intermediate-range missile carries a warhead of 1,000 pounds to a distance of 180 miles, and the one with the shortest range (90 miles) has 2,000 pounds of explosives. The Prithvi has apparently been inducted in all three services. The army appears to have the largest number (75 in a specially designated artillery regiment). However, the Indian Army has such limited battlefield surveillance capability that the missile cannot be used at its full range. Therefore, its utility is questionable against Pakistan and negligible against China. The IRBM, Agni is still under development. The second generation Agni, with its range of 1,500 miles, would be capable of hitting a dozen major population centers in China. Finally, India will have to create secure and tested command, control, and communication (C3) systems for targeting and for ordering nuclear strikes. Conversely, such systems must ensure against the unauthorized or accidental attack by these forces.

The strength and cost of strike forces

The total strength of the strike aircraft mentioned above is approximately 325 warplanes. Not all 325 aircraft would be configured to deliver nuclear weapons. Perhaps, 150 would suffice. In this regard, the Indian fleet could use the British model. The United Kingdom produced 324 aircraft for the V-Bomber fleet, but only 144 were designed to carry nuclear explosives. Based on French and British projections, at least one-third of the force was expected to survive a surprise first strike by the enemy. Therefore, about 50 out of the 150 Indian aircraft should survive a preemptive strike and be operational for retaliation. Considering Anglo-French calculations, an average of three aircraft per target should be committed. Accordingly, India could strike at a minimum of a dozen major targets in the region—obviously a telling deterrent capability. India has produced an estimated 350 to 500 kilograms of weapons-grade Plutonium—enough to manufacture at least 100 nuclear bombs with yields ranging from 40 to 300 kilotons.[12] About 60 such bombs are widely considered as sufficient deterrence against China. A smaller number should suffice against Pakistan. In addition to the strike aircraft, India could produce about 50 land-based missiles in hardened silos as a credible deterrent.

Deployment of the bomb accounted for 55.7 percent ($3,241 billion) of the vast U. S. nuclear arsenal, whereas the cost of the warheads was only 7 percent ($409.4 billion using 1996 as the constant for the purposes of computation). However, for the much smaller and regionally-directed Indian program, the further costs should not be so daunting. India has already paid for the aircraft, the nuclear reactors, fuel reprocessing plants, et cetera. The additional cost of fabrication of the warheads, the missiles and silos, and related infrastructure is estimated at $3.5 billion over a seven-to-ten year period. Nuclear submarine-based deterrence is regarded as the most desirable option as the detection and destruction of submarines is harder to guarantee in a preemptive strike. A fleet of three missile-equipped submarines (two at sea at any given time, while the remaining one is in port for servicing, upgrading, training, et cetera.) is likely to incur an expense of an additional $7.0 billion. Recurring costs of operating, maintaining, and upgrading the strategic force would be around $100 million per year.[13]

The indirect cost of going nuclear has been considerable and is ongoing. In the late 1960s, plans were drawn up in India for the construction of power plants based on the CANDU (Canadian Deuterium-Uranium) Pressurized Heavy Water Reactors (PHWRs) to generate 15,000-20,000 megawatts of electric power over the next 30 years. After the 1974 nuclear test, Canadian and American cooperation in developing these power plants ceased. As a result, by 1995, only 2,200 megawatts of capacity was installed. Thus, nuclear power provided only 1.9-2.7 percent of the 80,000 megawatts of electricity generated in India. The annual cost to the Indian economy by the shortage of 15 percent of electric power is computed to be $2.7 billion.[14]

The California-based think-tank, the RAND Corporation, with its close ties to the American armed forces developed flow charts to optimize civilian-military interaction. These charts are particularly relevant in the Indian environment where the civilian authorities are much more ill-informed about military matters than their American counterparts. The charts from RAND are summarized below:

1. The uniformed services must take a pro-active role in formulating, defining, demonstrating, and proposing new concepts like the strategy for nuclear weapons.
2. Concepts do not automatically exist. They must be formulated, evaluated, and demonstrated by the armed forces.
3. The right concepts must be judged as: operationally viable, technically feasible, fiscally affordable, and politically acceptable.[15]

The technical feasibility and political acceptability of nuclear weapons are now beyond debate and doubt in India. It is now for the end-users to ensure systems that are viable, adaptable to changing circumstances, and do not waste financial resources. In the past, close civil-military interaction in India was not vital. The inherited colonial systems, with some modifications, had fitfully and barely sufficed. However, by going nuclear, a new paradigm has emerged: Nuclear bombs are primarily political, not military weapons. In addition, the weapon systems are much more expensive than conventional ones and are often morally reprehensible to both the users and to most of the world. Moreover, these are not only weapons of mass destruction and terror but also imperil succeeding generations by the effects of radiation on genetic codes and on the environment. Therefore, it is incumbent on the armed forces to be pro-actively involved. The uniformed services have to not only deter an aggressor, but should also bear in mind the following considerations.

Tactical nuclear weapons
The official statements notwithstanding, the services are likely to develop doctrines for the use of tactical nuclear weapons in the event of an all-out war with Pakistan and/or China or when the country is threatened with nuclear blackmail or by military intervention by a third country. Nuclear Depth Bombs (NDBs) have an obvious anti-submarine warfare (ASW) role, whereas 155 mm nuclear shells or tactical nuclear airstrikes would demonstrate India's political will and induce an opponent to stop aggression or intervention.

Create another paradigm
Nuclear bombs do not have to be just tactical or strategic weapons. They may be used in a substrategic or a prestrategic role. Under the French Army's Plan Lorraine, a prestrategic strike was to be made against an advancing enemy at selected locations. The targeted areas had to be at a distance of at least four kilometers from urban centers with a population of 5,000 or more. In addition, the French deployed bombs that would release as little radioactive fallout as possible. In the Indian context such a strike could be launched against Chinese troop concentrations on the vast and sparsely populated Tibetan plateau at a distance of 40 miles from the Himalayan ranges. At that distance, the impact should be little on the Himalayas, sacred to Hindus as the abode of the gods and too fragile and geomorphologically active to be subjected to nuclear explosives. Against Pakistan or against a naval expeditionary force, a series of 50-100 kiloton underwater explosions at a distance of 100 miles from the target could generate massive waves (Very High Sea States—VHSS) of 100 feet or more. Such waves would wreak havoc on a harbor and cause much damage and disruption to a flotilla.[16]

Avoid turf wars
To fund a nuclear arsenal, some conventional systems will have to be pared down. Inter-service rivalry for the reduced funds is a logical consequence. For example, during the past decade, the Army has already been subjected to reduction of its projected armor strength from 80 to 59 regiments. Further reduc-

tions, even if deemed logical, are likely to be resented and resisted. Despite such pressures, the uniformed services should try to minimize turf wars.

Develop an integrated higher defense organization
Modern wars are not fought by just one service. At least, two, if not all three services are involved. In addition, support and input are essential from intelligence agencies and various civil services (police, railways, post and telegraph, administrative, et cetera). An apex body, like a National Security Council, is obviously needed. In India, such a Council was first mooted in 1990. It was revived in September 1998. Accordingly, a task force headed by former Defense Minister K. C. Pant was created. Little consideration was reportedly given to the recommendations of the task force for the revived six member National Security Council was little different from the Cabinet Committee on Defense: The NSC as constituted in November 1998, was headed by the Prime Minister. Four of the other members were the Ministers of Defense, Home Affairs, External Affairs and Finance. The new addition was the Principal Secretary to the Prime Minister who was given the supplementary designation of National Security Advisor. The thus constituted NSC attracted considerable negative comment: It was deemed as being too political in its membership; it included no specialists on defense matters; and, the National Security Advisor was viewed as being burdened with too many other administrative duties to be further encumbered with the responsibility for the security of the nation. These criticisms notwithstanding, India had taken a step towards a holistic approach towards the management of the defense of the country.

The seriousness of its intent was underscored by providing the NSC with three back-up bodies–the Strategic Policy Group (SPG), the National Security Advisory Board (NSAB) and the secretariat of the Joint Intelligence Committee (JIC). The 27-member SPG was composed of serving secretary level officers from the Cabinet Secretariat, Home Affairs, Defense, Finance and Defense Production, Revenue, and Space and Atomic Energy. The SPG also included the three Service Chiefs, the Governor of the Reserve Bank of India, the Director of the Intelligence Bureau, the Secretary of the Research and Analysis Wing, the Chairman of the JIC, and the Scientific Advisor to the Defense Minister. The Group marked the highest level of participation by the military. The 22-member National Security Advisory Board consisted of nonofficial or retired specialists in military and economic security from a more diverse background such as members of the academe and the media. Only 4 out of the 22 were retired military officers. The board's prestige was enhanced by appointment of the highly articulate, retired bureaucrat K. Subrahmanyam as its chairman. He was widely acknowledged as the country's leading strategic thinker. The board met at monthly intervals. Apparently, two groups emerged: the doves who proposed a smaller nuclear arsenal of 60 to 150 warheads with regional strike capability and the hawks, who sought 350 to 400 bombs with global reach.

In late August 1999, on the eve of a general election, the board produced a six-page document titled, "Indian Nuclear Doctrine." The report was, in fact, a doctrine-cum-strategy paper. It reiterated India's need for nuclear weapons, the importance of a credible minimum deterrence, and vested the prime minister with the sole authority to order the use of nuclear devices. The document also vaguely implied an option for future tests, the possibility of developing tactical bombs, and flexibility on the no-first-use pledge made by the Indian government. It went on to recommend the well-known triad of aircraft, mobile land-based missiles, and sea-borne weapons with a space-based early-warning system that could respond to an attack in the shortest possible time. One of the presumed hawks, Bharat Karnad, soothingly reiterated his calculations regarding the costs of the triad. He felt it would be quite affordable at Rs. 700 billion (approximately U. S. $17 billion) over 30 years. However, he added a caveat: The cost could be ten times as much in the face of trade embargoes and other punitive measures by the international community. The Indian Prime Minister was quick to add that the document was only a draft, subject to amendments. Others, including members of the board itself, too, made similar observations. All the same, it appeared that the hawks had dominated the deliberations, at least in the short term.

This multilayered cumbersome system was also to revamp the defense organization of the country. Out of the 55 persons involved, only a dozen or so members, whether civilian or military, possessed expertise in defense matters. Not unexpectedly, more than a year after the Indian tests even a basic principle like the creation of tri-service theater commands, instead of the current individual service field commands, was not enunciated. Only the concept of forming a specially designated strategic command, to cater exclusively for nuclear and related forces, was privately and unofficially aired.[17] In conclusion, on the threshold of a new millennium, India was a state with nuclear weapons (SNW), but not a nuclear weapons state (NWS) in more ways than one.

Notes

1. Department of Atomic Energy, Annual Report (New Delhi: Government of India Publications, March 31, 1999).
2. Amitav Ghosh, "Countdown: In South Asia, Nuclear Catastrophe in the Making," The New Yorker, October 26, 1998, p. 191.
3. General V. N. Sharma, "India's Security Environment," USI Journal, vol. CXXII, no. 510, p. 434.
4. Kuldip Nayar, "We have the A-bomb, says, Pakistan's 'Dr Strangelove'," The Observer, London, March 1, 1987.
5. K. Subrahmanyam, "Nuclear India In Global Politics," World Affairs, vol. II, no. 3, pp. 12-40. Jaswant Singh, "Against Nuclear Apartheid," Foreign Affairs, vol. LXXVII, no. 5, pp. 41-52. See also Jaswant Singh, Defending India (Chennai: Macmillan, 1999); Chris Smith et al. Defense and Insecurity in Southern Asia: The Conventional and Nuclear Dimensions, Occasional Paper no. 21, The Henry L. Stimson Center, May 1995; General K. Sundarji, Blind Men of

Hindoostan (New Delhi: UBSPD, 1993); The Asia Society Study Group, *Preventing Nuclear Proliferation in South Asia* (New York: The Asia Society, 1995); P. R. Chari, Pervaiz Iqbal Cheema, et al. *Nuclear Non-Proliferation in India and Pakistan: South Asian Perspectives* (New Delhi: Manohar, 1996); and Stephen P. Cohen, *The Security of South Asia: American and Asian Perspectives* (Urbana and Chicago: University of Illinois, 1987).

6. Robert S. Norris, Andrew S. Burrows, et al. *Nuclear Weapons Databook: British, French and Chinese Nuclear Weapons* (Boulder: Westview, 1994), p. 54 (British situation), p.183 (French compulsions). See also John C. Hopkins and Weixing Hu, eds., *Strategic Views from the Second Tier: The Nuclear Weapons Policies of France, Britain, and China* (San Diego: University of California, 1994) and Sir Solly Zuckerman, *Nuclear Illusion and Reality* (New York: Vintage, 1963).

7. Ministere de la defense, *La Defense de la France: Une action inscrite dans la duree* (Paris: Service d'Information et de Relations Publiques des Armees, October 1990), p.13.

8. Editorial, "Effets d'annonce," *Le Monde,* February 10, 1991.

9. Stephen P. Rosen, "Lessons from the 1991 US-Iraq War: Hypothetical Nuclear Weapons Use," Paper for Los Alamos National Laboratory, August 31, 1991, pp. 1-8.

10. Commander Ranjit Pisharoty, "The Indian Navy Takes On High-Tech Marvels," *Sainik Samachar,* vol. XL, nos. 48, 49 & 50, p. 19. See also Rahul Roy-Choudhury, *Sea Power & Indian Security* (London: Brassey, 1995).

11. Andrew R. Koch, "Nuclear Powered Submarines: India's Strategic Trump Card," *Janes Intelligence Review,* June 1998, pp. 29-31.

12. David Albright, Frans Berkhout, and William Walker, *Plutonium and Highly Enriched Uranium: World Inventories, Capabilities and Policies* (New York: Oxford University Press, 1997), p. 269.

13. Kanti Bajpai, "The Challenges to India's diplomacy and Defense After Pokhran II," Paper at seminar, "After Pokhran II: The National Way Ahead," New Delhi, September 19-20, 1998; Ernest W. Lefever, *Nuclear Arms In The Third World: U. S. Policy Dilemma* (Washington DC: Brookings, 1979), pp. 15-19; George Perkovich, "Nuclear Proliferation" *Foreign Policy,* Fall 1998 pp. 12-23; K. Subrahmanyam, "Nuclear Force Design and Minimum Strategy for India," pp.176-195 in Bharat Karnad, ed., *Future Imperilled: India's Security in the 1990s and Beyond* (New Delhi: Viking, 1994); Ian Smart, *Future Conditional: The Prospect for Anglo-French Nuclear Cooperation,* Adelphi Paper 78 (London: International Institute for Strategic Studies, 1971), p.5; General K. Sundarji, "Imperatives of Indian Minimum Nuclear Deterrence," *Agni: Studies in International Strategic Issues,* vol. II, no. 1, p. 18.

14. Rodney W. Jones, Mark G. McDonough et al. *Tracking Nuclear Proliferation: A Guide in Maps and Charts, 1998* (Washington DC: Carnegie Endowment for International Peace, 1998), pp. 113, 120.

15. "Providing Forces (New Capabilities) To Meet The Needs Of The Future," (Santa Monica: RAND, 3/22/95).

16. Norman Friedman, "SUBROC, ASROC & Terrier Retire," *Proceedings USNI,* July 1989, p. 118.

17. Air Marshal B. D. Jayal, "Higher Defense Organization In India: The Strategic Dimension" *Indian Defense Review,* vol. XIII, no. 2, pp. 34-39.

Part IV

Economic Dimensions

CHAPTER ELEVEN

The Economic Costs and Benefits of Nuclear Weapons[1]

Deepak Lal

Summary

Assessing the economic costs of a nuclear weapons program is problematic. An analysis of the economic burden of nuclear defense cannot be isolated from the costs of its delivery systems, the trade-offs between nuclear defense and conventional defense, the opportunity costs of a nuclear deterrence program on the civilian development program, and the intangible and immeasurable value added to a nation's international prestige. This chapter explores this minefield by assessing the determinants of military expenditures, and providing a framework for assessing the cost-benefits of a nuclear weapons program.

Introduction

It is virtually impossible to write a paper on the economic costs and benefits of nuclear weapons based on available studies because of two insurmountable problems. The first concerns the natural secrecy surrounding the nuclear programs of most Third World countries, including those—China, India and Pakistan—that have demonstrated a nuclear capability through nuclear explosions, and others that are known as recessed nuclear powers—Israel, South Africa, Brazil, North Korea—with existing material and technology to manufacture nuclear weapons. This makes it difficult to provide any hard estimates of the costs of nuclear proliferation: A problem that is compounded when the costs of different delivery systems (such as missile systems) have to be added to those of producing the bombs. If government budgets did provide a detailed breakdown of these costs in terms of the costs of capital outlays and labor distinguished by skill levels, then standard techniques of cost benefit analysis could be used to compute the real resource costs of the development and deployment of these weapons for particular countries.[2] No such accounts are available.

Equally problematic is the computation of the benefits from having nuclear weapons. The motives for acquiring these weapons encompass not only considerations of military security but also prestige.[3] When the international pecking order is coterminous with the existing nuclear powers as reflected in the permanent membership of the Security Council, other aspirants to a similar status (notably India and Brazil in the Third World) will not ignore this aspect of acquiring prestige. The preaching and pressures of the existing nuclear powers, for others to desist from acquiring these weapons will be seen as hypocritical by countries like India. It is virtually impossible to put a "value" on such national prestige. Attempts through the revealed preferences of particular countries, on what they are willing to spend in real resource costs to acquire nuclear weapons merely tell us how much particular countries (or more precisely their "elites") are willing to pay for this "noneconomic" benefit. That it remains an important motive in international relations is shown by the continuing attempts by the United Kingdom and France to maintain independent nuclear deterrent capacities, even though the justifications for them died with the Cold War. As the former UK Secretary of State Douglas Hurd maintained, being a nuclear power and a member of the Security Council allows the UK to punch beyond its weight in the international arena. Whether the ordinary UK citizen, as opposed to the politicians and bureaucrats desirous of "eating at the top table," derive any utility from such "prestige" is questionable. But it would be rash to predict that these nuclear powers will be forced by their democratic political processes to give up these symbols of past "greatness."

Given the continuing and (as Lawrence Freedman has argued) essentially circular and inconclusive debate in the industrialized West about the strategic and tactical usefulness of nuclear weapons, the benefits in terms of military security provided by nuclear weapons are also problematic. For, despite the axiomatic abhorrence of nuclear weapons in many circles and their apocalyptic potential, the fact remains that—apart from the devastation of Hiroshima and Nagasaki by the United States—nuclear weapons have not killed anyone since the end of the World War II. Also as Lawrence Freedman notes: "What we do know is that since 1945 Europe has been at peace. This underlines the point that nuclear deterrence maybe a viable policy even if it is not credible. . . . The Emperor Deterrence may have no clothes, but he is still Emperor."[4] Similarly, it is worth noting that after having fought three bloody wars between themselves till the early 1970s, there has been no such Indo-Pakistan conflict since the Indian "peaceful nuclear explosion" of 1974! Where even military experts and strategic thinkers are seriously divided about the usefulness of nuclear weapons, it would be folly for a mere economist to tread.

For these reasons, I will only be able to provide something analytical. I begin by discussing the sparse literature on the determinants of military spending across countries, concentrating on one study in particular (by Michael Beenstock) that provides an analytical framework that I believe is the right one to think about the costs and benefits of nuclear proliferation. This leads on in the final section to outlining the type of cost benefit analysis which someone with greater time and resources than those available to me should conduct to determine the true opportunity costs of nuclear proliferation for particular countries or regions.

The Determinants of Military Expenditure

The simplest way for an economist to understand the demand for defense expenditure is to look upon it as an insurance policy. Beenstock makes this precise. His and Maizel and Nisanke's study are the two major ones for developing countries dealing with this question.

Governments spend money on defense for three main reasons according to Maizel and Nissanke. The first is to quell internal rebellions. Most of the conflicts more recently have involved civil wars.[5] The second reason Maizel and Niskane state "is political tension with, or potential aggression from, neighboring countries. The Arab/Israeli and Iran/Iraq conflicts, and the political tensions between India and Pakistan, and Greece and Turkey, are good examples of such concern."[6] The third reason they give and which was particularly important during the Cold war was "the degree of involvement in either of the global power blocs."[7] In addition Maizel and Niskane also emphasize a number of political and economic variables (degree of internal repression, military dictatorship, level of economic development, size of the government budget, etc.) They estimated cross section regressions for 83 developing countries for 1978-80, with separate regressions for the three regions of Africa, Asia and Latin America for the determinants of the rate of military expenditure in GDP. They concluded: "The differences among developing countries in the relative size of their military burdens thus appear to reflect a complex of factors—domestic, regional and global—which are not easy to disentangle, and which no doubt vary in emphasis from country to country."[8]

Much more satisfactory is Beenstock's attempt to explain the determinants of military spending in terms of a model where "military spending is incurred to promote security and may be regarded as the insurance premium on a policy that is designed to deter war and to limit the deductible in the event that war breaks out. The analogy with insurance is complete."[9] He estimated a cross-section regression of 137 countries (including developed ones) for 1984, incorporating the various variables that emerge as relevant in the reduced form of his model. He finds: "(i) Defense spending is strictly proportionate to income and does not depend on population. (ii) Countries undergoing active internal conflicts typically spend 48% more on defense. (iii) Countries undergoing active external conflict typically spend more than four times more on defense. (iv) Countries experiencing a latent external threat spend more than five times more on defense. (v) NATO countries spend on average 40% more on defense while the WP [Warsaw Pact] countries spend 115% more than countries that are not members of NATO or the Warsaw Pact. (vi) Military aid boosts defense spending."[10]

Beenstock provides some indicators for determining country specific norms based on the predicted value from his international regression line for defense spending. He finds for 1984, that: "If countries are ranked by their defense spending as a percentage of GNP it turns out that Iceland is the smallest and Qatar the largest. These countries retain their positions even after normalizing with respect to the international regression line. Other countries, however, change their position quite radically. For example Egypt, ranked 124 (out of 137) in absolute terms, is only ranked 29 in relative terms, while Uruguay, ranked 63 in absolute terms, is ranked 91 in relative terms. Thus Egypt 'under-spends' on defense while Uruguay 'overspends.' Other perhaps interesting cases are the USA (absolute 106, relative 110), the former Soviet Union (absolute 125, relative 22), Pakistan (absolute 101, relative 16), South Korea (absolute 99, relative 14), and Kuwait (absolute 98, relative 121)."[11]

A Framework for Analyzing the Costs–Benefits of Nuclear Weapons

The Beenstock model can moreover be extended to examine the question of the costs and benefits of nuclear weapons. Though for the reasons set out in the introduction actual quantification maybe well nigh impossible. Having seen that the question of the appropriate level of defense expenditure for a particular country is likely to be more complicated than a simple computation of the losses in foregone growth and output as a result of the necessary diversion of resources from civilian issues, the further question of the appropriate composition of this aggregate expenditure will raise even more difficult and country specific issues. But the "insurance" analogy of Beenstock's model allows some illuminating comments on the relevant choices in the development and deployment of nuclear weapons.

The basic question is whether nuclear weapons offer the required degree of security with a lower insurance premium and a lower deductible than conventional weapons? First, it needs to be noted that the security nuclear weapons provide relates to external conflicts. They are hardly relevant for the more prevalent internal conflicts. For, if a government is seeking to pacify or regain control of parts of its own territory, it would hardly make sense for it to threaten to obliterate that territory in a nuclear holocaust. (I of course rule out those cases—which regrettably cannot be considered as purely theoretical—

where the government seeks to eliminate some regionally confined section of its population). So what we need to consider is the composition of that part of defense expenditure that seeks to meet external threats.

Analytically, it is simplest to think of what economists call the "expected utility"—denoted by "E"—the government derives in dealing with the external threat in two alternative cases: one when it only has conventional weapons (c), the other when it has nuclear weapons (n). Though of course in the latter case, in principle, the nuclear weapons need not be a substitute but an addition to conventional weapons.

Attached to these alternative cases or "projects" are the respective probabilities of war occurring. It being assumed that the function of these alternative forms of defense expenditure is to deter a foreign aggressor and hence to lower the probability of war denoted by "p," with the superscripts "c," or "n," referring to the conventional and nuclear alternatives.

If a war does occur there will be a loss (L) including the loss of men, material, and also possibly political and territorial losses (gains) if the country loses (wins). These losses are likely to differ in the two alternative cases, and in the nuclear case depending upon whether the potential foreign adversary does or does not possess nuclear weapons. As my subject is nuclear proliferation, and to simplify the argument, I will assume for the two polar cases that in one neither party to a possible war possesses nuclear weapons, and in the other that both do.

The costs of the defense expenditure on the two alternative systems will also differ. These will consist of various physical inputs of labor (differentiated by skill), capital goods and land. They need to be priced at their true opportunity costs (by what economists call "shadow prices"), which could be different for well–known reasons from market prices. The simplest and most general method of shadow pricing that can readily take account of various distortions in the working of the domestic price mechanism in developing countries (including problems such as unemployment or underemployment, shortage of savings, government budget constraints) are the rules developed by Ian Little and James Mirrlees.[12] Valuing each physical input m^i at its shadow price p^i and aggregating will yield the true social cost of the two alternative defense programs denoted by M^c for the conventional and M^n for the nuclear alternatives.

If the level of national income is denoted by "Y," and the population by "N," then the level of per capita welfare (W) that will prevail in either the nuclear or conventional case will depend upon whether there is war (W1) or there is peace (W2). Thus where i, j = n, c:

$$W1 = [Y-L^j-M^i]/N$$
$$W2 = [Y-M^i]/N(1)$$

Whilst the expected utility (E) from the two projects will then just be these two outcomes (W1,W2) weighted by their respective probabilities (p), so that where k = n, c:

$$E^k = p^k(W1) + (1-p^k)(W2)(2)$$

We can now readily derive an expression for the difference in expected utility from the nuclear over the conventional option by using (1) and (2) to obtain[13]:

$$E^n-E^C = [(M^c-M^n) + (p^{c''}L^c-p^{n''}L^n)]/N(3)$$

This expression succinctly summarizes the relative costs and benefits of the two options. The first expression in brackets is the difference in the costs at shadow prices of the physical inputs of the two alternative "projects." As the costs of the nuclear alternative are likely to be greater than that of the conventional one, we would expect this expression to be negative. The net benefits of the nuclear alternative then turn essentially upon whether or not the second expression within brackets that shows the relative expected "losses" from the conventional and nuclear options is positive enough to outweigh the negative expression for relative costs. *Ceteris paribus,* the lower the expected losses from the nuclear option, the more likely it is to produce net benefits. These in turn will depend on the probability of war if a country has nuclear weapons. This in turn will reflect the deterrent effect of these weapons. If one subscribes to the deterrence provided by mutual assured destruction, this probability essentially diminishes to zero. Then irrespective of the loss (L^n), which could be horrendously large, ($p^{n''}L^n$) will approach zero. But if with Greenpeace you believe that the loss from a nuclear war is infinite, and that there is always a finite possibility that nuclear powers will go to war, then as with Pascal's wager, the expected loss from possessing nuclear weapons will approach infinity!

There is unfortunately no rational basis for assessing these probabilities, and hence for providing any definitive quantification of expression (3), even if we could estimate the relative costs of the nuclear option at shadow prices. But for what it is worth, for one of the currently recessed nuclear powers—India— it has been estimated by "retired Air Commodore Jasjit Singh, who heads the Institute of Defense Studies and Analysis that India needs to allocate a minimum of 3% of its GDP to ensure credible conventional defense, if geopolitical threats remain unchanged in the next decade. A 2.5% GDP spending would be adequate if India were to deploy its nuclear capability."[14] But this comparison rests on assuming that the past costs of developing nuclear weapons and delivery systems are sunk costs, which is correct for countries that have already invested in creating a nuclear capability. For those seeking to acquire it, the capital costs of making the bomb can be considerable.[15] Whether these are worth undertaking must ultimately depend, as expression 3 shows, upon the relative probabilities of war and hence of deterrence under the two alternatives.

I know of no rational way to judge these probabilities. In conclusion, however, I might cite a piece of casual empiricism. When I was a student at Oxford in the early 1960s, a board game called Diplomacy was very popular amongst us. This was based on the map of Europe before the World War I, with players assigned particular countries and their armed forces reflecting the relative strengths of the countries at that time. It was amazing how often the game ended up repeating the pattern of alliances and events leading to the First World War. Sometime later this board game was overtaken by a new one invented in America, which was based on the Middle East situation in the 1960s. This version also provided nuclear as well as conventional arms to the various players. No matter how often we played the game with different permutations of players and countries, using the rational tactics for a repeated game of chicken, or the tit for tat strategy of the prisoners dilemma, or no strategy at all, within about half an hour the game usually ended with nuclear bombs having been unleashed on all the major population centers of the Middle East! It is this rather than any rational cost-benefit analysis of nuclear proliferation that at least would give me cause to pause.

Notes

1. This paper is based on part of my paper "Arms and the Man" in S. Spiegel (ed), *Dynamics of Middle Eastern Nuclear Proliferation*, Mellen Press, New York (in press) and reprinted in D. Lal: *Unfinished Business*, Oxford University Press, New Delhi, 1999.

2. See I. M. D. Little, and J. A. Mirrlees, *Project Appraisal and Planning for Developing Countries*, Heinemann Educational Books, London, 1974.

3. See L. Beaton, *Must the Bomb Spread*, Penguin Books, Harmondsworth, 1966.

4. L. Freedman, *The Evolution of Nuclear Strategy*, Macmillan, London, 1981, p. 399.

5. The study by Grobar and Gnanaselvam provides some estimates of the recent—and continuing—Sri Lankan civil war. They find that the opportunity cost of "the war during 1983-88 was about $1.5 billion, an amount equal to over 20% of 1988 GDP. Furthermore, the estimated opportunity cost is predicted to increase dramatically (to the range of $7-$15 billion) in the event that war continues through 1995" (p. 404). See L. M. Grobar and S. Gnanaselvam: "The Economic Effects of the Sri Lankan Civil War," *Economic Development and Cultural Change*, v. 41, no. 2, Jan. 1993.

6. A. Maizel and M. K. Nisanke: "The Determinants of Military Expenditures in Developing Countries," *World Development*, v. 14, no. 9, Sept. 1986, p. 1129.

7. Ibid.

8. Maizel and Niskane, p. 1137.

9. M. Beenstock, "International Patterns in Military Spending," *Economic Development and Cultural Change*, v. 41, no. 3, April 1993, p. 637.

10. Beenstock, p. 643.

11. Beenstock, p. 646.

12. For an exposition and derivation of shadow prices for India see Deepak Lal, *Prices for Planning*, Heinemann Educational Books, London, 1980.

13. This can be readily derived from:

$$E^n = [''(Y-L^n-M^n) + (1-p^n)(Y-M^n)]/N$$
$$E^c = [p^c(Y-L^c-M^c) + (1-p^c)(Y-M^c)]/N$$

14. Shekhar Gupta, *India Redefines Its Role*, Adelphi Paper 293, IISS, Oxford University Press, Oxford, 1995, p. 39.
15. See Beaton.

References

Beaton, L. *Must the Bomb Spread*. Penguin Books, Harmondsworth, 1966.

Beenstock, M. "International Patterns in Military Spending." *Economic Development and Cultural Change*, v. 41, no. 3, April 1993.

Grobar, L. M., and S. Gnanaselvam. "The Economic Effects of the Sri Lankan Civil War." *Economic Development and Cultural Change*, v. 41, no. 2, Jan. 1993.

Freedman, L. *The Evolution of Nuclear Strategy*. Macmillan, London, 1981.

Gupta, Shekhar. *India Redefines Its Role*. Adelphi Paper 293, IISS, Oxford University Press, Oxford, 1995.

Keegan, J. *A History of Warfare*. Pimlico, London, 1993.

Lal, D. *Prices for Planning*. Heinemann Educational Books, London, 1980.

———. *The Hindu Equilibrium: vol. 2—Aspects of Indian Labor*, Clarendon Press, Oxford, 1989.

———. *Poverty, Markets and Democracy*. The 1995 Nestle Annual Lecture on the Developing World, Nestle UK, 1995.

———. *Unfinished Business: India in the world economy*. Oxford University Press, New Delhi, 1999.

———. and H. Myint. *The Political Economy of Poverty Equity and Growth—A Comparative Study*. Clarendon Press, Oxford, 1996.

Little, I. M. D., and J. A. Mirrlees. *Project Appraisal and Planning for Developing Countries*. Heinemann Educational Books, London, 1974.

Maizels, A., and M. K. Nissanke. "The Determinants of Military Expenditures in Developing Countries," *World Development*, v. 14, no. 9, Sept. 1986.

CHAPTER TWELVE

The Domestic Consequences of India's Nuclear Tests

Devesh Kapur

Summary

This chapter examines two consequences of India's nuclear tests. First it analyzes the impact of the sanctions that were imposed subsequent to the tests. And second, it examines the proposition that the tests would result in an arms race, whose consequences would be ruinous for the subcontinent. In both cases the negative impact was quite limited. India's economy was not particularly vulnerable and the sanctions were not comprehensive either in the issue areas they were applied to or on with regard to the multilateral regime. If anything the sanctions had a modest positive economic impact in that they sell economic reforms within the BJP (albeit to a limited extent), the dominant partner in the ruling coalition. The cognitive impact of the sanctions was more significant in the short-term, especially on India's scientific community and underlined the need for a greater commitment by the Indian scientific community to deepen domestic technological development, particularly on defense. This chapter further argues that endogenous economic, institutional, and technological constraints will sharply limit any possibility of India launching into an arms race, notwithstanding the claims of some of the more breathless commentaries on the subject.

Introduction

India's decision to conduct nuclear tests in May 1998 was received with dismay by the world's major powers. The immediate official U. S. reaction was one of severe disapprobation, and the imposition of economic sanctions was the most visible manifestation of a decided chill in relations. Yet, barely a year later, relations between the two countries had thawed and indeed seemed to be warming to a degree not seen in decades. The Indian foreign policy establishment became much more upbeat about what it perceived was a much greater U. S. understanding of India's security concerns. Referring to the parity with Pakistan, long a thorny bone of contention in India-U. S. relations, Matt Daley, a U. S. diplomat was blunt in saying that "the days of even-handedness and balance in U. S. policy in the subcontinent are now over."[1] While admittedly given the lukewarm nature of relations between the two countries for most of the last half-century this new found warmth has its limitations (as evident by changes in U. S. policy in the subcontinent after the September 2001 World Trade Center terrorist attacks), the rapid turn around in relations in the aftermath of the tests needs explanation. Eventually, although the reasons for the sanctions—India's nuclear tests—could not of course be reversed, most of the other key conditions under which the sanctions would be revoked remained largely unmet when they were finally removed by the United States in the aftermath of the terrorist attacks on the World Trade Center.

Following the tests, many gigabytes were consumed in trying to explain the factors that prompted them. These explanations focused on domestic and exogenous factors, both short and long–term. The domestic explanations ranged from the changing political culture in India to bureaucratic imperatives, particularly pressures emanating from India's nuclear establishment.[2] Others placed the onus on the arrival of the BJP, the pressures of fractious coalition governments and a supposed "centralizing" feature inherent in nuclear weapons that would countervail growing pressures for a more federal Indian polity.[3] For some India's tests were a crude form of saber-rattling designed to intimidate its neighbor, Pakistan. Another set of explanations focused on the changing international context—the demise of India's strategic partner, the Former Soviet Union, the parallel rise of China and its perceived regional hegemonic tendencies,[4] and the fear of being cornered by the indefinite extension of the Non-Proliferation Treaty (NPT) and the specific features built into the entry-into force provisions of the NPT.[5] While the relative weight of these factors (which no doubt had a cumulative effect) will remain a matter of debate, an independent cognitive factor, India's anxieties— the "palpable, if quiet, crisis of confidence," about itself and its place in the world—undoubtedly played into the decision to conduct the tests.[6] The tests in this view were "a primal scream for self-assertion," with Indian policy elites regarding nuclear bombs as "harmless icons of empowerment."[7]

The focus of this chapter, however, is not on the factors leading to the tests but on the consequences of the tests. In particular, the chapter examines two issues that resulted from the tests. One, what was the impact of the sanctions that were imposed subsequent to the tests? And second, did the tests propel a ruinous arms race in the subcontinent? The paper argues that the immediate negative economic impact of the sanctions on India was modest. India was not particularly vulnerable and the sanctions were not comprehensive either in the issue areas they were applied to or on with regard to the multilateral regime. If anything the sanctions had a mild positive economic impact in that they helped sell economic reforms within the BJP, the dominant partner in the ruling coalition, albeit to a limited degree. The cognitive impact of the sanctions was more significant in the short–term, especially on India's scientific community and at the margin appeared to signal a greater commitment by the Indian scientific community to deepen domestic technological development, particularly on defense. The chapter further argues that endogenous economic, institutional, and technological constraints will sharply limit any possibility of India launching into an arms race, notwithstanding the claims of some of the more breathless commentaries on the subject.

Nature of the Sanctions

Although India's nuclear tests evoked strong condemnatory reactions from the international community, few countries went beyond a rhetorical flourish. The G-7, European Union, Australia, and New Zealand imposed sanctions that targeted bilateral aid programs, reduced support for multilateral assistance, continued the existing blockage of technological support for India's civilian nuclear programs, and curtailed military and diplomatic exchanges. Imports from India were not targeted in any way (and if so were bound to have been challenged in the WTO).

The most comprehensive scope of sanctions was announced by the United States in Presidential Proclamation 98-22 as required by the Glenn Amendment (Section 826-a of the Nuclear Proliferation Prevention Act of 1994) that mandates the United States to impose sanctions against nonnuclear states that detonate nuclear devices. As a result the United States:

1. Terminated assistance under the Foreign Assistance Act of 1961.
2. Banned sales of defense articles and defense services.
3. Ended Foreign Military Financing.
4. Denied credit and risk guarantees by U. S. government entities (Exim Bank and the Overseas Private Investment Corporation [OPIC]).
5. Announced U. S. opposition to any loans or financial assistance by International Financial Institutions.
6. Prohibited U. S. banks from making loans or extending credit to the government of India.

India's Economic Vulnerability and Consequences

The economic impact of sanctions depends on several factors. One, the relative economic resilience of the country in general and especially of sectors targeted;

second, the comprehensiveness of the sanctions with respect to the issue areas they are applied to; and three, the comprehensiveness of the multilateral sanctions regime. In an era of globalization, the fewer the number of countries willing to be part of the sanctions regime, the greater the ease with which embargoes can be sidestepped. In recent years as sanctions have been increasingly deployed as an instrument of coercive diplomacy, particularly by the United States, a burgeoning literature has sought to examine the effectiveness of the sanctions. By and large these studies conclude that sanctions are largely unsuccessful in achieving their foreign policy goals, especially if they are unilateral and even when applied within a multilateral regime, but their insignificant costs on the sender country make them quite popular.[8]

India was not particularly vulnerable to economic sanctions for the same reason that it was one of the few countries in Asia (or for that matter amongst all emerging markets, barring China) to remain unaffected by the Asian financial crisis in 1997–98. Despite the 1991 reforms, India remains a large, relatively closed economy, with foreign capital and foreign trade playing only a modest role. Unlike many other low-income countries, foreign aid is also relatively small, about 0.5 percent of GDP (1997 figures), largely in infrastructure, social sectors, and environment related projects and evenly divided between bilateral and multilateral sources.

The sanctions had targeted loans from international financial institutions. Since India was not vulnerable on its external accounts, the lack of recourse to the International Monetary Fund (IMF) was moot. The effects on loans from the World Bank and Asian Development Bank were potentially more serious, but in reality they were modest. After India's first nuclear test in 1974 the United States, again under Congressional mandate, voted against all loans to India (until 1978) but World Bank lending to India increased every year during that period. While this is not the case today, the multilateral banks are contractually obligated to disburse on existing pipeline loans—which in the case of the World Bank alone exceeded $8 billion in June 1998. Furthermore, with an exception made for humanitarian loans (all loans deemed to be poverty oriented), only new infrastructure loans were put on hold affecting about half of new lending by the multilateral development banks.[9]

India has always been cautious in external liberalization. India's prudence on its external accounts (in stark contrast to its domestic finances) has been intrinsic to its development and foreign policy ideologies, a marriage of economic autarky and nonalignment. While in recent years this attitude has changed with respect to trade and foreign investment, it persists with respect to financial sector liberalization and capital account convertibility. India had crossed the hump in external debt service payments in 1996–1997 when $14.1 billion was paid out in debt service, the bulk of which were debt obligations that accrued after the country had raised funds commercially and from the IMF to tide over the balance of payments crisis in 1991. A cautious policy of restricting overall external liabilities, and within that the short-term component of external debt liabilities, allowed the country to weather both the Asian crisis and the sanctions (see Table 12.1).

The impact of sanctions on private flows was relatively greater, albeit limited. The U. S. sanctions legislation seemed to imply that private credits to the Indian government would have to be curtailed, but immediately ran into major obstacles. First of all the law was ambiguous as to whether this extended to public enterprises and state governments. Second, even if the law was narrowly applied it placed U. S. banks like Citibank and Bank of America with highly profitable operations in India that had been build over decades, in a quandary. Under Indian banking regulations all banks are required to hold a certain fraction of their assets in government securities (standard in most countries). Under sanction laws they would be required to divest. The banks were faced with a damaging dilemma: If they conformed with U. S. sanction laws, they would violate Indian law and lose their license, a prospect that was perceived with considerable equanimity by other foreign banks operating in India, especially UK banks.[10] While the United States Treasury found a creative way to interpret the law and exempted U. S. banks from this requirement, in so doing it undermined the bite of the sanctions. U. S. companies, who have been the largest source of FDI in India in recent years, put their investment plans on hold as a result of the curbing of Exim Bank and OPIC guarantees. This part of the sanctions was however, waived almost immediately (in November).

The indirect impact of the sanctions on private flows was greater in so far as they increased the uncertainty about India's external environment. Between 1997–98 and 1998–99, FDI flows declined from $3.5 billion to $2.5 billion while portfolio flows declined from $1.8 billion to $-0.07 billion.[11] While it is difficult to disentangle causality, the fact that flows have again increased in 1999 suggests that the uncertain domestic political environment in India in 1998, and the resulting uncertainty regarding the course of economic reforms, together with the systemic crisis in capital flows to emerging markets were more important than the sanctions in the decline in private capital inflows to India. With economic reforms faltering and capital markets already spooked, the sanctions added to the negative factors that led to a lowering of India's sovereign ratings. It has been argued that the sanctions had a large opportunity cost for India. In May 1998, India looked like an island of stability in Asia and was poised to receive large capital flows that were lost in the aftermath of the sanctions. While this is true to an extent, nonetheless by August, following the Russian bond default, that argument was no longer valid. The contagion effect was so severe and that all emerging markets—even those far from Asia—were dragged down, as evidenced by weakening capital flows to Latin America. In other words, in the absence of the tests, given the conditions prevailing in international capital markets and the weaknesses in India's domestic economy, substantially larger capital inflows would not have materialized. It is interesting to note that in recent years, even as the Washington policy community stresses the primacy of factors internal to an economy as

Table 12.1   External Vulnerability

	India		Asian Crisis Countries*
	1997-1998	1998-1999	1997
Current Account Deficit (percent of GDP)	-1.3	-1.0	-5.3
Short-term debt/total debt (percent)	7	5	36
Short-term debt/reserves (percent)	26	17	130
Debt Service ratio (percent of exports)	19.8	19.9	15.5
Capital Account Convertibility	No	No	No

* Indonesia, Korea, Malaysia and Thailand
Source: IMF
Note: Data for India are on a fiscal year basis, from April 1 to March 30.

the principal determinant of a country's economic well being, when it comes to sanctions, external factors are suddenly deemed as central to a country's economic health that hence render it vulnerable to sanctions. India faces many economic problems, but these are largely endogenous and sanctions had little bearing on them.

Furthermore, any potential financial pressures from the sanctions were severely undercut by the resounding success of the Resurgent India Bonds (RIBs) bonds that raised $4.23 billion in just 20 days based on the support of over 74,000 expatriate Indians in over 30 countries.[12] The issue was a major boost for the Indian government. In undermining the effects of the U. S.-led sanctions it sent strong geopolitical signals. Furthermore, it resulted in significant financial gains to the government even though the bonds were technically not sovereign borrowing.[13]

Additional light on the likely consequences of the present sanctions regime may be cast by examining previous episodes when pressure was brought upon India. There are three examples from history that are worth examining in this regard.[14] In the mid-1960s the United States at the behest of President Johnson "short-tethered" wheat exports to India, at a time when India was extremely vulnerable on this front. That policy left Indian policymakers determined they would not allow the country to be exposed to such pressures again—grain production emerged as a core concern and during the 1970s India became self-sufficient in food and at least on this score has never again been politically vulnerable.[15]

The sanctions legislation also banned sales of military equipment and dual-use technology. This had an impact on a number of Indian defense programs where procurement of key equipment (such as engines for the Light Combat Aircraft and radar-guided mountain howitzers) was stalled. To an extent, however, the sanctions simply expanded the sanctions regime already in place that had serendipitous pay-offs. In the 1980s the United States refused to allow the sale of Cray supercomputers leading India to set up CDAC (Center for Development of Advanced Computing) which rigged together small machines in parallel to enhance processing speeds. Serendipitously, parallel processing emerged as the preferred choice in supercomputing technologies worldwide, handing India for once a technological advantage.

A more protracted technology embargo has been under the Missile Technology Control Regime. According to one analysis while this embargo delayed and increased costs of India's space projects, they did not halt any.[16] If anything ISRO (Indian Space Research Organization) and Indian industry, after being denied certain imports, indigenously developed a number of space missile technologies.[17] Typically programs were delayed by about five years and resulted in approximately ten percent increase in expenditures. The highly publicized US sanctions against ISRO and the Russian firm Glavkosinos in 1992-94 for the supply of cryogenic engines to ISRO for its geoearth orbit satellite launch vehicle did result in the latter not supplying the technology to ISRO. Eventually, however, ISRO did obtain the engines and subsequently initiated a program to develop indigenous cryogenic engines.

It should be emphasized that India's ambitious plans at developing conventional weapons systems indigenously have, in the time honored fashion of most government projects, suffered from time and cost overruns. But that is a feature intrinsic to all GOI projects be it in civilian or defense sectors. If anything, embargoes ignite a nascent streak of nationalism that have improved the quality and quantity of effort. Technology controls and sanctions have led to India becoming self-reliant in several key areas thus paradoxically considerably reducing any future leverage on India's military programs.

If India's limited *ex ante* vulnerability undermined the impact of the sanctions, the lack of agreement within the G-8 on their comprehensiveness and the muted enthusiasm in actually applying the sanctions forcefully meant that *ex post* effects were bound to be even less consequential. Both Russia and France had only weakly supported the G-8 stance. Russia, which historically has cultivated close ties with India, signaled its break with the P-5 when the Russian Prime Minster Yevgeny Primakov visited India in December 1997—the first by a member of the P-5—and signed a ten-year military cooperation pact, replacing the 1994 India-Russia Defense Agreement which was due to expire in 2000. While the strengthening of a "strategic dialogue" between France and India may have been due to the traditionally independent course chartered by the former, the position of the countries of the EU, and other members of the G-8, was broadly similar—a strongly condemnatory view of

India's nuclear tests, some reduction of bilateral cooperation with GOI projects, but otherwise pretty much business as usual.[18]

Amongst other key countries, the sharp negative reaction of Japan had the greatest potential for a significant economic impact on India. It called off scheduled bilateral meetings, even refusing India's offer to send a senior official to Tokyo to explain the rationale of the tests. As India's largest supplier of bilateral aid (about as large as all other countries combined), Japan's suspension of its aid program with its inevitable implications for Japanese investment was indeed problematic for India. But, unlike the United States, Japan did not impose restrictions in areas connected with trade, investment, and other dealings between the private sectors of the two countries.

Political and Cognitive Consequences

Analysts of economic sanctions generally agree that while they rarely work as intended they do have consequences.[19] This was the case here as well. An interesting political consequence of the sanctions was to positively nudge economic reforms in India. During the 1990s there was an increasing awareness of the congruence of security and economic policies in policy circles in India. This led to greater prominence to economics in strategic policy analysis. Paralleling this shift there was an increasing recognition that an India that was more involved in the global economy was more likely to build webs of economic interdependence which offered it greater political security. If the demise of the Soviet Union and the rise of China gave a greater impetus to economic reforms in general, the lessons of American business lobbies in shaping U. S. policies with regard to China was not lost on Indian policy makers.

Sanctions helped tip the balance of power within the ruling BJP, strengthening the hands of the reform faction in the party at the expense of the *swadeshi* (or economic nationalist) faction. Three prominent examples of this shift in the party's stance was with regard to foreign entry in insurance, strengthening the patent regime in line with WTO commitments (both of which it had opposed in the past), and sharply expanding the automatic list related to trade and foreign investment.

The second inadvertent but important cognitive impact of the U.S sanctions has been on the Indian scientific community. The sanctions targeted specific scientific disciplines—physics, aerospace, engineering, and space technology—and within them subgroups associated with the nuclear and missile program, affecting a total of 240 Indian educational and scientific entities. The list included academic departments of virtually all of India's leading universities and research institutions, whose faculty are largely U. S. trained. The ostensible object of drawing up the list was to monitor possible transfers of sensitive technologies by making special import applications obligatory for the named entities.

Although scientific exchanges at international conferences were not considered to fall in the category of sensitive exports, they became so with the Department of Energy (DoE) insisting that scientists from institutions funded by it be denied the opportunity to interact with their counterparts in India (given the international nature of science DoE scientists would in any case be rubbing shoulders with their Indian counterparts in some other conference outside the United States). The sanctions expelled Indian scientists visiting the United States on collaborative projects, unusual even in the case of visiting Soviet scientists at the height of the Cold War.[20] DoE installations (Argonne and Fermi Labs) not only curtailed scientific exchanges but Indian scientists were not allowed to continue their collaboration and asked to leave behind half million dollars of detection equipment. U. S. scientists were prevented from participating in international science conferences in India, despite it being a clear violation of the principles of the ICSU (International Commission of Science Unions).[21] The Director of Fermi Labs, John Peeples, reported that the DOE ordered him in writing to remove the Indian flag from the UN like display in front of Fermi Labs main building: "We never even did this with the Russians at the worst part of the Cold War."[22]

At one level the sanctions increased the transactions costs of Indian scientific research in India. India's principal scientific and research institutions faced a variety of constraints arising out of the sanctions, principally the denial of equipment and services by U. S. firms, in many cases despite existing contractual obligations be it lab equipment, computers, and processors. In some cases, such as the refusal by the Center for Disease Control to send out a rabies virus clone (citing the nuclear tests as the reason), the decision may reflect normal bureaucratic risk averseness. In other cases—for instance the refusal to renew the license for the usage of structural analysis software used by IIT Mumbai's mechanical and civil engineering departments[23]—the risk averseness probably reflects the inherent ambiguity of interpretation of dual-use technologies.

There can be no doubt that a small section of the Indian scientific establishment—concentrated in the Defense Research and Development Organization (DRDO) and the Atomic Energy Commission (AEC)—has played a critical political role in pushing India's nuclear program.[24] But the symbolic effects of these actions have been much more potent and can be understood only in the broader context of the constraints faced by the scientific community in India. More than in almost any other society, technology and tradition have an uneasy coexistence in India.[25] This ambivalence—perhaps best exemplified by the sharply contrasting views on modern technology held by Gandhi and Nehru—continues to date. The intellectual excitement of the of post-independence scientific endeavor had run aground by the 1970s, a victim of the increasing bureaucratization of the scientific establishment and the growing institutional malaise afflicting Indian universities. The output of the majority of the 40-odd laboratories of the Indian Council for Scientific and Industrial Research (CSIR) was mediocre science. At the same time it also failed to help Indian industry become more technologically dynamic, undermined by its goal to support autarkic import substitution policies, not globally competitive technology.

Although post–1991, the CSIR has become a more dynamic institution, the goal of combining good science with commercially useful R&D remains a daunting task.[26] Contemporary Indian science continues to be plagued by meager funding, a state bureaucratic apparatus that continues to pose formidable obstacles and a society that continues to be harbor strong negative perceptions of modern technology (largely because of a strongly held belief that technology threatens jobs).[27] It also strongly perceives that it faces a strong bias in the West.

The consequences of these manifold pressures have been apparent in the wake of India's nuclear tests. In a series of letters and articles in *Science,* G. Padmanaban, Director of the Indian Institute of Science, Banglore, India's leading research university, and a prominent biochemist, argued that:

> "a feeling of alienation permeates segments of Indian society that have anything to do with the West, the U. S. in particular. The general perception among Indian scientists in leading institutions, most of whom are U. S. trained, is that they are discriminated against. Even if I manage to publish in one of the best journals it will be seldom be quoted unless I have a U. S. western pedigree or a connection with an inner circle. There seems to be an inherent disbelief in the West, that good research can be done in India. Even if I am invited to deliver a lecture at an international research conference, I am made to feel like an outsider or am aware that I have been invited to satisfy a condition that someone from a developing country be included in the conference to be eligible for funds from an international agency. Our scientists are appalled by how the U. S. which values intellectual challenges and academic freedom can have such a discriminating attitude towards a country struggling to develop its science."[28]

This strongly held perception of alienation and discrimination underlay the strong sentiment in India's scientific community that the nuclear tests were a reminder to the world that, "India is not a push over . . . at times force is the only language that is taken note of."[29] The scientific disputes surrounding the size of the Indian blasts further reflected this tension.[30] Padmanaban was rewarded for his insights when the Indian Institute of Science was put on the watch list of the United States because it was thought to be a think-tank for India's defense effort. Reflecting on the sanctions, the Director-General of CSIR, who has had strong personal and scientific ties with U. S. institutions, recently argued that, "the new round of sanctions can easily be brushed aside, as India has literally grown up in this atmosphere of technology denials." The cognitive effects of the U. S. action succeeded only in converting leading sections of the broader Indian scientific community, many of who were at best lukewarm about the nuclear tests, into one whose nationalism was recharged.

"Feel-Good" Sanctions?

The sanctions imposed on India consequent to its nuclear tests were largely spearheaded and put into place by the United States. Mandated by Congress, the United States placed five key demands on India (and Pakistan) aimed at satisfying its nonproliferation concerns. At the time the sanctions were imposed it demanded that as a precondition for lifting them the countries should:

1. sign and ratify the CTBT;
2. halt production of fissile material and participate constructively in the Fissile Material Cutoff Treaty (FMCT);
3. accept International Atomic Energy Agency (IAEA) safeguards on all nuclear facilities;
4. agree not to deploy or test missile systems;
5. maintain existing export controls on nuclear and missile technology exports.

In the following years any changes in India's position were driven—like the tests themselves—from perceived national self-interest and domestic constituencies, and sanctions were of little import in the changes (or lack thereof). India agreed in principle to sign the CTBT but the change in its position was not a result of the sanctions but because the tests had removed the rationale in not signing the treaty. If anything it could be argued that the continuation of sanctions (despite the temporary waiver) made it more difficult for the government in India to move from accepting the CTBT in principle to actually signing it, since it would seen domestically as giving in to duress. In any case, the failure of the United States itself to ratify the treaty undermined a critical premise of the sanctions. There was little movement on the remaining conditions (except the last but that was moot in any case in India's case), although India signaled its willingness to participate "constructively" in the FMCT.

The marginal economic impact of the sanctions was also the conclusion reached by an Institute for International Economics (IIE) case study on the impact of the U.S. sanctions on India. The study calculated the economic impact of the sanctions at $554 million (or 0.13 percent of GDP in 1997-98). The sanctions, the study concluded were an outright failure, and gave it its lowest success score, a combination of poor policy results and virtually no contribution from the sanctions in achieving this policy result.[31]

Despite this failure, analysts concerned with nonproliferation continued to press for maintaining them arguing that they were essential to maintaining US "credibility." The success of sanctions, it was argued, was measured not by their impact on the country (countries) they were imposed on but by their "signaling" effect—in this case on would-be proliferators—and hence their preventive function. A more plausible rationale for maintaining them were that they were aimed as much at domestic constituencies, who would not easily countenance change. Eventually, the sanctions were put paid to by changing

Table 12.2   Indian Sanctions Scorecard

* Policy result scaled from 1 (failed) to 4 (success)	1
* Sanctions contribution scaled from 1 (none) to 4 (significant)	1
* Success score (policy result times sanctions contribution) scaled from 1 (outright failure) to 16 (significant success)	1

U. S. foreign policy priorities in the aftermath of the World Trade Center terrorist attacks, rather than any changes in the policies of the countries they were meant to alter.

An Arms Race?

If the rationale for India's nuclear tests were unconvincing to many in the United States, fears were expressed that efforts at weaponization and ratcheting effects would trigger an arms race in the sub-continent. But the fiscal basis of these fears was unproven. An arms race would presumably involve large budgetary outlays. But does the Indian state have the financial capacity to sustain large increases in defense expenditures?

The parlous state of government finances in India preclude any possibility of substantially greater commitments to defense. Indian defense expenditures peaked in the mid-1980s at around 3.5 percent of GDP and 18.5 percent of central government expenditure. During the 1980s they have averaged 2.5 percent of GDP and around 15 percent of central government expenditure. However, unlike the 1980s, a sustained legacy of fiscal profligacy has sharply increased the interest component of central government expenditures (Figure 12.1). The political inability to contain the fiscal deficit will mean that interest payments will continue to consume about 40 percent of central government expenditures. With the capital expenditure component of the central government's budget already half (as a share of GDP) of its levels at the beginning of the decade, and subsidies and a wage bill that is politically impossible to curb, defense expenditures can at best increase modestly.

If the *level* of defense expenditures is increasingly constrained, its *composition* is equally so. Although all budgets reflect a strong hysteria effect, defense expenditure rationalization has been difficult in the Indian case, bedeviled both by interservice bureaucratic rivalries on the one hand and the penchant for big-ticket purchases, at the cost of operations and maintenance efforts, on the other. Thus despite broad agreement within India's strategic and defense com-

Figure 12.1   Composition of Central Government Expenditures (CGE)

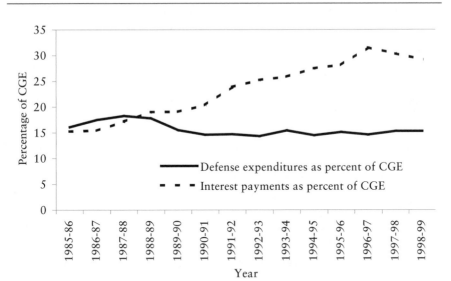

munity that China constitutes its principal long term strategic threat, capital expenditure patterns still reflect past rivalries with Pakistan.[32] The capacity to restructure defense expenditures even within a constrained resource environment has been further reduced by the ramifications of the excessively generous recommendations of the Fifth Pay Commission.[33] The latter has mean that capital expenditures as a fraction of defense expenditure has sharply fallen over the last few years (Figure 12.2) and are unlikely to reverse significantly soon.

An analysis of Indian government finances lends little credence to the arms race alarmist views that followed the tests of May 1998. Indeed, defense expenditures in the 1999–2000 budget, the first post-nuclear test budget, fell both as a share of GDP (from 2.56 percent in 1998–99 to 2.28 percent) and as a share of overall government expenditure (from 15.4 percent in 1998-99 to 14 percent). The ceiling on the rate of growth of military expenditures will be set by the rate of GDP growth that, in turn is a good indicator of the buoyancy of government revenues needed to finance that expenditure. Within these limits, the capital component of defense expenditures is constrained by the large share of irreversible revenue expenditures.[34]

However, in response to costly military clashes with Pakistan in May–June 1999, Indian defense expenditures are set to increase. It may be argued that Pakistan was emboldened by its nuclear tests (in response to India's tests) in precipitating the Kargil crisis and keeping the pot of militancy boiling, and hence the nuclear tests did indeed result in increasing defense expenditures. While this is possible, it is also the case that the absence of nuclear weapons

Figure 12.2   Composition of Defense Expenditures. Ratio of Capital to
Revenue Expenditures

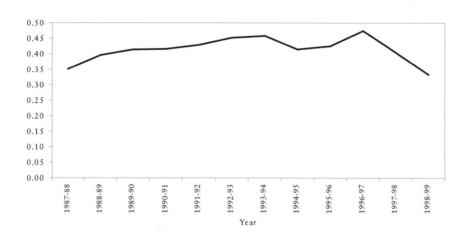

had not ruled out military adventurism in earlier years. In any case, because of
the fiscal pressures mentioned above, India's military expenditures will continue to be under three percent of GDP. And in so far as increases in expenditures will take place (in the short and medium term), most of it will be in
upgrading depleted conventional weapons capabilities rather than the sorts of
strategic weapon systems that critics of the nuclear tests had feared.

The fiscal constraints on India's military posture are compounded by three
additional structural weaknesses. For one, it has been argued that India's social
divisions reduce its effective military power—that case has been carefully examined elsewhere, and will not be addressed here.[35] However, to the extent that
the ongoing "revolution in military affairs" is changing the structural basis of
military power, relevant technological prowess are likely to matter more than
India's social diversity. This would, at first sight place India at an advantage,
if the much touted numbers of its scientists and engineers are to be believed.[36]
But for a variety of reasons India has not been technologically dynamic and
the quality of its scientific output has also been relatively modest. A protected
economy did not create the incentives and pressures that would lead to a grater
demand for innovation. A rapid expansion in the university system was paral-
leled by an almost equally precipitous decline in the quality of the median institution. In the case of elite institutions, their effective "yield" (availability to the
Indian science and technological enterprise) has not been more than a few percent, the result of human capital flight out of the country or to managerial and
administrative jobs within the country.

Although the incentive structure is changing, the changes are gradual. The lack of technological dynamism in the broader economy has been reflected in India's defense related research and development. While the capital component of India's military expenditures has declined in recent years, the research and development component had grown steadily, accounting for 6.5 percent of total military expenditures by the end of the 1990s. Some notable exceptions apart these expenditures have not been translated into potent military capabilities, at least as far as the indigenous conventional arms industry is concerned. The output of India's military industries is a third less than at the beginning of the decade. Meanwhile almost all large showpiece projects show little signs of progress.[37] This should not be surprising. India had paid a high price for its misguided policies in trade autarky. The goal of an independent arms industry eludes even West European countries, and it is unambiguously unattainable for India is the foreseeable future.

The emergence of the informatics sector, especially software, as the most dynamic technology sector in its economy holds by far the most promising portends for enhancing its defense capabilities. Leveraging India's growing strengths in information technologies, the Indian armed forces have begun working closely with private industry that has developed the requisite expertise, experience and human resource to undertake this tasks.[38] But the success of the software industry is proving to be a double edged sword for India's military capabilities in the near future. In the aerospace sector for example skyrocketing salaries (by Indian standards) are leading to an exodus by scientists and engineers to the lucrative information technology sector at annual rate in the range of 20 to 50 percent depending on the laboratory.[39]

Although these are not insurmountable problems, they pose formidable challenges for the Indian state to solve in a reasonably quick manner. And that brings us to the third factor why India, intentions notwithstanding, will not be able to enter into an arms race. The India state today does not have the functional autonomy, the bureaucratic capability, and the political stability that easily allows for policy innovation and strategic policy making in a non-incremental manner. The changing domestic political landscape has meant that governments are less stable and ministerial tenure is much shorter. For instance, the tenure of a defense minister in India in the 1950s was double that in the 1990s (Figure 12.3). A deterioration in the quality of India's public institutions is perhaps most apparent in the declining capabilities of its bureaucracy even as it continues to be locked-in into a control mind-set. This mind-set has been changing very gradually in the economic sphere, partly because of external pressure. However, the civilian bureaucracy's control mind-set continues unabated with regard to the military, be it in keeping the military at bay with regard to the country's nuclear program, or minute expenditure controls or even on staff promotions. For all these reasons decision making and implementation, never a bright spot for the GOI, remains slow.[40] It took a quarter of century for India to move from Pokharan-I to Pokharan-II. And that is about the pace that its weaponization program is likely to continue unless there is a precipitous decline in its external environment.

Figure 12.3   Average Tenure of Indian Defense Ministers

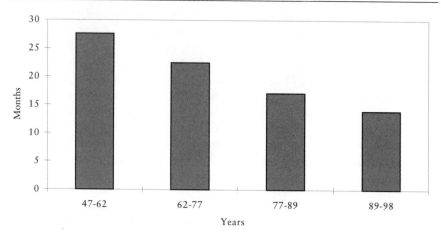

1947–62: Baldev Singh to V. K. Krishna Menon
1962–77: Jawahar Lal Nehru to Bansi Lal
1977–89: Jagjivan Ram to K.C. Pant
1989–98: V.P. Singh to George Fernandes

Conclusion

The continued popularity of sanctions amongst policymakers despite their limited direct effects has been seen to be due to their indirect effects. Sanctions, it is claimed serve as cognitive packets signaling the sender's preferences not just to the target but to a broader audience, both domestic and international. And by following through on them leaders supposedly increase the credibility of their commitment to carry out their threats.[41]

But at a deeper level sanctions can also signal a failure of policy, little more than a case of trying to lock the barn door after the horse has bolted. They can be an effective smokescreen, a decoy that focuses attention on the action itself while deflecting attention from what may well be a fundamental failure of policy to come to grips with the underlying causes that prompted the action.[42] No degree of sanctions can undo the reality of the tests by India and Pakistan. The claim that sanctions signal a toughness to would-be proliferators has limited currency, at least in the case of nuclear proliferation. The set is so small, and includes countries such as North Korea and Iraq for which such signals are meaningless given what they already face, that the only rationale can be a presumed signaling for other proliferation regimes.

This chapter has argued that while the direct economic consequences of sanctions on India were minor, their indirect and cognitive effects were somewhat greater. On the one hand they tipped the balance in India's governing coalition in favor of continued economic liberalization. On the other they energized civil society actors particularly the scientific community that had been specifically targeted by the sanctions. Since sanctions often occur in an international legal vacuum and combine in the source the role of lawmaker, judge, jury, and prosecutor, they need a degree of legitimacy to have at least a cognitive impact. This is particularly important in a democratic polity such as India's. However, even the substantial minority of India's elites who were opposed to or ambivalent about the nuclear tests were alienated by the reactions of the G-7 and P-5 and the United States in particular. The last was expected in the case of the ideological left, comprising the communist parties who were the most strident domestic critics of the tests. But even other groups whose opposition was based on a deeper Indian ethos that is deeply uncomfortable with the ramifications of nuclear weaponization were alienated by the perceived illegitimacy of a stance whose logic appeared to be "do as we say, not as we do." If the initial domestic reaction within India to its nuclear tests was divisive to a limited extent, even these divisions were cemented by the sanctions.

Finally, the fears that the nuclear tests would trigger an arms-race in the subcontinent proved unfounded. Fiscal exhaustion and domestic political constraints mean that an arms "race" will occur at a crawl even if hawkish sentiments in India were inclined otherwise.

Notes

1. Speech by Mathew Daley, Senior Adviser for South Asia, U. S. State Department, July 22, 1999.
2. Itty Abraham. *The Making of the Indian Atomic Bomb—Science, Secrecy and the Post Colonial State.* New York: Zed Books, 1998.
3. Stephen Cohen. "Nuclear Weapons and International Conflict in South Asia." paper presented to the Harvard/MIT Transnational Security Project Seminar, November 1998, Cambridge, MA.
4. Cited as the reason by Indian Prime Minster Vajpayee in his letter of May 1997 to President Clinton after the tests.
5. K. Subrahmanyam. "Indian Nuclear Policy," in Jasjit Singh, ed., *Nuclear India.* New Delhi, Knowledge World, 1998. Ted Carpenter, "Roiling Asia," *Foreign Affairs.* November/December 1998.
6. Pratap Bhanu Mehta. "A Nuclear Subcontinent," *Harvard Magazine.* September-October, 1998.
7. Amitav Ghosh. *Countdown.* New Delhi: Ravi Dayal, 1999.
8. Kimberly Ann Elliott and Gary Hufbauer. "Ineffectiveness of economic sanctions: Same song, same refrain? Economic sanctions in the 1990s," *American Economic Review*, Papers and proceedings, vol. 89, no. 2, May 1999, pp. 403-408; Robert Pape, "Why Economic Sanctions Do Not Work," *International*

Security, vol. 22, 1997, pp. 90-136. For a contrary view see Jesse Helms, "What Sanctions Epidemic," *Foreign Affairs*, January/February 1999.

9. New World Bank loans to India dropped from $2.1 billion in 1997–98 to $1.05 billion in 1998-99. It should be noted that pressing the IFIs to withhold lending for political reasons is a violation of their charter and corrodes their credibility when they press for the importance of governance and the rule of law in their borrowers.

10. "Banks lobby Washington for slack in Indian sanctions," *Wall Street Journal*, May 22, 1998.

11. CMIE Economic Review, July 13, 1999. The data correspond to India's fiscal year that runs from April to March.

12. Kala Rao. "Resurgent Bond Taps Indian Diaspora," *Euromoney*, October 1998. The five-year bonds constituted the single largest debt offer out of India. The dollar bonds carried a coupon of 7.75 percent, a spread of 225 basis points over U. S. treasuries at a time when markets roiled by Russia's debt default, were pricing emerging market sovereign debt at more than 500 basis points over comparable U. S. Treasuries.

13. Besides boosting foreign exchange reserves, the issue built up confidence in the foreign exchange market and increased the central bank's room for maneuver to manage the exchange rate, which stabilized after about a 10 percent decline since the beginning of the year. To be sure, there was a cost. The government will bear nearly the entire exchange loss that is expected to accrue over the life of the bonds. Assuming a rupee depreciation of 5 percent every year, the total cost of RIBs works out to around 12.5 percent, comparable to the 11.8 percent yield on five-year government bonds.

14. The threat of U. S. sanctions because of India's nuclear policies dates back to 1953 when India was considering selling its thorium reserves to the FSU (via China). The threat waned only after the U. S. and the FSU veered towards supporting programs for the "peaceful use of nuclear energy." Robert Anderson, "Why Lord Buddha Smiled," *Times Literary Supplement*, January 8, 1998.

15. An excellent account of this episode can be found in John P. Lewis, *India's Political Economy*. New Delhi: Oxford University Press, 1995, especially chapter 5. Foodgrain output in India more than tripled between 1965 and 1999 from 65 million tons to 205 million tons.

16. Dinshaw Mistry. "India's Emerging Space Program," *Pacific Affairs*, vol. 71, no. 2, Summer 1998, pp. 151-174.

17. Examples include shell catalysts for rocket fuel; magnesium plates for the Prithvi missile; radiation hardened chips; maraging steel for rocket motor casing. Ibid.

18. This was attested by the spate of high ranking visits by senior officials to India within months of the tests—whether the Belgian crown prince or Swiss President accompanied by a panoply of business executives—to cultivate better relations and commercial and business ties.

19. See for instance, Richard Haas, ed., *Economic Sanctions and American Diplomacy*, New York: Council on Foreign Relations, 1998.

20. Pallava Bagla. "Indian Scientists Shaken by Bomb Test Aftershocks," Science, July 24, 1998, vol. 281, pp.494-495.

21. For instance in January 1999, physicists from Fermi National and Argonne National labs were denied requests to travel to the 13th international conference on Hadron Collidor Physics at TIFR, Mumbai.

22. *Science* vol. 283, January 15, 1999, p. 307.
23. *Computers Today*, January 15, 1999, p. 10.
24. Abraham. *The Making of the Indian Atom Bomb*, 1998.
25. For historical and contemporary analysis of science and technology in India, see Michael Adas, *Machines as the Measure of Men*, Ithaca: Cornell University Press, 1989; Baldev Raj Nayar, *India's Quest for Technological Independence*, New Delhi: Lancer Publishers, 1983; and the survey on "Science in India," *Nature*, December 16, 1993.
26. The turnaround is generally credited to R. A. Mashelkar who became the director-general of CSIR in 1995 after a distinguished stint at the National Chemical Laboratory (NCL) in Pune.
27. Survey by the National Council of Applied Economic Research, New Delhi, 1998, cited in *Nature*, vol. 397, January 7, 1999.
28. G. Padmanaban "The Indian Psyche," *Science*, vol. 281, July 10, 1998, p. 175.
29. T. Balakrishna Reddy and G. Padmanaban, "Indian Science," *Science*, vol. 281, August 7, 1998, p. 78.
30. Compare for instance the differing estimates of Indian physicists at BARC (S. K. Sikka et. al. *Current Science*, September 10 1998) with these from US academic and government seismologists (Borian Barker et al., "Policy Forum," *Science*, vol. 281, 25 September 1998, pp. 1967-1968.
31. Institute for International Economics, case study 98-1, available at website www.iie.com/hotopics/sanction/india2.htm
32. Jaswant Singh, *Defending India*, especially the chapter on "Defence Spending and Force Structure."
33. Pay Commissions are a statutory body constituted periodically. Although their recommendations directly affect federal employees, they ricochet rapidly onto public enterprises and state governments who are politically unable to concede demands of wage "parity" by their employees.
34. Unlike Pakistan, the Indian defense budget excludes pension payments that are met by general government expenditures. Pensions constitute an escalating contingent liability, which will further constrain fiscal maneuverability.
35. Stephen Rosen. *India and Its Armies*. New Delhi: Oxford University Press, 1996.
36. The popular conception is that India has the "third-largest" number of scientists and engineers in the world. The figure is dominated by those with degrees in science of indifferent quality. Even Korea, whose population is a fifteenth that of India, has more engineers.
37. These include the Arjun tank, the Advanced Light Helicopter and the Light Combat Aircraft that have consumed the lion's share of resources and has been 15 years in the making without yet making even a test-flight.
38. Rahul Bedi. "India develops latest secure data system," *Jane's Defence Weekly*, vol. 30, no. 17, October 28, 1998. According to the article, the Indian Navy has developed a secure data transmission system matching that used by US and NATO forces. Also, "India launches IT network programme," *Jane's Defence Weekly*; October 7, 1998.
39. The figures are from a recent report by S.Suryanarayan of IIT Mumbai's aerospace engineering department as quoted in *The Times of India*, January 30, 1999.
40. The fifteen year wait on acquiring new fast jet training aircraft for the air force is a good example. Between 1991 and 1998, 172 jet fighters have crashed dur-

ing training, most of them MiG-21s, killing more than 60 pilots. India's Air Force loses four aircraft for every 10,000 hours flying time, against 0.21 for the British air force. If decision making had not been paralyzed by politics and officialdom, the savings that India could achieve in having better trained pilots (and not losing aircraft and pilots at the appalling high rates) would exceed the $1 billion cost involved in buying new trainers. Mark Nicholson, "India's $1 bn defence contract emerges from bureaucratic thicket after 12 years," *Financial Times*, December 11, 1998.

41. An argument on these lines can be found in James Fearon, "Signaling Foreign Policy Interests: Tying hands versus Sinking Costs," *Journal of Conflict Resolution*, vol. 41, 1997, pp. 68-90.

42. For instance the view that the failure of the policy was due to the "rather patronizing attitude towards India," a "stubborn" refusal to view India's position beyond the India-Pakistan context, which inevitably meant that "none of [the signals from India], was enough to open deliberately closed eyes." Therese Delpech, "Nuclear Weapons and the 'New World Order': Early Warnings from Asia," *Survival*, vol. 40, no. 4, Winter 1998-99, pp. 57-76.

CHAPTER THIRTEEN

The Costs of Nuclear Weapons in South Asia

Peter R. Lavoy[1]

Summary

Officials in India and Pakistan insist that no expense should be spared to achieve national security. The development of nuclear weapons and missiles, they contend, is required to deter foreign hostility and political coercion. This claim could be correct: Nuclear deterrence might foster peace and security in South Asia. But at what cost? Will Indian or Pakistan replicate the Soviet experience, whereby the costs of creating and maintaining a credible nuclear deterrent bankrupt the government and society? Are India and Pakistan threatening their future prosperity, prestige, and security for questionable security gains? This chapter identifies the costs of the nuclear deterrent programs pursued by India and Pakistan. Five categories of costs are examined: the financial burden, the opportunity costs, the domestic political reverberations, and the international political price This discussion is followed by a brief assessment of the military risks that India and Pakistan now face in the aftermath of the 1998 nuclear tests.

Introduction

The nuclear explosive tests conducted by India and Pakistan in May 1998 received wide and vocal support in each country. Patriotic Indians and Pakistanis initially believed that they had much to celebrate. Their scientists had surmounted enormous political, financial, and technical barriers to achieve what only five other states had done: develop and detonate nuclear weapons. The fact that their leaders authorized these tests in the face of intense international political pressure, including the certainty of severe economic sanctions, only spurred the nationalist fervor in India and Pakistan. Three years after the Pokhran and Chagai Hills explosions, however, public confusion and anxiety are as commonplace as expressions of pride and euphoria. Periodic military clashes bordering on open warfare in Kashmir, including a major 1999 clash in Kargil, make even ardent nuclear advocates question the utility of nuclear deterrence, or whether it actually exists in South Asia. And in the face of deep poverty, outdated economies, persistent social problems, and teetering governments, Indians and Pakistanis now question whether they can afford their nuclear arms competition.

Government officials in New Delhi and Islamabad insist that no expense should be spared to achieve national security. The development of nuclear weapons and missiles, they contend, is required to deter foreign hostility and political coercion. This claim could be correct: nuclear deterrence might foster peace and security in South Asia. But then again, it might fail. India and Pakistan could be drawn into a fourth conventional war—one that could go nuclear. Or, as the Soviet experience suggests, the cost of creating and maintaining a credible nuclear deterrent could bankrupt the government and society supporting the development of weapons of mass destruction. In short, India and Pakistan could be threatening their future prosperity, prestige, and security for questionable strategic gains.

This chapter identifies the costs of the nuclear deterrent programs pursued by India and Pakistan. Five categories of costs are examined:

1. the financial burden of Indian and Pakistani efforts to achieve nuclear deterrence;
2. the opportunity costs of these expenses on the fragile economies and industries of both states;
3. the opportunity costs of the Indian and Pakistani nuclear and missile programs on the conventional military capabilities of each country;
4. the domestic political reverberations that the South Asian nuclear programs have created; and
5. the international political price New Delhi and Islamabad are paying to become nuclear weapons powers.

This discussion is followed by a brief assessment of the military risks that India and Pakistan now face in the aftermath of the 1998 nuclear tests.

Readers might wonder why this discussion focuses so heavily on the costs and risks of the Indian and Pakistani nuclear and missile programs. Why not also calculate the short–and long-term benefits that could accrue to India or Pakistan as a result of their efforts to establish nuclear deterrence? The answer is not that there are no advantages to producing nuclear arms and missiles. Although there is a fiery debate on this matter, New Delhi and Islamabad very well could reap some of the security and symbolic gains that Washington, Moscow, London, Paris, and Beijing have enjoyed.[2] However, the cost of achieving nuclear deterrence for India and Pakistan, like for the first five nuclear powers, will be very high. Until recently, claims about the merits of nuclear proliferation in South Asia (and elsewhere) have turned on different assessments of the potential benefits and risks to Indian and Pakistani security.[3] But the costs need to be calculated as well; and the estimated costs ought to be weighed against the presumed benefits. There is little informed discussion of what nuclear and missile proliferation costs India and Pakistan, although this is a matter of growing concern to the populations of both countries. This chapter seeks to stimulate a more balanced deliberation about the costs of nuclear weapons in South Asia.

The Financial Burden of Nuclear Deterrence

It is not a simple task to calculate the costs of the nuclear weapons and missile programs of any country. Citing the need for secrecy, the New Delhi and Islamabad governments refuse to reveal what they spend to develop nuclear explosives and other nuclear weapons components or delivery systems. Some official statements about the costs of the Indian and Pakistani nuclear programs have been made in the past, but generally these interventions were designed to legitimize a particular policy position, not to provide an objective assessment of the expenditure required to produce and sustain a viable nuclear deterrent arsenal.

Take the case of India in 1964. Nine days after China conducted its first nuclear explosive test, Homi Bhabha, then chairman of the Indian Atomic Energy Commission, told the listeners of All-India Radio that the production of a ten-kiloton nuclear explosive device would cost India $350,000 (about 1.75 million rupees) and that a two-megaton weapon would cost $600,000 (about 3 million rupees). He further argued that atomic explosives were some 20 times cheaper than conventional explosives.[4] Bhabha knew that this claim was not entirely correct: His cost estimates were based on figures presented at the Third International Conference on the Peaceful Uses of Atomic Energy that did not account for the expense of manufacturing nuclear production facilities or actually producing fissile material and other weapons components. In fact, U. S. officials secretly calculated at the time that the production of a low-yield plutonium device would cost India "$30-40 million over a three-year period" beyond its existing nuclear expenditures.[5] Bhabha himself confided to a U. S. official that "he could make and test a crude nuclear device for approximately ten million dollars."[6] Bhabha's strategically timed statements were intended to persuade Indian politicians of the economic feasibility of making nuclear weapons, not to inform the Indian public of true costs of going nuclear.

Two weeks after Bhabha's radio address, Prime Minister Lal Bahadur Shastri, together with India's former defense minister, Krishna Menon, criticized Bhabha's cost estimates. In a public statement, the anti-nuclear Krishna Menon criticized Bhabha, without mentioning him by name, for using his position to manipulate elite opinion on the nuclear issue. "By common consent, we do not discuss the Atomic Energy Commission even in Parliament," Krishna Menon declared. "If it has any information to give, then such information is the sole and secret property of the government and the government alone. It has no business to discuss in the open press the cost structure and technical possibility of India producing the bomb. It has still less business to give incorrect data under the cloak of expertise." Menon went on to say that cost of building a nuclear bomb was at least 25 million rupees.[7] Prime Minister Shastri, who also opposed India's production of nuclear weapons (but ultimately approved developmental work toward this end), stated that the cost of manufacturing nuclear weapons was even higher—about 40 to 50 million rupees apiece.[8] During India's 1964 nuclear debate—and indeed in the three plus decades afterward—the financial cost of "going nuclear" was never settled.

Several nongovernmental analyses have calculated the cost of nuclear weapons development for small nuclear weapons programs, such as the ones being pursued by India and Pakistan. Although these estimates vary in terms of the assumptions they make—such as about construction cost estimates, plant technology, and industrial infrastructure, as well as about the scale and character of the nuclear weapons arsenal that is to be assembled—they do provide unofficial standards of comparison where no official data exist. Two kinds of cost estimates have been made: those for "generic," small nuclear powers and those for India.[9]

Generic Cost Estimates

In December 1966 the United Nations General Assembly commissioned a study on the security and economic implications of acquiring and possibly using nuclear weapons. Thirteen experts from various nations (including Vikram Sarabhai, then chairman of India's Atomic Energy Commission) authored a report that estimated the costs of several nuclear-weapons production programs.[10] The expenditure required to produce ten 20-kiloton plutonium-based warheads over ten years was estimated in 1968 U. S. dollars at $104 million, or about $11 million per warhead. The cost of producing one hundred 20-kiloton warheads over a ten-year period was calculated to be $188 million, or $1.9 million per warhead.[11]

In 1976 Albert Wohlstetter and his colleagues at the Pan Heuristics organization calculated the cost of a program to manufacture five plutonium-based fission weapons per year at about $200 million in 1976 dollars.[12] One year later the U. S. Office of Technology Assessment (OTA) published a study that calculated the cost of producing various amounts of weapons-grade plutonium and highly enriched uranium (HEU), which were assumed to be the largest costs involved in nuclear weapons production.[13] OTA estimated that the cost of manufacturing and operating a reactor and reprocessing plant capable of producing 9 kilograms (kg) of plutonium per year would be $40-55 million in 1977 dollars and that the cost of producing 100 kg of plutonium per year would be $175-350 million. The expenditure required to produce 30 kg of HEU per year was estimated at $2-5 million and $198-231 million was the cost of producing 300 kg of HEU per year. Finally, in 1984 Stephen Meyer calculated that the development of a small plutonium-based nuclear weapons program would cost slightly over $60 million in 1960 dollars.[14]

How much light do these generic estimates shed on the actual costs of the Indian and Pakistan nuclear weapons programs? Although the paucity of detail and the variance in assumptions underlying each of the four estimates make it difficult to single out any one as being particularly relevant to India or Pakistan, they do identify several factors that should be assessed when calculating the cost of nuclear arms production in South Asia (or anywhere else).

First, the scale of the weapons program clearly matters. Economies of scale obtain both in the construction of larger nuclear facilities (although generally less so with uranium enrichment plants than with reactors and reprocessing plants) and in the production of larger quantities of fissile material.[15] If India embarks on the path outlined in 1999 by the National Security Advisory Board in the draft Indian Nuclear Doctrine, which calls for a triad-based nuclear arsenal for "credible minimum deterrence," then the unit cost of each kilogram of plutonium produced presumably will be much less expensive than the plutonium India has produced to date. The same logic should apply to Pakistan's production of HEU for its nuclear weapons program.

The second factor is the degree to which the nuclear weapons production program is embedded in a civil nuclear power program. In the case of India, the cost of many of the country's nuclear weapons-related facilities and that of the education and training of its nuclear scientists, engineers, and technicians are born by India's ambitious, civil nuclear energy program. Since Pakistan's nuclear weapons program appears to be a dedicated military effort that is separate from its modest civil nuclear power program, its costs cannot be diffused as widely as in India. (Pakistan's nuclear weapons program, however, does not have to bear the burden of sustaining a large and relatively inefficient energy production program.)

Third, technology choices matter. As the OTA study indicates, the production of highly enriched uranium is generally much less expensive than the production of plutonium, because a costly nuclear reactor is required in the latter case. Therefore, the bombs exploded by Pakistan in May 1998, which are reported to have used HEU as the explosive material, probably cost less than those detonated by India several days earlier, which are reported to have used plutonium.[16] Regardless of whether the HEU or the plutonium path to weapons production is selected, the country still faces difficult cost-benefit choices in the specific fissile material production technology it decides to employ. At some point, India and Pakistan might choose to acquire more sophisticated plutonium reprocessing and uranium enrichment systems than those they currently possess. If they do, their short-term costs will skyrocket, but over time more efficient and reliable systems might drive down fissile material production costs. A commitment to produce both plutonium and HEU will be much more costly than the pursuit of a single path to fissile material production.

Fourth, producing nuclear weapons indigenously is likely to be far more costly than importing some or all of the components of a nuclear bomb program. Self-reliance was highlighted as a crucial goal of the Indian nuclear program from its origins in the late 1940s and early 1950s. As a result, India has been willing to spend vast sums of money to develop the infrastructure, technology, and skills needed to produce both nuclear power and nuclear weapons domestically. In contrast, Pakistan, which followed India by more than a decade in initiating its civil nuclear program, has relied heavily on foreign imports of nuclear technology and materials. Although Pakistan has had to create elaborate and presumably costly international procurement networks to circumvent export controls and acquire essential nuclear weapons-related components, these foreign purchases probably were less costly than investing in local development and production of the required goods.[17]

Finally, local labor and industrial market costs (such as for materials, safety and security, transportation, land, and interest) will affect the cost of nuclear weapons production. In this respect, the Indian and Pakistani nuclear weapons development costs ought to be similar to one another, but quite different from related costs in the United States, Britain, and France where labor, materials, and regulatory costs are much higher (China and Russia probably fall in between). Of course, low local labor costs can be offset by quality control problems that could lead to construction delays and poor facility operating practices. Numerous construction delays and technical operating difficulties have plagued India's civil nuclear power program. During the month of March 1994, for example, six of India's ten operable nuclear power reactors were shut down for various technical reasons.[18]

Based partly on the aforementioned generic cost estimates, partly on deductions from the costs of nuclear weapons production in the United States, and taking into account approximate labor, facility, and material costs in India and Pakistan, one can estimate that each state has allocated more than $5 billion (in 1999 dollars) for the production of fissile materials and the manufacture of a few nuclear weapons.[19] This level of public expenditure might seem reasonable when compared to the more than $400 billion the United States reportedly paid from 1940 to 1996 to manufacture its arsenal of nuclear weapons.[20] But building bombs consumed just 7 percent of the total cost of the U. S. nuclear weapons program. Washington reportedly spent over $3 trillion on delivery systems and weapons deployment, nearly $1 trillion on nuclear targeting and command-and-control, another $1 trillion on active and passive defenses against nuclear threats, and about $400 million for dismantling old nuclear bombs, managing nuclear waste, and cleaning up the environment.[21] One inescapable implication is that India and Pakistan are embarking on a course of enormous—and partially hidden—financial costs.

Estimates of the Indian Nuclear Weapons Program

Notwithstanding the deceptive figures Homi Bhabha provided in 1964, Indian nuclear analysts have been relatively realistic in calculating many of the "hidden costs" that will be associated with their country's pursuit of a minimal nuclear deterrent capability. As early as 1966, retired Major General Som Dutt, the first director of the Institute for Defense Studies and Analyses (IDSA), calculated that the development of a survivable nuclear arsenal capable of threatening significant Chinese targets would cost India at least $220 million (in 1966 dollars) per year over ten years.[22] Because such a program would amount to a 20 percent increase in India's defense budget, which already consumed nearly a third of India's government expenditure, Dutt concluded that the cost of going nuclear would be too expensive for India.

Two years later, K. Subrahmanyam, who replaced Dutt as IDSA director, took issue with his predecessor's analysis. Ironically, Subrahmanyam estimated a greater cost for India to obtain a nuclear deterrent, but argued that the benefit outweighed the expense.[23] He stated that "the production of fissile material or the fabrication of a nuclear weapon alone cannot confer on a nation a credible deterrent nuclear posture. A nation must have a delivery system, invulnerable to enemy pre-emptive attack and an effective command-and-control system to wield that capability operationally."[24] Specifically, Subrahmanyam wrote that a credible nuclear deterrent "will require, apart from nuclear and thermonuclear warheads, a missile delivery system—aircraft, silo and submarine based; sophisticated high-performance, low-flying, long-range aircraft; nuclear propelled or long-range diesel propelled, missile-firing submarines; a comprehensive radar warning system and a command and control network to operate the entire system."[25] He estimated the cost of this ambitious program—which looks much like the one advocated in the 1999 draft Indian Nuclear Doctrine (perhaps understandably since Subrahmanyam is one of its authors)—at $10-15 billion (in 1968 dollars) spread over ten years.[26]

While the public Indian debate over the cost of nuclear weapons quieted somewhat during the 1970s and 1980s,[27] K. Subrahmanyam revealed that in 1985, when Indian concerns about Pakistan's nuclear weapons program were mounting, the Indian military tasked a small group of officers and scientists to prepare a secret estimate of the expenditure required for a "balanced deterrent program."[28] Admiral Tahliani, who was serving temporarily as Chairman of the Chiefs of Staff Committee, formed a group composed of Vice Chief of Army Staff Lieutenant General K. Sundarji, Vice Chief of Naval Staff Vice Admiral K. K. Nayyar, Deputy Chief of Air Staff Air Marshall John Greene, and Rajgopala Chidambaram from the Department of Atomic Energy, and A. P. J. Abdul Kalam, from the Defense Research and Development Organization. The report they produced concluded that a force of warheads "in low three digit figures" with aircraft and Agni and Prithvi missile delivery systems would cost 70 billion rupees (180 billion in 1999 rupees, or $5 billion). Prime Minister Rajiv Gandhi reportedly rejected this option because of the high expense.[29]

The Indian public debate resurfaced energetically in the 1990s. One notable exchange took place in late 1990 between respected Indian journalist Pran Chopra, who criticized the "costly status of mutual deterrence,"[30] and the former chief of the Indian army, K. Sundarji, who contended that India must develop the means to deter China and that the cost of doing so would be an affordable "one half to one percent of the GDP (Gross Domestic Product)."[31] Sundarji later wrote that the cost of a nuclear deterrent consisting of 150 warheads and Prithvi and Agni missiles would be slightly over 27 billion rupees.[32] In 1992 retired Brigadier Vijai K. Nair calculated that the production of 132 warheads over ten years would cost nearly 12 billion rupees, or 90 million rupees for each device. Nuclear testing would cost an additional 1.86 billion rupees over ten years. Command and control requirements would cost more than 2 billion rupees annually. And the cost of 12 short-range ballistic missile (SRBM), 36 intercontinental-range ballistic missile (ICBM), and 80 submarine-launched ballistic missile (SLBM) delivery systems would amount to just under 14 billion rupees over 15 years. Nair estimated that the entire nuclear deterrent program could be funded for about 70 billion rupees ($2.8 billion in 1992 dollars) with an annual price tag of 6 billion rupees ($240 million), or 3.47 percent of India's fiscal year 1991/92 defense expenditure.[33]

After the May 1998 nuclear tests, the financial debate has intensified, but elite opinion in India remains divided as ever—both on the desired size of the deterrent arsenal and on the cost of different options. At the high end, Indian defense analyst Bharat Karnad calls for a robust "thermonuclear deterrent" triad of 328 warheads deployed on submarines and land–and air-based missiles and a sophisticated command and control system—a program that would cost just over 600 billion rupees ($13.3 billion in 1999 dollars).[34] Retired Lieutenant General Jasbir Singh estimates that a deterrent capability almost half this size (150 warheads) would cost 400-500 billion rupees over ten years.[35] Some supporters of a "minimum deterrent" argue that India can get away with fewer nuclear weapons but generally agree with the nuclear triad concept. For example, Uday Bhaskar, Deputy Director of IDSA, estimates that an arsenal of 60 Agni nuclear warheads and a suitable command and control system would cost 36 billion rupees ($800 million).[36] At the other end of the spectrum, a growing number of Indian analysts, social leaders, and journalists argue that the pursuit of a nuclear deterrent program would make India less secure and ruin the economy in the process.[37]

Economic and Industrial Opportunity Costs

India and Pakistan might be able to finance their deterrent programs, lavish as they may be, but what are the opportunity costs? Although they have relatively modern industrial sectors with expertise in nuclear energy, missile development, and armaments production (and space, satellite communications, and software design for India), India and Pakistan are afflicted with some of the world's worst poverty. Widespread unemployment, outdated infrastructure, rising food prices, and low living standards beset each society. India's 1998 per capita GDP of $390 ranks in the bottom fifth worldwide; Pakistan's is only slightly better. Each country ranks in the bottom quarter of the world in the United Nations Development Program (UNDP) Human Development Index.[38] According to one Indian estimate, a single Agni missile costs as much as the annual operation of 13,000 health care centers.[39] More than 3,000 public housing units could be built for the price of one nuclear warhead.[40] The expenditures required to develop India's "minimum" deterrent could meet 25 percent of the yearly costs of sending every Indian child to school.[41] Nearly all Pakistani children could be educated and fed for the cost of the nuclear and missile arsenal that is being created for their "protection."[42]

The energy sectors suffer directly from the nuclear arms race. If India and Pakistan were to abandon their nuclear deterrent programs, sign the Nuclear Non-Proliferation Treaty (NPT) as nonnuclear-weapons states, and accept full-scope safeguards on their civilian nuclear power plants, the energy benefits could be tremendous. Fifteen years ago Indian Atomic Energy officials planned on producing 10,000 megawatts of installed nuclear power by the year 2000. India's ten aging reactors now produce one fifth of that amount.[43] While nuclear power production has tapped scarce resources for more than four decades, it generates less than 3 percent of India's electricity.[44] In Pakistan, where energy shortfalls have slowed economic growth for years, the situation is even worse. China recently built a 300-megawatt reactor at Chashma, but if this facility is used for military purposes, Pakistan's only nuclear energy source will remain the 34-year-old Karachi nuclear power plant, which produces less than 100 megawatts of electricity annually.[45] By becoming NPT members in good standing, Pakistan and India might be able to draw critical infusions of capital and technology to jump-start their ailing nuclear power industries. This investment could stimulate economic growth and lessen dependence on foreign energy sources, thereby enhancing national security.

Conventional Military Costs Also Are Rising

The guns-versus-butter tradeoff is one way to assess the costs of South Asia's nuclear arms competition. The guns-versus-guns tradeoff is another. Following in the footsteps of the United States and other nuclear weapons advocates,[46] Indian and Pakistani nuclear hawks argue that developing nuclear deterrent forces will make conventional military buildups unnecessary and reduce overall defense costs. In October 1996, for example, the IDSA argued that if the Indian government does not allocate at least 2.5 percent of the GDP on defense, the country will have to deploy nuclear weapons, that are relatively less expensive than effective conventional forces.[47] More recently, P. K. Iyengar, former chairman of the Indian Atomic Energy Commission, stated that while a nuclear device costs only 10 million rupees, conventional armaments such as fighter aircraft cost many times more.[48] In defiance of this logic, Indian defense spending rose 11 percent after the May 1998 tests.[49] Pakistan's defense spending rose as well. In the aftermath of the Kargil conflict, moreover, it appears that conventional military expenditures are likely to soar even higher alongside rising nuclear and missile costs.

During the summer of 1999, Indian and Pakistani troops (and Pakistan-backed rebels) fought the fiercest military battles ever waged in the mountains of Kashmir. Journalists report that each side lost more than 1,000 lives.[50] In financial terms, local media place the daily expense of Indian military operations at $3–6 million.[51] While Pakistani costs probably are lower because of smaller force commitments, they too are onerous. To offset the expense of staging military operations around Kargil, India's parliament authorized an emergency grant of $135 million to purchase ordnance, hardware, and high-altitude clothing. The cost of the Kashmir conflict is still climbing. Fighting has subsided since its peak in summer 1999, but it has not ended. Indian and Pakistani politicians state that they will meet the financial needs of their militaries to replenish equipment and ammunition and to prepare for more conflict.

The fighting in Kargil shows that nuclear deterrence is unstable between India and Pakistan, if it exists at all. The economic costs of this conflict also hint at the serious damage that will be inflicted against both economies by a general war. The large military spending increases that a broader war would cause would trigger higher interest rates and inflation, and the war-time destruction of industrial and infrastructure facilities would reduce productivity and drain already-limited foreign exchange reserves. The threat of follow-on hostilities or the breakdown of domestic order in parts of India or Pakistan would discourage foreign investment and financial assistance that is crucial for the long-range economic growth and development in each country. In short, a conventional war could ruin India and Pakistan. The human and economic costs of a nuclear war are beyond calculation.

Mounting Domestic Political Costs

The political expense that India and Pakistan will pay to become nuclear powers might rival the economic burden created by their weapons programs. Despite the immediate outpouring of support for the nuclear tests in India and Pakistan, ironically, the domestic standing of the governments in New Delhi and Islamabad is now lower than it was before the tests. Considering the outbursts of pride and support that swept South Asia last May, it is striking that the Indian coalition government led by Atal Behari Vajpayee's Bharatiya Janata Party (BJP) fell less than a year after the tests. The same tragic fate befell Pakistani Prime Minister Nawaz Sharif. One and a half years after he authorized the Chagai Hills explosions, Sharif was ousted in a bloodless coup by Pakistan's Chief of Army Staff, General Pervez Musharraf.

In India, the BJP lost support because it failed to implement crucial economic reforms and curb rising food prices. These problems provided effective political ammunition for BJP opponents both within and outside the ruling coalition. Opposition and coalition leaders criticized the diversion of scarce resources into the nuclear program. Predictably, nuclear deterrence is less salient to India's population than clean water and affordable food. By all accounts, the return to power of Prime Minister Vajpayee and the BJP in the October 1999 elections was seen more as a comment on the lack of viable alternatives to the BJP than an expression of support for the BJP's record as a ruling party, especially regarding its defense policies.

A similar political deterioration occurred in Pakistan where domestic opposition to Prime Minister Nawaz Sharif rose precipitously in the wake of the nuclear tests and especially after the Kargil fiasco. Sharif's declaration of a national emergency after the Indian nuclear tests, his suspension of foreign exchange accounts, his vastly unpopular decision to build the Kalabagh dam, the steady deterioration of law and order throughout the country, and his humiliating retreat from Kargil had resulted in widespread speculation that his days were numbered.[52] When Nawaz Sharif attempted to preempt the issue by unceremoniously ousting Musharraf as Army chief on October 12, 1999, the latter immediately deposed the unpopular prime minister.[53]

Sharif's nuclear policies certainly did not cause his ouster, but neither did they dramatically improve his popularity. Immediately following the nuclear tests, a Gallup poll showed that 85 percent of the respondents approved of Sharif's decision, but his popularity rapidly plummeted.[54] After the May 1998 nuclear tests, Pakistan People's Party (PPP) leaders gradually came to question the need for carrying these tests if a balance of terror could not be achieved with India.[55] In the province where the nuclear explosions were conducted, the Baluchistan National Party criticized the government's nuclear policy for diverting scarce resources from development to defense. The majority party in Pakistan's Northwest Frontier Province also condemned these policies.[56]

International Political Costs:
They Are Bad, But They Could Be Worse

Internationally, the May 1998 nuclear tests produced outrage in many parts of the world and spurred costly economic sanctions. The five permanent members of the UN Security Council (P-5) issued a communiqué on June 4, 1998 condemning the nuclear policies of India and Pakistan. This was followed on June 6 by a Security Council resolution deploring the tests and similar criticisms by the Group of Eight industrial nations (G-8), the European Union, key nonaligned states, and other international bodies. The United States, Japan, Australia, and other nations imposed costly economic sanctions and trade restrictions against the two South Asian countries. Officials in India and

Pakistan alike condemned these sanctions as discriminatory and claimed that they would have only marginal economic effects and absolutely no impact on their nuclear weapons policies.

U. S. sanctions on India and Pakistan, which were required by the 1994 Glenn Amendment, included the termination of foreign economic assistance, foreign military sales and licenses, government credits, credit guarantees and financial assistance (such as that provided by the Export-Import bank), U. S. support for loans from International Financial Institutions (IFIs), such as the World Bank, private bank lending to Indian and Pakistani government entities, and a ban on certain dual-use exports.[57] Because U. S. export controls restricting nuclear–and missile-related sales to India and Pakistan were imposed prior to the 1998 tests, and because Washington provided only a small level of economic aid and military sales to India and none to Pakistan (President Bush had cut off economic assistance and arms sales to Pakistan in 1990 under the Pressler Amendment), the effect of U. S. sanctions was minimal in these areas. However, the curtailment of IFI assistance and the termination of Japanese aid, which collectively accounted for most of the foreign assistance going to India and Pakistan, had a huge impact.[58]

Although the imposition in November 1998 of new restrictions on U. S. trade with all Indian (and Pakistani) entities "involved in nuclear and missile activities" created serious difficulties for over 200 Indian firms and agencies, the overall impact of U. S. and international economic sanctions on India has not been enormous.[59] International investor confidence in India flagged and the flow of capital to India plummeted after the May 1998 tests.[60] But India's foreign exchange reserves remain stable and the country's economic growth has not been too disappointing (growth fluctuated between 4.7 percent in the second quarter of 1998 to 8 percent in the first quarter of 1999—as compared to 5 percent in 1997/98 and 7.8 percent in 1996/97).[61]

Pakistan is more reliant on foreign assistance; therefore, sanctions have had a much greater impact on that state than on India. Pakistan's current economic recession began before May 1998, but it worsened considerably after the imposition of international sanctions. Output growth slowed from 4.3 percent in 1997/98 to 3.1 percent in 1998/99, and exports and investment had plummeted.[62] Pakistan is experiencing a deep balance-of-payments crisis. If the International Monetary Fund did not provide an emergency $1.56 billion loan, Pakistan would have defaulted on its vast external debt.

Even if the international sanctions imposed after May 1998 were not severe enough to cause India and Pakistan to reverse their nuclear weapons policies, their impact has been significant enough to create growing pockets of domestic opposition to these policies in each country. And even if the international consensus underpinning sanctions has started to fray,[63] the nuclear weapons development efforts of India and Pakistan have kept them at political loggerheads with the world's most powerful nations and organizations. If the Indian and Pakistani governments had expected the nuclear tests to improve their domestic and international standing, the results must be disappointing.

Rising Military Risks

Continued fighting over Kashmir and the downing of aircraft in other areas indicate that nuclear deterrence has not yet emerged in South Asia. The risk of another India-Pakistan conventional war seems higher than ever before and India's relations with China also have deteriorated. Added to these problems are new risks of inadvertent or accidental nuclear use because of unsophisticated nuclear command-and-control systems and poorly defined nuclear doctrines. And, even if India and Pakistan do manage to establish nuclear deterrence, the effect will be that every Indian and Pakistani will live under the threat of nuclear annihilation. Welcome to the nuclear club.

Security and Prosperity without Nuclear Weapons

As former U. S. Deputy Secretary of State Strobe Talbott stated, "India and Pakistan need security, deserve security, and have a right to determine what is necessary to attain security."[64] Are there ways for India and Pakistan to enhance their security without deploying nuclear weapons and missiles? Considering the dangerous and expensive record of the U. S.-Soviet arms race, the enormous political and economic costs of Indian and Pakistani deterrent programs, and the growing risk of nuclear war in South Asia, India and Pakistan should make every effort to pursue non-nuclear sources of security. And, all concerned states should help them to achieve that security.

Notes

1. The views expressed in this chapter are the author's alone; they do not represent those of the Department of Defense or any other U. S. government agency. The author wishes to thank Samina Ahmed, Tom Clements, Sumit Ganguly, Robert Hehl, Khidhir Hamza, Neil Joeck, Debra Lavoy, and Jim Wirtz for their helpful comments. An earlier, briefer version of this chapter appeared in "Responding to the Challenge of Proliferation," vol. 4, no. 2 of *U. S. Foreign Policy Agenda* (September 1999), pp. 31-34.

2. For a prominent optimistic view of deterrence in South Asia and elsewhere, see Kenneth N. Waltz, "More May Be Better," in Scott D. Sagan and Kenneth N. Waltz, eds., *The Spread of Nuclear Weapons: A Debate* (New York: Norton, 1995), pp. 1-45. An application of this logic to India and Pakistan is Devin T. Hagerty, *The Consequences of Nuclear Proliferation: Lessons from South Asia* (Cambridge, Mass.: MIT Press, 1998). For a pessimistic perspective on the security effects of nuclear proliferation, see Scott D. Sagan, "More Will Be Worse" and "Sagan Responds to Waltz," both in *The Spread of Nuclear Weapons*, pp.

47-91, 115-136. For a pessimistic view of nuclear proliferation in South Asia, see George Perkovich, *India's Nuclear Bomb: The Impact on Global Proliferation* (Berkeley: University of California Press, 1999).

3. For an analysis of the logic and evidence used by each side in this debate, see Peter R. Lavoy, "Strategic Consequences of Nuclear Proliferation," *Security Studies* vol. 4, no. 4 (Summer 1995), pp. 695-753.

4. *Hindu*, October 27, 1964; *New York Times*, October 27, 1964.

5. See U. S. Arms Control and Disarmament Agency, "The Indian Nuclear Program: Proposed Course of Action," declassified report produced by the Committee on Nuclear Weapons Capabilities (Thompson Committee), October 13, 1964, p. 3.

6. Jerome Weisner, declassified cable from U. S. Embassy, New Delhi, to U. S. Secretary of State, January 21, 1965, nuclear nonproliferation collection, National Security Archives, record no. 22456.

7. *Blitz*, November 14, 1964.

8. During this debate, Prime Minister Shastri argued that building nuclear bombs was counter to the peaceful and nonviolent tradition that Gandhi and Nehru had created for India; that having exploded only one bomb, China need not be taken seriously; and that the cost of making weapons might be 40 to 50 million rupees, a huge drain on economic development goals. *Hindu,* November 9, 1964. For background on this and other Indian political debates over nuclear weapons, see Peter R. Lavoy, "Learning to Live with the Bomb: India and Nuclear Weapons, 1947–1974" (Ph.D. Dissertation, University of California, Berkeley, Spring 1997).

9. Although there has been little public debate about the financial cost of Pakistan's nuclear weapons program, the Pakistani government has considered this issue very carefully from the start. For example, when the question of developing nuclear weapons was first seriously considered in 1966 (during Zulfikar Ali Bhutto's last days as foreign minister), President Ayub Khan rejected the option largely because the Secretaries of Finance, Foreign Affairs, and Defense raised spirited financial objections. See Iqbal Akhund, *Memoirs of a Bystander: A Life in Diplomacy* (Karachi: Oxford University Press, 1997), pp. 262-64.

10. United Nations, Department of Political and Security Council Affairs, "Effects of the Possible Use of Nuclear Weapons and the Security and Economic Implications for States of the Acquisition and Further Development of These Weapons," report of the Secretary-General transmitting the study of his consultative group, A/6858 (New York: United Nations, 1968). For a detailed comparison of this study with the three other generic cost estimates described here, see Katherine Starr, James Tomashoff, and Joseph Yager, "The Cost of Proliferation," unpublished report by Science Applications International Corporation (SAIC), November 15, 1993. See also Thomas W. Graham, "The Economics of Producing Nuclear Weapons in Nth Countries," in Dagobert L. Brito, et al. eds., *Strategies for Managing Nuclear Proliferation*, (Lexington, Mass.: Lexington Books, 1983), pp. 9-27.

11. The 100-warhead program was not estimated to be ten times more expensive than the ten-warhead effort because a 40-50 megawatt heavy water reactor was assumed for the latter whereas a 250 megawatt production reactor was assumed for the former and also because of significant economies of scale were presumed to accrue to the larger program.

12. Albert Wohlstetter et al., *Moving toward Life in a Nuclear Armed Crowd* (Los Angeles: Pan Heuristics, 1976).

13. Office of Technology Assessment, *Nuclear Proliferation and Safeguards* (New York: Praeger, 1977).

14. Stephen M. Meyer, *The Dynamics of Nuclear Proliferation* (Chicago: University of Chicago Press, 1984), pp. 194-203.

15. This section is based on Starr, Tomashoff, and Yager, "The Cost of Proliferation," pp. 21-32.

16. For background on the May 1998 Indian and Pakistani nuclear tests, see Program for Promoting Nuclear Non-Proliferation, "Proliferation-Related Developments: India and Pakistan," *Newsbrief*, no. 42 (insert), 2nd quarter 1998.

17. See Director of Central Intelligence Nonproliferation Center, "Unclassified Report to Congress on the Acquisition of Technology Relating to Weapons of Mass Destruction and Advanced Conventional Munitions, 1 January through 30 June 1998" (http://www.cia.gov/cia/publications/bian/bian.html#pakistan); and Starr, Tomashoff, and Yager, "The Cost of Proliferation," p. 28.

18. Tarapur-1 was closed for refueling and maintenance; Rajasthan-1 had been closed frequently since the 1980s, when it was deemed "sick" and derated to 100 MWe; Narora-1 had been closed since March 1993, when a fire broke out in its turbine hall; Kakrapar-1 was down for annual maintenance; Madras-2 was shut down when the temperature in the generator seal exceeded designed limits; and Madras-1 had been closed since July 1993, when it was shut down for turbine inspection and repair in the wake of the Narora fire. See "On Line, Off Line," *Nuclear Engineering International* (May 1994), p. 8.

19. These rough estimates are derived from calculations provided by specialists in the U. S. scientific and defense communities and take into account differences in labor, material, and other local costs between the United States and South Asia. Each state probably has allocated close to $1 billion on the design and manufacture of a small number of nuclear-capable missiles (Prithvi and Agni for India, Ghauri and Shaheen for Pakistan).

20. A recent study organized by the Brookings Institution calculates that the United States spent $409.4 billion between 1946 and 1996 to manufacture nuclear weapons. See Kevin O'Neill, "Building the Bomb," in Stephen I. Schwartz, ed., *Atomic Audit: The Costs and Consequences of U. S. Nuclear Weapons since 1940* (Washington, D. C.: Brookings Institution Press, 1998), pp. 32-103.

21. Schwartz, *Atomic Audit*.

22. Retired Major General D. Som Dutt, *India and the Bomb*, Adelphi Paper no. 30 (London: International Institute for Strategic Studies, 1966), p. 7.

23. Institute for Defense Studies and Analyses (IDSA), *A Strategy for India for a Credible Posture against a Nuclear Adversary* (New Delhi: IDSA, 1968). In a conversation with me, K Subrahmanyam revealed that he was the author of this document.

24. Ibid., p. 6.

25. Ibid., pp. 7-8.

26. Ibid., p. 6.

27. However, there was a relatively vigorous debate in the early 1970s. See K. Subrahmanyam, "Costing of Nuclear Weapons Programme," in *Nuclear Weapons and India's Security*, special issue of *Institute for Defence Studies and Analyses Journal*, vol. 3, no. 1 (July 1970), pp. 82-88; Sampooran Singh, *India*

and the Nuclear Bomb (New Delhi: S. Chand & Co., 1971); and Narasimhiah Seshagiri, *The Bomb! Fallout of India's Nuclear Explosion* (Delhi: Vikas, 1975), p. 69.

28. K. Subrahmanyam, "Indian Nuclear Policy—1964–98 (A Personal Recollection)," in Jasjit Singh, ed., *Nuclear India* (New Delhi: IDSA, 1998), p. 41. All information in this paragraph derives from this source.

29. Ibid..

30. Pran Chopra, "The Nuclear Trap," *Hindu*, November 29, 1990.

31. K. Sundarji, "Minimum Nuclear Deterrence—Where Third World Differs from the West," *Hindu*, December 12, 1990.

32. K. Sundarji, "Imperatives of Indian Minimum Deterrence," *Agni: Studies in International Strategic Issues*, vol. 2, no. 1 (May 1996), p. 21.

33. Vijai K. Nair, *Nuclear India* (New Delhi: Lancer International, 1992), pp. 195-219.

34. Bharat Karnad, "A Thermonuclear Deterrent," in Amitabh Mattoo, ed. *India's Nuclear Deterrent: Pokhran II and Beyond* (New Delhi: Har-Anand, 1999), pp. 108-49.

35. Lieutenant General R. K. Jasbir Singh, "The Costs of Nuclear Weaponisation," in R. K. Jasbir Singh, ed. *Indian Defence Yearbook: 1999* (Dehra Dun: Natraj, 1999), pp. 128-36.

36. C. Uday Bhaskar, "Nukes: Can We Afford Them?" *Economic Times*, September 13, 1999. See also Brahma Chellaney, "Nukes: Can We Afford Them?" *Economic Times*, September 13, 1999.

37. For a sample, see Kanti Bajpai, "The Fallacy of an Indian Deterrent," in *India's Nuclear Deterrent*, pp. 150-88; Arundhati Roy, "The End of Imagination," *Outlook* (August 3, 1998), pp. 62-71; T. V. Rajeshwar, "Costly Deterrence," *Hindustan Times* (September 6, 1999); T. Jayaraman, "Deterrence and Other Myths," *Frontline*, vol. 16 no. 10 (May 8-21, 1999); and Jayati Ghosh, "The Bomb and the Economy," *Frontline*, vol. 16 no. 10 (May 8-21, 1999).

38. United Nations Development Program, *Human Development Report 1999* (New York: Oxford University Press, 1999), pp. 134-37.

39. Singh, "The Costs of Nuclear Weaponisation," p. 135.

40. Ibid.

41. Ibid., 136.

42. There are additional opportunity costs to the economic and educational sectors of India and Pakistan that result from the incentives provided to leading scientists and engineers to work on the nuclear weapons and missile programs.

43. The Indian Department of Atomic Energy had a program to overcome the nearly 8,000 MW shortfall, but according to a recent report of the Comptroller and Auditor General of India, the DAE has failed to generate any additional nuclear power despite having spent 50 billion rupees as of the end of March 1998. "Atomic Energy 'Profile' Flayed," *Business Line*, November 9, 1999.

44. The International Atomic Energy Agency (IAEA) reports that nuclear reactors generated 2.51 percent of India's total electricity consumption in 1998. *IAEA Press Release*, 1999/04 (29 April 1999).

45. This single operating nuclear reactor generated 0.65 percent of total Pakistani electricity production in 1998. *IAEA Press Release*, 1999/04 (April 29, 1999).

46. In September 1951, for example, Senator Brien McMahon, chairman of the Joint Committee on Atomic Energy, claimed: "The cost of military fire power based on atomic bombs is hundreds of times cheaper, dollar for dollar, than conven-

tional explosives." Senate Resolution. 46, 82nd Congress, 1st session, introduced September 18, 1951.

47. See Avirook Sen, "The Budget: Casualties of the Funds Crunch," *India Today* (October 15, 1996), pp. 90-92.

48. P. K. Iyengar, "N-arms cheaper than conventional weapons," *Hindu*, May 19, 1998.

49. Sabyasachi Mitra, "India Readies to Pay the Bill for Kashmir Conflict," *Reuters*, July 15, 1999.

50. See Raj Chengappa, "Kargil: Holding the Heights," *India Today*, August 16, 1999; and Rahul Bedi, "The Real Cost of Victory," *Asiaweek*, August 13, 1999.

51. Chengappa, "Kargil: Holding the Heights;" and Bedi, "The Real Cost of Victory."

52. Smruti S. Pattanaik, "Pakistan: The Post-Chagai Challenges," *Strategic Analysis* (September 1998), pp. 883-902.

53. For background on the events leading up to the coup, see Najam Sethi, "Saviours," *Friday Times*, October 15-21, 1999, pp. 1, 5.

54. See Neil Joeck, "Nuclear Developments in India and Pakistan," *AccessAsia Review*, vol. 2, no. 2 (July 1999): p. 23.

55. On August 10, 1998, during a Senate debate on the Kargil conflict, the Senate opposition leader, the PPP's Senator Aitzaz Ahsen criticized the nuclear tests. See "Senate Debates Kargil Crisis: Pakistan Will Be Declared Terrorist State: Aitzaz," *Dawn*, August 11, 1999.

56. Samina Ahmed, "Pakistan's Nuclear Weapons Program: Turning Points and Nuclear Choices," *International Security*, vol. 23, no. 4 (Spring 1999), pp. 198-99.

57. The Glenn amendment is reprinted in *After the Tests: U. S. Policy toward India and Pakistan*, Report of an Independent Task Force Co-sponsored by the Brookings Institution and the Council on Foreign Relations (New York: Council on Foreign Relations Press, 1998), pp. 35-40. Two exemptions were granted immediately by the United States: Humanitarian assistance was continued as were export credits permitting wheat sales by American farmers.

58. Prior to May 1998 Pakistan annually was receiving $100-200 million from the International Monetary Fund (IMF), $250-300 million from Japan, and $1-1.5 billion from IFIs. Meanwhile, India was receiving annual aid worth $2 billion from the World Bank and other IFIs and $1 billion from Japan. See Dinshaw Mistry, "Diplomacy, Sanctions, and the U. S. Nonproliferation Dialogue with India and Pakistan," *Asian Survey*, vol. 39, no. 5 (September/October 1999), pp. 753-771.

59. R. Ramachandran, "Sanctions: The Bark and the Bite," *Frontline*, vol. 16, no. 10 (May 8-21, 1999).

60. Foreign investors withdrew more than $400 million from Indian stock markets in May and June 1998 and Moody's downgraded India's credit rating to below investment grade. See "The Indian Economy: A Fine Balance," *South Asia Monitor* (published by the South Asia Program, Center for Strategic and International Studies), no. 3 (1 November 1998).

61. Dinshaw Mistry, "Diplomacy, Sanctions, and the U. S. Nonproliferation Dialogue," p. 3.

62. See "Pakistan: A Fragile Economy," *South Asia Monitor* (published by the South Asia Program, Center for Strategic and International Studies), no. 11 (July 1, 1999).

63. See C. Raja Mohan, "Cracks within G-8 over Nuclear Issue," *Hindu*, September 17, 1999.
64. Strobe Talbott, "U. S. Diplomacy in South Asia: A Progress Report," official press release, November 12, 1998, p. 2.

CHAPTER FOURTEEN

India's Energy Policy and Nuclear Weapons Program

Raju G. C. Thomas

Summary

Unlike Israel and Pakistan, and earlier South Africa under its apartheid regime, all three of which sought the dedicated path towards a nuclear weapons capability, India's nuclear weapons program is mainly an offshoot of its nuclear energy program. From an economic development standpoint, India has rationalized the necessity of a nuclear energy program to fill shortfalls in its overall electricity needs. Especially given the costs of mining and transporting coal throughout India from its location in the northeast-central regions, and that the great rivers of India cannot all be harnessed appropriately for hydro-electric power to service the major cities of India, a case is made for nuclear energy. Elsewhere in the world, especially in France, Japan, South Korea, Taiwan, and much of the European Union countries, nuclear energy is viewed now as essential for meeting increasing energy demands and for reducing reliance on Middle East oil. Oil supply and prices are subject to manipulation by the Organization of Petroleum Exporting Countries (OPEC), and coal mining and coal-fired power plants are seen as health hazards. The chapter concludes that while the U. S. nonproliferation policy failed to contain India's nuclear weapons program, international technological and economic sanctions severely curtailed the development of India's nuclear energy program which lags far behind other countries such as the United States, France, Japan, South Korea, and Taiwan. This has caused shortfalls in India's energy requirements thereby also affecting its infrastructure and economic growth potential.

Nuclear Choices and Consequences

"Nuclear deterrent posture" and "energy security policy" are different aspects of India's overall security environment and economic development policy. Using the terminology of Joseph Nye and others, the first may be perceived as a part of "high politics" or "hard security," and the second an aspect of "low politics" or "soft security." However, military and civilian nuclear technologies cannot be separated, and the terminology of "high" and "low" politics appear irrelevant in the nuclear political context. The links between nuclear energy and nuclear weapons arise not only from the dual-use nature of the technology, but also the opportunity costs that nuclear security poses for energy and economic development. India's decision to become a nuclear-weapons state 1998 in defiance of the primarily U. S. sponsored nuclear nonproliferation regime, has provoked severe sanctions on a wide array of civilian technology transfers which also carry military applications. The security and development dimensions of the problem, and the linkages between the two, are examined in this chapter.

The security dimension pertains to the level of nuclear weapons capabilities required to maintain a minimum credible deterrence, the relationship between conventional and nuclear weapons strategies, and of political and military strategies to be adopted in case nuclear deterrence fails. Discussion here must relate to global anti-proliferation politics, domestic political choices, the development of nuclear doctrines, the numbers and the yields of atomic and thermonuclear bombs, the different modes of delivery systems available, and degrees of accuracy that may be needed for a purely counter-value deterrent posture, or for a counter-force war-fighting posture. Stripped of the jargon, the essential question here is whether nuclear weapons generate greater or less real security, and whether they are held to prevent nuclear war, or intended to be used in a nuclear war.

The development dimension concerns issues of accessibility, availability and affordability of energy in general, the degree of reliance on foreign and domestic sources, and the role that nuclear energy plays in alternative sources of energy development to advance the national economy. Energy is a crucial component of the infrastructure, and the denial of access to foreign sources, or the inability to develop domestic sources because of international sanctions could lead to severe economic dislocation and destruction.

For instance, during the early part of the energy crisis in 1974, Secretary of State Henry Kissinger declared that the West had a right to intervene militarily in the Middle East if the Arab oil-exporting states were to "strangulate" the Western economies by denying Western nations who supported Israel access to their oil resources. India is also dependent on foreign oil. More than half of India's annual consumption of oil is imported mainly from the Organization of Petroleum Exporting Countries (OPEC). Nor can India afford Western economic sanctions that may "strangulate" its economy. India does not have the inclination or the capacity to go to war against the members of OPEC in the Middle East. It may just hope that the United States and others would conduct the military intervention for the good of all oil-importing states. And it does not have the military capabilities to confront NATO if its members choose to undermine the Indian economy in retaliation for developing nuclear weapons and missile launchers.

The experience across the border is relevant. After Pakistan conducted its nuclear tests in May 1998, Western economic sanctions nearly brought the country to the verge of bankruptcy. However, following the U. S. war in Afghanistan in Fall 2001, economic sanctions were lifted on both India and Pakistan. Pakistan's external debt of about $32 billion was rescheduled and partly written off as a reward for Pakistani president Pervez Musharraf's support for the American campaign in Afghanistan. An additional $1.3 billion has been offered in economic assistance.

The oil crisis of the mid 1970s intensified arguments in India for nuclear power. Whereas India's first atomic test in May 1974 obtained the necessary plutonium from the Canadian supplied Cirus Research reactor and allegedly other materials from the American supplied Tarapur Light Water reactor, the subsequent buildup of India's nuclear energy facilities was undertaken with unsafeguarded indigenous resources and technology. This has given India a large nuclear weapons capacity and potential. Currently, it possesses sufficient fissile materials to make between 80 and 100 thermonuclear weapons from the plutonium extracted from the waste fuel of its Heavy Water reactors.

The consequences of India's nuclear tests in May 1998 on India's economic, technological and military objectives are varied. The imposition of international economic sanctions was expected to have a major impact on the development of India's infrastructure, especially through the denial of loans from the World Bank, the IMF and the Export-Import Bank for power projects and telecommunications. Technological assistance and cooperation between India and the West, particularly with the United States and Japan, declined drastically and in many areas ended. Indian scientists working or studying at U. S. establishments in areas considered to have implications for India's nuclear and missile capabilities were terminated. These actions affect a range of critical civilian technologies in India that contribute to the growth of India's economy.

On the military front, the end or the reduction of technological cooperation between India and the West was expected to slow down or even spell the end of several indigenous and licensed co-production projects in aircraft, helicopter, tank, and submarine development. In particular, U. S. sanctions were expected to end India's prolonged and expensive Light Combat Aircraft (LCA) project. However, all of these adverse consequences were reversed suddenly during the Afghanistan crisis of 2001. Almost all economic sanctions imposed after the 1998 tests were lifted. The United States resumed its aid for the LCA project.

Energy Sources of Proliferation in South Asia

The nuclear weapons option that India's Bharatiya Janata Party (BJP)-led government exercised in early May 1998 at its underground testing site in Rajasthan may be perceived as a spinoff from its nuclear energy program, specifically from its capacity to generate plutonium from existing reprocessing facilities at the Kalpakkam power plant near Chennai and the Dhruva research reactor at Mumbai. Plutonium was the fissile material used in the making of India's nuclear bombs. This is in contrast to Pakistan's dedicated path towards nuclear weapons capability through the acquisition of enriched uranium from its Kahuta plant. The clandestine transfer to Pakistan by its agents of nuclear technology and materials from the West in the 1970s and 1980s, culminated in the Pakistani nuclear tests in Baluchistan in late May 1998, a quick response to India's earlier tests.

Pakistan's nuclear motives were first demonstrated by its failed attempt in the 1970s under the leadership of Munir Khan to acquire a reprocessing plant from France to be set up at Chasma. This was followed by its successful attempt in the 1980s under the leadership of Abdul Qadir Khan to set up a uranium enrichment plant at Kahuta. Both waste fuel reprocessing and uranium enrichment facilities are legitimate needs of a nuclear energy program if the program is to become self-sufficient through the autarkic control of the nuclear fuel cycle. However, Pakistan's pursuit of such facilities without the prior establishment of a genuine nuclear energy program, was generally considered indications of its weapons procurement motives. But over the last 20 years, Pakistan has made a case for nuclear energy in its power development program. It has no coal or oil, and its hydroelectric power generation from harnessing the Indus river and its tributaries carry some serious technical problems because of high siltation conditions. But this new Pakistani rationale for nuclear energy, if it was genuine at all, appeared to be secondary to Pakistan's nuclear weapons ambitions.

There is, therefore, a fundamental difference in the origins and sources of the May 1998 nuclear tests on the subcontinent. In India it arose from its nuclear energy program which is considered essential to fill in shortfalls in its overall power program for the industrial sector of its economy. The nuclear energy program, in turn, provided India with weapons capability. Therefore, the sources of India's nuclearization tendencies may be seen as an "Energy-to-Security" phenomenon. On the other hand, since the rationalization for the nuclear energy program in Pakistan follows its primary objective of acquiring a nuclear weapons capability, the Pakistan case may seen as a "Security-to-Energy" phenomena. This distinction is important. In order to restrain Pakistan's proliferation motives, one needs to address its security fears. In order to restrain India's proliferation tendencies, one needs to watch its nuclear energy program.

The energy-to-security tendency in India essentially takes the following path:

1. The development and growth of coal-fired thermal power plants and hydro-electric power plants in India carry several inherent weaknesses in the nature, location and availability of such electricity generating capacity.
2. Nuclear energy is expected to fill the critical gaps in total energy needs of its rapidly growing industrial and agricultural sectors that are obtained mainly from coal-fired thermal plants and hydroelectric power.
3. Given the lack of any technological fix separating a peaceful nuclear energy program from a nuclear weapons program, India's nuclear science and engineering community would be able to develop nuclear weapons should such security needs arise.
4. As a spinoff from the nuclear energy program, an Indian nuclear weapons program will prove economically viable and affordable when calculated as an incremental cost over its civilian program.

Irrespective of whether the civilian nuclear energy program is economically viable, and irrespective of whether the program is intended primarily to maintain India's nuclear weapons option, the nuclear program has achieved considerable "technological self-sufficiency." Frank Barnaby noted that India had "developed and constructed a self-sufficient nuclear fuel cycle, with uranium mines and mills, a uranium purification UO2 plant, fuel fabrication plants, plutonium reprocessing plants, nuclear power reactors and research reactors. In addition, it has a small uranium conversion UF6 plant, a pilot uranium-enrichment plant, and heavy-water production plants. . . . India is experimenting with gas centrifuges for the enrichment of uranium."[1]

Since India also has about 50,000 tons of uranium deposits found mainly in Bihar and substantial resources of thorium in Kerala, it is almost self-sufficient in the basic raw materials needed to conduct the nuclear program. But the civilian program has run into technological snags and breakdowns. India's projected goal in 1970 of attaining 10,000 megawatts of electricity by the year 2000 is likely to produce in reality only 5,770. However, the Indian ability to swiftly siphon off a major nuclear weapons program is not in doubt. The gestation period of converting civilian programs to weapons programs was at one time as long as two years, the period needed to test the first atomic device at Pokharan in Rajasthan in May 1974. However, today the period my be much less as demonstrated by Pokharan-II in early May 1998, less than two months after the BJP-led coalition government took office in mid March.

By the end of 1995, India's stock of weapons-grade plutonium was estimated to be about 420 kilograms, enough for about 85 nuclear weapons.[2] Following the 1998 tests, an estimated 375 kilograms of plutonium remain, enough for at least 75 bombs. Much of the plutonium came from the Dhruva Research Reactor which is not under international safeguards, and partly also from the Canadian-supplied Cirus Research reactor which began operating in 1960. Further progress on India's Fast Breeder Reactor (FBR) program (a research FBR has already been established at Kalpakkam in Madras) and waste fuel generated at other reactors at Kota, Kakrapur, and Kaiga, would provide India

Table 14.1   Nuclear Capabilities

India	- Atomic test (1974) Fission: 15-20 Kt - Atomic & Thermo- nuclear tests (1998) Fusion: 43 Kt; Fission: 12 Kt and 3 sub-kiloton devices - 1997 Stockpile: 370 kg weapons grade plutonium for 75 bombs - Plutonium from Dhruva reactor: 20 kg/5 bombs p.a. - No. of Bombs from Kalpakkam & other reactors undetermined
Pakistan	- Atomic & Thermo-nuclear tests (1998) - Total yield claimed by Pakistan: 43 Kt - Indian & US estimates of yield: 8 Kt - 1998 Stockpile: 400 Kg weapons grade uranium for 16-20 bombs - Khushab reactor plutonium: 1-3 bombs per annum
China	Number of nuclear warheads: Not available

with more plutonium for bombs.[3] On the other hand, problems of safety in the civilian program may slow down India's weapons technological capabilities. Periodic reports in the Indian media have pointed to serious safety problems and close calls that escaped serious accidents at atomic power plants at Kota, Kalpakkam, Kakrapur and Kaiga. According to one report, 24 "incidents" took place in India's nuclear plants between 1988 and May 1994.[4]

Energy Politics in India

The two major events of 1974—oil pricing shocks and the Indian atomic test—highlighted some of the linkages of energy, security, and development policies in India. Heavy dependence on oil imports at the time from the Persian Gulf states, Libya, and the Soviet Union had implications for Indian diplomatic, economic, and military policies. Apart from the obvious need not to alienate these states if oil was to keep flowing on affordable commercial terms, India had to step up exports to the oil-supplying countries to prevent a massive foreign exchange deficit that would have crippled the Indian development program. There was also a military dimension to the international oil crisis. The Middle East oil-exporting states were some of the largest buyers of technologically advanced weapons systems from the industrialized West, which offset the cost of Western oil imports. The proximity of these OPEC arms importers to the subcontinent, and the overt or latent military links of states such as Saudi Arabia, Libya, and the Shah's Iran with Pakistan, carried strategic implications for India. Special purchases of oil and military equipment from the Soviet Union also accentuated India's economic and military dependence on the communist regime in Moscow.

The passing of the international energy crisis by the mid-1980s brought greater economic prosperity to India, both because of successful efforts to tap domestic oil resources, especially in the offshore Bombay High oilfields on the western coast, and because of the decline and stabilization of international oil prices. The favorable energy environment since the 1980s was supported by a series of good annual monsoon rains, with the exception of the drought of 1987. This was offset by the economic growth of the 1980s and the buffer food stocks that had been accumulated. Since socialism ended and marketization began in 1991, the Indian economy has grown at a healthy average rate of almost 7 percent per annum. There was a short phase when Indian oil imports from, and commercial goods exports to Iraq were dislocated following the 1992 Gulf War. But this problem was overcome through higher oil imports from Saudi Arabia and the Gulf Sheikdoms to offset the loss of Iraqi oil imports. Memories of the energy crisis have now faded.

India has three conventional sources of commercial and industrial energy: oil, coal and hydroelectric power. Oil of various kinds, and oil products are used primarily in the transportation, petrochemical and household sectors of the economy. The other two energy sources—coal-fired thermal and hydro-electric power—provide some 70 and 25 percent of electricity generation in India. Coal is still used marginally in locomotives in some sectors of the Indian railway network. In the rural economy, where about 70 percent of the Indian population lives, there is still considerable use of firewood and agricultural and animal waste. The extensive use of dried cow dung as fuel in the rural areas has led to the setting up of several biogas plants under the earlier Indian Five Year Plans. The Government of India has also been exploring the potential use of geothermal, tidal and solar power. Development and annual growth rates in these various sources of energy have been uneven. (See Tables 14.2 and 14.3.)

At the height of the oil crisis in the 1970s and early 1980s, oil imports consumed nearly 80 percent of India's export earnings. Now with half of India's annual oil requirements coming from the offshore Bombay High oilfields and from the onshore Assam oilfields, and with international oil prices down to about $15-18 per barrel in the mid 1990s from the earlier highs of $32-42 per barrel in the early 1980s, the cost of oil imports now constitute only about 20 percent of India's export earnings. Oil in India is not used for power plant electricity generation (except for small generators used as emergency fallbacks in hospitals and luxury hotels), but it is absorbed entirely in the household and transportation sectors. The needs of India's transportation industry, including diesel locomotives, require no explanation. But the utilization of oil in the household sector does. Cooking on kerosene stoves is still widespread in India, and in a country with a population of nearly one billion, kerosene oil consumption is very high.

Before the Gulf War of early 1992, much of India's oil imports came from Kuwait, and from both Iran and Iraq even at the height of the 1980–89 Iran-Iraq war. After the Gulf War, oil imports came from Iran, the United Arab Emirates and Saudi Arabia. In a rather remarkable diplomatic policy, today

Table 14.2   Trends in the Performance of Infrastructure Sectors (Percentage Growth)

Energy	Units	91-92	92-93	93-94	94-95	95-96	96-97	97-98
Coal Production	tonnes in ml	8.3	3.9	3.3	3.2	6.4	5.7	3.9
Electricty generated (Utilities only)	Kwh billion	8.5	5	7.4	8.5	8.3	3.8	6.7
Hydroelectric	Kwh billion	1.4	-4	0.8	17.2	-12.1	-5.4	6.2
Thermal Including Nuclear power	Kwh billion	11.1	8.1	9.5	6.1	14.6	5.9	6.8
Petroleum								
Crude Oil	Tonnes mil	-8.1	11.2	0.3	19.3	9.1	-6.5	3.3
refinery throughput	Tonnes mil	-0.7	4	1.5	3.8	3.9	6.9	3.6
GDP Growth rate at factor cost			5.3	6.2	7.8	7.2	7.5	5.1
Inflation rate		10.1	8.4	10.8	7.7	8.9		

Source: *Indian Economic Profile, Federation of Indian Chambers of Commerce and Industry, 1998*

India has close ties with Israel, Iran and Iraq, three mutually antagonistic states. It should be noted that in the past, India's refusal to recognize Israel was for at least two reasons; in part to avoid alienating the Arab states and the Muslim world in general, so as to remain on good economic terms with these countries and to keep the oil flowing to India; and to ensure, at the minimum, the neutrality of the Muslim world over the Kashmir issue.

Coal, the main source of commercial energy in India, provides about 80 percent of total electricity generated. Coal reserves in India are substantial, projected to last another 80–100 years at compound rates of consumption. Despite such large proven reserves, the productivity of operations under the government-owned corporation Coal India Limited and its subdivisions is low when compared with Western standards. The average output per man-shift for Coal India is 0.8 MT in underground mines, considerably lower than the range of about 2.5 to 4 MT in Western Europe, and 8 to 12 in the United States, Australia and South Africa.[5] Indian productivity, however, compares favorably with China where it is 0.5 MT. (For estimates of production in the coal, hydro-electric and nuclear energy sectors, see Table 14.4 and 14.5. For electricity consumption patterns see Table 14.6.)

The problem with coal utilization is the location where it is found: West Bengal, Bihar, Orissa and Madhya Pradesh. Political conditions in the first two states have been particularly volatile over the decades where labor strikes and general political unrest have been extensive. The location of coal resources in the northeast sector of India implies that it has to be transported and distributed throughout the country railway. This makes it vulnerable to disruption or interruption if the powerful labor union, the All-India Railwaymen's Federation, with a membership of between 2 and 3 million employees, were to go on a nation-wide strike. This would not only bring all railway passenger and goods traffic to a halt, but would also paralyze coal-fired thermal plants and thereby industrial activity throughout India. The seriousness of this internal security threat was probably best exemplified by the crisis of 1974 when the All-India Railwaymen's Federation successfully launched a nation-wide strike of its 2 million-plus members. With most power plants carrying less than 2 weeks of coal supplies, power had to be severely rationed in major industrial cities that were dependent on electricity from coal thermal plants. Apart from this, there is the usual criticism that coal mining is hazardous to the health of the miners, and that its utilization causes considerable pollution of the atmosphere.

Assessing the total potential of hydroelectric power resources in India is difficult because the flows of Indian rivers vary widely, ranging from thousands of cusecs in the monsoon season to a few cusecs in the dry season. Consequently, estimates of hydroelectric potential in India usually amount to identifying specific targets in each river basin where the potential for hydroelectric power generation is both technically feasible and economically viable. The Indian government estimated in 1978 that the potential annual energy generation from hydel plants to be about 400 Tetrawatt-Hours (TWH). However,

Table 14.3   Procurement of Coal and Petroleum in India (millions of tons)

	1991-92	1993-94	1995-96	1996-97
Coal Production	243.8	264.1	292.3	308.2
Crude Oil				
Onshore	11.4	11.6	11.9	11.4
off shore	19.0	15.4	23.3	21.5
Production Total	30.4	27.0	35.2	32.9
Oil Imports	24.0	30.8	27.3	33.9

Source: *Economic Survey,* Ministry of Finance, 1998

Table 14.4   Total Installed Electric Generating Capacity as of March 2000 (MW)

Hydro	23527.28	24.54%
Thermal	69474.76	72.47%
Nuclear	1840	1.92%
Wind	1024	1.07%
Total	95866.04	100%

Source: Annual Report, 1999–2000, Ministry of Power, Government of India

the installed hydroelectric generating capacity at that time was only 40 TWH, or just 10 percent of estimated potential, a share that has changed little during the next two decades. This meant that a 90 percent potential for clean and renewable hydroelectric power was being wasted annually because of the failure to harness India's rivers. Part of the problem has been the social opposition to large dam building for irrigation and hydroelectric power as this is perceived to cause environmental damage and uproot several hundred thousand villagers from the traditional homes. This opposition eventually killed the huge Narmada Dam project in the mid 1990s, despite a World Bank approval and offer of a loan. The Narmada project involved the building of 30 major dams and several hundred smaller dams. On the other hand, China has decided to go through with its highly controversial massive Three Gorges Dam project on the Yangtse River. Critics have alleged that the Three Gorges Dam project could lead to another major Chinese disaster like the "The Great Leap Forward" of the 1950s.

In the 50 years since independence in 1947, electricity generation capacity in India grew by more than 60 times. In 1947, India generated 1,362 MW of electricity. In 1997, this capacity reached 83,288 MW.[6] Energy projections in India beyond the year 2000 suggest serious shortfalls of about 11 percent but rising to a high of 19 percent during peak periods. Demand for electricity is expected to rise at the rate of 8 percent per annum over the next decade, this

Table 14.5   Domestic Oil Production and Petroleum Products
Consumption (1991–1997 actual and 1997–2007 estimates)

	Domestic Production MMT	Consumption/Demand MMT	% Self Sufficency
1990-91	33.02	55.0	55.60%
1991-92	30.35	56.9	49.3
1992-93	26.95	58.9	42.4
1993-94	27.17	61.5	40.9
1994-95	32.24	67.4	44.3
1995-96	35.20	74.4	43.7
1996-97	36.31	80.9	41.6
2001-02	38.69	112.8	31.8
2006-07	39.61	155.8	23.5

Source: *Indian Economic Profile*, Federation of Indian Chambers of Commerce and Industry, 1998

Table 14.6   Electricity Consumption in India (in thousand Gwh)

	1991–92	1993–94	1995–96	1996–97	
Minning & Manfg	110.62	121.38	137.13	140.87	44.20%
Transport	4.52	5.62	6.22	6.65	2.10%
Domestic	35.85	43.34	51.74	56.29	17.60%
Agriculture	58.56	70.70	85.73	84.33	26.50%
Others	21.42	24.41	28.65	30.59	9.60%
Total	230.97	265.45	309.47	318.73	100%

Source: Central Electricity Authority, Power Data Bank & Information Directorate, Government of India

despite the fact overall generating capacity increased from 287 Billion Units (BU) in 1991–92 to 420 BU in 1997–98, and to an expected 502 BU in 1999-2000. With Indian economic reforms since 1991 now generating a growth rate of about 7 percent, the main obstacle to more rapid growth is the poor infrastructure of roads, water supply, telecommunications and especially power.

The Case for Nuclear Energy

There remains the question, however, whether nuclear-generated electricity is commercially viable and affordable compared to the conventional sources of energy. The pro-nuclear power lobby in India suggest that this source of energy may have a cost advantage over coal-fired thermal plants. This was disputed earlier in Germany and Britain who decided to cut back on their nuclear power programs. However, France, Japan, and South Korea are convinced that nuclear power is a critical source of electricity. None of these states possess much oil, coal, and hydroelectric power resources.

Today there is renewed interest in nuclear power in Europe, Japan and the United States, the main guardians of the nuclear non-proliferation regime. In an article on the nuclear industry, Simon Holberton claimed that "as the European nuclear industry approaches the end of the millennium, there is reason to think that its prospects are better than they have been for 20 years. With memories of the Chernobyl disaster fading and public concern about global warming growing, the industry has been presented with an opportunity to change its public perception and possibly its future." Taken collectively, the European Union's nuclear industry is the biggest in the world with more than 140 nuclear reactors in operation producing one-third of the total electricity generated. France obtains 80 percent of its electricity from nuclear power plants. Japan has embarked on a major nuclear energy program and expects to obtain almost 50 percent of its electricity from nuclear power plants. Table 14.7 is one comparative cost assessment of electricity production costs in the European Union countries.

After shunning nuclear energy for more than 2 decades, especially following the accident at Three Mile Island in Pennsylvania, the United States is now seeking salvation for its energy crunch through nuclear power. The problem has been most acute in California.[7] As Richard Rhodes noted in his article "Nuclear Power's New Day": "The population of the United States is growing, adding the equivalent of California every ten years. Demand has caught up with supply even with significant improvements in energy efficiency and conservation, and the United States has become the world's largest greenhouse gas emitter. These factors make a renewal of nuclear power likely. . . . France once burned coal. That nation's electricity is now 80 percent nuclear, with five times less air pollution and with carbon dioxide emissions 10 times lower than Germany's and 13 times lower than Denmark's."[8]

Arguments for nuclear power in the midst of the energy crisis in California, Brazil, and other states, have raised concern among those seeking to stop the spread of nuclear weapons. In an article entitled "More Nuclear Power Means More Risk," Paul Leventhal claimed that the "nuclear industry's safety and security claims are often misleading. They don't acknowledge that the core of at the Three Mile Island plant was within hours of an uncontrolled meltdown, with Chernobyl-like consequences, when a new shift operator came on duty" and shut the plant down.[9] Leventhal continued: "A rapid expansion of nuclear power would compound the existing dangers of nuclear weapons proliferation. International inspections of nuclear facilities provide uncertain protection. Iran, for example, has pledged to put the reactors it will build under inspection but is still suspected of using civilian nuclear power as a cover for a nascent nuclear weapons program." George Perkovich, in his book *India's Nuclear Bomb,*

Table 14.7   Cost of Electricity Production in the European Union (Ecu/1000KWH)

		Investment	Operation & maintenance	Fuel	Total
5% per annum	Nuclear	11-22	3.7-11	4-8	22-40
Discount rate	Coal	17-15	3.7-11	13-26	28-74
	Gas	4.5-9	1.8-5.2	19-42	26-56
10% per annum	Nuclear	19-74	4-12	4.5-7	33-60
Discount rate	Coal	15-26	7-11	13-26	33-60
	Gas	7-17	2.2-5.2	19-38	30-60

Assumption: 1,000 Mwe PWR commissioning in the year 2000 at 1991 prices.
Source: from Simon Holberton, "The Nuclear Industry," *Financial Times, November 14, 1974.*

reports that a bomb tested by India in 1998 was made from the grade of plutonium produced in its 10 uninspected power reactors. If nuclear energy is the energy of the future, and if the West perceives this as a critical source of energy, then there will be limits to the American ability to contain further nuclear proliferation in the future.

Although there are limitations and liabilities in developing coal-fired thermal, hydel and oil as sources of energy in India, these will continue to generate the bulk of electricity in India for several decades to come. But the growth in thermal and hydroelectric generating capacity is not expected to keep pace with industrial and urban demand. Projected energy needs beyond the year 2000 suggest serious shortfalls of up to 20 percent. The crucial gap cannot be filled by increasing oil production, since domestic oil reserves are too limited to meet industrial demand and, in any case, are being depleted rapidly. Almost all of future oil imports are expected to be absorbed by the petrochemical, household, and transportation sectors of the economy. The concentrated geographic location of coal in the northeast of India, and the vulnerability of transporting coal throughout India, imply that coal cannot be guaranteed for the generation of electricity in the major industrial cities. Indian planners and politicians perceive nuclear power as critical.

India has always claimed that nuclear power was essential to its developmental needs. First, given the location of coal resources and the costs and security risks of transportation throughout India, and given the fact that hydel power projects needs to located along major rivers, some of the major cities of India such as Bombay and Madras do not have ready and reliable access to electricity. Nuclear power plants can be located right next to India's major cities. Apart from accidental leakages of radioactive materials and the likelihood of nuclear meltdowns, nuclear power is clean and non-polluting compared to coal-fired thermal plants. Major accidents such as the one at Three Mile Island in Pennsylvania and the Chernobyl disaster in the Ukraine are not likely to happen again, as technology and safety standards have advanced.

Indian nuclear scientists and economic planners are convinced that nuclear power is the only long-term solution to India's energy needs. The following statement in 1980 by Raja Ramana, then Chairman of the Indian Atomic Energy Commission, is reflective of the views of many members of the nuclear scientific community in India: "Looking at it [the future of nuclear energy] with the experience of the past and the terrifying energy problems of the future, I can think of no other source of energy that has been discovered to date except nuclear energy, which can solve the energy problems of this country during the next 25 years and beyond. If I do not make the case now and point out to the urgency of accepting its inevitability, I will have done a great disservice."[10]

According to Raja Ramana, the apparent higher cost of nuclear power over thermal power as alleged by the critics, arises from the nature of cost accounting applied to these two sources of energy. An assessment of the average cost of nuclear-generated electricity in India usually includes the capital outlay in areas like the production of heavy water and the setting up of a means of controlling the nuclear fuel cycle to enable domestic self-reliance. Compared to this, Raja Ramana pointed out that the extensive costs of developing coal mines and transporting the coal to power plants throughout India are not included in the assessment of the average cost of coal-generated electricity, mainly because the development of coal mines, the construction of railway lines, and the acquisition of wagons and locomotives are not undertaken exclusively for generating electricity from coal-fired thermal plants. Ramana observed: "The point usually overlooked is that for each coal-fired power station replaced by a nuclear power station, the need to develop coal mines and to organize transportation facilities will be proportionately reduced, and thus, the capital outlay required for these purposes would be significantly reduced."[11]

On Table 14.8, Raja Ramana provided this comparative cost assessment of coal and nuclear power in 1980:

Table 14.8 Comparative Costs of Power Production in 1980

Coal Fired Cost Component Investment Rs/Kwe		Nuclear Cost Component Investment Rs/Kwe	
Power Station	4,500	Power Station	5,000
Coal Mines	750	Heavy water plants	495
Coal Transportation	1,000	Uranium exploration	65
na	na	Uranium mining	295
na	na	Fuel fabrication	185
na	na	Fuel Reprocessing	135
Total	6,250	Total	6,175

Source: Raja Ramana, "Inevitability of Atomic Energy in India's Power Programme," in Rajendra K. Pachauri, Ed., *Energy Policy for India*, Delhi: Macmillan of India, 1980, p. 221.

U. S. Non-Proliferation Policy and India's Nuclear Energy Program

The fertile global conditions for nuclear weapons proliferation were set probably in 1953 when President Eisenhower introduced his "Atoms for Peace" plan whereby the United States would share the benefits of the peaceful atom with the rest of the world. At the time, this meant that the industrialized countries with nuclear technology would be willing to sell nuclear power reactors to the rest of the world, at least to those who could afford to buy them. The United States sold light water reactors to Japan, South Korea, Taiwan and Iran setting up their nuclear power base. Germany and France sold reactors to Argentina, Brazil, Chile, South Africa and Iraq.

Canada sold and set up two heavy water reactors in Rajasthan in India (the Rajasthan Atomic Power Plant—RAPP I and II) of 450 megawatts each, and gave a small research reactor called "Cyrus" installed at the Bhabha Atomic Research Center (BARC) in Bombay. Canada also provided a small 125 megawatt heavy water reactor to Pakistan installed in Karachi. In 1961, the United States gave India two 400 megawatt light water reactors which were stationed in Trombay, a suburb of Bombay (the Trombay Atomic Power Plant—TAPP I and II). When India conducted its Peaceful Nuclear Explosion (PNE) the plutonium was alleged to have come from the Canadian-supplied Cyrus research reactor, from RAPP, and from the American supplied TAPP. India denied these allegations since it had already developed and established its own heavy water reactors based on the CANDU design at Kalpakkam, a suburb of Madras (the Madras Atomic Power Plants—MAPP I and II).

Since then India set up other indigenously built nuclear reactors in many other states, and also an experimental Fast Breeder Reactor in Madras. While India has allowed the Canadian and American supplied RAPP and TAPP to be placed under IAEA safeguards, none of the Indian built reactors are under international safeguards. Two Russian-supplied 1000 megawatt light water reactors being installed at Koodanakulum in Tamil Nadu, are also under mutually agreed upon IAE safeguards. This leaves a dozen Indian build heavy water reactors throughout India that are capable of diverting the plutonium extracted from the reprocessing of its waste fuel to be used for weapons purposes. Following India's PNE in May 1974, Pakistan tried to buy a reprocessing plant from France. When that failed because of U. S. pressure on France, Pakistan sought to piece together a uranium enrichment plant at Kahuta through a variety of clandestine transfers of materials and technology from the Netherlands, Germany, Switzerland, Canada and the United States. Thus, India and Pakistan took two separate routes to nuclear weapons capability. The Indian nuclear tests of 1998 were plutonium technology-based, and the Pakistani nuclear tests were enriched uranium technology-based.

Perhaps Eisenhower's Atoms for Peace program is at least partially to blame for this chain of events, although shortly thereafter the United States successfully established the International Atomic Energy Agency (IAEA) in 1957 to monitor the recipient countries nuclear energy facilities. Even with the periodic inspections by the IAEA, a determined state could divert to nuclear weapons capability as Iraq and North Korea demonstrated decades later. The ability of not just India, but also South Korea, Taiwan, South Africa, Argentina and Brazil to make nuclear weapons may be traced to the Atoms for Peace program. On the other hand, the Israeli determination to acquire its variously estimated 100–200 "bombs in the basement" would appear to have happened anyway, whether Israel pursued a nuclear energy program or not.

However, back in 1953 it would have been difficult for the United States and other Western industrialized countries not to have offered the sharing of the anticipated wonders of the peaceful atom. Nuclear energy was perceived then as the energy of the future promising energy salvation for all countries. There was no nonproliferation treaty in existence at the time, and no restrictions on the transfer of "peaceful" nuclear technology. The competition for the lucrative nuclear reactor market would have meant that France, Germany and the Soviet Union would have sold them anyway. The United States would then have been compelled to pre-empt them on the grounds that "it would better if we do it than they," thereby guaranteeing profits for American corporations, and American control over possible diversions to military purposes.

Western economic and technological sanctions did not contain India's nuclear weapons capabilities. Instead, U. S. nonproliferation policy essentially retarded India's nuclear energy program relative to nuclear energy programs elsewhere in the world. There has been little or no Western assistance for India's nuclear energy and weapons programs since India tested its first atomic device in May 1974. These sanctions were further increased and tightened after the test of 1998. The denial of external technology assistance has prevented India from fulfilling its nuclear energy goals. India's nuclear energy performance has been comparatively dismal. (See Tables 14.9 and 14.10.)

Projections made back in the 1970s that nuclear energy would constitute 10 percent of India's electric power by the year 2000, have proven woefully short of expectations. In 2000, nuclear power constituted about 2.5 percent of total electricity generated in India. In France, electricity generated from nuclear power plants is about 80 percent, in Belgium 62 percent, South Korea 50 percent, Sweden 48 percent, Japan 35 percent, Germany 32 percent, and the United Kingdom and the United States about 25 percent.[12] France and Japan have established major nuclear energy programs and its reliance on this source of energy is expected to grow. France has almost 60 power plants with an electricity generating capacity of about 55 gigawatts. The United Kingdom has 35 nuclear reactors with a generating capacity of 13 gigawatts, Germany 20 reactors with a generating capacity of 22 gigawatts.

India had only 10 operating reactors in 2000, two each at Tarapur near Bombay, Kota in Rajasthan, Kalpakkam near Madras, Narora in Uttar Pradesh, and Kakrapar in Gujerat. Site preparation or construction for two nuclear reactors each were being conducted at Tarapur, Kaiga in Karnataka,

Table 14.9 Comparative Energy Capabilities (1995)

Country	Coal Production Mil Short	Hydro Electric Power Generation BillionKWH	Crude Oil Production 1000 BPD	Natural Gas Production Liquid & Dry 1000BPD/CuFT	Nuclear Electric Power Generation Billion KWH
India	311.06	71.00	703.4	47 & 0.66	7.23
China	1,478.07	175.00	2,990.0	Na & 0.60	12.38
Pakistan	3.27	18.50	57.1	5 & 0.64	0.50
Indonesia	41.47	12.30	1,502.6	76 & 2.23	na
Taiwan	0.32	8.77	1.2	0.5 & 0.03	33.93
South Korea	6.31	5.42	Na	na & na	63.68
Japan	7.40	79.70	11.0	na & na	275.22
Brazil	5.24	245.00	695.4	40 & 0.16	2.39
Argentina	0.21	30.00	715.0	42 & 0.89	7.07
Mexico	10.23	27.25	2,617.5	447 & 0.94	8.02
Russia	310.03	179.23	5,995.1	180 & 21.01	94.34
France	9.99	71.37	50.0	12 & 0.11	358.60
U.K.	52.36	3.99	2,489.1	267 & na	76.57
U.S.A.	1,032.97	323.52	6,559.6	762 & 18.80	673.46

Table 14.10   Comparative Per Capita Consumption of Electricity (KWH)

Bangladesh	84	Mexico	1,486	Germany	6,513
Kenya	139	Brazil	1,783	France	7,126
India	314	Canada	17,347	Japan	7,281
Pakistan	416	Italy	4,588	USA	12,308
China	719	U.K.	5,843	Sweden	16,534

From: *India's Means Business; Investment Opportunities in Infrastructure.* Ministry of External Affairs, Investment Promotion and Publicity Division, Government of India, 1997

and Koodankulam in Tamil Nadu. On the other hand, South Korea and Taiwan had far greater nuclear generating capacity than India. A 1998 news report indicated that China is in the market for 150 nuclear reactors which led to extensive lobbying in the U. S. Congress by General Electric, and other nuclear power plant suppliers to ease up congressional sanctions or restrictions on China because of China's dismal human rights record. These figures indicate that India's indigenous nuclear energy program which has been denied external assistance since its atomic test of 1974, needs all the foreign assistance it can get if nuclear energy is to make a significant contribution to the severe deficiency in the power sector.

Nuclear Energy and Nuclear Weapons

Despite the relatively small contribution of nuclear power to the Indian economy, it plays a critical role. However, the current and projected uses of nuclear energy carry political, economic, and security implications. Energy shortages in India have demanded adept diplomacy and adequate bargaining power abroad to fill the breaches. Lack of energy can undermine economic growth and stability and lead to political instability and violence. External and internal security, as well as external trade policies and economic development plans, have roots in the successful or unsuccessful management of energy policy. While the international energy crises may now lie behind us, the basic linkages among India's energy programs, security policies and economic development plans remain. Indian energy management must aim at either maintaining the present equilibrium or advancing to safer levels. Energy crises, in short, strike at both the economic and defense sectors. India has determined that nuclear energy is essential for the economy and nuclear weapons for security.

However, the basic question remains: Are nuclear energy programs in India intended to maintain India's nuclear weapons capability? The answer is twofold: (1) Conventional energy shortages in India not only retards or stymies India's economic reforms by creating severe bottlenecks for industrial growth, but it also leads to the increasing perception that energy salvation may be found only through greater reliance on nuclear energy. (2) This reliance on nuclear energy and thereby also the dual civilian-military uses of nuclear technology increases the general perception that meeting threats from China and Pakistan, or dealing with the general problems of discrimination between nuclear "haves" and "have-nots," is properly addressed through the policy of a nuclear weapons program.

The above conclusion is not intended to suggest that India can have its cake and eat it too. No doubt, India's nuclear weapons program, which may be obtained at an incremental cost from its nuclear energy program, does seem like the best of all worlds. It helps resolve the energy problem in India, and it may provide India with a credible two-way nuclear deterrent against China and Pakistan when combined with appropriate delivery systems. Against Pakistan, the Prithvi-II is sufficient. Against China, the Agni-II version gives India a reach up to China's cities in the southeast. Meanwhile the missile technology derived from the development of the Polar Satellite Launch Vehicle from the Indian space program will eventually give India a global reach to deter all nuclear powers. But recent reassessment of the nuclear arms race between the United States and the Soviet Union indicate that the costs and the burden of defense were phenomenal, especially for the Soviet Union. It destroyed the Soviet Union.

Maintaining the nuclear weapons option, and now an overt nuclear weapons capability, will continue to deny India access to advanced technology in the field of nuclear power plants. The indigenous nuclear energy program is woefully slow, basic and inadequate. It is the equivalent of continuing to build the domestic "Hindustan Ambassador" and "Premier President" cars based on the technology of the British Morris and Italian Fiat cars of the 1950s. Moreover, the obsolete technology and the inefficiency of the domestic nuclear energy program have resulted in serious safety problems. Molly Moore reported that India's reactors "are judged among the world's least efficient and most accident prone."[13] Nuclear Engineering International assessed the Indian nuclear power plants as worse than those in the ex-Soviet republics. On a scale of 1 to 7, where the Chernobyl nuclear accident is considered a 7, India has had several accidents that would rate between 1 and 3, with a Chernobyl waiting to happen. Moore observed that in north India near the Rajasthan and Narora nuclear plants, some serious accidents have occurred causing a high incidence of cancer, infertility, tumors, premature aging among villagers living in the vicinity. According to Moore, "all of India's nine nuclear power plants have encountered safety problems, and each has been closed down for months—or, in one instance, years. All the plants operate at only a fraction of their promised capacity and provide less than 3 percent of India's power needs."

If nuclear energy is considered critical for India's economic development, and if external technology and assistance may be received only if India signs the NPT and the CTBT, then India may have to make a choice between a viable nuclear energy program and a credible nuclear weapons deterrent.

Notes

1. Frank Barnaby, *How Nuclear Weapons Spread: Nuclear-Weapon Proliferation in the 1990s*, London: Routledge, 1993, p. 68.
2. Barnaby, p. 73.
3. See S. B. Bhoje, "Need for Fast Breeder Reactors," *The Hindu*, June 14, 2001, and M. V. Ramana, "Fast Breeders: Tall Promises, Poor Performance," *The Hindu*, July 16, 2001.
4. *The Pioneer*, September 24, 1995. See also *Frontline*, June 6, 1994; *The Telegraph*, June 23, 1994; *The Statesman*, December 26, 1994; and *The Economic Times*, May 22, 1995.
5. See Raju G. C. Thomas, "India," in Raju G. C. Thomas and Bennett Ramberg, eds., *Energy and Security in the Industrializing World*, Lexington: University Press of Kentucky, 1990, 19-20.
6. *India Economic Profile*, Federation of Indian Chambers of Commerce and Industry, New Delhi, 1998, p. 14.
7. For a debate on the pros and cons of nuclear energy in the context of the California energy crisis, see the following two articles: William Tucker, "The Nuclear Option Revisted: As Fossil Fuels Become Scarce, We Must Look to the Atom's Great Reservoir of Energy," and Amory B. Lovins and L. Hunter Lovins, "The Nuclear Option Revisited: Too Expensive and Unacceptably Risky, Nuclear Power was Declared Dead Long Ago," both in the *Los Angeles Times*, July 8. 2001.
8. Richard Rhodes, "Nuclear Power's New Day," *New York Times*, May 7, 2001.
9. Paul L. Leventhal, "Nuclear Power Means More Risk," *New York Times*, May 17, 2001.
10. See Raja Ramana, "Inevitability of Atomic Energy in India's Power Programme," in Rajendra K. Pachauri, ed., *Energy Policy for India*, New Delhi: Macmillan, 1980, p. 221. M. T. Srinivasan who later became Chairman of the IAEC, also made similar assessments in his "Where should all the Energy Come From?" *Times of India*, December 7, 1980.
11. Ramana, p. 226.
12. From Simon Holberton, "The Nuclear Industry: Future Calls for Power to Persuade," *Financial Times*, November 14, 1997.
13. See Molly Moore, "Nuclear Power in India: Boon or Burden?" *Washington Post*, August 21, 1994.

Part V

*Proliferation Lessons
and Security Prospects*

CHAPTER FIFTEEN

On The "Lessons" of South Asian Proliferation

George H. Quester

Summary

A series of optimistic or pessimistic lessons can be extracted from the aftermath of the 1998 nuclear detonations by India and Pakistan. If pessimistic "lessons" are accepted, these may well be self-confirming. If the outside world sees important distinctions between South Asia and the situation in other regions, however, some more optimistic conclusions may be in order.

South Asia is peculiar in that most knowledgeable outsiders had already assumed that India and Pakistan had significant numbers of nuclear weapons. It was special also in that both countries, at the time of the detonation, were governed as democracies, with this producing a pessimistic contradiction of theories of the "democratic peace." The region seems to have shifted from a pattern of "mutual deterrence of nuclear weapons acquisition" to "mutual deterrence of use." The theory that nuclear proliferation reduces the incidence of conventional fighting does not seem borne out by events since 1998. And finally, the idea that Pakistan and India stood up to the outside world with these detonations, and thus served their own national interests, will be judged on the outside by whether the two states now truly seem better off as a result.

Introduction

The news of the Indian and Pakistani nuclear detonations of May 1998 induced an initial wave of pessimism among supporters of a nuclear nonproliferation regime, as the "lessons" for the outside world might have seemed to be that this "regime" would fail, that nations all around the world would emulate the South Asian states in deciding that it now made sense to acquire nuclear weapons.[1]

This chapter will seek to sort out the pessimistic or optimistic lessons that can be drawn from these detonations and from the world's reaction to them. If "dominos" fall in a series of similar acquisitions of nuclear weapons, pessimism among the arms controllers would be well taken. If a pessimistic analysis of the impact of South Asian precedents is widely adopted, such an analysis can indeed turn out to be self-confirming. But if the outside world sees important distinctions between South Asia and other regions, or if the outside world is consumed by problems having little to do with nuclear weapons, then there may have been much less damage to the non-proliferation regime. And, to repeat the emphasis on the tendency of predictions to confirm themselves, if the outside world concludes that nuclear proliferation is still not so likely to happen, then it may indeed *not* happen. Will Argentina and Brazil, or Israel and Egypt, or Australia and Japan, or North and South Korea, now draw important lessons from the behavior of Pakistan and India, or will they not? And what in fact will be these "lessons?"[2]

The Peculiar Setting of the Stage

While it is always difficult to be objective about measuring the extent of the excitement caused by such events, and thus to predict the damage done to previous degrees of stability, the first, less pessimistic, review of the responses to South Asia's nuclear moves would indeed be that the world did not get transfixed by these events.

In part this would have to be because India had already detonated a nuclear device in 1974, labeling it a test of a "peaceful nuclear explosive," and because Pakistan was widely suspected of having accumulated enriched uranium to produce more than ten nuclear warheads over the years since then, in a period where India was conversely suspected of having acquired enough plutonium to produce perhaps more than 100 such warheads.[3]

The world had thus become accustomed to assuming that India and Pakistan were already locked in the mutual deterrence of a nuclear confrontation, as each had "bombs in the basement" and the means of delivering them to some densely populated cities on the other side of their mutual border. No one really assumes anymore that a test detonation is required to be certain that a plutonium or uranium atomic bomb will work as a weapon. India had detonated before 1998, while Pakistan had not, but either of these states already had to fear a massive retaliation from the other, and the world may thus have already taken this into account.

There was a time when an actual detonation may have made a great deal of difference for whether the world concluded that proliferation had occurred; and, for those observers who are less conversant with the realities of nuclear technology, the actual explosion of such a device is still an important benchmark (a benchmark that in the Indian case, was of course already crossed some two decades ago). But, for those who have been more attuned to the rumors of the spreading of expertise and the accumulation of fissionable materials, the actual detonations would be much less of a punctuation mark, less exciting (with some cynics writing these off as nothing more than a very verifiable reduction in the total of such weapons that Islamabad or New Delhi would hold at its disposal).

Where the possession of such "bombs in the basement" had already thus been widely assumed, as has long been true for Israel, and for Pakistan and India, the shock of a detonation can not be as great. This is hardly to be so sanguine as to conclude that such detonations did no damage for the stability of the rest of the world, so that the United States and other powers would not have wished to forestall them. There was indeed some important gains to holding back these states from detonations and from any explicit claims of weapons; our question here pertains to assessing *how much* damage was done when this could no longer be held back.

A second important difference in the stage that had been set in South Asia is, of course, that neither India nor Pakistan had adhered to the Nuclear Non-Proliferation Treaty (NPT), which is very different from the state of play for Iran and Iraq, and North Korea, or South Korea and Japan.[4] If the detonations of 1998 had come as explicit and blatant violations of treaty commitments, there would have been much more to the argument that the United States, and its partners in the resistance to nuclear proliferation, had failed in a major contest of resolve. With the exception of Israel, every other state that since 1968 has seemed as close to acquiring nuclear weapons as India and Pakistan has also been induced to become a party to the NPT.

The Impact of Democracy

A somewhat more pessimistic impact of the South Asian nuclear interaction would emerge for anyone who has examined the decision processes in New Delhi and Islamabad at all closely.

At the end of the Cold War, in the general enthusiasm about the spread of political democracy with the collapse of the Soviet Union and the Warsaw Pact, one saw a number of political scientists around the world speculating that this triumph of liberal institutions would make wars and arms races extremely unlikely, or perhaps impossible. The plausible generalization was advanced that there may never have been a war between two such democracies and that arms races between two "governments by the consent of the governed" might therefore also be highly unlikely.[5]

Yet the evidence is that the nuclear detonations in both India and Pakistan drew substantial popular support, and that they were indeed made more likely by the way political parties had to advocate such weapons programs as the way of winning election. Democracy may have made nuclear proliferation less likely in Argentina and Brazil, but it made it more likely in Pakistan and India.

The proposition that wars never occur between democracies might indeed have faced one of its strongest tests in the confrontation between India and Pakistan, even if there were no nuclear weapons being developed there. The major wars between the two countries had thus far indeed occurred only when Pakistan was not governed democratically, which might save the "iron law" for those who see an ending of violent power politics in the spread of free elections.

But there had been continuous military tensions between the two states even when civilian democratic rule was in effect in Islamabad; and, to repeat, an important impetus for the shift to outright nuclear proliferation and open detonations was indeed the workings of democratic electoral politics in both countries.

As Pakistan has now been subjected once again to military rule, any conventional or nuclear war with India would not disprove our "iron law" that democracies never war with each other. However much Americans and others want to have their faith in democracy maintained, however, no one will be feeling relieved about avoiding the difficult test for this faith, because the lives of so many millions of South Asians are now in direct danger.

The outside world thus prays that the deterrence theorists in New Delhi and Islamabad will be correct, in their prediction that nuclear weapons will actually work to prevent war in South Asia, with such theorists arguing that the same mechanism that prevented conventional war between the Soviet Union and the United States can work as well, or even better, between India and Pakistan. If these theorists were incorrect, however, the outside world might be dismayed to see a war at last break out between two democracies (democracy will almost surely be restored for another round in Pakistan, even as Pakistani nuclear weapons will just as surely be retained when such democracy is restored), and would be appalled at the risk of millions of people being killed if the nuclear arsenals of the two states came into use in such a war.

Deterrence of Use vs. Deterrence of Possession

The nuclear non-proliferation "regime" around the globe has not depended, as many of its critics would contend, simply on the selfish policy dictation of Washington and Moscow, the "haves" allegedly imposing their will on the "have-nots."[6] Rather it has been derived from another form of the very same mutual deterrence argument that now draws so much endorsement in South Asia.

The basic mutual deterrence argument pits two possessors of nuclear weapons into a confrontation where each tells the other that "we will not use nuclear weapons against your cities as long as you do not launch such attacks against our cities, and we will definitely retaliate with such weapons if you do launch such attacks." This is the mutual assured destruction confrontation that never failed between the United States and the Soviet Union, which Indians and Pakistanis now claim they intend to emulate.

But there is a prior mutual deterrence argument that may now have come into play between Argentina and Brazil, or Japan and Australia, or in many other pairs of countries, where each side is definitely known to be technologically *capable* of producing nuclear weapons, but where each in effect is saying to the other "we will not *produce* nuclear weapons as long as you do not, and we will definitely retaliate by producing nuclear weapons if you do so." The basic logic is the same, but at one further remove from the possibility of a nuclear holocaust, as each country feels itself better off when neither has nuclear weapons, as compared with the alternative, where *both* would possess such weapons.

Here we thus confront a very different kind of important "lesson" proffered by the South Asian example, whether the mutual deterrence of forces-in-being is actually preferable to the mutual deterrence of *potential* forces. It has to be stipulated that there are now many countries around the world that have the technological skills to convert fissionable materials into nuclear weapons and that will acquire substantial amounts of such materials as a byproduct of the production of electric power by nuclear reactors.[7] Most of such countries have neighbors or near-neighbors that are similarly able to acquire such weapons. When confronting the basic choice between neither country having atomic bombs, and *both* countries having such bombs, most states will thus welcome the NPT, regarding it not as an imposition of the superpowers, but as a vehicle by which states can make a treaty pledge to avoid such weapons and by which International Atomic Energy Agency (IAEA) inspection will reassure each side that the other is keeping its pledge.

Having seen India and Pakistan unable to stay at the no-first-possession line of nuclear weapons, so that the two South Asian powers now instead have to try to hold the line at no-first-use, will other pairs of countries around the globe shift their focus of mutual deterrence here? Happily, the odds are that such countries will not feel the need to make such a shift.

To begin, India had already upset the terrain by detonating its device in May of 1974. From the point of view of outsiders opposed to nuclear proliferation, Indira Gandhi's choice here was extremely regrettable. (Yet the same outsiders would then have had to congratulate India on its restraint thereafter, as India set the world record for time elapsed between the first and second nuclear detonations—an interval of 23 years, perhaps a record which will never be broken—, and similar congratulations would have gone to Pakistan for its patience in face of the asymmetry that New Delhi had created.)[8]

Leaving aside the fact that South Asia was already a special case, with "nuclear proliferation" by many definitions having already occurred by the Indian detonation of 1974, one can indeed find a reinforcement for nonproliferation in the clarity of the logic of mutual deterrence that gets voiced so often by Pakistanis and Indians.

Each side sounds just like the other, in telling Americans and other outsiders that there is no reason why the bombs that have been produced will ever have to be used, as the mere potential of such bombs will suffice, will keep the bombs of others from coming into use.

Yet this clarity of potential working as a deterrent can, to repeat, also be applied one step further back, as the mere potential of producing bombs is held in reserve to keep others from exercising an identical potential. Mutual deterrence is a very clear concept. It is made clearer as Indians and Pakistanis match Americans and Russians and Frenchmen in enunciating it. But this clear concept is indeed one of the strongest underpinnings for nonproliferation. "If you make the bomb, we will too. As long as you do not, we will not."

Reduced Conventional War

If an Indian or a Pakistani had been asked to describe the benefits of the advance to outright possession of nuclear weapons, he might have argued that such proliferation might actually put a damper on risks of conventional war between these two adversaries, much as analysts of the NATO confrontation with the Warsaw Pact had for decades credited the presence of nuclear warheads with having deterred the use of the Soviet advantage in tanks.[9]

Indeed, there had been no major outbreaks of South Asian warfare since the Indian detonation of 1974. If this had indeed been the original "proliferation" act of the region, one could have thus ascribed benefits to it even from then (which would of course then beg the question of why the Indian—and responsive Pakistani—detonations of 1998 were at all necessary).

Yet the direct aftermath of the 1998 detonations was not then to be a more relaxed military confrontation between the two South Asian rivals, but the outbreak of more serious armed conflict in Kashmir, including an escalation into conventional aerial warfare. One can argue about which side is to blame for this. But one can hardly argue that the nuclear moves of 1998 had led to a more robust mutual deterrence, taking the steam out of the confrontation of conventional arms. As the outside world watches events in South Asia for lessons on the desirability of acquiring nuclear weapons, or on the possibility that such proliferation is indeed very undesirable, it will indeed be assessing whether the Indian-Pakistani rivalry seems to be at all eased now, or instead worsened.

In the immediate aftermath of the Indian and Pakistani nuclear tests, there was an optimism for a time that New Delhi and Islamabad were capable of a special mutual understanding, perhaps reinforced by various confidence building measures and explicit or subtle pledges to a no-first-use policy. Becoming more political in the analysis, there was even a hope that the democratically-elected governments of these two countries, having proven that they could stand up to the outside world, and stand up to each other, by acquiring nuclear weapons, would then be able to make some meaningful and statesmanlike concessions to resolve the political disputes that have poisoned relations ever since 1947.

However, since then such optimistic hopes have largely faded, as the vehemence of the conflict over Kashmir intensified. The pledges of no-first-use that have been exchanged with regard to nuclear weapons are welcome, of course; but those outsiders who worry about the future safety of the cities of India and Pakistan would still have much preferred an abstention from nuclear weapons possession in the first place. A no-first-use pledge might at best work to partially relieve the inherent threat posed by the presence of such weapons.

In short, if a dyad like Argentina and Brazil is watching the Indian-Pakistan dyad for lessons, it might, as of the end of the millennium, deduce that the risk of nuclear war has been increased by the proliferation that has taken place (it was of course increased already in 1974, with the Indian detonation, and then with all the Pakistani effort to acquire enriched uranium which followed this), with mutual declarations only partially reducing this threat. And any such outside dyad of countries might similarly conclude that a benign influence of nuclear weapons, in reducing the risk of conventional war, has for the moment not really been demonstrated.

Standing Up to Outside Powers

A retired Indian General let himself make an offhand comment that has come much to be quoted since then, that the lesson of Iraq's experience in Desert Storm was that a state confronting the United States should acquire nuclear weapons first. If the major pattern of international interactions is now indeed to be one of small states fending off the dictates of the "hegemonic" United States, or the dictates of the other major powers, then the outside world would have to be exploring the logic of this comment, comparing what Iraq or Iran or North Korea can obtain with or without nuclear weapons, with what Pakistan and India now obtain.

Indians and Pakistanis indeed often depict the NPT itself as an example of American hegemonic dictation to the world, and earlier as an imposition by the "duopoly" of the two superpowers, the United States and the Soviet Union. Saddam Hussein's regime in Iraq would of course similarly depict the international action forcing him out of Kuwait as an act of naked American power.

Happily, almost all of the world saw the issues of Desert Storm substantially differently, as the United States was not simply indulging itself in an exercise of power in Desert Storm, but was responding to a blatant Iraqi aggression that would have amounted to a very dangerous precedent if the world had not stood up to it. (Indian commentators sometimes claimed to see the issues as Saddam Hussein saw them, but one wonders about whether this was their sincere feeling.) And, to repeat, most of the world has not seen the NPT as a power trip by Washington and Moscow, even if such a picture sometimes lends itself to General Assembly eloquence, but rather as something benefiting regions and countries by the mutual reassurances of a "no-first-proliferation" regime.

What nations gain or lose by having acquired nuclear weapons, in terms of being able to bargain with Washington and with any other state, or what they gain or lose by even hinting at such proliferation and becoming physically capable of it, is of course one of the major background questions affecting whether the nonproliferation regime will ultimately succeed.

Countries all around the world will watch to see what kinds of help and treatment Indian and Pakistan get from the United States, now that nuclear weapons have been openly acquired, and will be watching what North Korea gets as it seems to move into greater compliance with the obligations it has already undertaken by its 1985 adherence to the NPT. They will compare this with the bargaining position of Japan, South Korea, and Taiwan, as these countries retain latent abilities to do things with plutonium, and with what Israel has extracted over the years, by the mere rumors that it has acquired nuclear weapons, rumors never confirmed by an open declaration or a detonation.

As the world thus watches once again to see whether there are any apparent political or strategic benefits to be gained by nuclear proliferation, it will be alert to the conflicts that might have emerged otherwise between India and the United States, or between India and China or any other powers, and similarly between Pakistan and other powers, to see whether such weapons really amount to a reassurance against a smaller power's getting pushed around. The results will always be somewhat speculative and untestable, as it would remain possible that India would not have been subjected to the dictates of any global hegemony even if it had not crossed the nuclear line in 1974 and then again in 1998. The proposition has not yet really been disproved that democracies do not threaten war against each other, but rather bargain with each other as participants in a more civilized process of international law and order.

In the aftermath of the proliferation that has indeed occurred, one can also watch a different, more secondary, lesson of the gains of proliferation. Americans and others may conclude that the spread of nuclear weapons to South Asia is indeed an irreversible fact, and that it might make general sense for outside assistance to be offered to India and Pakistan for making these new nuclear arsenals more responsible and secure.

Should the "reward" for having defied the nonproliferation regime be that India and Pakistan now receive help on Permissive Action Link (PAL) devices to keep nuclear weapons from unauthorized use? Should they even be assisted with more secure second-strike delivery systems, reducing the temptations and risks of a preemptive nuclear war in South Asia?

If all an American or anyone else wished to do was to reduce the risk of a nuclear holocaust in South Asia, such assistance should be rushed to the area. But the generic concern will always be that this would send a very different "lesson" to the outside world, perhaps encouraging *more* countries to acquire such weapons, a lesson that the acquisition of a rudimentary and dangerous nuclear arsenal induces the outside world to replace this with a more reliable arsenal.

The Bottom Line of "Lessons"

The resolution of this last tough choice, on whether to attempt to stabilize the South Asian nuclear confrontation, despite the precedent being set, will depend, for Washington and for other players, on much of the rest of what has been discussed here, whether there are indeed any larger numbers of erstwhile nuclear proliferants being prodded along by the "lesson" of India and Pakistan.

The world will watch to see whether India and Pakistan, in the processes of ongoing diplomacy and pursuit of national interest, have really improved their position by their joint crossing of the nuclear line. If, as is indeed very plausible, the diplomats and strategists of the outside world conclude that there has been more of a loss than a gain for India and Pakistan here, the "lesson" of 1998 may not be a disaster for the nonproliferation regime.

The "regime" phrase was always likely to be misleading, suggesting dictation by some leading countries, dictating to others that were reluctant. If nuclear proliferation can be contained, and there is still every reason to conclude that it can be, this will emerge by the self-interested policies of a great many countries that are indeed physically capable of producing nuclear weapons.

Notes

1. Valuable observations on the future possibilities here can be found in George Perkovich, "Nuclear Proliferation," *Foreign Policy* No. 112 (Fall 1998) pp. 12-23.
2. A useful discussion of the general state of play on nuclear proliferation can be found in Rebecca Johnson, "Is the NPT Tottering?" *Bulletin of the Atomic Scientists* Vol. 55, No. 2 (March/April, 1999) pp. 16-18.
3. For this author's earlier interpretation of the South Asian nuclear confrontation, see George H. Quester, *Nuclear Pakistan and Nuclear India: Stable Deterrent or Proliferation Challenge?* (Carlisle, Pennsylvania: U. S. Army War College Strategic Studies Institute, 1992).
4. On the special damage done when treaty commitments are violated here, see Michael Mazarr, *North Korea and the Bomb* (New York: Macmillan, 1995).
5. The potential importance of democracy as a contribution to peace is discussed in Bruce Russett, *Grasping the Democratic Peace* (Princeton, New Jersey: Princeton University Press, 1993).
6. Such a critical interpretation of the nonproliferation effort can be found in Ashok Kapur, "New Nuclear States and the International Nuclear Order," in T. V. Paul,

Richard Harknett and James Wirtz, eds., *The Absolute Weapon Revisited* (Ann Arbor: University of Michigan Press, 1998) pp. 237-262.

7. Leonard Spector, *Nuclear Ambitions* (Boulder, Colorado: Westview, 1990) offers a very comprehensive overview of the spread of "dual-use" nuclear technology.

8. An interesting and useful earlier analysis of the India-Pakistan confrontation is to be found in George Perkovich, "A Nuclear Third Way in South Asia," *Foreign Policy* No. 91 (Summer, 1993) pp. 85-104.

9. A good analysis of the nuclear role in the NATO-Warsaw Pact confrontation can be found in Ivo Daalder, *The Nature and Practice of Flexible Response* (New York: Columbia University Press, 1991).

INDEX